# The Essentials of American History
to 1877

**RICHARD N. CURRENT**

University of North Carolina at Greensboro

**T. HARRY WILLIAMS**

Louisiana State University

**FRANK FREIDEL**

Harvard University

**W. ELLIOT BROWNLEE**

University of California, Santa Barbara

# The Essentials of American History
## to 1877

Second Edition

ALFRED A. KNOPF    NEW YORK

*THIS IS A BORZOI BOOK PUBLISHED BY ALFRED A. KNOPF, INC.*

Second Edition
987654321
Copyright © 1977 by Alfred A. Knopf, Inc.

**Library of Congress Cataloging in Publication Data**
Main entry under title:

The Essentials of American history to 1877.

   Text consists of the 1st pt. of the 1-vol. 2d ed.
published in 1976 under title:   The Essentials of
American history.
   Bibliography:   p.
   Includes index.
   1.   United States—History—Colonial period, ca.
1600-1775.   2.   United States—History—Revolution,
1775—1783.   3.   United States—History—1783-1865.
4.   Reconstruction.   I.   Current, Richard Nelson.
E188.E882   1976      973      76-40492
ISBN 0-394-31283-X

Design: Meryl Sussman Levavi
Manufactured in the United States of America

To the Memory of William Best Hesseltine (1902–1963)

# PREFACE

The four years since the first edition of this book appeared have witnessed a swift torrent of historical scholarship and an even more rapid flow of national events. In revising *The Essentials of American History* we have sought to bring the book up to date in terms of both recent scholarship and current history. As part of that effort we have expanded our treatment of the role of minorities and women in American history. Also, we have revised the historiographical essays, "Where Historians Disagree," expanded the treatment of economic and social history, and reorganized the coverage of politics since 1865.

Despite substantial revision, *The Essentials of American History* remains a brief textbook that provides the main themes of American history while omitting much of the factual and illustrative material commonly found in longer texts. The organization—with chapters grouped in chronological units and with an introduction for each period—is intended to make the overall structure quite clear and at the same time to allow a good deal of flexibility in assignments. The list of readings at the end of each unit is highly selective, presenting examples of the best available writings as judged by both readability and scholarly importance. Books published in

comparatively low-priced softcover editions are so indicated on each list. Since the variety of paperbacks on the market continually grows and changes, current issues of the quarterly publication *Paperbound Books in Print* should also be consulted. The brief historiographical essays included in the text introduce the student to several of the most serious conflicts of historical interpretation and thus, it is hoped, help him to understand that the study of history involves far more than merely collecting and memorizing "facts."

In preparing this revision, we have profited from the expertise of the editors at Alfred A. Knopf, Inc. Of particularly great assistance was Suzanne Thibodeau, the project editor of this edition. We also want to thank Edward D. Bridges, Douglas L. Crane, Jr., Virginia M. Noelke, and Germaine M. Reed for their helpful critiques of the first edition. We shall be grateful for suggestions regarding improvements to be made in future reprintings and revisions of this text.

R.N.C.

T.H.W.

F.F.

W.E.B.

# CONTENTS

## 1823–1848 • PART THREE
### Sectionalism Contends with Nationalism as the Country Expands

## 1848–1877 • PART FOUR

### North and South Separate, Fight, and Rejoin, while the Slaves Gain Partial Freedom    136

### Appendices

### Index

## Maps

## Where Historians Disagree

# The Essentials of American History
## to 1877

# Englishmen Become Americans and Gain Their Independence

The history of the United States from its colonial beginnings is fairly short. It covers a period of less than 400 years, a period that can be spanned by the overlapping lifetimes of a mere half-dozen men. Yet the roots of American civilization go deep into the human past. These roots are to be traced mostly to the Old World, not the New. American history is an extension of European and particularly English history.

The colonists who came to English America in the seventeenth century were transplanted Englishmen. They had no desire to lose their Englishness. Rather, they hoped to build in the New World a better England, one that would be free from the imperfections of their native land, one that would give them greater opportunities for personal happiness.

Even the first arrivals, however, began to depart from many of their accustomed ways. As new generations grew up in America they developed a more and more distinctive character. In the course of the eighteenth century they became provincial "Americans"—a term that had been applied to them even before 1700 but did not come into general use until after 1750.

There were three main reasons for the divergence between the culture of the colonies and that of the homeland. First, English society was not transplanted as a whole. The people who left for America were not entirely typical of England: usually they were the more discontented or the more adventurous; they were themselves in some degree "different." Second, they found in the New World an unfamiliar environment with its own challenges and opportunities. Certain elements of the English inheritance flourished and adapted themselves to the strange surroundings, while others withered or never took root at all. Third, some of the early colonists (the Dutch, for example) had come from countries other than England, and during the eighteenth century new arrivals in much larger numbers came from other places—Scotland and Ireland, the European continent, and Africa. Hence, in America, there was a mixture of peoples and cultures, though the English continued to predominate.

In the developing American society there were variations from colony to colony and from region to region. The New England colonies had much in common with one another, less in common with the middle colonies (Pennsylvania, New Jersey, New York), and still less in common with the southern colonies. These last fell into two subgroups with important differences between the two: the tobacco colonies (Maryland, Virginia, and North Carolina) and the others (South Carolina and Georgia).

Looking back two centuries later, it is easy enough to see that the people of the thirteen colonies, for all their diversity, had come to share some distinctive characteristics by the middle of the eighteenth century. From the viewpoint of England at that time, these people seemed already to be Americans rather than, in a strict sense, Englishmen. As yet, however, few of the colonists thought of themselves as Americans. Their "country," as they saw it, was first of all their particular colony, and then perhaps their region (at least in the case of the Southerners and the New Englanders), and finally the British Empire.

As of 1763 the Empire appeared to be an imposing success, having just disposed of its last great imperial rival in North America—France. Yet it was about to prove a failure, at least so far as its ability to hold the thirteen colonies was concerned. After the great victory over the French, the policy makers in London undertook to bind the outlying provinces more closely than ever to the metropolitan center. Instead of consolidating the Empire, however, its rulers unwittingly prepared the way for its early disruption.

The colonies by then had long been used to a large measure of self-rule, and to preserve this they resisted the imperial program of George III's government. In the course of their resistance they developed a new sense of common cause and new forms of political cooperation. They were not yet conscious of belonging to, or of desiring to create, a separate country, but they eventually found themselves engaged in the first battles of a war that was to lead to independence.

The actual fighting seems insignificant in comparison with more recent wars. Battle deaths on the American side totaled less than 5,000. Cannons tossed out iron balls that did no damage unless they made a direct hit, and an alert soldier could see them coming and get out of the way. The Pennsylvania rifle, which some of the Patriots carried, was fairly accurate at a range of one hundred yards, but the more common smoothbore musket was not, and its flintlock misfired when wet. A military campaign was almost out of the question except in good weather.

Yet the war as the Patriots fought it, old-fashioned though it was in some respects, had one feature that made it new and revolutionary in itself. In previous wars the battles had been fought by comparatively small numbers of professional soldiers, serving only for pay. In this one the people on the American side took up arms in their own cause. Though their armies seldom numbered more than a few thousand at any one time, a total of almost 400,000 men enlisted (most of them for short terms) during the eight years (1775–1783) that the war lasted.

Its consequences also were revolutionary. The first of the modern wars against colonialism, it brought into being a new nation which, though weak and insecure at the start, was eventually to grow into one of the greatest powers of all time. The ideals the war aroused provided inspiration for future generations not only in the United States but also in other countries. One of the leading revolutionaries of 1776, Thomas Paine, averred that the war "contributed more to enlighten the world, and diffuse a spirit of freedom and liberality among mankind, than any human event . . . that ever preceded it."

# Chapter 1.   TRANSPLANTED ENGLISHMEN: THE SEVENTEENTH CENTURY

## Interest in Colonization

The innovative and powerful merchants who led in the development of the English interest in colonization were part of a rising class of merchant capitalists who prospered from the expansion of foreign trade. During the century before the discovery of America these merchant capitalists had risen to wealth and power by shrewdly turning from the export of raw wool to the export of woolen cloth. They gathered up the raw material, put it out for spinning and weaving in individual households, and then sold the finished product both in England and abroad. Beside trading in cloth, the merchants bought and sold a vast array of products, fish and wine most importantly, and their trading network stretched from the Mediterranean in the east to Ireland and Iceland in the west. Their relentless search for new markets for their cloth and for new sources of fish to feed Catholic Europe led them to sail to North American shores by the end of the fifteenth century and to plant permanent colonies there by the beginning of the seventeenth century. To support these activities they formed chartered companies, each with a monopoly from the sovereign of England for trading in a particular part of the world. Some of these were joint-stock companies, much like modern corporations, with stockholders sharing risk and profit.

To further their profitable trade, spokesmen for the merchant capitalists developed a set of ideas about the proper relation of government and business—ideas supporting the argument that the whole nation benefited from the activities of the overseas traders. The trade of England as a whole, it was said, was basically like that of any individual or firm: transactions were worthwhile if sales exceeded purchases in value. The difference in value would have to be paid in money (gold and silver), and the inflow of money into England would stimulate business and strengthen the national economy by raising commodity prices and lowering interest rates. Merchant capitalists depended upon loans to carry on their business, and interest was considered now as a cost of production, whereas in medieval times it had been regarded as sinful usury. According to their theory, the government should act to encourage a "favorable" balance of trade—that is, an excess of exports over imports. This economic philosophy came to be known as "mercantilism." It guided the economic policies not only of England but also of Spain, France, and other nation-states.

Colonies would fit well into this mercantilist program, or so it seemed to a number of thoughtful Englishmen in the late sixteenth and early seventeenth centuries. These men argued that colonies would provide an additional market for English manufacturers and that colonial commerce, while yielding profit for shipowners and customs duties for the government, would bring from the colonies products for which England previously had depended upon foreigners—products such as lumber, naval stores, furs, and above all, silver and gold. To further augment English wealth, and thereby the power of the English state and the Protestant faith, colonies would serve as bases for raiding and looting the Spanish ships that carried gold bullion, for promoting slave revolts in Spanish domains, and for controlling a westward passage to the Asian marketplace.

There was yet another reason for the growing interest in colonies. The Church of England, in the form it took under Queen Elizabeth, by no means satisfied all her subjects. It was much too Protestant to suit those Englishmen who held on to the Roman Catholic faith, and at the same time it seemed too "popish" to many who opposed the ways and influence of Rome. Among these were the Puritans, who, affected in varying degrees by the teachings of John Calvin, wished to "purify" the Church. The majority of the Puritans were content to remain within the Anglican fold but hoped to simplify the forms of worship and lessen the power of the bishops, who were appointed by the throne. A minority, the Separatists, were determined to worship as they pleased in their own independent congregations. Like all subjects, however, they were forbidden by law to absent themselves from regular Anglican services or to hold unauthorized religious meetings, and they were taxed to support the established Church. Religious nonconformists began to look for places of refuge outside the kingdom.

## The Wilderness Setting

The fate of the English colonies—their success or failure, the kind of development they took—was to depend in large measure upon the environment in which they were planted along the Atlantic seaboard of North America.

To the first colonists, America was trees. From the Atlantic to the Appalachians and beyond stretched a great forest, unbroken except for occasional small clearings made by the elements or by the Indians, and thick with tall pines, maples, oaks, and countless other varieties of trees as well as shrubs. This made a refreshing contrast with comparatively treeless England, rapidly being deforested to meet the fuel needs of industry and a rapidly growing population.

Apart from the great forest, the geographical fact that most distinguished the new from the old country and most influenced the economic development of the colonies was sheer space. Not that all the land was readily accessible. The need for clearing the forest, the presence of hostile tribes, the dependence upon water transport, and ultimately the difficulty of crossing the mountain barrier—all these considerations hindered the actual occupation of the land, and increasingly so in proportion to the remoteness from seaports. Hence the English settlements, scattered though they might seem, remained on the whole fairly compact throughout the colonial period, at least in comparison with the Spanish and French settlements in the New World, though not in comparison with the crowded towns and countryside of the Old World. There populations teemed and lacked sufficient room. Here land was plentiful and people relatively scarce.

European diseases preceded European colonies to American shores. The native population lacked immunity to European childhood diseases, such as measles and mumps. Whenever the Indians encountered the first wave of European traders and fishermen, they were attacked by these diseases, as well as smallpox and syphilis, with fatal results. Death swept ahead of settlement and cleared the Atlantic seaboard of much of the native people. By 1600 a native population of about 125,000—perhaps only half the number in 1500—remained along the coast south of the St. Lawrence River.

Concentrated in southern New England and around Chesapeake Bay, most of the tribes carried on a primitive form of agriculture. They made clearings by cutting into trees to kill them and by setting fires in the forest. Among the dead and blackened trunks they planted pumpkins, squash, beans, and corn—crops they had learned of indirectly from the Indians of Mexico and South America. A tribe abandoned its clearing and made a new one when the yields fell, or when the accumulated filth of the village became too deep to endure. The Indian "old fields," especially in New England and the sites abandoned by tribes decimated by disease attracted incoming settlers as convenient places to begin settlement. The newcomers eagerly adopted the cultivation of native crops, above all corn. Without the clearings and the crops that the Indians provided, the Englishmen would have had much greater difficulty than they did in getting a start in the New World.

To Englishmen the Indians were of interest as customers for English goods and as suppliers of woodland commodities, especially hides and skins. Trade brought the white man and the red man together. It was a disadvantage to the Indian, for while he obtained guns, knives, blankets, and iron pots, he also became increasingly dependent upon the white man, his commerce, and his culture.

In English America there was not to be the fusion of Indian and European people and culture that developed in the Spanish empire. The reasons for this were various, but one of them was the fact that the Englishmen, unlike the Spaniards (and the Frenchmen), almost always came as family men, with their womenfolk, and hence had much less occasion to intermarry with the aborigines.

Nevertheless, American history without the Indians would have lacked much of its special character. Not only did the colonists receive from them a number of new things to eat, such as corn, but the English language in America was enriched by words of native origin (*moccasin* and *succotash*, to mention only two), and American thought was colored by numerous elements of Indian lore. Yet, even though they aided the first European arrivals, the Indians attempted to obstruct the expansion of white settlement, and life on the frontier derived many of its peculiarly "American" qualities from the Indian danger and the Indian wars.

In the wilderness the English were to encounter threats not only from Indians but also from rival Europeans. To the south and southwest were scattered the outposts of the Spaniards who, despite a peace that Spain and England made in 1604, continued to look upon the English as intruders. The English in their settlements along the coast could not for many years feel entirely safe from attack by Spanish ships.

On the north and northwest were beginning to appear the outposts of another and eventually more dangerous rival, France. The French founded their first permanent settlement in America at Quebec in 1608, less than a year after the English had started their first at Jamestown. The English were soon to find a third rival, the Dutch. Shortly after the planting of the English colonies at Jamestown and Plymouth, the Dutch began to wedge themselves in between, when the Dutch West India Company established posts on the Hudson, Delaware, and Connecticut rivers.

## Virginia and Maryland

Virginia was the name that—in honor of Elizabeth, the Virgin Queen—had been given to an indefinite stretch of the North American mainland bordering the Atlantic coast. In 1606 a company of London merchants obtained from King James I a charter giving them the right to start a colony in Virginia. They intended to found not an agricultural settlement but a trading post. To it they expected to send English manufacturers for barter with the Indians, and from it they hoped to bring back American commodities procured in exchange or produced by the labor of their own employees.

Their first expedition of three small ships (the *Godspeed,* the *Discovery,* and the *Susan Constant*) carrying about 100 men sailed into Chesapeake Bay and up the James River in the spring of 1607. The colonists—too many of whom were

adventurous gentlemen-soldiers and too few of whom were willing laborers—ran into serious difficulties from the moment they landed and began to build the palisaded settlement of Jamestown. Though beautiful to look at, the site was low and swampy and unhealthful. It was surrounded by thick woods, which were hard to clear for cultivation, and it was threatened by hostile Indians under the imperial chief Powhatan.

By January 1608, when ships appeared with additional men and supplies, all but thirty-eight of the first arrivals were dead. The winter of 1609–1610 turned into a "starving time" worse than anything before. While Indians killed off the livestock in the woods and kept the settlers within the palisade, these unfortunates were reduced to eating "dogs, cats, rats, snakes, toadstools, horsehides," and even the "corpses of dead men," as one survivor recalled. No one could see much point in staying, and soon all were on their way downriver, leaving the town to its decay. Yet the colony was to begin again. The refugees met a relief ship coming up the river and were persuaded to go back to Jamestown.

The basis of Virginia's future prosperity was laid when one of the planters, John Rolfe, experimented successfully with the growing and curing of tobacco. And a truce with the Indians was cemented when Rolfe married Powhatan's daughter Pocahontas, who afterward was entertained as a princess on a visit to England, where she died. But Powhatan's brother and successor, Opechancanough, broke the peace with a massacre of more than 350 unsuspecting Virginians.

The lack of adequate defenses in the colony, the general mismanagement of the Virginia Company, and the bickerings among its directors led James I, in 1624, to revoke the charter and take the government of Virginia into his own hands. As a profit-making venture for its investors the colony was a failure, yet in a larger sense it was a success, for it demonstrated that English men and women could survive and prosper in America.

One of the stockholders of the Virginia Company, George Calvert, Lord Baltimore, conceived the idea of undertaking a new colony on his own. Himself a convert to the Roman Catholic faith, Calvert had in mind primarily a gigantic speculation in real estate and incidentally the establishment of a refuge for Roman Catholics, victims of political discrimination in England. From Charles I he obtained a patent to a wedge of Virginia's territory which lay north of the Potomac and east of Chesapeake Bay, and which the King now christened Maryland in honor of his Roman Catholic wife, the Frenchwoman Henrietta Maria.

In March of 1634 the *Ark* and the *Dove,* bearing 200 or 300 passengers, entered the Potomac and turned into one of its eastern tributaries. On a high and dry bluff these first arrivals laid out the village of St. Mary's, while the neighboring Indians, already withdrawing to avoid native enemies, assisted by providing stocks of corn. The early Marylanders knew no massacres, no plagues, no starving time. Their most serious trouble arose from border disputes with the Virginians, disputes which provoked some bloodshed but finally were ended by the King's decision in favor of Maryland.

Spending a large part of the family fortune in the development of their American possessions, the Calverts had to attract many thousands of settlers if their venture was to pay. They encouraged the immigration of Protestants as well as Roman Catholics, and since relatively few of the latter were inclined to leave England, the Protestant settlers soon far outnumbered them.

## Chesapeake Society

Tobacco growing quickly spread throughout the Chesapeake settlements—in both Maryland and Virginia—as England and English merchants welcomed the opportunity to reduce their imports of tobacco from the Spanish empire. Tobacco shaped the society that developed in the region in a variety of ways. One way was that in taking up land along the bay and navigable streams, the early settlers acquired extensive tracts. Thus most of the people came to be widely scattered, living on isolated farms. Villages or towns were few.

Even if a man owned a thousand acres or more, he actually farmed only a small part of his land, because of the difficulty of clearing it. He worked in his fields alongside his boys and his servants or slaves—if he had any. His servants might have come with him from England. Or they might have come later, binding themselves to their master in return for their passage over. Some were sold into servitude against their will.

Upon completing his term (usually four or five years) the servant was entitled to certain benefits—clothing, tools, and occasionally land—in addition to his freedom and the privilege, if he could afford it, of acquiring servants of his own.

In Jamestown John Rolfe had recorded in 1619: "About the last of August came in a Dutch man of war that sold us twenty negars." These black men were bought, it seems, not as slaves but as servants to be held for a term of years and then freed, like the white servants with whom the planters already were familiar. The number of black workers on the tobacco farms increased rather slowly. In Virginia there were fewer than 300 Negroes in 1640, and only about 2,000 in 1670, when the total population of the colony had reached 40,000. By that time blacks were being treated as permanent slaves and no longer as temporary servants. But the day of the great tobacco plantation, with its labor force consisting almost entirely of Negro slaves, still lay in the future.

Though there was more religious diversity in Maryland than in Virginia, Anglicans predominated in both colonies, but Anglicanism soon ceased to be quite the same thing that it was in England. Virginia laws dating from 1643 directed all members to conform to the Church of England, ordered the expulsion of nonconformists, and required the payment of tithes to support the established church. The Bishop of London was supposed to watch over the far-flung American parishes, but he left the responsibility to the colonial governors, who most of the time were preoccupied with political affairs. Actual control gravitated to the parishes themselves. They worked out relatively democratic and independent church organizations of their own. Local vestries (governing boards of laymen) hired pastors on a yearly basis and provided salaries.

On July 30, 1619, in the Jamestown church, delegates from the various communities met as the House of Burgesses to consider, along with the governor and his council, the enactment of laws for the Virginia colony. This was a bright example for the future—the first meeting of an elected legislature, a representative assembly, within what was to become the United States. The members of this House of Burgesses were chosen in county elections in which all men aged seventeen or older were entitled to vote. When, five years later, the King took over the government of the province, he allowed the burgesses to continue to meet. From then on, however, Virginia was a "royal" colony, and the King rather than the Virginia Company was responsible for the appointment of the governor and the governor's council.

As Virginia grew in population, the House of Burgesses became less democratic than it had been in the beginning. Each county continued to have only two representatives, even though some of the new counties of the back country contained many more people than the old ones of the tidewater area; hence the more recent settlers on the frontier were underrepresented. After 1670 the vote was restricted to landowners, and elections were seldom held, the same burgesses remaining in office year after year. One long-serving governor, Sir William Berkeley, corrupted the council and the burgesses and made himself an autocrat.

Discontent with the Berkeley regime flared into violence in 1676. The frontier followers of Nathaniel Bacon, exasperated at the governor's neglect of Indian defenses, marched on Jamestown, attacked and defeated the governor's troops, and set fire to the place. After Bacon died of fever, the rebellion came to a sudden end. Berkeley took a bloody revenge, seeing to the execution of thirty-seven of the leading rebels.

Politics in Maryland were complicated by the hostility of the Protestants toward the Catholic minority and the Catholic proprietor. Lord Baltimore appointed the governor and council and, in 1635, invited the landholders to meet with them and approve laws. By 1650, Maryland had a legislature similar to Virginia's, but the proprietor, insisting that he as well as the governor had a right to veto laws, allowed little power to the elected assembly, the House of Delegates. He also tried to collect high annual quitrents from the settlers who occupied his lands, and who claimed to own them outright. Between 1652 and 1681 the discontented Marylanders took part in four revolts against the proprietary government.

## Plymouth and Massachusetts Bay

New England from the 1620s to the 1670s took its character as a colony in part from the Pilgrims who settled at Plymouth, but in a much larger measure from the Puritans who later landed at nearby Massachusetts Bay and then spread out from there. These Puritans would have liked to remake the institutions of England, but they faced too much opposition there. In the wilderness of America they saw an opportunity to create society anew and to set an example for the Old World.

Slipping away a few at a time, the members of a Separatist congregation from Scrooby, in Nottinghamshire, had crossed the English Channel and begun their lives anew in Holland. There they were allowed to meet and worship freely, but, as aliens, they were not allowed to join the Dutch guilds of craftsmen, and so they had to work long and hard at unskilled and poorly paid jobs. Some of them decided to move again, this time across the Atlantic, where they might find opportunity for happier living and also for propagating "the gospel of the Kingdom of Christ in those remote parts of the world." These Pilgrims made arrangements with English merchants for financing their venture, and they got permission from the Virginia Company to settle as an independent community on its land. They tried, and failed, to get from James I a guarantee of religious freedom, but they learned "that he would . . . not molest them, provided they carried themselves peaceably." This was an historic concession on the part of the King, for it opened English America to settlement by dissenting Protestants.

From Plymouth, England, the *Mayflower* took its 102 passengers to Plymouth in New England, where on a bleak December day in 1620 they disembarked, though they had not reached their intended destination. During the first winter half of them died from scurvy and exposure, but the rest managed to put their colony on its feet. Among the Indians thereabout, who as a result of a recent plague had been decimated even worse than they, the Englishmen discovered friends—Squanto, Samoset, Massasoit—who showed them how to gather seafood and cultivate corn. On their sandy and marshy soil the settlers could not aspire to rich farms, but they developed a profitable trade in fish and furs. As citizens of a virtually independent republic they went their way for over seventy years, until Plymouth was annexed to the much larger colony of Massachusetts Bay.

Englishmen were first attracted to Massachusetts Bay by its fisheries. From these a plan developed for establishing a permanent fishing and trading station and then a missionary outpost at Salem. A corporation, formed to raise funds for putting the struggling colony on a sounder basis, was reorganized in 1629 as the Massachusetts Bay Company, with a royal charter that granted a strip of land between the Charles River and the Merrimack.

Some members of the company, alarmed by the high-church and anti-Parliament attitudes of the new King, Charles I, were beginning to look upon the colony less as a business venture and more as a Puritan refuge. Some were eager to migrate themselves if they could do so and still control the company. They arranged to buy the stock of those who preferred to stay at home. Then, in 1630, they sailed under the lead of the company's governor, John Winthrop, a gentleman of means, with a university education, a deep but narrow piety, a cool and calculating way, and a remarkably forceful and stubborn character. The expedition, with 17 ships and 1,000 people, was the largest of its kind in the seventeenth century. These colonists founded a number of new towns, among them Boston, which was to be both the company's headquarters and the colony's capital.

The Massachusetts enterprise seemed especially blessed. After the first winter (1629–1630), when nearly 200 died and many others decided to leave, the colony grew and prospered. The nearby Pilgrims helped with food and advice. Incoming settlers, many of them well-to-do, brought needed tools and other goods, which they exchanged for the cattle, corn, and other produce of the established colonists. During the 1630s, while Charles I ruled England without a Parliament, Puritans escaping from his tyranny migrated in such numbers that by 1643 the colony had a population of about 15,000.

## The Puritan Way of Life

The Massachusetts Bay Company soon was transformed into the Massachusetts colonial government. Governor Winthrop brought with him the company charter. According to its terms, the "freemen" (the stockholders) were to meet as a General Court to choose officers and adopt rules for the corporation. After their arrival in America the freemen proceeded to elect officials and pass laws for the colony.

To be a freeman, to take any part in the colonial government, a man had to be a member of the Puritan (Congregational) Church. This was not easy. The Puritans in England (and the Pilgrims in Plymouth) had required for church membership only that a person profess the faith, sign the covenant, and live an upright life. The Puritans in Massachusetts, however, soon began to limit membership to the "visible saints," that is, to those who could demonstrate that they had experienced God's saving grace and hence belonged to the elect, the group whom He had chosen for eventual salvation.

Winthrop and the other Massachusetts founders saw themselves as starting a holy commonwealth, a model for the corrupt world to see. The problem was to keep it holy. In this effort the preachers and the politicians worked together. The ministers did not run the government, but they supported it, and they exerted great influence upon the church members who alone could vote or hold public office. The government in turn protected the ministers, taxed the people (members and nonmembers alike) to support the Church, and enforced the law requiring attendance at services. In this Puritan oligarchy the dissidents had no more freedom of worship than the Puritans themselves had had in England.

The early settlers almost always took up land in groups. A congregation arriving from England received from the General Court the grant of a town (township), an area of twenty-five square miles or so. Its distribution was left to the leaders of the new settlement. They laid out a village, in which they set aside a "common" as pasture and timberland, chose a site for a meeting house (church) and for a fort, and assigned each family a strip of land as a home lot on either side of the one village street. They also divided up the outlying fields in the town, the size of a field and the desirability of its location depending on the family's numbers, wealth, and social standing. Wherever he went to work his fields, the typical seventeenth-century New Englander lived not in a lonely farmhouse but in a village with neighbors close by, and he maintained a strong sense of community.

Once established, the town was left to go pretty much its own way, with little interference from the colonial government except in cases where the townspeople could not agree among themselves. They held a yearly "town meeting" in the meeting house to decide important local questions and to choose a group of "selectmen" who governed the town until the next general gathering.

Coastal towns developed an overseas trade through fishing, shipping, shipbuilding, and related enterprises. With the growth of commerce, the colonial shipowning merchants came to dominate the New England economy. These rich businessmen might be good Puritans — though many were not — and yet their way to wealth inevitably created tensions within Puritan society. The Puritan oligarchy gradually lost some of its political power and the ministers lost some of their authority, while the merchants gained in influence.

As the first generation of American Puritans passed away, the number of church members declined, for few of the second generation could show the saving grace that church membership required. Eventually in most communities the Congregational Church came to include all who cared to join and could profess the faith. As the number of church members rose, so did the number of men who could take part in colonial politics as voters and officeholders. Orthodox Puritans continued to oppose the transformation that was coming over the erstwhile land of the saints.

Yet Puritanism remained an important element in the life of New Englanders, and it was in some degree to affect the outlook of most Americans for many generations. It left its lasting mark not in the form of theological doctrines or religious practices but in the form of attitudes that were real though hard to define — a sense of duty, of hard work and of success as its reward, and of mission to make the world a better place.

## Expansion of New England

Meanwhile, an outpouring from Massachusetts Bay to various parts of New England (and to other places in English America) had begun. This exodus was motivated by several considerations: the unproductiveness of the stony soil around Boston, the intolerance of established Puritan communities, and the oppressiveness of the Massachusetts government.

The Connecticut Valley, one hundred miles beyond the settled frontier, contained fertile meadows that invited pioneering despite the presence of warlike Indians and the claims of the already fortified Dutch. By the early 1630s a few Englishmen were already living there. In 1635 a number of families from Massachusetts towns moved west with the General Court's approval, on the understanding that they would "continue still under this government." But the settlers of Hartford, Windsor, and Wethersfield on the Connecticut River decided to set up a colonial government of their own in 1639.

A separate colony had grown up around New Haven on the Connecticut coast. Eventually the governor of Connecticut obtained a royal charter (1662) that not only authorized his colony but also extended its jurisdiction over the New Haven settlements.

Rhode Island had its origin in the religious dissent of Roger Williams, a likeable but troublesome young minister of Massachusetts Bay. Williams was an extreme Separatist who at first advocated not religious freedom but rather a church made even more pure and strict. Making friends with the neighboring Indians, he concluded that the land belonged to them and not to the King or to the Massachusetts Bay Company. The colonial government, considering Williams a dangerous man, decided to deport him, but he escaped. He took refuge with Narragansett tribesmen during a bitter winter, then bought a tract of land from them and in 1636, with a few of his friends, created the town of Providence on it.

Anne Hutchinson, the charming and strong-minded wife of a substantial Bostonian, attracted many more followers than Williams with her heretical doctrine that the Holy Spirit dwelled within and guided every true believer. If this were so, the Bible would have no more authority than anyone's personal revelation, and both the church and the government would be exposed to anarchy, or so it seemed to Governor Winthrop and his associates. In 1638 she was convicted of sedition and banished as "a woman not fit for our society." With her family and some of her followers she moved to a point on Narragansett Bay not far from Providence.

In time other communities of dissidents arose in that vicinity. They quarreled with one another and with Williams, who began to advocate complete freedom of worship and absolute separation of church and state. In 1644 he got from Parliament a charter authorizing a government for the combined settlements. The government, though based on the Massachusetts pattern, did not restrict the vote to church members nor did it tax the people for church support. A royal charter of 1663 confirmed the existing arrangement and added a guarantee of "liberty in religious concernments."

New Hampshire and Maine had become the separate possessions of two proprietors. Few settlers were drawn to these northern regions until the religious disruption of Massachusetts Bay. In 1638 John Wheelwright, a disciple of Anne Hutchinson, led a party of his fellow heretics to Exeter, in New Hampshire. Thereafter a number of towns in that province and in Maine were peopled by orthodox or unorthodox Puritans from Massachusetts or by Anglicans from across the sea. The Massachusetts Bay Company claimed the whole territory to the north but ultimately lost its cases against the proprietors' heirs. New Hampshire then (1679) was set up as a separate royal province. Maine, the proprietary family having sold their rights to it, remained a part of Massachusetts until admitted to the Union as a state in 1820.

As New England spread, the settlers ran into trouble with the Indians. With a few exceptions like Roger Williams, the Puritans viewed the redmen as "pernicious creatures" who deserved extermination unless they would adopt the white man's ways. In 1637 the exasperated Pequots went on the warpath in the Connecticut Valley. The Connecticut frontiersmen marched against a palisaded Pequot stronghold and set it afire. About 500 Pequots were burned to death or massacred when trying to escape, and most of the survivors were hunted down, captured, and sold as slaves. The Pequot tribe was almost wiped out.

To provide frontier protection, to adjust boundary disputes among themselves, and to further their mutual interests in other ways, four of the colonies joined (1643) in "The Confederation of the United Colonies of New England." These four were Massachusetts, Plymouth, Connecticut, and New Haven. The other settlements—those of Rhode Island, New Hampshire, and Maine—were excluded, since Massachusetts aspired to annex them and objected to recognizing them as equals.

By 1675 the New England Confederation had deteriorated so much that it could no longer be relied on for organizing frontier defense. In that year war broke out between Massachusetts towns and the Wampanoag Indians, who lived by Narragansett Bay and were led by King Philip. During the three years of King Philip's War the Indians were able to destroy completely twelve towns, to damage half of the towns in New England, and to kill one out of every sixteen New England men of military age.

## Carolina

Carolina (after the Latin *Carolinus,* meaning Charles), partly taken like Maryland from the Virginia grant, was awarded by Charles II to a group of eight of his favorites, all prominent politicians active in colonial affairs. One was the Virginia governor, Sir William Berkeley, but the man who was to do the most for the development of Carolina was Sir Anthony Ashley Cooper, about to become the Earl of Shaftesbury. In successive charters (1663, 1665) the eight proprietors received joint title to a vast territory.

They expected to profit as landlords and land speculators, reserving tremendous estates for their own development, selling or giving away the rest in smaller tracts, and collecting annual payments as quitrents from the settlers. They hoped to attract settlers from the existing American colonies and thus to avoid the expense of financing expeditions from England. The proprietors, four of whom had investments in the African slave trade, also intended to introduce slaves into the colony so as to profit both from selling them and from using their labor. Early settlers were offered a bonus of extra land for every black bondsman or woman they brought in. Negro slavery existed from the outset in Carolina, with no transitional period of temporary servitude as in Virginia.

The northern part of Carolina, the first part to be settled, suffered from geographical handicaps —the coastal region being isolated by the Dismal Swamp, by the southeastwardly flow of the rivers, and by the lack of natural harbors usable for ocean-going ships. As a Carolina proprietor, Virginia's Governor Berkeley worked hard to induce Virginians to take up land on the other side of the colonial boundary, and gradually the Albemarle settlements grew. Virginians were inclined to look upon the neighboring Carolinians as a lazy and immoral set of runaway servants, debtors, thieves, and pirates. Actually, most of these people—like many in the Virginia they had left behind—were honest but poor tobacco-growing farmers, though they showed the marks of their primitive, backwoods existence, having few roads and practically no villages, churches, schools—or slaves.

The southern part of Carolina was favored with an excellent harbor at the point where the Ashley and Cooper rivers joined. Here in 1670 a fleet bringing colonists arrived whom the Earl of Shaftesbury had sent out after realizing that settlers from existing colonies were not going to flock in. Then in 1680 he saw to the laying-out of the city of Charleston, which soon had its wharves, fortifications, and fine houses, and its wide streets running at right angles to one another. Settlers took up land along the two rivers, down which they began to send large quantities of corn, lumber, cattle, pork, and (in the 1690s) some rice to Charleston, for shipment to Barbados in the British West Indies. To Charleston also came furs, hides, and Indian slaves obtained by traders who were advancing farther and farther into the interior, around the southern end of the Appalachians, to deal with the southwestern tribes. The wealthy planters and merchants, centering in Charleston, dominated the region's economy, social life, and politics. Charleston became the capital of Carolina in 1690, when the governor took up his residence there, leaving a deputy to take charge of the Albemarle settlements.

Already there were in fact two Carolinas, each having a distinctive way of life, long before the colony was formally divided (1729) into North and South Carolina, with completely separate governments.

## New York

The year after making his Carolina grant, Charles II bestowed (1664) upon his brother, the Duke of York, all the territory lying between the Connecticut and Delaware rivers. A large part of this land presumably belonged to the Massachusetts Bay Company by virtue of the company's sea-to-sea grant. The whole region was claimed by the Dutch, who occupied strategic points within it.

The Dutch republic, after winning independence from Spain in 1648, had launched upon its own career of overseas trading and empire building in Asia, Africa, and America. On the basis of Hudson's explorations, the Dutch staked an American claim and proceeded promptly to exploit it with a busy trade in furs. To add permanence to the business, the Dutch West India Company began to encourage settlement, transporting whole families on such voyages as that of the *New Netherland* in 1624, and later offering vast feudal estates to "patroons" who would bring over immigrants to work the land. So developed the colony of New Netherland. It centered around New Amsterdam with its blockhouse on Manhattan Island and included thinly scattered settlements on the Hudson, the Delaware, and the Connecticut rivers, with forts for their protection. In 1655 the Dutch extended their sway over the few Swedes and Finns settled along the lower Delaware. In the Connecticut Valley, they had to give in to the superior numbers of the English moving out from Massachusetts Bay.

Three Anglo-Dutch wars arose from the commercial and colonial rivalry of England and the Netherlands throughout the world and particularly in America. The Dutch dominated the lucrative trade with the Caribbean Spanish empire and competed effectively (and illegally) with English merchants in the trade with the English West Indian colonies. The ambitious English wished to reduce the power of the Dutch. They viewed the New Amsterdam colony as a dangerous stronghold that posed a military threat to their northern and southern mainland colonies; the colony also supported Dutch commerce, particularly smuggling with English colonies. In 1664 troop-carrying vessels of the English navy put in at New Amsterdam and extracted a surrender from the arbitrary and unpopular governor, the peg-legged Peter Stuyvesant. During the final conflict the Dutch reconquered and briefly held their old provincial capital (1673–1674), then lost it again for good.

New York, formerly New Netherland, already the property of the Duke of York and renamed by him, was his to rule as virtually an absolute monarch. The Duke confirmed the Dutch patroonships already in existence, the most notable of them being Rensselaerswyck with its 700,000 acres around Albany, and he gave comparable estates to Englishmen in order to create a class of influential landowners loyal to him. Wealthy English and Dutch landlords, shipowners, and fur traders, along with the Duke's political appointees, dominated the colonial government.

## The Quaker Colonies

The Society of Friends originated in mid-seventeenth-century England in response to the preachings of George Fox, a Nottingham shoemaker, whose followers came to be known as Quakers from his admonition to them to "tremble at the name of the Lord." The essence of Fox's teachings was the doctrine of the Inner Light, the illumination from God within each soul, the divine conscience, which when rightly heeded could guide human beings along the paths of righteousness.

Like the Puritans earlier, Fox and his followers looked to America for asylum. As the head of a sect despised in England, however, he could not get the necessary colonial grant without the aid of someone influential at the court. Fortunately for his cause, his teachings had struck the hearts of a number of wealthy and prominent men, one of whom in particular made possible a large-scale effort to realize the Quaker dream. This was William Penn—whose father was Sir William Penn, an admiral in the Royal Navy and a landlord of valuable Irish estates.

New Jersey had been given by the Duke of York to two of the Carolina proprietors, one of whom sold his half-interest to two Quakers. The colony received Penn's attention when he was asked to assist the two Quakers with their debts. In their behalf he helped to see to the division of the province into East and West Jersey, one of the original proprietors keeping the East, and the Quakers the West. West Jersey soon began to fill up with Friends from England while East Jersey was being populated mostly by Puritans from New England. Before long Penn together with other wealthy Quakers purchased the eastern property (1682), and eventually the two Jerseys were reunited as one colony (1702), second in Quaker population only to Pennsylvania itself.

Pennsylvania—which Charles II insisted on naming for his old ally the admiral—was based on the King's grant of 1681. Penn had inherited his father's Irish lands and also his claim to a small fortune owed by the King. Charles II, possessing more real estate than ready cash, paid the debt with a grant of territory larger than England and Wales combined.

Much more than a mere real-estate promoter, Penn undertook in Pennsylvania what he called a Holy Experiment. Colonies, he said, were the "seeds of nations," and he proposed to plant the seeds of brotherly love. Closely supervising the planting, he devised a liberal Frame of Government with a representative assembly. He personally voyaged to Pennsylvania (1682) to oversee the laying-out, between the Delaware and Schuylkill rivers, of the city he appropriately named Philadelphia ("Brotherly Love"), which with its rectangular streets, like those of Charleston, helped to set the pattern for most later cities in America. Penn believed, as had Roger Williams, that the land belonged to the Indians, and he was careful to see that they were reimbursed for it, as well as to see that they were not debauched by the fur traders' firewater. With the Indians, who honored him as a rarity, an honest white man, his colony had no trouble during his lifetime. It prospered from the outset because of his thoughtful planning and also because of favorable circumstances, including the mildness of the climate and the fertility of the soil. The settlers were well-to-do and well-equipped, and they received assitance from the people of other colonies and from the Hollanders and Swedes and Finns already there—for Pennsylvania when Penn first saw it was no such wilderness as Virginia had been when the first Englishmen arrived.

Delaware, after its transfer to Penn from the Duke of York (1682), was treated as a part of Pennsylvania (and was known as "the lower counties") but was given the privilege of setting up its own representative assembly. The three counties did so in 1703, and thereafter Delaware was considered a separate colony, though until the Revolution it continued to have the same governor as Pennsylvania.

## The "Glorious Revolution"

The colonies, for the most part, had originated as quite separate projects and had grown up in rather independent ways, with little thought for a long time that they belonged, or ought to belong, to a unified empire. A kind of union, imposing the King's authority on the colonies, was attempted in the 1680s with the establishment of the Dominion of New England. This was intended to help enforce the mercantile system.

One of the arguments for colonization in the first place had been that colonies would increase the wealth of the mother country and lessen her dependence on other nations. According to the mercantile theory, she would prosper and grow strong by exporting more and more to foreigners and importing less and less from them. Colonies would aid by providing a source of supply for raw materials she could not produce at home. To get the full benefit, she would have to exclude foreigners (as Spain had done) from her colonial trade.

Hence in 1660 Parliament began to pass the Navigation Acts, which were aimed at the Dutch. These acts closed the colonies to all trade except that carried in English ships, which were defined as ships built in England or the colonies and manned by sailors of whom three-fourths were Englishmen or colonists. This law also required that certain enumerated items, among them tobacco, be exported from the colonies only to England or to an English possession. Another act (1663) provided that all goods sent from Europe to the colonies had to go by way of England and that taxes could be put on the goods during their transshipment. If the Navigation Acts were to be strictly enforced, the King would have to get more direct control over the colonial governments than he had.

Only in Virginia, a "royal colony" since 1624, did the King as yet have the right to appoint the governor. In Massachusetts, a "corporate colony," the people elected their own governor, as they also did in Plymouth. In Maryland, a "proprietary colony," the appointing power had been delegated to the proprietor. When Charles II created other proprietary colonies—Carolina, New York, New Jersey, Pennsylvania—he himself followed the Maryland example. And when he gave royal charters to Connecticut and Rhode Island, he accepted these two as "corporate colonies" by allowing them to go on choosing their officials. Moreover, he and his predecessors had permitted the development of an assembly representing the people (or some of the people) in each of the colonies—royal, corporate, or proprietary. And the assemblies were claiming more and more power for themselves.

Massachusetts, the worst offender, behaved practically like an independent republic. Charles II decided to take action for controlling and chastising this colony in particular and for tightening control over the American empire in general. He struck a blow at Massachusetts when, in 1679, he denied her authority over New Hampshire and chartered a separate, royal colony whose governor he would himself appoint. He wished to make a royal colony of Massachusetts as well, and he started legal proceedings that led, in 1684, to the revocation of the corporate charter.

His brother and successor, James II, went much further when he came to the throne in 1685. He combined Massachusetts and the rest of the New England colonies into one Dominion of New England, and later he added New York and New Jersey to it. Within this dominion he eliminated the existing assemblies, and over it he placed a single governor, Sir Edmund Andros, with headquarters in Boston. An able but stern and tactless administrator, Andros thoroughly antagonized the people as he proceeded to levy taxes and enforce the Navigation Acts.

Soon after the Bostonians heard of the 1688 movement to overthrow James II in England, they determined to overthrow his viceroy in New England. A mob set out after Andros and other royal officials: he escaped but later surrendered and was imprisoned.

The Massachusetts leaders now hoped to get back their old corporate charter, but the new sovereigns, William and Mary, combined Plymouth with Massachusetts and claimed the land as a royal colony (1691). Under the new charter, they themselves appointed the governor, but they restored the General Court with its elected lower house and allowed the General Court to choose the members of the upper house. This charter also did away with the religious test for voting and officeholding. Though there remained a property requirement, the great majority of Massachusetts men could meet it. Thus the Massachusetts government, no longer a Puritan oligarchy, began to be fairly democratic.

Andros had been ruling New York through a lieutenant governor, Captain Francis Nicholson, who enjoyed the support of the wealthy merchants and fur traders of the province. The groups that were excluded from a fair share in the government—farmers, mechanics, small traders, and shopkeepers—already had a long accumulation of grievances when news came of James' fall and Andros' arrest. Rebellious militiamen promptly seized the New York City fort, and Lieutenant Governor Nicholson sailed away to England.

The leadership of the New York rebels fell to Jacob Leisler, who had come from Germany, succeeded as a merchant, and married into a prominent Dutch family, but had never gained acceptance as one of the colony's ruling class. Leisler's followers proclaimed him commander in chief, and he declared his loyalty to William and Mary. These sovereigns finally appointed a new governor, who was given authority to call an elected assembly. When, ahead of the new governor, a British officer appeared with a contingent of troops, Leisler refused to surrender the fort to him. Leisler afterward yielded, but the delay gave his political enemies, soon back in power, a pretext for charging him with treason. He and a son-in-law were hanged, drawn, and quartered.

In Maryland the people at first assumed (erroneously) that the Catholic Lord Baltimore had sided with the Catholic James II and had opposed the accession of William and Mary. So, in 1689, an old opponent of the proprietor's government, John Coode, started a new revolt as head of an organization calling itself "An Association in Arms for the Defense of the Protestant Religion, and for Asserting the Right of King William and Queen Mary to the Province of Maryland and All the English Dominions." The insurgents drove out Lord Baltimore's officials and, through an elected convention, chose a committee to run the government for the time being. In 1691 William and Mary took advantage of their opportunity to deprive the proprietor of his authority and transform Maryland into a royal colony. (It became a proprietary colony again in 1715, after the fifth Lord Baltimore had joined the Anglican Church.)

Thus the Glorious Revolution of 1688 in England touched off revolutions, mostly bloodless, in the colonies. Under the new regime the representative assemblies that had been abolished were revived, but not the scheme for colonial unification from above. Several of the provinces, however, were now royal colonies in which the King appointed the governor, and over which he potentially had greater direct control than he once had had.

# Chapter 2.  PROVINCIAL AMERICANS, 1700–1763

## The Scarcity of Labor

The transplanted Europeans discovered an abundance of land in North America but faced an acute shortage of labor, which was necessary to unlock the continent's vast wealth. However, the wide availability of land proved to be a powerful attraction for European immigrants; it also provided a need for importing Africans. Immigration and the high rate at which the established population multiplied led to a rate of growth in the population and the labor force far greater than that of contemporary England and Europe.

After 1700 few European immigrants went to either New England or to the South. The largest numbers went to Pennsylvania, where opportunities were more attractive than in stony, intolerant New England or in the slave South. At least half of these people arrived not as free men, but in various states of voluntary servitude. Conditions were most difficult for the "redemptioners" who gave their indentures to the captain of the ship they boarded. He auctioned off their contracts after putting in at an American port, and each buyer then claimed his servants.

Although the terms under which the redemptioners labored were very poor, they were flexible and lenient compared to those the African slaves were subjected to. The slaves found themselves almost completely under the control of their owners. Identifiable by their color, black slaves could not run away and merge themselves with the mass of free humanity as white servants could. Nor could slaves rise out of their bondage to compete with their masters for wealth and political influence as the servants sometimes did. It was, of course, this total control of labor that made slavery increasingly attractive to southern planters. Planters in Virginia and Maryland had developed a highly marketable crop in tobacco, but they discovered that few Englishmen would willingly contract to provide the needed labor. Tobacco planters thus turned to African slaves, in spite of the tendency of the wealthier sugar planters in the West Indies to drive up the price of slaves. By 1700 Negroes accounted for as much as 15 percent of the population of the southern colonies.

During the eighteenth century, tobacco planters became even more committed to slavery, especially after European demand for their product increased dramatically during the 1720s. In 1720 only 25 percent of the planters in the Chesapeake were slaveholders, but by 1770 over half owned slaves. By the time of the Revolution the slave population amounted to well over one-third of the total population of the South, as the exceptionally heavy demands of Carolina rice planters for unskilled labor came to reinforce the needs of the tobacco growers. At the same time, the number of slaves supplied by American and European traders increased rapidly.

The slave trade was dominated by ships owned in England but was shared by others owned in New England. The latter often followed a "triangular" route. That is, a ship took rum and other items from a New England port to the Guinea Coast of Africa, slaves from Africa to the West Indies, and sugar and molasses as well as specie and bills from the West Indies to the home port. There some of the cargo would be distilled into rum for another voyage of the same kind. On the African coast the slave marts were kept supplied by native chieftains who made a business of capturing enemy tribesmen in warfare and bringing them, tied together in long lines known as "coffles," out of the jungle. Then, after some haggling on the seashore, came the horrors of the "middle passage" – so called because it was the second of the three legs of the voyage – during which the slaves were packed in the dark and stinking hold, with no sanitary facilities, no room to stand up, and scarcely air enough to breathe. Those who died en route were thrown overboard, and the losses from disease were generally high. Those who survived were "seasoned" for a time in the West Indies before being shipped on to the mainland.

Economic conditions throughout much of North America appeared conducive to the spread of slavery. The combination of very cheap land and very expensive labor existed not only in the southern colonies. Yet, while men owned slaves in all the colonies, only 20 percent of the slave population lived in New England and the middle colonies in 1763 (45,000 out of 230,000 slaves). Slavery spread extensively only in the South. The higher costs of clothing and sheltering slaves in the more northerly colonies and the less expansive condition of agriculture in the North placed even the wealthiest northern landowners at a disadvantage in bidding for slaves.

## Population Growth

Besides the Africans, other non-English peoples came in large numbers to the colonies after the end of the seventeenth century, while immigration from England itself fell off. Recovering from a prolonged depression in the 1630s, England thereafter began to develop more and more industries which demanded workmen, so that the talk of overpopulation ceased to be heard. Instead of encouraging emigration from its own shores, the government tried to check the loss of English manpower by prohibiting the departure of skilled artisans, while continuing to unload the unemployable or the undesirable upon the defenseless colonies. Although, during the eighteenth century, the colonies received relatively few newcomers from England, the populations of several of them were swelled by vast numbers of arrivals from France, Germany, Switzerland, Ireland, and Scotland.

Of these immigrants the earliest though not the most numerous were the French Calvinists, or Huguenots. Under the Edict of Nantes (1598) they had enjoyed liberties and privileges that enabled them to constitute practically a state within the state in Roman Catholic France. In 1685 the edict was revoked, and singly and in groups the Huguenots took the first opportunity to leave the country, until a total of about 300,000 had left for England, the Netherlands, America, and elsewhere, only a small minority of them going to the English colonies.

Like the French Protestants, many German Protestants suffered from the arbitrary enactments of their rulers, and German Catholics as well as Protestants suffered even more from the devastating wars of the Sun King of France, Louis XIV. The Rhineland of southwestern Germany, the area known as the Palatinate, was especially exposed to the slaughter of its people and the ruin of its farms. For the Palatine Germans, the unusually cold winter of 1708–1709 came as the last straw, and more than 12,000 of them sought refuge in England. The Catholics among them were shipped back to Germany and the rest were resettled in England, Ireland, or the colonies. Pennsylvania was the usual destination of Germans, who sailed for America in growing numbers, to form the largest body of eighteenth-century white immigrants except for the Scotch-Irish.

The Scotch-Irish, the most numerous of the newcomers, were not Irishmen at all, though coming from Ireland, and they were distinct from the Scots who came to America directly from Scotland. In the early 1600s King James I, to further the conquest of Ireland, had seen to the peopling of the northern county of Ulster with his subjects from the Scottish Lowlands, who as good Presbyterians might be relied upon to hold their ground against the Irish Catholics. These Ulster colonists—the Scotch-Irish—eventually prospered despite the handicap of a barren soil and the necessity of border fighting with the Irish tribesmen. Then, after about a century, the English government destroyed their prosperity by prohibiting the export of their woolens and other products, and at the same time threatened their religion by virtually outlawing it and insisting upon conformity with the Anglican Church. As the long-term leases of the Scotch-Irish terminated, in the years after 1710, the English landlords doubled and even tripled the rents. Rather than sign new leases, thousands upon thousands of the ill-used tenants embarked in successive waves of emigration. Understandably a cantankerous and troublesome lot, these people often were coldly received at the colonial ports, and most of them pushed out to the edge of the American wilderness.

The Scots and the Irish, as migrants to America, had no connection with the Scotch-Irish. Scottish Highlanders, some of them Roman Catholics frustrated in the rebellions of 1715 and 1745, went with their tartans and kilts and bagpipes to more than one of the colonies, but mostly to North Carolina. Presbyterian Lowlanders, afflicted with high rents in the country and unemployment in town, left in largest numbers shortly before the American Revolution. The Irish had migrated in trickles over a long period and, by the time of the Revolution, were about as numerous as the Scots, though less conspicuous, many of them having lost their Roman Catholic religion and their identity as Irishmen.

All these various immigrants contributed to the remarkable growth of the colonies. In 1700 the colonial population totaled a quarter of a million or less; by 1775 it was nearly ten times as large, more than two million. Its rate of growth was more than twice that common in Europe during the same period. Important as the continuing immigration was, the rapid growth of the colonial population was mainly due to natural increase, to the excess of births over deaths. As a consequence, only about one-tenth of the white population alive at the end of the colonial period had been born abroad. Contributing to the high rate of natural increase was the fact that colonists married earlier and had more children. The abundance of land and opportunity made it possible for young couples to set up households and follow the Biblical advice: "Be ye fruitful and multiply." Even more important for rapid population growth was a low mortality rate. In an average year, the American mortality rate was about one-half of that prevailing in Europe. Crops were more abundant, sharply reducing periods of famine, and although the winters were harsher in much of America, families were better able to protect themselves because of the great availability of wood for building of houses and for fuel for heating and cooking. The infant mortality rate, in particular, was lower, because pregnant and nursing women were better able to sustain their own health.

The colonial population was surprisingly mobile; New Englanders resettling in New Jersey and other colonies to the south, and Pennsylvanians (Scotch-Irish and Germans) swarming up the Shenandoah Valley to people the back country of the Carolinas. In all the colonies men and women pushed upstream toward the unsettled wilderness, until with Daniel Boone leading the way into Kentucky (1769) they began even to occupy the land beyond the mountains.

Along the seacoast a number of villages grew into small cities. For more than a century after its founding, Boston remained the largest town, but eventually it was overtaken by Philadelphia. After 1700 these and other colonial towns increased more rapidly than most English cities. Indeed, by 1775 Philadelphia, with its 40,000 inhabitants, had become larger than any English city with the exception of London. Eight out of a hundred Americans lived in towns in 1720. The rest of the people—the overwhelming majority throughout the colonial period—were scattered over the countryside and lived on farms of one description or another.

## The Founding of Georgia

The population increase from 1700 to 1775 mainly reflected the growth of existing colonies; only a single new one was founded during these years. Georgia, the last of the mainland colonies, was unique in its origins. It was founded by neither a corporation nor a proprietorship, and its guiding purpose was neither to make profits nor to create a sectarian refuge. In the beginning Georgia was the work of trustees serving without pay. Their main purpose was twofold: to provide a new start in life for Englishmen imprisoned for debt, and to erect a military barrier against the Spaniards on the southern border of English America.

The charter from George II (1732) transferred the land between the Savannah and Altamaha rivers to the trustees for a period of twenty-one years. In their colonization policies they were to keep in mind the needs of military security. Landholdings were limited in size so as to make settlement compact. Negroes—free or slave—were excluded, and Roman Catholics also, to forestall the danger of wartime insurrection and of collusion with enemy coreligionists. And the Indian trade was strictly regulated, with rum prohibited, to lessen the risk of Indian complications. The first expedition built a fortified town at the mouth of the Savannah in 1733. Newcomers generally preferred to settle in South Carolina, where there were no laws against big plantations, slaves, and rum. Before the twenty-one years of the trusteeship were up, these restrictions were repealed, and after 1750 Georgia developed along lines similar to those of South Carolina.

## Agriculture

In the shaping of the provincial economy—that is, in the determination of the ways the colonists made their living – four forces were especially important. One of these was the policy of the British government, which discouraged certain occupations, such as iron finishing, and encouraged others, such as shipbuilding, in accordance with mercantilist principles. A second and more important influence derived from the geographical conditions in America, which favored some lines of activity, such as wheat farming, and made others, such as growing sugar cane, impracticable. A third consisted of the aims and energies of the individual settlers, who brought with them from the British Isles and the European Continent (and, in the case of the slaves, from Africa) their own skills and habits and aspirations for personal success, including the desire for a higher standard of living. A fourth was the rapidly growing demand of European and West Indian consumers for a wide variety of products. As a result of these diverse factors, there flourished in the eighteenth century a variety of agricultural, industrial, and commercial pursuits, not all of which conformed to the broad mercantilistic plan.

In George Washington's time the tools and methods of farming were not much advanced beyond what they had been in the day of the Pharaohs, and in provincial America there was even less care of the soil than there had been in ancient Egypt. Most of the colonists gave little thought to conserving their land by rotating crops, applying fertilizers, or checking erosion. Their attitude was reasonable enough in their circumstances: it paid them to economize on labor and capital, not on land.

Near the frontier – that ever-expanding arc from Maine to Georgia, which bounded the area of settlement – subsistence farming was the rule. The frontiersman planted his corn and beans amid the stumps in patches he had incompletely reclaimed from the forest, and with his crops and his catch of wild game he fed himself and his family. Eventually some of the backwoodsmen went in for cattle raising on a fairly large scale, especially in Pennsylvania and the Carolinas.

In New England – where farmers once had lived on village lots, shared the "commons" as pasture and timberland, and tilled outlying fields – the system of landholding gradually changed. After 1700 the commons were partly divided into private property, and the fields were consolidated into separate farms. The typical farm became one that was small enough to be worked by the farmer, his sons, and perhaps an occasional hired hand, with the aid of neighbors at harvests and at house or barn raisings. It was bounded by fences made of stones that had been laboriously cleared off the fields. A fairly self-sufficient unit, producing mainly for use rather than for sale, it contained a variety of livestock, apple and other orchards, and fields devoted chiefly to hay and corn, the prevalence of the "blast" or black-stem rust having discouraged the cultivation of wheat.

In New York, despite the abundance of excellent soil, agricultural productivity lagged because of the engrossment of the land in great estates, running to thousands and even hundreds of thousands of acres, on which few people were willing to work as tenants when they could get farms of their own in other colonies. In Pennsylvania, of all the colonies the most favored by nature for farming, the Germans applied the intensive cultivation they had learned in the old country. Their neat and substantial barns were their pride, but the work of their womenfolk in the fields was sometimes shocking to non-Germans. With fairly large holdings, these farmers needed all the labor they could get, and in addition to their wives and daughters they employed indentured servants, women as well as men. In both New York and Pennsylvania the farmers concentrated on the production of staples to be sold abroad and at home. After ceasing to produce enough food to feed all its own people, particularly those living in the port cities, New England depended upon these "bread colonies" for its wheat. The most important demand for wheat was that of the West Indian planters, who specialized heavily in sugar production. By 1763 exports of wheat exceeded those of any crop except tobacco.

In the Chesapeake region there still existed tobacco farms as small as a hundred acres, cultivated by the owners, their families, and perhaps a servant or a slave or two. Such farms, however, had come to be overshadowed by large plantations with thousands of acres and dozens or even hundreds of Negroes. On the tobacco plantations slave labor was easily adapted to the simple and repetitive round of tasks that the crop required – sowing, transplanting, weeding, worming, picking, curing, stripping, and packing.

Slave labor was also fairly well suited to rice culture along the Georgia and Carolina coasts. Here dikes and ditches leading from the tidal rivers permitted the necessary flooding and draining of the paddies, while care was taken to see that no salt water reached the rice with the incoming tide. To cultivate the growing rice, men had to stand knee-deep in mud, their bare backs exposed to malarial mosquitoes and to the broiling sun. Since white men could not be hired to do it, slaves were compelled to perform this torturing and unhealthful work. But the rice plantations were smaller than the tobacco plantations and did not provide a similar year-round routine that would utilize slave labor to the full.

Indigo supplemented rice after the successful cultivation of the dye plant (1743) by Eliza Lucas, the daughter of a West Indian planter. Grown on high ground, the indigo did not get in the way of the rice on the river bottoms, and it occupied the slaves at times when they were not busy with the rice. They tended the indigo fields, cut the leaves, soaked them in vats, and extracted the residue as a blue powder. Glad for a chance to be freed from foreign sources of the dye, Parliament granted a bounty of sixpence a pound.

The British government tried to encourage the production of other crops that would meet the needs of mercantilism. It gave bounties for hemp, and a little was grown in the colonies, particularly in North Carolina, but not enough to make the experiment pay. The government also attempted to force the growth of grapes for wine and of mulberry trees for silk, but had even less success with these than with hemp. Too much skilled labor was required for such products. Obstinately the colonial farmers and planters stuck to those lines of production in which they had a comparative advantage over producers elsewhere in the world. In some cases, as with tobacco and indigo, the colonial products happened to supplement those grown in England and thus fit the mercantilistic pattern. In other cases, as with wheat, the produce of the colonies competed with that of the mother country and was either irrelevant to the mercantile system or incompatible with it.

## Industries

In the 1700s, as in earlier times, most families produced nearly all their necessities within the household, but an increasing quantity of goods was manufactured outside the home, in shops.

In the rising towns, artisans of many kinds appeared — carpenters, chandlers (candlemakers), coopers (barrelmakers), cordwainers (shoemakers), weavers, tailors, wheelwrights, and dozens of others. In such lines as millinery and dressmaking, women artisans were common and often a widow took over her husband's work and succeeded as a cobbler, tinworker, or even blacksmith. By 1750 almost a third of the people of Philadelphia owed their living to a craft of some kind.

Colonial craftsmanship became notable for quantity as well as quality. As late as 1700 all but a tiny fraction of the manufactures that the colonists bought were made in England. Before the Revolution, most of the manufactures were made in America. The rise of the provincial craftsman was watched with concern by men in London who took the doctrines of mercantilism seriously.

Water power was widely used in various kinds of colonial mills. At the rapids of streams small enough to be easily dammed, grist and fulling mills were set up to take some of the heavier labor out of the household, grinding grain and fulling cloth (shrinking and tightening the weave by a process of soaking and pounding) for the farmers in the area. The millowner was usually a farmer himself in his spare time. He frequently used his water wheel to power a sawmill for cutting his neighbors' logs.

Like lumbering, the fur trade and the fisheries were extractive industries, depending closely upon the resources provided by nature. Both fishing and fur trading became big businesses employing what were, by colonial standards, large amounts of capital. The fisheries led to shipbuilding, the first colonial-built ships being put together on the New England coast for the use of fishermen, and the abundance of timber and naval stores enabled the industry in the provinces to expand to the point of outdoing that of England itself. So cheap and yet so seaworthy were the materials that, despite the high wages of colonial labor, excellent ships could be produced at as little as half the cost of those built in English yards. By the Revolution almost one-third of all British-owned ships were of colonial construction.

From the beginning of colonization, the home government encouraged the colonial production of iron in a crude form, as a raw material for English mills and foundries. When provincial ironmakers began to produce more than merely the crude metal, their competitors in England induced Parliament to pass the Iron Act of 1750, which removed the English duty on pig and bar iron but forbade the colonists to erect new mills for the secondary processing of iron or steel. This prohibition was in line with other acts intended to limit the rise of advanced manufactures in America. The Woolen Act (1699) prohibited the export of wool or woolens from a colony to any place outside its boundaries, and the Hat Act (1732) similarly prohibited the export of hats, which could be cheaply made in America because of the availability of beaver skins. But the colonists usually disregarded such legislation when it was in their interest to do so and by the Revolution colonial iron makers produced 15 percent of the world's iron.

## Money and Commerce

Though the colonists produced most of what they consumed, they by no means achieved economic self-sufficiency. The colonies as a whole could not supply their entire wants from their own agriculture and industry. Neither could any of the separate colonies, nor could an individual household except at an extremely low level of living. To maintain and raise their living standards the mainland colonists had to have the benefits of trade with one another and with people overseas.

The central problem in the overseas commerce of the colonies was to find the means of payment for the increasing imports. Money was scarce in the colonies. All of them experimented at one time or another with paper currency, often securing it with land. But Parliament suppressed this expedient by legislating against the Massachusetts land bank in 1740, and by outlawing paper money as legal tender in New England in 1751 and in the rest of the colonies later on. Anyhow, this kind of paper was not acceptable in payment for imported goods and services, which had to be bought with specie or with bills of exchange arising from colonial exports. In short, the colonies had to sell abroad in order to buy from abroad, but British policy attempted to limit and control their selling opportunities.

Though the tobacco planters had an abundant staple for export, they were not allowed to dispose of it to the highest bidder in the markets of the world. According to the Navigation Acts, tobacco was one of the "enumerated items" that must be exported only to the British Isles, whence more than half of it was reexported to other places. The laws also prohibited the growing of tobacco in the British Isles, but protection against competition in the mother country did not quite offset the disadvantages of the colonial planter.

He usually sold his annual crop to an English merchant (or after the 1720s to a Scottish merchant) either directly or through a factor in the colonies, and the merchant credited him with its value, after deducting charges for shipping, insurance, and a merchant's commission. Through the merchant he bought slaves and manufactured goods, and the merchant deducted the cost of these from the planter's credit on the books. After tobacco prices had begun to fall, the planter often found at the end of a year that his crop did not pay for all the goods he had ordered in return. The merchant then carried him until the next year and charged interest on the extension of credit. As the years went by, the planter went more and more deeply into debt, eventually leaving his indebtedness to his heirs.

The colonial merchant in such ports as Boston, New York, and Philadelphia did not have the same difficulties as the tobacco planter, though he had others of his own. He was favored by the Navigation Acts, passed in 1650 and after, which excluded foreign ships from practically all the colonial carrying trade. And he found a market in England for the furs, timber, naval stores, and vessels produced in the northern colonies. But he could not profitably sell in England all the fish, flour, wheat, and meat that the colonies produced for export. He had to find other markets for these commodities if he was to obtain adequate means of paying for his imports from England. Wherever he traded, his profits would be reduced if he obeyed the laws and paid the duties imposed on most of the colonial goods that went to England and on all the European goods that went through England to the colonies.

In the English island colonies of the West Indies the colonial merchant found a ready outlet for mainland foodstuffs and livestock. In the French, Dutch, and Spanish islands of the Caribbean he also got eager customers—and often better prices. Responding to pressure from English sugar planters, who wished to monopolize the growing mainland sugar market, Parliament in the Molasses Act of 1733 put a high duty on foreign sugar taken to the continental colonies. The molasses duty was intended to discourage commerce with the foreign islands. But the Northern merchant could evade the tax by smuggling, and he often did.

To and from England, to and from the West Indies—these were much the most important routes of trade for the Northern merchant. He also worked out a number of routes of indirect trade with the mother country; some of them complex and frequently changing, others fairly stable and somewhat "triangular" in their simplicity. Thus he might direct his ships to Catholic southern Europe with fish, then to England with wine and other proceeds in cash or bills of exchange, and then back home with manufactured goods.

## The Class Structure

In provincial America the generous economic basis of life supported a society in which the benefits of physical well-being were more widely diffused than anywhere else in the world. It was a comparatively open society, in which people had more opportunity than elsewhere to rise in economic and social status. Yet it was also a society with great inequalities, one that offered only hardship and poverty to many of its members and especially to those of African descent.

In the colonies the English class arrangement was not reproduced. Few or none of the nobility became colonists, though some of them were colonial enterprisers. A relatively small number of untitled gentlemen and a great many members of the middle and lower orders migrated to Virginia, Massachusetts, and other colonies. Some of these arrivals doubtless hoped to reconstruct in America something like the social system they had known in England, only here they hoped to occupy the higher levels themselves. A fortunate few did acquire extensive landholdings and proceeded to mimic the aristocrats back home, but no true aristocracy was transplanted to the colonies.

A colonial class system nevertheless grew up. Once social differentiation was well developed, as it was by the middle of the eighteenth century, the upper classes in the colonies consisted of the royal officials, the proprietary families, the great landholders in the North and the planters in the South, and the leading merchants with their investments mostly in forms of property other than land. The middle classes included most of the landowning farmers and, in the towns, the lesser merchants, shopkeepers, ship captains, professional men, and self-employed artisans. The lower classes comprised the indentured servants and the poorest farmers, together with the comparatively small number of wage earners, including farm hands, sailors, and fishermen. Forming a separate class or caste, though often working in the fields alongside white servants and even alongside men of the master class, were the Negro slaves, the lowest of all.

All except the slaves could aspire to a higher place for themselves or at least for their children. Once a man had made a fortune, he was usually accepted by those who theretofore had considered him their social inferior. The colonists, believing in enterprise and material success, honored the self-made man. Afterward his descendants were inclined to forget the humble and even grubby origins of the family fortune and to think of themselves as thoroughgoing aristocrats. For example, one of the "first families" of eighteenth-century Virginia, the Byrds, enjoyed a fortune that William Byrd I had put together in the seventeenth century by selling pots, pans, guns, and rum to the Indians in exchange for furs and hides, as well as by dealing in Indian and African slaves.

As some of the rich grew richer, some of the poor became more impoverished. There was a widening of extremes. If many of the early indentured servants acquired valuable land and respectable status after completing their servitude, many of the later ones either took up subsistence farming on the frontier or sank to the level of the "poor whites" on worn-out lands in the neighborhood of the planters. Yet, especially in New England and Pennsylvania, the majority of the people came to form a self-respecting, property-owning middle class.

The institution of slavery grew more and more rigid, with slave codes that were increasingly severe. This was especially true in South Carolina, where whites had reason to fear the blacks who greatly outnumbered them. There, slave conspiracies or mere rumors of them brought savage retribution and further tightenings of the already strict laws governing slavery. Near Charleston several slaves accused of conspiring to revolt were burned to death in 1720. In the city itself fifty were hanged in 1740, and when a disastrous fire followed, two more were executed for arson.

Such events were not confined to the South. In New York City a Negro insurrection led in 1712 to the execution of twenty-one participants, three of whom were burned at the stake while another was chained up without food or drink until he died. Again, in 1741, 101 Negroes were convicted of plotting with poor whites to burn the city; eighteen of the blacks were hanged, thirteen burned alive, and the rest banished; four whites, two of them women, went to the gallows. Even in New England, where slaves were relatively few and slavery relatively mild, there were occasional instances of blacks attacking whites.

## The Pattern of Religions

Though originating abroad, religions developed a new and distinctive pattern in America. With the immigration of diverse sectarians from several countries, the colonies became an ecclesiastical patchwork made up of a great variety of churches. Toleration flourished to a degree remarkable for the time, not because it was deliberately sought but because conditions favored its growth. No single religious establishment predominated in the colonies as the Church of England did in the British Isles and as other state churches, Lutheran or Roman Catholic, did in Western Europe.

By law, the Church of England was established in Virginia, Maryland, New York, the Carolinas, and Georgia. In these colonies everyone regardless of belief or affiliation was supposed to be taxed for the support of the Church. Actually, except in Virginia and Maryland, the Church of England succeeded in maintaining its position as the established church only in certain localities.

Protestants extended toleration to one another more readily than to Roman Catholics. To strict Puritans the Pope seemed no less than Antichrist. Their border enemies in New France, being "papists," seemed agents of the devil bent on frustrating the divine mission of the wilderness Zion in New England. In most of the Eng-

lish colonies, however, the Roman Catholics were far too small a minority to occasion serious conflict. They were most numerous in Maryland, and even there they numbered no more than 3,000. Ironically, they suffered their worst persecution in that colony, which had been founded as a refuge for them and had been distinguished by its Toleration Act of 1649. According to Maryland laws passed after 1691, Catholics not only were deprived of political rights but also were forbidden to hold religious services except in private houses.

Even fewer than the Catholics, the Jews in provincial America totaled no more than about 2,000 at any time. There was relatively little social discrimination against the Jews, but there was political discrimination: in no colony could they vote or hold office.

## The Great Awakening

During the early 1700s the pious outlook gave way more and more to a worldly view. With the westward movement and the wide scattering of the colonial population, many of the frontiersmen lost touch with organized religion. With the rise of towns and the multiplication of material comforts, the inhabitants of the more densely settled areas were inclined toward an increasingly secular outlook. With the appearance of numerous and diverse sects, some people were tempted to doubt whether any particular denomination, even their own, possessed a monopoly of truth and grace. And with the progress of science and free thought in Europe, at least a few Americans began to adopt a rational and skeptical philosophy.

For thousands of the colonists, the trend away from religion was reversed by a revival movement known as the Great Awakening, which reached a climax in the 1740s. Wandering exhorters from abroad did much to stimulate the revivalistic spirit. John and Charles Wesley, founders of Methodism, which began as a reform movement within the Church of England, visited Georgia and other colonies in the 1730s with the intention of revitalizing religion and converting Indians and Negroes. George Whitefield, a powerful open-air preacher from England and for a time an associate of the Wesleys, made several evangelizing tours through the colonies.

Yet the outstanding preacher of the Great

Awakening in New England was Jonathan Edwards—one of the most profound theologians in the history of American religious thought. From his pulpit in Northampton, Massachusetts, Edwards attacked the new doctrines of easy salvation for all. He called upon his people to return to the faith of their fathers. He preached afresh the old Puritan ideas of the absolute sovereignty of God, the depravity of man, predestination, the necessity of experiencing a sense of election, and election by God's grace alone. Describing hell as vividly as if he had been there, he brought his listeners to their knees in terror of divine wrath. Day after day the agonized sinners crowded his parsonage to seek his aid; at least one committed suicide.

The Great Awakening spread over the colonies like a religious epidemic. It was most contagious in frontier areas and among the comparatively poor and uneducated folk, especially in the South. It led to the division of existing congregations and the founding of schools for the preparation of ministers. To some extent, too, it aroused a spirit of humanitarianism, a concern for the physical as well as the spiritual welfare of the poor and oppressed. The widely preached doctrine of salvation for all—of equal opportunity to share in God's grace—encouraged the notion of equal rights to share also in the good things on earth. Thus it stimulated feelings of democracy.

Though the Great Awakening had these important and lasting consequences, many of the converted soon backslid, and by the end of the colonial period English America contained fewer church members for its population than did any other Christian country of the time, and fewer than the United States has today.

## Reading and Writing

As an American variant of English culture developed in the colonies, it was reflected in the partial Americanization of the English language. After 1700 English travelers in America began to notice a strangeness in accent as well as vocabulary, and in 1756 the great lexicographer Dr. Samuel Johnson mentioned the existence of an "American dialect."

Dr. Johnson thought of Americans as barbarians, and some no doubt were, but from the beginning many had been concerned lest civili-

zation be lost in the wilderness. They continued to provide schooling for their children as best they could, particularly in New England. In various colonies, the advancement of religion being one motive for education, the Quakers and other sects operated church schools. Here and there a widow or an old maid conducted a "dame school," holding private classes in her home. In some of the cities master craftsmen set up evening schools for their apprentices, at least a hundred such schools appearing between 1723 and 1770. Far more people learned to read than ever attended school, yet a great many—perhaps a great majority—never learned to read at all.

Founded in 1704, the first regular newspaper in the colonies, though not a very newsy one, was the weekly Boston *News-Letter,* a small folded sheet of four pages with two columns to a page. By the 1760s one or more weekly papers were being published in each of the colonies except New Jersey and Delaware, both of which were well enough supplied by the presses of New York and Philadelphia. Several monthly magazines, notably the *American Magazine* of Philadelphia, were started after about 1750, with hopes of wide circulation. One after another they appeared for a year or two and then expired. More successful and more widely read were the yearly almanacs. Originally mere collections of weather data, these turned into small magazines of a sort, containing a great variety of literary fare. *Poor Richard's Almanac,* now well remembered, was only one of many, though a superior one.

Its publisher, Benjamin Franklin, was one of a few colonial-born men of letters who wrote works of lasting literary merit. As a rule, provincial authors had no time for belles-lettres, for fiction, poetry, drama, and the like. Writers concentrated upon sermons, religious tracts, and subjects of urgent, practical concern.

## The Higher Learning

Of the six colleges in actual operation by 1763, all but two were founded by religious groups primarily for the training of preachers. Harvard (1636) was established by Congregationalists, William and Mary (1693) by Anglicans, and Yale (1701) by conservative Congregationalists who were dissatisfied with the growing religious liberalism of Harvard. The College of New Jersey (1746), later known as Princeton, was set up by Presbyterians in response to the Great Awakening. At any of these institutions a student with secular interests could derive something of a liberal education from the prevailing curricula, which included logic, ethics, physics, geometry, astronomy, rhetoric, Latin, Hebrew, and Greek. From the beginning Harvard was intended not only to provide an educated ministry but also to "advance learning and perpetuate it to posterity." King's College (1754), afterward Columbia, had no theological faculty and was interdenominational from the start. The Academy and College of Philadelphia (1755), which grew into the University of Pennsylvania, was a completely secular institution, founded by a group of laymen under the inspiration of Benjamin Franklin. It offered courses in utilitarian subjects as well as the liberal arts—in mechanics, chemistry, agriculture, government, commerce, and modern languages. Though the colonies were thus well supplied with colleges, at least in comparison with other countries at the time, some Americans continued to go to English universities. But the great majority of colonial leaders, after 1700, received their entire education in America.

In the provincial colleges, considerable attention was given to scientific subjects. Chairs in "natural philosophy," or physical science, were endowed at William and Mary and at Harvard. The most advanced scientific thought of Europe —Copernican astronomy and Newtonian physics—eventually made its way into American teaching. But scientific speculation and experiment were not the exclusively academic, professional occupations that they later became.

Mather, Edwards, and many other ministers, merchants, and planters in America were active as amateur scientists. The Royal Society of London, founded in 1662 for the advancement of science, honored a number of them by electing them as fellows. To this society the American members and nonmember correspondents sent samples and descriptions of plants, animals, and remarkable phenomena. By means of their contributions the colonial amateurs added a good deal to the accumulation of data upon which later scientific progress was to be based. They also sent in plans for mechanical inventions and helped to start the reputation of Americans as a mechanically ingenious people.

The greatest of colonial scientists and inventors, Benjamin Franklin, gained world-wide fame with his kite experiment (1752) which demonstrated that lightning and electricity were one and the same. He interested himself in countless subjects besides electricity, and he was a theoretical or "philosophical" scientist as well as a practical one. He also was a promoter of science. In 1727 he and his Philadelphia friends organized the Junto, a club for the discussion of intellectual and practical matters of mutual interest. In 1744 he led in the founding of the American Philosophical Society, the first learned society in America.

## Toward Self-government

After England's Glorious Revolution of 1688 and the collapse of the Dominion of New England, the English government (or the British government after 1707, when Great Britain was created by the union of England and Scotland) made no serious or sustained effort for more than seventy years to tighten its control over the colonies. During that time, it is true, additions were made to the list of royal colonies (New Jersey, 1702; North and South Carolina, 1729; Georgia, 1754) until they numbered eight, in all of which the King had the power of appointing governors and other colonial officials. During that time, also, Parliament passed new laws supplementing the original Navigation Acts and elaborating on the mercantilist program — laws restricting colonial manufactures, limiting paper currency, and regulating trade. Nevertheless, the British government itself remained uncertain and divided about the extent to which it ought to interfere in colonial affairs. The colonies were left, within broad limits, to go their separate ways, and they were able to assert fairly extensive rights of self-government.

Resistance to imperial authority centered in the colonial assemblies. By the 1750s they had established the right to levy taxes, make appropriations, approve appointments, and pass laws for their respective colonies. Their legislation was subject to veto by the governor and to disallowance by the Privy Council (the central administrative agency in England), but they could often sway the governor by means of their money powers, and they could get around the Privy Council by repassing disallowed laws in slightly altered form. The assemblies came to look upon themselves as little parliaments, each practically as powerful within its colony as Parliament itself was in England.

Meanwhile some developments were laying a basis for the eventual growth of a sense of intercolonial community. The increase of population, which produced an almost continuous line of settlement along the seacoast, brought the people of the various colonies into closer and closer contact, as did the gradual construction of roads, the rise of intercolonial trade, and the improvement of the colonial post office. In 1691 the postal service operated only from Massachusetts to New York and Pennsylvania. In 1711 it was extended to New Hampshire on the north, in 1732 to Virginia on the south, and ultimately all the way to Georgia. After 1753 Franklin, a deputy postmaster, improved the service, providing weekly instead of biweekly posts and speeding them up so that, for example, mail was delivered from Boston to Philadelphia in about three weeks instead of six. Post riders carried newspapers as well as letters and thus enlarged and unified the colonial reading public.

Still, the colonists were loath to cooperate even when, in 1754, they faced a new threat from old and dreaded enemies, the French and their Indian allies. A conference of colonial leaders — with delegates on hand from Pennsylvania, Maryland, New York, and the New England colonies — was meeting in Albany to negotiate a treaty with the Iroquois. The delegates stayed on to talk about forming a colonial federation for defense. Benjamin Franklin proposed to his fellow delegates a plan by which Parliament would set up in America "one general government" for all the colonies, each of which would "retain its present constitution" except for the powers to be given the general government. The King would appoint a President-General, and the colonial assemblies would elect representatives to a Grand Council. The President-General in consultation with the Council would take charge of all relations with the Indians; the Council, subject to his veto, would make laws and levy taxes for raising troops, building forts, waging war, and carrying on other Indian affairs.

War with the French and Indians was already beginning when this Albany Plan was presented to the colonial assemblies for their consideration. Yet none of them approved it, and none except the Massachusetts assembly even gave it very serious attention. "Everyone cries, a union is necessary," Franklin wrote to the Massachusetts governor, "but when they come to the manner and form of the union, their weak noodles are perfectly distracted."

## New France

The French had founded a string of widely separated communities, strategically located fortresses, and far-flung missions and trading posts. On Cape Breton Island they established Fort Louisbourg, one of the most redoubtable strongholds in all the New World, to guard the approach to the Gulf of St. Lawrence. From both banks of the St. Lawrence River the strips of land ("seigneuries") of would-be feudal lords stretched to the edge of the clearings. On a high bluff above the river stood Quebec, the pride of the French empire in America. Farther up the river was Montreal, even more "provincial" and less sophisticated than Quebec. Hundreds of miles to the northwest, near the juncture of Lake Superior with Lakes Michigan and Huron, was the tiny outpost of Sault Sainte Marie. Hundreds of miles to the southwest, at the juncture of Lakes Huron and Erie, was the well-fortified Detroit. Still farther in the same direction, along the Mississippi between the Missouri and the Ohio, was a cluster of hamlets—Cahokia, Kaskaskia, Fort Chartres, Sainte Genevieve—each with its outlying common fields of black earth under cultivation. Over on the Wabash was the fifth tiny settlement of the Illinois country, Vincennes.

On the lower Mississippi were plantations much like those in the Southern colonies of English America, plantations worked by Negro slaves and supporting a race-conscious class of "Creoles," who had far more pretensions to grandeur than did the comparatively poor and necessarily democratic seigneurs of Canada. Louisiana became relatively populous, especially after thousands of settlers had been brought in by the land-speculation schemes of John Law, whose "Mississippi Bubble" burst in 1721, to the ruin of investors in Europe and the disillusionment of recently arrived Louisianans. Founded in 1718, New Orleans soon grew into a city comparable in size with some of those on the Atlantic seaboard but quainter than most, with its houses built of cypress logs and bark roofs and set upon stilts above the swampy ground. To the east of New Orleans, along the Gulf of Mexico, were the towns of Biloxi (founded 1699) and Mobile (1702), completing the string of mainland settlements which stretched all the way around from Fort Louisbourg.

## Anglo-French Conflict

Spacious though it was, the continent of North America seemed too small to contain both the English and the French. The English, as Protestants, and the French, as Roman Catholics, eyed each other with suspicion and fear. As fishermen and fur traders they competed for the profits of the forest and the sea. Each national group began ultimately to feel that its very survival in America depended upon the elimination of the other's influence. No serious trouble between English and French colonists occurred, however, so long as their homelands remained at peace.

Eventually two wars spread from Europe to America, where they were known to the English colonists as King William's War (1689–1697) and Queen Anne's War (1701–1713). The first, which involved few of the colonists except in northern New England, led to no decisive result. The second, which entailed border fighting with the Spaniards in the South as well as the French and their Indian allies in the North, ended in one of the great and far-reaching international settlements of modern history—the Treaty of Utrecht (1713). At Utrecht the English were awarded some sizable territorial gains in North America at the expense of the French: Acadia (Nova Scotia), Newfoundland, and the shores of Hudson Bay.

After about a quarter of a century of European and American peace, England went to war with Spain over the question of English trading rights in the Spanish colonies, and the English in Georgia came to blows with the Spaniards in Florida. The Anglo-Spanish conflict soon merged in a general European war. Again New England and New France were involved in the hostilities—in what the English colonists referred to as King George's War (1744–1748). New Englanders captured the French bastion at Louisbourg on Cape Breton Island, but to their bitter disappointment they had to abandon it in accordance with the peace treaty, which provided for the mutual restoration of conquered territory.

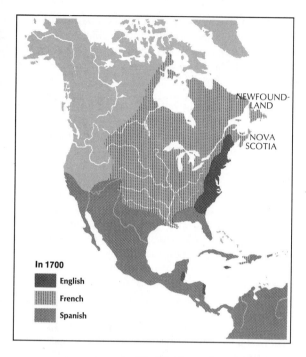

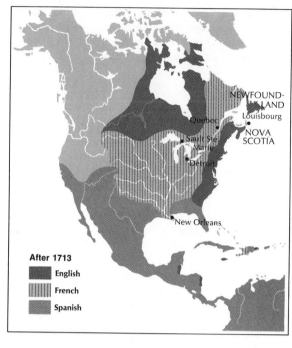

**North American Empires**

The next conflict was different. Known to the colonists as the French and Indian War, it was in fact a "Great War for the Empire." Unlike the preliminaries, this climactic struggle originated in the interior of North America.

## The Great War for the Empire

Within the American wilderness a number of border disputes arose, but the most serious of them concerned the ownership of the Ohio Valley. The French, desiring to control this direct route between Canada and Louisiana, began to build a chain of fortifications to make good their claim. Pennsylvania fur traders and Virginia land speculators (the latter organized as the Ohio Company) looked to the country across the Alleghenies as a profitable field for their operations, and the British government, aroused to the defense of its territorial rights, gave instructions to the colonial governors to resist French encroachments.

Acting on these instructions, the governor of Virginia sent George Washington, then only twenty-one, to protest to the commanders of the French forts newly built between Lake Erie and the Allegheny River, but these commanders politely replied that the land was French. While Washington was on his fruitless mission, a band of Virginians tried to forestall the French by erecting a fort of their own at the strategic key to the Ohio Valley—the forks of the Ohio, where the Allegheny and Monongahela rivers join. A stronger band of Canadians drove the Virginians away, completed the work, and named it Fort Duquesne. Arriving with the advance guard of a relief force from Virginia, Washington met a French detachment in a brief but bloody skirmish. He then fell back to a hastily constructed stockade, Fort Necessity, where he was overwhelmed by troops from Fort Duquesne and compelled to surrender (July 4, 1754). The first shots of the French and Indian War had been fired.

At first the overall direction of British strategy was weak. Then, in 1757, William Pitt, as prime minister, was allowed to act as practically a wartime dictator of the Empire. With Pitt as organizer, the British regulars in America, together with colonial troops, proceeded to take one French stronghold after another, including Fort Duquesne in 1758. The next year, after a siege

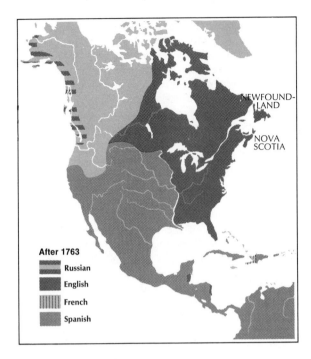

After 1763

▨ Russian

■ English

▥ French

▦ Spanish

French and Indian War, the English government did not attempt to tax or draft the colonists directly but called upon the assemblies to provide quotas of soldiers and supplies. This requisition system, itself a concession to provincial prejudice, heightened the self-importance of the assemblies, and most of them further asserted their autonomy by complying in a slow and niggardly way. Some of them, unwilling to be taxed by Parliament, also refused to tax themselves; they issued paper money instead.

In Virginia the legislature not only issued paper money but, when the price of tobacco rose, also passed a law to deprive the Anglican clergy (who were paid in tobacco) of the benefits of the price rise. When this law was disallowed (1759), one of the ministers sued his vestrymen for his full pay. At the trial of the "parson's cause" the young lawyer Patrick Henry, defending the vestrymen, denounced the Privy Council for its tyranny and told his fellow Virginians to ignore its action. Roused by Henry's oratory, the jurors awarded the parson damages of only one penny. Thus did they defy the authority of the British government.

In Massachusetts the merchants disregarded the laws of the Empire even more flagrantly than did the planters in Virginia. Throughout the war these merchants persisted in trading with the enemy in Canada and in the French West Indies. British officials resorted to general search warrants — "writs of assistance" — for discovering smuggled goods and stamping out the illegal and unpatriotic trade. As attorney for the Massachusetts merchants, James Otis maintained that these searches violated the ancient rights of Englishmen and that the law of Parliament authorizing the warrants was therefore null and void. With eloquence as stirring as Henry's, Otis insisted that Parliament had only a limited power in legislating for the colonies.

Believing in a kind of commercial imperialism, most English merchants opposed the acquisition of territory for its own sake. But some Englishmen and Americans began to believe that land itself should be acquired for the Empire because of the population the land would support, the demand for English manufactures and the taxes it would produce, and the sense of imperial greatness it would confer. Both William Pitt and Benjamin Franklin were among the advocates of this new territorial imperialism. Franklin wrote powerfully upon the future greatness of the Brit-

of Quebec, supposedly impregnable atop its towering cliff, the army of General James Wolfe struggled up a hidden ravine, surprised the larger forces of the Marquis de Montcalm, and defeated them in a battle in which both commanders were slain. The fall of Quebec marked the climax of the American phase of the war.

Peace finally came after the accession of the peace-minded George III and the resignation of Pitt, who disagreed with the new King and wished to continue hostilities. Yet Pitt's aims were pretty well realized in the treaty signed at Paris in 1763. By its terms the French ceded to Great Britain some of their West Indian islands and all their colonies in India except two. The French also transferred Canada and all other French territory east of the Mississippi, except the island of New Orleans, to Great Britain, and New Orleans and the French claims west of the Mississippi to Spain. Thus the French gave up all their title to the mainland of North America.

## Burdens of Victory

So strong had grown the colonial feeling against direct legislation by Parliament that, during the ish Empire in America, stressing the need for vast spaces to accommodate the rapid and limitless growth of the American people. Old-fashioned mercantilists, however, continued to think of trade and the importation of raw materials as the essences of empire, and of island and coastal possessions as bases for trade and centers of agricultural production.

The issue came to a head with the peace-making at the end of the French and Indian War. Commercial imperialists urged that Canada be returned to France in exchange for the most valuable of her sugar islands, Guadeloupe. Territorial imperialists, Franklin among them, and English sugar planters in the West Indies argued in favor of keeping Canada and leaving Guadeloupe in French hands. The decision to retain Canada marked a change in the emphasis of imperial policy.

With the acquisition of Canada and the other fruits of war in 1763, the area of the British Empire was more than doubled and the problems of governing it were made many times more complex. The war had left the British government with a staggering burden of debt, and English landlords and merchants objected violently to increased taxes. The rather half-hearted war effort of the colonists had shown the cumulative evils of the Empire's rather loose administration. And, by giving Great Britain undisputed title to the transmontane West as well as Canada, the peace had brought new problems of administration and defense. British statesmen feared that France, by no means crushed, might soon launch an attack somewhere in America for the recovery of her lost territories and prestige.

## The New Imperialism

As the war ended, the London policy makers faced a dilemma, though they were not fully aware of it. On the one hand, they could revert to the old colonial system with its half-hearted enforcement of the mercantilist program, but that would mean virtual independence for the colonies. On the other hand, the men in London could renew their efforts to reform the Empire and enforce the laws, but that would lead to revolt and absolute independence. The problem was further complicated by both the costs and the rewards of the war — the debts and the territory that it brought.

Responsibility for the solution of these post-war problems fell to the young monarch George III. More immediately responsible was George Grenville, whom the King made prime minister in 1763. Grenville, a brother-in-law of William Pitt, did not share Pitt's sympathy with the colonial point of view. He agreed with the prevailing British opinion that the colonists should be compelled to obey the laws and to pay a part of the cost of defending and administering the Empire. Promptly he undertook to impose system upon what had been a rather unsystematic aggregation of colonial possessions in America.

The Western problem was the most urgent. With the repulse of the French, frontiersmen from the English colonies had begun promptly to move over the mountains and into the upper Ohio Valley. Objecting to this intrusion, an alliance of Indian tribes, under the remarkable Ottawa chieftain Pontiac, raised the war cry. As an emergency measure the British government issued a proclamation forbidding settlers to advance beyond a line drawn along the mountain divide between the Atlantic and the interior.

Though the emergency passed, the principle of the Proclamation Line of 1763 remained — the principle of controlling the westward movement of population. This was something new. Earlier the government had encouraged the rapid peopling of the frontier for reasons of both defense and trade. In time the official attitude had begun to change, because of a fear that the interior might draw away so many people as to weaken markets and investments nearer the coast, and because of a desire to reserve land-speculating and fur-trading opportunities for English rather than colonial enterprisers. Then, having tentatively announced a new policy in 1763, the government soon extended and elaborated it. A definite Indian boundary was to be located, and from time to time relocated, in agreement with the various tribes. Western lands were to be opened for occupation gradually, and settlement was to be carefully supervised to see that it proceeded in a compact and orderly way.

To provide further for the defense of the colonies, and to raise revenue and enforce imperial law within them, the Grenville ministry with the cooperation of Parliament meanwhile instituted a series of measures, some of which were familiar in principle and others fairly novel. Regular troops were now to be stationed permanently in the provinces, and the colonists were called upon to assist in provisioning and maintaining the army. Ships of the navy were assigned to patrol American waters and look out for smugglers. The customs service was reorganized and enlarged, and vice-admiralty courts were set up in America to try accused smugglers without the benefit of sympathetic local juries. The Sugar Act (1764), designed in part to eliminate the illegal trade between the continental colonies and the foreign West Indies, lowered the high molasses duty of the Molasses Act of 1733, but imposed new duties on a number of items and made provision for more effective collection. The Currency Act (1764) drastically restricted the ability of colonial assemblies to create paper money. Most momentous of all, the Stamp Act (1765) imposed a tax to be paid on every legal document in the colonies, every newspaper, almanac, or pamphlet, and every deck of cards or pair of dice.

Thus the new imperial program with its reapplication of old mercantilist principles began to be put into effect. In a sense it proved highly effective. British officials soon were collecting more than ten times as much annual revenue in America as before 1763. But the new policy was not a lasting success.

## Colonial Self-interest

The colonists still had much to gain by remaining within the Empire and enjoying its many benefits. They still held grievances against one another as well as against the authorities in London. In 1763, for example, a band of Pennsylvania frontiersmen known as the Paxton Boys descended on Philadelphia to demand defense money and changes in the tax laws, and bloodshed was averted only by concessions from the colonial government.

In 1771 a small-scale civil war broke out as a consequence of the Regulator movement in North Carolina. The Regulators were farmers of the Carolina upcountry who organized to oppose the extortionate taxes that the sheriffs collected. These sheriffs, along with other local officials, were appointed by the governor. At first the Regulators tried to redress their grievances peaceably, by electing their leaders to the colonial assembly. The western counties were badly underrepresented in the assembly, and the Regulators were unable to get control of it. They

finally armed themselves and undertook to resist tax collections by force. To suppress the revolt, Governor William Tryon raised an army of militiamen, mostly from the eastern counties. The militiamen met and defeated the Regulators, some 2,000 strong, in the Battle of Alamance, in which nine on each side were killed and many others wounded. Afterward, six Regulators were hanged for treason.

Though such bloodshed was exceptional, the people of the colonies were divided by numerous conflicts of interest. After 1763, however, the policies of the British government increasingly offset the divisive tendencies within the colonies and caused Americans to look at the disadvantages of empire more closely than at its benefits. These policies threatened, in some degree or other, the well-being of nearly all classes in America.

Northern merchants would suffer from the various restraints upon their commerce, from the closing of the West to their ventures in land speculation and fur trading, from the denial of opportunities in manufacturing, and from the increased load of taxation. Southern planters, already burdened with debts to English merchants, would not only have to pay additional taxes but would also be deprived of the chance to lessen their debts by selling Western land, in which George Washington and others were much interested. Professional men—preachers, lawyers, and professors—considered the interests of merchants and planters to be identical with their own. Small farmers, clearly the largest group in the colonies, stood to lose as a result of reduced markets and hence lower prices for their crops, together with an increase in their taxes and other costs. Town workers faced the prospect of narrowing opportunities, particularly because of the restraints on manufacturing.

At the end of the French and Indian War, the colonists already were beginning to feel the pinch of a postwar depression. Previously the British government, pouring money into their midst to finance the fighting, had stimulated a wartime boom. Now the government was going to take money out of the colonies instead of putting it in. Also, the Currency Act had a decided deflationary impact on colonial prices. If all the government's measures should be strictly enforced, the immediate effect would be to aggravate the hard times. The long-run effect would be to confine the enterprising spirit of the colonists and condemn them to a fixed or even a declining level of living.

Grievous as were the economic consequences of George III's program, its political consequences would be as bad or worse. While colonial democracy was far from all-inclusive, the colonists were used to a remarkably wide latitude in self-government. Nowhere else in the world at that time did so large a proportion of the people take an active interest in public affairs. The chief centers of American political activity were the provincial assemblies, and here the people (through their elected representatives) were able to assert themselves because the assemblies had established the right to give or withhold appropriations for the costs of government within the colonies. If, now, the British authorities should succeed in raising extensive revenues directly from America, the colonial voters and their representatives would lose control over public finance, and without such control their participation in politics would be very nearly meaningless.

Home rule was not something new and different that these Americans were striving to get. It was something old and familiar that they desired to keep. They would lose it if the London authorities were allowed to carry out the program of raising revenues from colonial taxation and providing unconditional salaries for royal officials. The discontented Americans eventually prepared themselves to lay down their lives for a movement that was both democratic and conservative — a movement to conserve the liberties they already possessed.

## The Stamp Act Crisis

The experience of the French and Indian War, while convincing prominent Englishmen of the need for tighter imperial control, had exerted an opposite effect on the attitude of colonials. The French threat having been removed from the frontier forest, many of the colonists felt a new surge of expansive energy and daring. In short, they concluded that they needed not more but rather less of imperial guidance and protection than they had previously received.

If Prime Minister Grenville had wished deliberately to antagonize and unify some of the most influential groups in the colonies (which, of

course, he did not) he could have chosen no means more effective than the Stamp Act. The tax fell upon all Americans, of whatever section, colony, or class. In particular, the stamps required for ship's papers and legal documents offended merchants and lawyers. Tavern owners, often the political oracles of their neighborhoods, now were supposed to buy stamps for their licenses; and printers, for their newspapers and other publications. Thus the tax antagonized those who could play most effectively upon public opinion.

Nevertheless, it occurred to few colonists that they could do more than grumble and buy the stamps, until the Virginia House of Burgesses sounded a "trumpet of sedition" that aroused Americans to action almost everywhere. Patrick Henry, ambitious to enlarge the fame he had gained in the "parson's cause," made a fiery speech in the House (May 1765), concluding with a hint that George III like earlier tyrants might lose his head. There were shocked cries of "Treason!" and, according to a man who was present, Henry apologized, though many years afterward he was quoted as having made the defiant reply: "If *this* be treason, make the most of it." In any case, he proceeded to introduce a set of resolutions declaring that Americans possessed all the rights of Englishmen, especially the right to be taxed only by their own representatives.

Stirred by the Virginia Resolves, mobs in various places began to take the law into their own hands, and during the summer of 1765 riots broke out in various places, the worst of them in Boston. Men belonging to the newly organized "Sons of Liberty" went about terrorizing stamp agents and burning the stamps. The agents, themselves Americans, hastily resigned, and very few stamps were sold in the continental colonies.

At about the time that Patrick Henry presented his resolutions to the Virginia assembly, James Otis proposed to his fellow legislators in Massachusetts that they call an intercolonial congress for concerted action against the new tax. In October 1765 the Stamp Act Congress met in New York, with delegates from nine of the colonies present. The delegates decided to petition both the King and the two houses of Parliament. Though admitting that Americans owed to Parliament "all due subordination," the congress denied that they could rightfully be taxed except by their provincial assemblies.

If the British government had tried to enforce the Stamp Act, possibly the Revolutionary War would have begun ten years earlier than it actually did. The government was not deterred by resolves, riots, and petitions, but the Americans also used something more persuasive than any of these—economic pressure. Already, in response to the Sugar Act of 1764, many New Englanders had quit buying English goods. Now the colonial boycott spread, and the Sons of Liberty intimidated those colonists who were reluctant to participate in it. The merchants of England, feeling the loss of much of their colonial market, begged Parliament to repeal the Stamp Act, while stories of unemployment, poverty, and discontent arose from English seaports and manufacturing towns.

King George III himself finally was convinced that the act must be repealed. Opponents of repeal, and they were strong and vociferous, insisted that unless the colonists were compelled to obey the Stamp Act, they would soon cease to obey any laws of Parliament. So Parliament passed the Declaratory Act, asserting parliamentary authority over the colonies in "all cases whatsoever," and then repealed the Stamp Act (1766). In their rejoicing over the repeal, most Americans paid little attention to the sweeping declaration of Parliament's power.

## The Townshend Program

A new chancellor of the exchequer, Charles Townshend, had to deal with imperial problems and colonial grievances left over from the Grenville ministry. By the Townshend Act (1767), duties were laid upon colonial imports of glass, lead, paint, paper, and tea. Townshend reasoned that the colonists could not logically object to taxation of this kind. For Benjamin Franklin, as a colonial agent in London trying to prevent the passage of the Stamp Act, had drawn a distinction between "internal" and "external" taxes and had denounced the stamp duties as internal taxation. While Townshend laughed at this distinction he was now recommending duties that, without question, were to be collected externally.

Townshend also took steps to enforce commercial regulations in the colonies more effectively than ever. The most fateful of these steps was the establishment of a board of customs commissioners in America. The commissioners, with headquarters in Boston, virtually ended the smuggling at that place, though smugglers continued to carry on a busy trade in other colonial seaports.

Naturally the Boston merchants were the most indignant, and they took the lead in organizing another boycott. In 1768 the merchants of Philadelphia and New York joined those of Boston in a nonimportation agreement, and later some of the Southern merchants and planters also agreed to cooperate. Throughout the colonies, crude American homespun became suddenly fashionable, while English luxuries were frowned upon.

Before the consequences of his program were fully apparent, Townshend died, leaving the question of revising his import duties to his successor, Lord North. Hoping to break the nonimportation agreement and divide the colonists, Lord North secured the repeal (1770) of all the Townshend duties except the tea tax.

Meanwhile the presence of the customs commissioners in Boston led to violence. The terrified officials were driven to take refuge in Castle William, out in the harbor. So that they could return safely to their duties, the British government placed four regiments (afterward reduced to two) within the city. The presence of the redcoats antagonized the Boston radical Samuel Adams and his followers. While his men ragged the soldiers and engaged them in brawls, Adams filled the newspapers with imaginary stories of rapes and other atrocities committed by the troops, and he spread throughout Boston a rumor that the soldiers were preparing for a concerted attack upon the citizens. On the night of March 5, 1770, a mob of dockworkers and other "liberty boys" fell upon the sentry at the custom house. Hastily Captain Preston lined up several of his men in front of the building to protect it. There was some scuffling, and one of the soldiers was knocked down. Other soldiers then fired into the crowd, killing five of its members.

These events quickly became known as the "Boston Massacre" through the efforts of Samuel Adams and his adherents, who published an account bearing the title *Innocent Blood Crying to God from the Streets of Boston* and giving the impression that the dead were victims of a deliberate plot. The soldiers, tried before a jury of Bostonians and defended by Samuel Adams' cousin John Adams, were found guilty of no more than manslaughter and were given only a token punishment.

## The Philosophy of Revolt

Though America quieted down for a while after 1770, Americans did not abandon their principles, and these principles were revolutionary, at least in implication. Very few of the people thought of outright independence, but many desired autonomy within the Empire. They argued that the English Constitution, correctly interpreted, supported their claims to individual liberty and colonial self-rule, and that the laws of nature and of God justified them in resisting infringements upon their rights.

Of these rights the most fundamental, according to the colonists, was the right to be taxed only with their own consent. When Townshend levied his "external" duties, the Philadelphia lawyer John Dickinson maintained in the *Letters of a Pennsylvania Farmer* that even external taxation was legal only when designed to regulate trade and not to raise a revenue. But Americans did not like trade regulations, either, when the regulations began to be enforced. Eventually the discontented colonists took an unqualified stand upon the slogan "No taxation without representation."

This clamor about "representation" made little sense to Englishmen. Only about one in twenty-five of them was entitled to vote for members of Parliament, and some populous boroughs in England had no representatives at all. According to the prevailing English theory, however, Parliament did not represent individuals or geographical areas. Instead, it represented the interests of the whole nation and indeed the whole Empire, no matter where the members happened to come from. The unenfranchised urban boroughs of England, the whole of Ireland, and the colonies 3,000 miles away—all were represented in the Parliament at London.

That was the theory of "virtual" representation, but Americans believed in actual representation. They felt they could be represented in Parliament only if they sent their quota of members to it. Some of them, even James Otis,

considered proposals for electing American representatives, but most of the colonists realized that if they should participate in the action of Parliament they would be bound by that action, even though they were outnumbered and outvoted. So they reverted to the argument that they could be fairly represented only in their own colonial assemblies.

According to the American view of the Empire, and according to actual fact, these assemblies were little parliaments, as competent to legislate for their respective colonies as Parliament was for England. The Empire was a sort of federation of commonwealths, each with its own legislative body, all tied together by common loyalty to the King (much as in the later British Commonwealth of Nations). This being their conception of the Empire, the Americans protested bitterly against the pretensions of Parliament but had nothing except kind words for George III—until they decided to cut their imperial ties completely and declare for independence. According to the English view, the Empire was a single, undivided unit, and everywhere within it the King and Parliament together were supreme.

The American doctrine of resistance to unconstitutional and tyrannical laws was based heavily upon the writings of John Locke. Locke (1632–1704) would probably have been shocked if he had lived to see the use that Americans made of his doctrines. In his *Two Treatises of Government* (1690) he had attempted to justify the English revolution of 1688 by which Parliament had won supremacy over the King. According to Locke's theory, men originally lived in a state of nature and enjoyed complete liberty, then agreed to a "compact" by which they set up a government to protect their "natural rights," especially their right to the ownership and enjoyment of private property. The government was limited by the terms of the compact and by "natural law." It was contrary to natural law for a government to take property without the consent of the owners. And, according to Locke, if a government should persist in exceeding its rightful powers, men would be released from their obligation to obey it. What was more, they would have the right to make a new compact and establish another government.

Also influential in developing revolutionary thought were the works of English radical publicists, such as John Trenchard and Thomas Gordon who joined to write the widely read and quoted *Cato's Letters* (1720). They argued that the English revolution had established a constitution that created a balance between the monarchy, the aristocracy, and the common people that could protect Englishmen against the abuses of absolute power. A continual battle to contain power was required to protect the rights of Englishmen won in 1688. These publicists maintained that this battle ought to be regarded as a natural part of the political order, and while the struggle ordinarily would be peaceful, it might require force to check the most absolute and corrupt form of power—the tyranny enforced by a standing army.

## The Tea Excitement

A dispute over the importation of tea broke the relative calm that had descended over Anglo-American politics during the early 1770s. The East India Company, with a large stock of unsalable tea on hand, was nearly bankrupt, and Lord North induced Parliament to go to the company's relief with the Tea Act of 1773. This law permitted the company to export its product to America without paying any of the usual taxes except the tea tax still remaining from the original Townshend duties. With these privileges the company could undersell American merchants who bought their tea supplies in England.

Lord North, like others in his office before him, was surprised by the reaction of the Americans. He had not expected the tea-importing merchants in the colonies to like the new law, for it threatened to drive them out of business and replace them with a giant monopoly. But the colonists—especially the women—were excessively fond of tea. Lord North thought they would be so glad to get it cheap that they would swallow the hated tea tax along with it. Instead, they renounced their beloved beverage and turned for the time being to such substitutes as coffee and chocolate.

Meanwhile, with strong popular support, leaders in various colonies made plans to prevent the East India Company from landing its cargoes in colonial ports. In Philadelphia and New York determined men kept the tea from leaving the company's ships, and in Charleston they stored it

away in a public warehouse. In Boston, having failed to turn back the three ships in the harbor, the followers of Samuel Adams staged a spectacular drama. On the evening of December 16, 1773, three companies of fifty men each, masquerading as "Mohawks," passed between the protecting lines of a tremendous crowd of spectators, went aboard, broke open the tea chests, and heaved them into the water. As the electrifying news of the Boston "tea party" spread, other seaports followed the example and held tea parties of their own.

When the Bostonians refused to pay for the property they had destroyed, George III and Lord North decided upon a policy of coercion, to be applied not against all the colonies but only against Massachusetts—the chief center of resistance. In four acts of 1774 Parliament proceeded to put this policy into effect. One of the laws closed the port of Boston, another drastically reduced the local and provincial powers of self-government in Massachusetts, still another permitted royal officers to be tried in other colonies or in England when accused of crimes, and the last provided for the quartering of troops in the colonists' barns and empty houses.

These Coercive Acts were followed by the Quebec Act, which was separate from them in origin and quite different in purpose. Its object was to provide a civil government for the French-speaking, Roman Catholic inhabitants of Canada and the Illinois country. The law extended the boundaries of Quebec to include the French communities between the Ohio and Mississippi rivers. It also granted political rights to Roman Catholics and recognized the legality of the Roman Catholic Church within the enlarged province. In many ways it was a liberal and much-needed piece of legislation.

To many Protestants in the thirteen colonies, however, the Quebec Act was anathema. They were already alarmed by rumors that the Church of England schemed to appoint a bishop for America with the intention of enforcing Anglican authority upon all the various sects. To them the line between the Church of England and the Church of Rome always had seemed dangerously thin. When Catholics ceased to be actively persecuted in the mother country, alarmists in the colonies began to fear that Catholicism and Anglicanism were about to merge, and at the passage of the Quebec Act they became convinced that a plot was afoot in London for subjecting Americans to the tyranny of the Pope. Moreover, those interested in Western lands believed that the act, by extending the boundaries of Quebec, would reinforce the land policy of the Proclamation Line of 1763 and put an additional obstacle in the way of westward progress.

Had it not been for the Quebec Act, Lord North might have come close to succeeding in his effort to divide and rule the colonies by isolating Massachusetts. As it was, the colonists generally lumped the Quebec law with the Massachusetts measures as the fifth in a set of "Intolerable Acts." From New Hampshire to South Carolina the people prepared to take a united stand.

# Chapter 4.  THE AMERICAN REVOLUTION

## Lexington and Concord

From 1765 on, colonial leaders had provided a variety of organizations for converting popular discontent into action, organizations which in time formed the basis for an independent government. The most famous and most effective were the committees of correspondence. Massachusetts took the lead (1772) with such committees on the local level, a network of them connecting Boston with the rural towns, but Virginia was the first to establish committees of correspondence on an intercolonial basis. These made possible cooperation among the colonies in a more continuous way than had the Stamp Act Congress, the first effort at intercolonial union for resistance against imperial authority. Virginia took the greatest step of all toward united action in 1774 when, the governor having dissolved the assembly, a rump session met in Williamsburg, declared that the Intolerable Acts menaced the liberties of every colony, and issued a call for a Continental Congress.

Variously elected by the assemblies or by extralegal meetings, delegates from all the thirteen colonies except Georgia were present when, in September 1774, the Continental Congress convened in Philadelphia. The delegates drew up a somewhat self-contradictory statement of grievances, conceding to Parliament the right to regulate colonial trade but demanding the elimination of all oppressive legislation passed since 1763. They agreed to nonimportation, nonexportation, and nonconsumption as means of stopping all trade with Great Britain, and they formed a "Continental Association" to see that these agreements were carried out. They also approved a series of resolutions from a Suffolk County (Massachusetts) convention recommending that military preparations be made for defense against possible attack by the British troops in Boston.

For months the farmers and townspeople of Massachusetts had been gathering arms and ammunition and training as "minutemen," ready to fight on a minute's notice. The Continental Congress having approved preparations for a defensive war, these citizen-soldiers only waited for an aggressive move by the British regulars.

In Boston, General Thomas Gage, commanding the British garrison, knew of the warlike bustle throughout the countryside but thought his army too small to do anything until reinforcements should arrive. But when he heard that the minutemen had stored a large supply of gunpowder in Concord (eighteen miles from Boston) he at last decided to act. On the night of April 18, 1775, he sent a detachment of about 1,000 men out from Boston on the road to Lexington and Concord. He intended to surprise the colonials with a bloodless coup.

But during the night the hard-riding horsemen William Dawes and Paul Revere warned the villages and farms, and when the redcoats arrived in Lexington the next day, several dozen minutemen awaited them on the common. Shots were fired and some of the minutemen fell, eight of them killed and ten more wounded. Advancing to Concord, the British burned what was left of the powder supply after the Americans hastily had removed most of it to safety. On the road from Concord back to Boston the 1,000 troops, along with 1,500 more who met them at Lexington, were harassed by the continual gunfire of farmers hiding behind trees, rocks, and stone fences.

A war was on, and most Americans believed the enemy had started it.

## Declaration of Independence

Three weeks after the battles of Lexington and Concord, when the Second Continental Congress met in Philadelphia, the delegates adopted a Declaration of the Causes and Necessity of Taking up Arms, announcing that the British government had left the American people with only two alternatives, "unconditional submission to the tyranny of irritated ministers or resistance by force," and that the people had decided to resist.

For the first year of the war, the Americans were fighting for a redress of grievances within the British Empire, not for independence. During that year, however, many of them began to change their minds, for various reasons. For one thing, they soon were making sacrifices so great that their original war aims seemed incommensurate with the cost. For another thing, they lost much of their lingering affection for the mother country when she prepared to use Indians, Negro slaves, and foreign mercenaries (the hated "Hessians") against them. And, most important, they felt that they were being forced into independence when the British government closed the colonies to all overseas trade and made no concession except an offer of pardon to repentant rebels. The Americans desperately needed military supplies to continue the war, and now they could get them from abroad in adequate amounts only if they broke completely with Great Britain and proceeded to behave in all respects as if they comprised a sovereign nation.

These feelings in America were not caused, but were clarified and crystallized, by the publication, in January 1776, of the pamphlet *Common Sense*. Its author, unmentioned on the title page, was Thomas Paine, who with letters of introduction from Benjamin Franklin had emigrated from England to America less than two years before. Though long a failure in various trades, Paine now proved a brilliant success as a revolutionary propagandist. In his pamphlet he argued with flashing phrases that it was plain common sense for Americans to separate from an England rotten with the corrupt monarchy of George III, brutal as an unnatural parent toward her colonies, responsible for dragging them in to fight her wars in the past, and no more fit as an island kingdom to rule the American Continent than a satellite was fit to rule the sun.

Despite the persuasion of *Common Sense*, the American people were far from unanimous, and they entered upon a bitter debate over the merits of dependence and independence. While the debate raged, the Continental Congress advanced step by step toward a final break. Congress opened the ports of America to all the world except Great Britain, entered into communication with foreign powers, and recommended to the various colonies that they establish governments without the authority of the Empire, as in fact they already were doing. On July 2, 1776, Congress adopted a resolution "That these United Colonies are, and, of right, ought to be, free and independent states. . . ." Two days later Congress approved the Declaration of Independence, which gave reasons for the action already taken.

The thirty-three-year-old Virginian Thomas Jefferson wrote the Declaration. In it he restated the familiar contract theory of John Locke, who had held that governments were formed to protect the rights of life, liberty, and property, but Jefferson gave the theory a more humane twist by referring instead to the rights of "life, liberty and the pursuit of happiness" and adding the democratic principle that "all men are created equal."

Some people in America had disapproved of the war from the beginning, and others had been willing to support it only so long as its aims did not conflict with their basic loyalty to the King. These people, numerous but in the minority, refused to cross the new line that had been drawn. Either openly or secretly they remained Loyalists, as they chose to call themselves, or Tories, as they were known to the Whig or Patriot majority.

## State Governments

While waging war, the Patriots also busied themselves with providing a government for the new nation. With the outbreak of war they set up provisional governments based upon existing assemblies or emergency conventions as the royal officials fled from their positions in one colony after another. When the colonies became states, the Patriots formed permanent governments with written constitutions. The constitution-making procedure varied from state to state. In Rhode Island and Connecticut the legislatures merely revised the old colonial charters, and in most of the other states the legislatures, though not elected for that purpose, took it upon themselves to draft new constitutions. Thomas Jefferson, for one, insisted that the fundamental law should come from the people of each state, who should elect constitutional conventions and then vote on ratification. Actually, conventions were held in only three states, referendums in only five, and both a convention and a referendum in only one — Massachusetts.

## "FACTS" VERSUS INTERPRETATIONS

**Why Historians Disagree**

Was the American Revolution essentially a civil war, in which the ordinary people of the colonies were struggling to get democracy at home? Did slaves in the Old South keep alive their African culture and maintain cohesive, well-knit families? Was the United States to blame for the start of the Cold War with the Soviet Union?

On these and many other questions, American historians have disagreed among themselves. Conflicting points of view on several of these issues are presented in this book in a series of essays entitled "Where Historians Disagree." Why do they disagree?

In totalitarian countries there are few controversies of this kind. In the Soviet Union, for example, historians are required to follow the official, Marxist-Leninist interpretation of history. They cannot openly discuss such questions as their own government's responsibility for the Cold War. Only in a free society do scholars have the right to seek to know the past as it actually was. In the search for truth they are obligated only to the impartial standards of historical scholarship. They are limited only by their personal infirmities and biases.

American historians, in writing about their country, have come to agree on most of the "facts." But there are countless facts, and historians have differed as to which are the most important and should therefore be emphasized. Hence the differences in the interpretation of certain phases of American history.

Historians may disagree because of differences in their personal backgrounds (geographic, social, religious, racial, ethnic) or in their historical philosophies (their theories or assumptions about the nature of history and about historical methods) — which lead them to focus on particular aspects of a subject. From one period to another the prevailing view of historians on some phase of the past may change as a result of new evidence coming to light or new public issues rising to prominence. Since the study of the past helps us to understand the problems of the present, it is only natural that historians in each generation should emphasize those features of earlier times that seem most relevant to contemporary preoccupations.

This is not to say that present concerns should dictate historical views. Present concerns can provide only the questions, not the answers. Nor is it to say that all interpretations are equally valid. In time one view may prove to be right and the opposing view wrong. More commonly there is something of value in both, or in several, interpretations. Often it is a matter of each of the contending historians getting hold of only one part of the subject — like the blind men examining the elephant in the fable. Usually the controversies lead to further research and to deepened understanding, if not also to a new consensus.

In these controversies (with few exceptions) the historians are, to repeat, not disputing the facts. The question is not "What happened?" but "What is the *significance* of what happened?" Even where historians disagree the most, they agree much more than they disagree.

The new constitutions, all pretty much alike in general outline though different in detail, were both conservative and democratic. They were conservative in retaining essentially the same structure as the old colonial governments. Ex-

cept in Georgia and Pennsylvania, both of which experimented with a unicameral legislature, each constitution provided for a two-house legislature, with an elected senate taking the place of the former governor's council. All the constitutions except Pennsylvania's continued the office of governor, though most of them denied the holder of this position the bulk of the executive powers he had enjoyed in colonial days. All the new documents confirmed and extended the ideas of popular rule that long had been put into practice; seven had fully-fledged bills of rights, and some had preambles stating that sovereignty (the ultimate power of government) resided in the people. To vote in any state a man had to own only a modest amount of property, in some states just enough so that he could qualify as a taxpayer. To hold office he had to meet a somewhat higher property requirement, essentially as in pre-Revolutionary times. Only in New Jersey were women allowed to vote, and eventually they were deprived of the suffrage even there. But, considering the widespread ownership of property, something approaching universal manhood suffrage existed from the beginning in all the states.

Once in operation, the new states proceeded to make advances in social as well as political democracy. New York and the Southern states, in which the Church of England had been tax-supported, soon saw to its complete disestablishment, and the New England states stripped the Congregational Church of some of its privileges. Virginia, in its Declaration of Rights, boldly announced the principle of complete toleration and, in 1786, enacted the principle in the Statute of Religious Liberty, which Jefferson long had championed.

The new states took steps toward personal as well as religious freedom. All of them except South Carolina and Georgia prohibited the importation of slaves, and even South Carolina laid temporary wartime bans on the slave trade. After the first antislavery society in America (founded in 1775) began its agitation, and prominent Southerners including Jefferson and Washington declared their opposition to slavery, Virginia and other Southern states changed their laws so as to encourage manumission; Pennsylvania passed a gradual-emancipation act (1780), and Massachusetts through a decision of its highest court (1783) held that the state's bill of rights outlawed the ownership of slaves. Besides all this, five of the new states put provisions into their constitutions for the establishment of public schools, and all soon began to revise their criminal codes so as to make the punishment more nearly fit the crime.

# The Confederation

While the separate states were fashioning constitutions and recasting their legal systems, the Second Continental Congress tried to create a written form of government for the states as a whole. No sooner had the Congress appointed a committee to draft a declaration of independence than it appointed another to draft a plan of union, and after much debate and many revisions the Congress, in November 1777, adopted the committee's plan, the Articles of Confederation.

The Articles of Confederation provided for a central government very similar to the one already in actual operation, though it increased the powers of Congress somewhat. Congress was to have the powers of conducting war, carrying on foreign relations, and appropriating, borrowing, and issuing money, but not the powers of regulating trade, levying taxes, or drafting troops. For troops and taxes it would have to petition the states. There was to be no separate, single, strong executive (the "President of the United States" was to be merely the presiding officer at the sessions of Congress), but Congress itself was to see to the execution of the laws through an executive committee of thirteen, made up of one member from each state, through ad hoc and standing committees for specific functions, and through such administrative departments as it might choose to create. There were to be no Confederation courts, except for courts of admiralty, but disputes between the states were to be settled by a complicated system of arbitration. The states were to retain their individual sovereignty, each of the legislatures electing and paying the salaries of two to seven delegates to Congress, and each delegation, no matter how numerous, having only one vote. At least nine of the states (through their delegations) would have to approve any important measure, such as a treaty, before Congress could pass it, and all thirteen state legislatures would have to approve before the Articles could be ratified or amended.

Ratification was delayed by differences of opinion about the proposed plan. Some Americans were willing enough to accept a relatively weak central government, but others preferred to see it strengthened. Above all, the states claiming Western lands wished to keep them, but the rest of the states demanded that the whole territory be turned over to the Confederation government. Except for New York, the "landed" states, among which Virginia had the largest and best claim, founded their claims upon colonial charters. The "landless" states, particularly Maryland, maintained that as the fruit of common sacrifices in war the Western land had become the rightful property of all the states. At last New York gave up its rather hazy claim, based upon a protectorate over the Iroquois Indians, and Virginia made a qualified offer to cede its lands to Congress. Then Maryland, the only state still holding out against ratification, approved the Articles of Confederation, and they went into effect in 1781.

The Confederation government came into being in time to conclude the war and make the peace. Meanwhile, during the years of fighting from 1775 to 1781, the Second Continental Congress served as the agency for directing and coordinating the war effort of the people of the thirteen states.

## Mobilizing for War

Congress and the states faced overwhelming tasks in raising and organizing armies, providing the necessary supplies and equipment, and paying the costs of war.

Some of the states offered bounties for the encouragement of manufactures, especially for the production of guns and powder, and Congress in 1777 established a government arsenal at Springfield, Massachusetts. Even so, the Americans themselves managed to manufacture only a small fraction of the equipment they used. They got most of their war materials through importations from Europe, particularly from France.

In trying to meet the expenses of war, Congress had no power to tax the people, and the states had little inclination to do so. Indeed, cash was scarce in the country, as it always had been. When Congress requisitioned the states for money, none of them contributed more than a tiny part of its share. At first Congress hesitated to requisition goods directly from the people, but finally allowed army purchasing agents to take supplies from farmers and pay with certificates of indebtedness. Congress could not raise much money by floating long-term loans at home, since few Americans could afford war bonds and those few usually preferred to invest

their funds in more profitable wartime ventures, such as privateering. So Congress had no choice but to issue paper money, and Continental currency came from the printing presses in large and repeated batches. The states added sizable currency issues of their own.

With goods and coin so scarce and paper money so plentiful, prices rose to fantastic heights and the value of paper money fell proportionately. Eventually, in 1780, Congress decided that the states should accept Continental currency from taxpayers at the rate of forty paper dollars to one silver dollar, then send it to Congress to be destroyed.

The states added to their financial resources by seizing lands belonging to the Crown and to colonial proprietors. In 1777 Congress recommended that the states also confiscate and sell the property of Loyalists active in the British cause, then lend the proceeds to the central government. The states were eager enough to expropriate the Loyalists, though not to make the requested loan. Around 100,000 of the Loyalists, either voluntarily or because of banishment, left the country during the course of the war, the most numerous group going to Quebec and laying the foundations of English-speaking Canada.

As for the Patriots, only a small proportion of them were willing to volunteer for the American armies once the first surge of patriotism at the start of the war had passed. The states had to resort to persuasion and force, to bounties and the draft, the bounties being commonly in the form of land scrip, since land was an asset with which the states were well supplied. Thus recruited, militiamen remained under the control of their respective states.

Foreseeing some of the disadvantages of separately organized militias, Congress called upon the states (while they were still colonies) to raise troops for a regular force, the Continental army, and agreed that it should have a single commander in chief. George Washington, forty-three years old, sober and responsible by nature, possessed more command experience than any other American-born officer available. And he had political as well as military qualifications. An early advocate of independence, he was admired and trusted by nearly all the Patriots. A Virginian, he had the support not only of Southerners but also of Northerners who feared that the appointment of a New Englander might jeop-

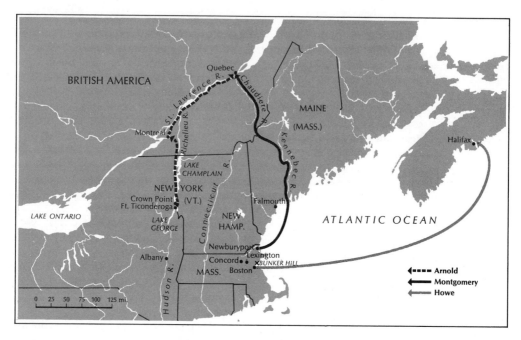

The War in the North 1775

ardize sectional harmony. As the unanimous choice of the delegates, he took command in June 1775.

## The Fighting, to 1777

For about the first year of the fighting (1775–1776) the colonial armed forces took the offensive. After the British retreat from Concord and Lexington, the Americans besieged the army of General Gage in Boston, and though suffering severe casualties in the Battle of Bunker Hill (June 17, 1775), they inflicted even greater losses upon the enemy and thereafter they continued to tighten the siege. Finally the British gave up their attempt to hold Boston and departed with hundreds of Loyalist refugees (March 17, 1776) for Halifax. Within a year from the firing of the first shots, the enemy had been driven from American soil.

The British soon returned, however, to put the Americans on the strategic defensive for the remainder of the war. During the summer of 1776, in the weeks immediately following the Declaration of Independence, the waters around the city of New York became filled with the most formidable military force Great Britain ever had sent abroad. Here were hundreds of

men-of-war and troopships and a host of 32,000 disciplined soldiers under the command of the tall and affable Sir William Howe. Having no grudge against the Americans, Howe would rather awe them into submission than shoot them, and he believed that most of them, if given a chance, would show that they were at heart loyal to the King. In a parley with commissioners from Congress he offered the alternatives of submission with royal pardon or battle against overwhelming odds.

To oppose Howe's awesome array, Washington could muster only about 19,000 poorly armed and trained soldiers, including both Continentals and state troops, and he had no navy at all. Yet without hesitation the Americans chose continued war, which meant inevitably a succession of defeats. The British pushed the defenders off Long Island, compelled them to abandon Manhattan Island, and drove them in slow retreat over the plains of New Jersey, across the Delaware River, and into Pennsylvania.

For the campaign of 1777 the British devised a strategy that, if Howe had stuck to it, might have cut the United States in two and prepared the way for final victory by Great Britain. According to this plan, Howe would move from New York up the Hudson to Albany, while another force, in a gigantic pincers movement,

## THE AMERICAN REVOLUTION

**Where Historians Disagree**

In their accounts of the American Revolution, historians at one time concentrated on the Patriot aim of autonomy within the British Empire and then complete independence from it. These historians differed among themselves in regard to revolutionary motivation; some of them emphasized political ideals, others stressed economic interests. But all of them took as their central theme the struggle between the American colonies and the British government.

Eventually, a number of writers began calling attention to struggles *within* the colonies as well. These writers maintained that the Revolution involved not only the question of home rule but also the question who should rule at home. It was, according to them, a movement toward both independence and democracy. Thus, in a study of New York politics from 1770 to 1776 (1909) and in *The Eve of the Revolution* (1918), Carl L. Becker described the Revolution as, in part, a kind of civil war, a contest for power between American radicals and conservatives, one that led to the "democratization of American politics and society." J. F. Jameson elaborated upon the idea in his slim but influential volume *The American Revolution Considered as a Social Movement* (1926). "The stream of revolution, once started, could not be confined within narrow banks, but spread abroad upon the land," Jameson wrote. "Many economic desires, many social aspirations were set free by the political struggle, many aspects of colonial society profoundly altered by the forces thus let loose." The social changes tended "in the direction of levelling democracy."

This view long prevailed, but recently it has been sharply challenged. Robert E. Brown shows in *Middle Class Democracy and the Revolution in Massachusetts, 1691–1780* (1955) that, before 1776, Massachusetts was already "very close to a complete democracy," with practically all men enjoying the right to vote. Brown argues that, at least in Massachusetts and probably also in other colonies, the aim of the Revolutionary leaders was to preserve the democratic liberties that already existed. And E. S. Morgan, in a bold and concise reinterpretation, *The Birth of the Republic, 1763–1789* (1956), holds that most Americans were in basic agreement on political principles; thus he endorses the older view of the Revolution as a struggle between the colonies and the British government. Bernard Bailyn, in *The Ideological Origins of the American Revolution* (1967), agrees, seeing the Revolution as an ideological and constitutional struggle in which Americans developed and acted upon a self-awareness of their political uniqueness.

The debate goes on, with the net result a broadening of our knowledge of the Revolutionary period.

---

would come down from Canada to meet him. One of Howe's ambitious younger officers, the dashing John Burgoyne, "Gentleman Johnny," secured command of this northern force and elaborated upon the plan by preparing for a two-pronged attack along both the Mohawk and the upper Hudson approaches to Albany.

Then, fortunately for the United States, Howe adopted a different plan for himself, intending to dispirit the Patriots and rally the Loyalists by seizing the rebel capital, Philadelphia.

Up north, Burgoyne was left to carry out his

twofold campaign without aid from Howe. He got off to a flying start, easily taking Fort Ticonderoga and an enormous store of powder and supplies, and causing such consternation that Congress removed General Philip Schuyler from command in the north and replaced him with Horatio Gates, in response to the demands of New Englanders.

By the time Gates took command, Burgoyne already faced a sudden reversal of his military fortunes in consequence of two staggering defeats. Short of materials, with all help cut off,

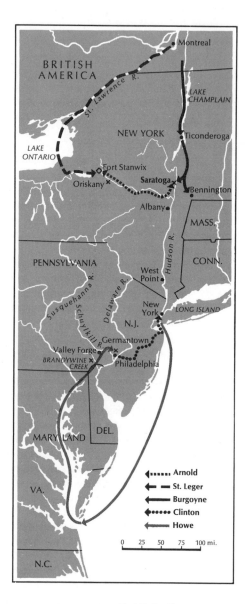

**British Campaigns**

Burgoyne withdrew to Saratoga, where Gates surrounded him. Burgoyne was through, and he knew it. On October 17, 1777, he ordered what was left of his army, nearly 5,000 men, to lay down their arms.

Not only the United States but also Europe took note of the amazing news from the woods of upstate New York, and France in particular was impressed. The British surrender at Saratoga, a great turning point in the war, led directly to an alliance between the United States and France.

## Foreign Friends

Of all the possible foreign friends of the United States, the most promising and most powerful was France, who still resented her defeat at the hands of Great Britain in 1763. France had an astute and determined foreign minister in the Count de Vergennes, an expert practitioner of Machiavellian principles, thoroughly trained in the cutthroat diplomacy of eighteenth-century Europe. Vergennes soon saw that France had a vital interest in the outcome of the American war. If the colonies should assert and maintain their independence, the power of Great Britain would be seriously weakened by the loss of a good part of her empire, and the power of France would be correspondingly increased.

Early in the war the French shipped large quantities of munitions to America through a fictitious trading firm that had been rigged up to disguise the fact that most of the shipments were financed by the King of France and the King of Spain. Whether this assistance was a gift or a loan later became a question of bitter dispute.

After the Declaration of Independence, Benjamin Franklin went to France to get further aid and outright recognition of the United States. A natural diplomat, the equal if not the superior of the world's best at that time, Franklin immediately captivated Frenchmen of all classes — and Frenchwomen too. But Vergennes hesitated. At the first news of the American Declaration, he was inclined to make a treaty recognizing United States independence, but he did not wish to act without Spain; and when reports came of Washington's defeat on Long Island he decided to wait and watch the military developments in America. If and when the Americans should show that they had a real chance of winning, then France would intervene. Meanwhile Vergennes was willing to go on financing the American war. He initiated a series of subsidies which in time amounted to nearly $62 million and a series of loans which totaled over $6 million.

The news that Vergennes and Franklin were waiting for — the news from Saratoga — arrived in Paris on December 4, 1777. Without waiting for Spain to go along with France, Vergennes on February 6, 1778, signed two treaties, one of commerce and amity, and the other of alliance. France (for her own reasons, of course) was the true friend in need of the Americans. Not only did she furnish them most of their money and munitions, but she also provided a navy and an expeditionary force that, with Washington's army made possible the decisive victory at Yorktown.

## Victory at Yorktown

During the final two years of fighting, all the significant action occurred in the South.

Sir Henry Clinton, who had replaced General Howe, planned a Southern offensive that was supposed to end the American will to resist, but he put the command of the operation in the hands of Lord Cornwallis, an able general but one as rash as Clinton himself was cautious. Clinton and Cornwallis based their strategy on assumptions that were not to prove facts. They assumed that seapower would enable them to move their troops from point to point along the coast with ease, that the difficulties of overland travel would make American counteraction ineffectual, and that Loyalists would rise en masse to welcome and assist the redcoats as liberators. With the conquered South as a base, Clinton and Cornwallis thought they could dispose of the rest of the country at their leisure.

The British succeeded in taking Savannah (December 29, 1778) and Charleston (May 20, 1780), inspiring many Loyalists to take up arms, and advancing far into the interior. At every turn they were harassed, however, by Patriot guerrillas. Penetrating to Camden, well up the Wateree River in South Carolina, Cornwallis met and crushed (August 16, 1780) a combined force of militiamen and Continentals under Horatio Gates, who did not quite deserve his fame as the hero of Saratoga. Congress recalled Gates, and Washington gave the Southern command to Nathanael Greene, a former Quaker blacksmith of Rhode Island and probably the ablest of all the American generals of the time next to Washington himself.

Greene combined all his forces and arranged to meet the British on ground of his own choosing at Guilford Court House, North Carolina. After a hard-fought battle (March 15, 1781) Greene was driven from the field, but Cornwallis lost so many men that he decided at last to abandon the Carolina campaign.

Cornwallis retreated to the peninsula between the York and James rivers and began to build fortifications at Yorktown. While Clinton

**Road to Yorktown**

worried about Cornwallis' moves, Washington made plans with the Count de Rochambeau, commander of the French expeditionary force in America, and with Admiral de Grasse, commander of a French fleet in American waters, for trapping Cornwallis. Washington and Rochambeau marched a Franco-American army from the New York vicinity to join Lafayette in Virginia while de Grasse sailed with additional troops for Chesapeake Bay and the York River. These joint operations, perfectly timed and executed, caught Cornwallis between land and sea. After a few shows of resistance, he asked for terms on October 17, 1781, four years to the day after the capitulation of Burgoyne, and two days later he surrendered his whole army of more than 7,000.

The fighting was over, but the war was not quite won. The United States continued to be something of an occupied country, with British forces holding the seaports of Savannah, Charleston, Wilmington, and New York. Before long a British fleet met and defeated Admiral de Grasse's fleet in the West Indies, ending Washington's hopes for further seapower assistance. So far as the naval and military situation was concerned, the British still held the upper hand in America. And peace was yet to be made.

## Winning the Peace

When, in 1779, Spain in the role of mediator proposed a peace conference, Congress promptly named John Adams as the American delegate and sent him instructions to enter into no negotiations unless Great Britain first recognized the United States as "sovereign, free, and independent." Later Congress replaced the single delegate with a whole delegation, including Franklin and John Jay as well as Adams, told the prospective peacemakers to keep in close touch with the French government, tell it everything, follow its advice. Thus the United States was put into the hands of Vergennes by the time (1781) Austria and Russia made their joint mediation offer that led eventually to a general peace settlement.

Then the victory at Yorktown, by giving the Americans new bargaining power, rescued them from the worst of their dependence upon Vergennes. In England, Cornwallis' defeat provoked outcries against continuing the war and demands for cultivating American friendship as an asset in international politics. British emissaries appeared in France to talk informally with Franklin. He suggested what he called "necessary" terms of peace, including independence and the establishment of the Mississippi as the western boundary of the United States, and "desirable" terms including the cession of Canada for the purpose of "reconciliation," a "sweet word," as he said. But John Jay, recently arrived from his fruitless mission to Spain, where he had acquired reason to be suspicious of Spaniards and all Europeans, objected to continuing the negotiations on the grounds that the Americans were addressed not as plenipotentiaries of a sovereign nation but as "persons" from "colonies or plantations." The negotiations were delayed until Jay was satisfied.

All along Franklin, Jay, and Adams had kept Vergennes informed of their conversations with British agents, in accordance with the instructions from Congress. Then, one day, Jay learned that Vergennes' private secretary was off on a secret mission to England. Jay feared that Vergennes was going to leave the United States in the lurch and make a separate peace by which Great Britain and Spain would divide between themselves the territory west of the Alleghenies and east of the Mississippi. Such a deal, as Franklin exclaimed, would have "cooped us up within the Allegheny Mountains." Though Jay was mistaken as to the details of the secret mission, he was right in thinking that Vergennes was suggesting separate negotiations that were to be kept from the American peacemakers and that might have proved disadvantageous to the United States. From that day on, Franklin, Jay, and Adams ceased to inform Vergennes of their diplomacy but went ahead on their own and soon drew up a preliminary treaty with Great Britain.

The final treaty was signed September 3, 1783, when Spain as well as France agreed to end hostilities. It included a number of provisions that Franklin and Jay and Adams had opposed, and some of these were to lead to serious friction with Great Britain and with Spain in the years ahead. Yet it also included essentially the "necessary" terms that Franklin originally had indicated, though not his "desirable" ones such as the cession of Canada. On the whole the peace was remarkably favorable to the United States in granting a clear-cut recognition of independence and a generous, though ambiguous, delimitation of territory — from the southern boundary of Canada to the northern boundary of Florida and from the Atlantic to the Mississippi. Indeed, by playing off the powers of Europe against one another, Franklin and his colleagues had achieved the greatest diplomatic success in the history of the United States. With good reason the American people celebrated as the last of the British occupation forces embarked from New York and General Washington at the head of his troops rode triumphantly in.

---

**SELECTED READINGS**    For general accounts of colonial life and culture see Clarence L. Ver Steeg, *The Formative Years, 1607–1763* (1964), and L. B. Wright, *The Cultural Life of the American Colonies, 1607–1763\** (1957). On seventeenth-century developments in New England see George Langdon, *Pilgrim Colony: A History of New Plymouth, 1620–1691* (1966); G. F. Willison, *Saints and Strangers\** (1945); C. M. Andrews, *The Fathers of New England* (1919); S. E.

Morison, *Builders of the Bay Colony** (1930); A. T. Vaughn, *New England Frontier: Puritans and Indians, 1620–1675* (1965); E. S. Morgan, *The Puritan Dilemma: The Story of John Winthrop** (1958); and Perry Miller, *The New England Mind: The Seventeenth Century** (1939). On the middle colonies in the seventeenth century: T. J. Wertenbaker, *The Founding of American Civilization: The Middle Colonies* (1938); E. B. Bronner, *William Penn's "Holy Experiment": The Founding of Pennsylvania, 1681–1701* (1962); and A. W. Trelease, *Indian Affairs in Colonial New York: The Seventeenth Century* (1960). On the seventeenth-century South: G. F. Willison, *Behold Virginia* (1951); W. F. Craven, *The Southern Colonies in the Seventeenth Century, 1607–1689* (1949); and Verner Crane, *The Southern Frontier, 1670–1732** (1956).

Aspects of life in the expanding settlements of the eighteenth century are treated in the following: T. R. Reese, *Colonial Georgia: A Study in British Imperial Policy in the Eighteenth Century* (1963); I. C. C. Graham, *Colonists from Scotland* (1956); R. B. Morris, *Government and Labor in Early America* (1946); W. D. Jordan, *White over Black: American Attitudes Toward the Negro, 1550–1812** (1968); Eugene Genovese, *The World the Slaveholders Made* (1970); F. B. Tolles, *Meeting House and Counting House** (1948); Carl Bridenbaugh, *Cities in the Wilderness, 1625–1742** (1938), and *Cities in Revolt, 1743–1776** (1955); Perry Miller, *Jonathan Edwards** (1949); Carl Van Doren, *Benjamin Franklin** (1938), an extensive biography; and W. R. Jacobs, *Dispossessing the American Indian** (1972).

Anglo-French conflict in America is the subject of Francis Parkman, *The Parkman Reader,** ed. by S. E. Morison (1955); H. H. Peckham, *The Colonial Wars, 1689–1762** (1964); and L. H. Gipson, *The British Empire Before the American Revolution* (13 vols., 1936–1967), vols. 6 and 7 — *The Great War for the Empire.*

Backgrounds of the American Revolution are discussed in J. C. Miller, *Origins of the American Revolution** (1957); L. H. Gipson, *The Coming of the Revolution, 1763–1775** (1954); A. M. Schlesinger, *The Colonial Merchants and the American Revolution 1763–1776** (1917); J. M. Sosin, *Agents and Merchants: British Colonial Policy and the Origins of the American Revolution, 1763–1776* (1965); Carl Becker, *The History of Political Parties in the Province of New York, 1760–1776** (1909); R. E. Brown, *Middle-Class Democracy and the Revolution in Massachusetts, 1691–1780* (1955); E. S. and H. M. Morgan, *The Stamp Act Crisis** (1953); John Shy, *Toward Lexington: The Role of the British Army in the Coming of the American Revolution* (1965); and Bernard Bailyn, *Ideological Origins of the American Revolution** (1967).

On the Revolutionary War the following are helpful: J. R. Alden, *The American Revolution, 1775–1783** (1954); J. C. Miller, *Triumph of Freedom, 1775–1783** (1949); W. H. Nelson, *The American Tory** (1961); W. M. Wallace, *Appeal to Arms** (1951); S. E. Morison, *John Paul Jones: A Sailor's Biography** (1959); S. F. Bemis, *The Diplomacy of the American Revolution** (1935); and R. B. Morris, *The Peacemakers: The Great Powers and American Independence* (1965).

* Titles available in paperback.

# PART TWO

# The Young Republic Makes a Successful Start under a New Constitution

William E. Gladstone, a nineteenth-century British statesman, once described the Constitution of the United States as the "most wonderful work ever struck off at a given time by the brain and purpose of man." Actually, the Constitution was not the result of a sudden stroke of genius. It was the product of generations of experience with colonial and state governments and with the Articles of Confederation. It took form in the heat of political controversy and was adopted in the face of bitter opposition. Yet, though far from flawless, it was indeed a wonderful work. Certainly it created, as it was intended to do, a "more perfect union" than existed at the time it was written. More than that, it provided a fundamental law capable of growth and adaptation to meet the needs of the nation for centuries to come.

From the beginning the Constitution took on some of the characteristics of a sacred writing, a holy mystery of the Americans. Among its virtues was its brevity (only about 7,000 words), but the defect of that virtue was a considerable ambiguity, which left room at certain points for a variety of interpretations. Political differences, no matter what the interests that underlay them, came to be expressed in constitutional terms. In discussing a governmental policy, men asked not only whether it was to their particular advantage, or whether it contributed to the public good, but also whether it was in accord with the Constitution. Those who had opposed the adoption of the Constitution joined in the discussion instead of advocating repeal. All were willing to obey the fundamental law, but not all agreed on what it permitted.

Two basic lines of interpretation quickly appeared. According to one, the words of the document were to be broadly construed, so as to give the new government "implied powers" beyond those literally specified. According to the other, the words were to be strictly followed, so as to leave to the states all powers not plainly delegated to the central government. Alexander Hamilton was the first great exponent of liberal or loose construction, and Thomas Jefferson of strict construction and state rights.

The party followers of Hamilton—the Federalists—controlled the Presidency during the first dozen years under the Constitution. The Federalists infused vigor into the federal government, putting it on a sound financial basis, and they set the young republic on the path of neutrality and diplomatic independence. In their grasp for power, however, they overreached themselves. They faced the dilemma of all rulers in a government that depends upon the will of the people—the dilemma of choosing between governmental strength and individual freedom—and they made their choice in favor of strong government at the expense of popular liberty and popular support. The Federalists never won another presidential election after 1796, yet their main achievements endured.

Once Jefferson and his party followers were in control, after 1801, they had to deal with situations that seemed to demand strong, unfet-

tered action. Soon the Jeffersonian Republicans were going even farther, in some respects, than the Federalists in the exercise of federal
authority. If Jefferson appeared to be inconsistent, so did many of his
opponents, for they now adopted the theory of state rights and turned
his former arguments against him. Some even objected to his greatest
achievement as President, when he doubled the territory of the
United States by acquiring Louisiana, which then consisted roughly
of the entire Mississippi Valley to the west of the great river, plus the
New Orleans area to the east of it.

A European war, which had begun in 1793 and was renewed in
1803, jeopardized the policy proclaimed by President Washington
and endorsed by President Jefferson—the policy of neutrality and
peace. Twice the United States got involved in the European struggle:
the first time with France (1798), the second time with Great Britain
(1812). The War of 1812, though avowedly waged for free seas and
sailors' rights, was resisted by the group most directly interested in
seagoing commerce, the New England merchants, who sneeringly
referred to it as "Mr. Madison's war." The war ended in what was at
best a draw. Yet it had important consequences. It broke the Indian
barriers that had blocked northwest and southwest expansion. It gave
a boost to the spirit of nationalism, which discredited the antiwar
party and helped overcome the divisive force of postwar sectionalism.
And it stimulated the growth of manufactures, thus accelerating the
progress of the nation toward industrial greatness.

The westward movement of population led to a sectional crisis
(1819–1821). The specific question was whether Missouri, which had
been organized out of a part of the Louisiana Purchase, should be admitted as a slaveholding state, but also at stake was the larger question of whether the North or the South should dominate the rising
West. The Missouri controversy was settled by a compromise, and
the ideal of a strong national government was vigorously reasserted in
the Supreme Court decisions of Chief Justice John Marshall and in
the foreign policies of President James Monroe.

The year the war ended, 1815, marks a turning point in the relations
of the United States with the rest of the world. Previously, this
country had become involved again and again in the broils of Europe,
and much of the time the requirements of diplomacy had dictated
domestic policies. Afterward, for almost a century, domestic politics
held a clear priority over foreign affairs as the country entered upon a
period of comparative "isolation."

# Chapter 5.  A MORE PERFECT UNION

## Failures in Foreign Affairs

The peace treaty of 1783 recognized the independence of the United States and granted the new nation a vast domain—on paper—but Americans found it hard to exercise their full sovereignty in fact. At once they ran into serious conflict with both Great Britain and Spain, yet they could not count on the support of France even though France remained technically America's ally.

Despite the treaty provision calling upon the British to evacuate American soil, British forces continued to occupy a string of frontier posts along the Great Lakes within the United States. The Spaniards claimed that their territory of Florida extended farther north than the boundary the United States and Great Britain had agreed upon. Possessing Louisiana as well as Florida and thus occupying both banks of the lower Mississippi, Spain had lawful power to close the river to American navigation, and did so in 1784.

Though commerce now flourished in new directions, most American trade persisted as much as possible in the old, prewar patterns. In the United States the bulk of imports continued to come from British sources, for Americans were used to British goods, and British merchants knew and catered to American tastes, offered attractive prices, and extended long and easy credit. To earn the British funds needed to pay for these imports, Americans desired free access to more British markets than were open to them after the war.

In 1784 Congress sent John Adams as minister to London with instructions to get a commercial treaty and speed up the evacuation of the frontier posts. Taunted by queries about whether he represented one nation or thirteen, Minister Adams made no headway in England, partly because Congress had no power to retaliate against the kind of commercial warfare that Great Britain was pursuing against the United States. Throughout the 1780s the British government refused even to return the courtesy of sending a minister to the American capital.

The Spanish government, by contrast, was willing to negotiate its differences with the United States, and in 1785 its representative, Don Diego de Gardoqui, arrived in New York (where Congress had moved from Philadelphia) to deal with the Secretary for Foreign Affairs, John Jay. After months of the most friendly conversations, Jay and Gardoqui initialed a treaty (1786). By its terms, the Spanish government would have granted Americans the right to trade with Spain but not with her colonies; would have conceded the American interpretation of the Florida boundary; and (in a secret article) would have joined in an alliance to protect American soil from British encroachments. The United States, besides guaranteeing Spanish possessions in America, would have agreed to "forbear" the navigation of the Mississippi for twenty years, though not to abandon the right of navigation. Jay found it hopeless, however, to secure the necessary nine state votes for the ratification of his treaty by Congress, since the delegates from the five Southern states objected bitterly and correctly that the interests of Southerners in Mississippi navigation were being sacrificed to the interests of Northerners in Spanish trade.

## The Needs of the West

Into the areas of postwar border conflict with Great Britain and Spain moved an unprecedented horde of American settlers during and after the Revolution. When the war began, only a few thousand lived west of the Appalachian divide; by 1790 their numbers had increased to 120,000. These frontiersmen needed protection from the Indians, access to outside markets for surplus crops, and courts with orderly processes of law. In dealing with the West, Congress inherited responsibilities that formerly had baffled King and Parliament.

With Virginia's cession in 1781, the landed states had begun to yield their Western claims to the Confederation. Congress soon began to make policy for the national domain. The most momentous decision was that settlements in the territory should not be held in permanent subjection as colonies but should be transformed ultimately into states equal with the original thirteen.

The Ordinance of 1785 provided a system of land survey and sale. The land to the north of the Ohio was to be surveyed and marked off in a rectangular pattern before any of it was sold. This land ordinance provided for east-west base lines, north-south "ranges," and townships with sides paralleling the ranges and base lines. Each township was to contain thirty-six square-mile sections. In every township four sections were to be set aside for the United States and one for the support of schools. The rest of the sections were to be sold at auction for not less than $1 an acre. Since there were 640 acres in a section, the prospective buyer of government land had to have at least $640 in ready cash or in United States certificates of indebtedness. These terms favored large speculators over the actual settlers. The Ordinance of 1787 provided for territorial government. This famous "Northwest Ordinance" established one Northwest Territory for the time being, provided for its subsequent division into several territories, not fewer than three nor more than five, and laid out three stages for the evolution of each territory into a state. In the first stage, Congress-appointed officials would govern the territory, in the second an elected legislature would share power with them, and in the third, when the people numbered 60,000 or more, they might frame a constitution and apply for statehood. These two ordinances constituted the Confederation's greatest accomplishment — the institution of enlightened management of western territory.

The Indian policy of Congress fell short of the requirements of land speculators as well as frontier settlers. In 1785 and 1786 congressional commissioners made treaties with representatives of the Iroquois and other tribes, who thereby surrendered their claims to a stretch of land north of the Ohio in return for comparatively worthless trinkets. Repudiating the treaties, many of the tribesmen went on the warpath. Congress vainly instructed Colonel Josiah Harmar, commanding the federal troops in the Ohio country, to drive the Indians back, then in desperation called upon the aging hero George Rogers Clark to save the frontier. While the campaign against the Indians in the Northwest faltered, a new threat arose in the Southwest, where the Creeks under the half-breed Alexander McGillivray not only repudiated their treaties ceding land but also formed an alliance with the Spaniards to resist the advance of American frontiersmen.

Some of the frontier leaders in the Southwest, instead of fighting the Spaniards, turned to collaborating with them. These leaders and their followers thought for a time that they saw advantages for themselves in the possible creation of a Southwestern confederacy under Spanish tutelage. They might thus get what the United States seemed unable to give them — protection from the Indians, cheap or free land, and an outlet to Eastern and foreign markets through the navigation of the Mississippi. At the same time another underground separatist movement was afoot on the far northern frontier. The aspirations of Vermont for statehood having been frustrated by the rival claims of New York and New Hampshire to its soil, some Vermonters intrigued with British agents for returning the Green Mountain country to the British Empire.

## Debts, Taxes, and Daniel Shays

At the end of the war foreign ships crowded into American seaports with cargoes of all kinds, and the American people bought extravagantly with cash or credit. In consequence the wartime accumulations of specie were drained out of the country, consumer indebtedness to importing merchants was multiplied, and a postwar depression lasting from 1784 to 1787 was made worse than it might otherwise have been. The depression, with its money scarcity, bore heavily upon debtors both public and private, complicating the financial problems of many citizens and of the Confederation and state governments.

The Confederation government had canceled most of its war debt to Americans by repudiating hundreds of millions of dollars in Continental currency. Yet it still owed a large domestic debt; and through continued borrowings from abroad, mostly from the Netherlands, its foreign debt increased. During the 1780s the government had to make do with uncertain and fluctuating revenues. It could only make requisitions on the states, and they paid an average of only about one-sixth of the total that was requested. This was barely enough to meet the government's ordinary operating expenses. To pay the interest on the foreign debt, the Secretary of the Treasury, Robert Morris, used the proceeds from the new loans. Thus he maintained an excellent credit rating with Dutch and other foreign bankers. But he could not keep up with the domestic obligations, and the government lost credit at home. At a fraction of the face value, shrewd speculators bought up Confederation certificates of indebtedness from former Revolutionary soldiers and others who lost hope of payment from Congress and who needed ready cash.

The states, too, came out of the war with large debts, and one by one they added to their obligations by taking over parts of the Confederation debt owed to their respective citizens. Taxable resources varied a good deal from state to state. The chief reliance everywhere was upon the direct tax on land and its improvements.

Suffering from the postwar deflation and from the tax burden upon their land, the debtor farmers of the country demanded relief in the form of paper money, and seven of the states responded by issuing such currency. The other six states refused to yield to the advocates of inflation and pursued policies of unrelieved taxation to support their public debts. To the state creditors — that is, the bondholders — all this was sound and honest public finance. But it seemed like robbery and tyranny to many of the poverty-stricken farmers, especially in New England, who felt that money was being extorted from them to swell the riches of the wealthy bondholders in Boston and other towns. At a time when cash was not to be had, these farmers were called upon to pay in specie not only state tax collectors but also mortgage holders and other private creditors. When debtors failed to pay they found their mortgages foreclosed and their property seized, and sometimes they found themselves in jail.

Mobs of distressed farmers rioted in various parts of New England but caused the most serious trouble in Massachusetts. There the malcontents of the Connecticut Valley and the Berkshire Hills, many of them Revolutionary veterans, found a leader in Daniel Shays, himself a former captain in the Continental army. Organizing and drilling his followers, Shays put forth a program of demands including paper money, tax relief, a moratorium on debts, the removal of the state capital from Boston to the interior, and the abolition of imprisonment for

debt. During the summer of 1786 the Shaysites concentrated upon the immediate task of preventing the collection of debts, private or public, and went in armed bands from place to place to break up court sittings and sheriff's sales. In Boston, members of the legislature, including Samuel Adams, denounced Shays and his men as rebels and traitors. When winter came these rebels, instead of laying down their arms, advanced upon Springfield to get more of them from the arsenal there. From Boston approached an army of state militiamen financed by a loan from wealthy merchants who feared a new revolution. In January 1787, this army met Shays' ragged troops, killed several of them, captured many more, and scattered the rest to the hills in a blinding snowstorm.

As a military enterprise, Shays' Rebellion was a fiasco, yet it had important consequences for the future of the United States. In Massachusetts it resulted in a few immediate gains for the discontented groups. Shays and his lieutenants, at first sentenced to death, were soon pardoned, and some concessions to Shays' earlier demands were granted in the way of tax relief and the postponement of debt payments. Far more significant, the rebellion also affected the country as a whole by giving added urgency to the movement for a new Constitution.

## Advocates of Centralization

Weak though the Confederation government was, it satisfied a great many — probably a majority — of the people. They did not want a strong central government. Having just fought the Revolutionary War to avert the danger of remote and, to them, tyrannical authority, they desired to keep the centers of political power close to home in the thirteen states.

Others, however, either disliked the Articles of Confederation from the outset or came eventually to desire something different. Disgruntled at the refusal of Congress to grant them half pay for life, some of the military men through their exclusive and hereditary Society of the Cincinnati hoped to control and to invigorate the government, some of them even aspiring to a kind of army dictatorship. Artisans or "mechanics," the manufacturers of the time, preferred a uniformly high national tariff to the varying state tariffs.

Merchants and shippers preferred a single and effective commercial policy to thirteen different and ineffective ones. Land speculators wished to see the "Indian menace" finally removed from their Western tracts, and creditors desired to stop the state issues of paper money. Investors in Confederation securities hoped to have the Confederation debt made good and the value of their securities enhanced. Large property owners in general looked for a reliable means of safety from the threat of mobs and noted that the Confederation had lacked any authority to intervene in Shays' Rebellion.

The issue was not whether the Confederation should be changed but how drastic the changes should be. Even its defenders reluctantly came to agree that the government needed strengthening at its weakest point — its lack of power to tax. To save the Articles of Confederation, its friends backed the import amendment of 1782, which would have authorized Congress to levy customs duties. All the states ratified the amendment except Rhode Island, whose single veto was enough to kill it. The next year a similar amendment was accepted by Rhode Island but defeated by New York. Later the state-rights advocates proposed that the states make to Congress a temporary and qualified grant of taxing authority (not an amendment to the Articles), but most of the centralizers had begun to lose interest in such remedies. They insisted upon a much more thoroughgoing change.

The most resourceful of the reformers was the political genius, New York lawyer, one-time military aide to General Washington, and illegitimate son of a Scottish merchant in the West Indies — Alexander Hamilton. From the beginning he had been dissatisfied with the Articles of Confederation, had seen little to be gained by piecemeal amendments, and had urged the holding of a national convention to overhaul the entire document. To achieve his aim he took advantage of a movement for interstate cooperation which began in 1785 when a group of Marylanders and Virginians met in Alexandria to settle differences between their two states.

One of the Virginians, James Madison, who was as eager as Hamilton to see a stronger government, induced the Virginia legislature to invite all the states to send delegates to a larger conference on commercial questions. This group met at Annapolis in 1786, but representatives from only five states appeared at the meeting. Hamilton, a delegate from New York, took satisfaction in seeing the conference adopt his report and send copies to the state legislatures and to Congress. His report recommended that Congress call a convention of special delegates from all the states to gather in Philadelphia the next year and consider ways to "render the constitution of the Federal government adequate to the exigencies of the union."

## A Divided Convention

Fifty-five men, representing all the states except Rhode Island, attended one or more sessions of the convention that sat in the Philadelphia State House from May to September, 1787. Practically all of them represented, both directly and indirectly, the great property interests of the country. Many feared what one of them called the "turbulence and follies" of democracy. Most agreed that the United States needed a stronger central government. There were differences of opinion, however, as to how much stronger the government should be, what specific powers it should have, and what structure it should be given. There were differences, in particular, over the relative influence the large and small states should exert in the new system.

The Virginians took the initiative from the moment the convention began. Washington was easily elected to preside, and then a resolution was passed to keep the proceedings absolutely secret. Next, Edmund Randolph of Virginia proposed that "a *national* government ought to be established, consisting of a *supreme* Legislative, Executive, and Judiciary." This being approved, Randolph introduced the plan that Madison already had worked out. The Virginia Plan, if adopted, would give the larger influence to the richer and more populous states. It would also mean abandoning the Articles of Confederation and building the government anew.

But the existing Congress had called the convention "for the sole and express purpose of revising the Articles of Confederation," and the states in commissioning their "deputies" had authorized them to do no more than revise the Articles. Some of the delegates — especially those from the smaller states — now raised doubts whether the convention properly could entertain such proposals as were embodied in the Virginia Plan. At first, however, these men had nothing to offer in its stead. After some delay, William Paterson of New Jersey submitted an alternative scheme for a "federal" as opposed to a "national" government. The New Jersey Plan was intended only to revise and strengthen the Articles.

The stage was now set for a full debate between large-state and small-state delegates. To the latter, one of the worst features of the Virginia Plan was the system of representation in the proposed two-house legislature. In the lower house, the states were to be represented in proportion to their population, and so the largest state (Virginia) would have about ten times as many representatives as the smallest (Delaware). In the upper house, the members were to be elected by the lower house, and some of the smaller states at any given time might have no members at all! To the small-state delegates the Congress of the Articles of Confederation, as well as the Congress of the New Jersey Plan, at least had the merit of equal representation for all the states, regardless of size. But the New Jersey Plan gained the support of only a minority in the convention and, after much argument, was tabled.

The Virginia Plan was left as the basis for discussion. Its proponents realized that they would have to make concessions to the small-state men if the convention were ever to reach a general agreement. The majority soon conceded an important point by consenting that the members of the upper house should be elected by the state legislatures rather than by the lower house of the national legislature. Thus each state would be sure of always having at least one member in the upper house, but there remained the question of how many members each state should have.

There remained also the question of the number of representatives each state should have in the lower house. If the number was to depend upon population, were slaves to be included in the population figure? The delegates from the states where slavery seemed a permanent institution—especially those from South Carolina—insisted that slaves should be counted as persons (though not, of course, entitled to vote) in determining a state's representation. But these delegates argued that slaves ought to be considered as property, not as persons, when it was proposed that the new legislature be allowed to levy a direct tax (such as a land or poll tax) on each state in proportion to its population. Men who came from states where slavery had disappeared or was expected to disappear argued that slaves should be included in calculating taxation but not representation. Thus an issue between slave and free states was added to the one between large and small states.

## Differences Compromised

On these and other matters, the delegates bickered day after day. By the end of June, as both temperature and tempers rose to uncomfortable heights, the convention seemed in danger of breaking up, with nothing accomplished. If this should happen, the men at Philadelphia would "become a reproach and byword down to future ages," said the venerable Franklin, the voice of calmness and conciliation throughout the summer. "And what is worse, mankind may hereafter, from this unfortunate instance, despair of establishing governments by human wisdom, and leave it to chance, war and conquest."

Through the calming influence of Franklin and others, especially Oliver Ellsworth of Connecticut, the delegates managed to settle the most serious of their disputes and go on with their work. A committee of twelve, with one member from each state, brought in a report that culminated in what afterwards was known as the "Great Compromise" (adopted on July 16, 1787). One part of this report provided that the states should be represented in the lower house in proportion to their population, and that three-fifths of the slaves should be included in determining the basis for both representation and direct taxation. The three-fifths formula, though seemingly rather arbitrary, gained some degree of logic from the assumption that, in contributing his labor to the wealth of a state, a slave was on the average three-fifths as productive as a freeman. Another part of the Great Compromise provided that in the upper house, the states should be represented equally with two members apiece.

In the ensuing weeks, while committees busied themselves with various parts of the document that was beginning to take shape, the convention as a whole effected another compromise, this one having to do with the legislative power to impose tariffs and regulate

## Background of the Constitution

Where Historians Disagree

The 1780s once seemed to historians like a "critical period," one of impending collapse and chaos from which the newly independent republic was rescued only by the timely adoption of the Constitution. This was the theme of a widely read book that John Fiske, a popularizer of both science and history, wrote a century afterward (1888). Fiske and other writers emphasized the difficulties and failures of the 1780s—the business depression, the weaknesses of the central government under the Articles of Confederation, the threats to American territory from Great Britain and Spain, the debts of the Confederation and of the states, the interstate jealousies and barriers to trade, the widespread resort to paper-money inflation, and the disorders and lawlessness culminating in Shays' Rebellion. All this, according to Fiske and those who followed him, represented the darkness before the dawn.

One of the greatest of American historians, Charles A. Beard, challenged the prevailing view in an arresting and controversial work, *An Economic Interpretation of the Constitution of the United States* (1913). Beard maintained that the 1780s had been a "critical period" only for certain business interests, not for the people as a whole. According to him, these interests desired a central government strong enough to promote industry and trade, safeguard private property, and make good the public debt. Many of the delegates to the constitutional convention, he said, stood to gain directly as well as indirectly from their efforts, for they had bought up the Confederation's "certificates of indebtedness" cheaply, and these would rise in value if a strong central government were set up. He added that the advocates of the Constitution succeeded in obtaining its ratification despite the indifference or opposition of a majority of the people. In a later book (1927) Beard suggested that the Articles of Confederation might still be serving quite satisfactorily as our twentieth-century frame of government if a comparatively small group of impatient and determined men had not managed to bring about a drastic change in 1787–1788.

Most historians promptly adopted Beard's conclusions, and some proceeded to elaborate upon his work. Merrill Jensen, for one, in *The Articles of Confederation* (1940) and *The New Nation* (1950), produced additional evidence to show that the 1780s were a time of hopeful striving rather than black despair, of economic recovery and not persisting depression, of governmental progress under the Articles despite temporary failures. Other historians disagreed with Beard, however, and in recent years the dissenters, notably Robert E. Brown and Forrest Mc-Donald, have criticized his methods and findings with increasing effectiveness. Today, few if any historians accept the Beard thesis without qualification. And some, like Gordon S. Wood in his *The Creation of the American Republic, 1776–1787* (1969), find that the 1780s were important primarily for the resolution of intellectual and constitutional issues; they see the writing of the Constitution as the orderly culmination of the Revolution.

commerce. The men from some of the Southern states feared that this power might be used for levying export duties on their crops, interfering with the slave trade, and making commercial agreements (as in the recent Jay-Gardoqui treaty) which would sacrifice the interests of rice and tobacco growers. The South Carolinians proposed that a two-thirds vote in the legislature be required not only to approve commercial treaties but also to pass commercial laws.

Though not accepting that proposal, the convention made concessions by forbidding the legislature to levy a tax on exports, to put a duty of more than ten dollars a head on imported slaves, or to prohibit slave importations until twenty years had elapsed.

Some differences of opinion the convention was unable to harmonize, and it disposed of them by evasion or omission. One of these concerned the question whether the new courts or some special agency should be empowered to review legislative acts and set them aside. The "council of revision," a part of the original Virginia Plan, was dropped, and no provision was added to confer the power of judicial review explicitly upon the courts.

The Constitution, as it finally took form at the end of summer in 1787, though an outgrowth of the Virginia Plan, was in some respects so different that Randolph himself refused to sign it. Yet it differed even more from the New Jersey Plan, and several refused on that account to give it their approval. Indeed, the completed document did not entirely satisfy any of the delegates. Nevertheless, thirty-nine of them affixed their signatures to it, doubtless with much the same feeling that Franklin expressed. "Thus I consent, Sir, to this Constitution," he said, *"because I expect no better, and because I am not sure that it is not the best."*

## The Constitution of 1787

Madison, who was responsible for most of the actual drafting, observed that it was, "in strictness, neither a national nor a federal Constitution, but a composition of both."

Certainly it possessed some strongly national features. The Constitution and all laws and treaties made under it were to be the "supreme law" of the land, regardless of anything to the contrary in the constitution or laws of any state. Broad powers were granted to the central government, including the congressional powers of taxation, regulation of commerce, control of money, and the passage of laws "necessary and proper" for carrying out its specific powers. At the same time, the individual states were deprived of a number of the powers—such as the issuance of money and the passage of laws "impairing the obligation of contracts," for example,

laws postponing the payment of debts—which the states had been free to exercise under the Articles of Confederation. Now all state officials were to be required to take an oath of allegiance to the Constitution, and the state militias were to be made available, upon call, for enforcing the new "supreme law." Nowhere were the former claims of the states to individual sovereignty recognized. Gone was the stipulation of the Articles that "each State shall retain every power, jurisdiction, and right not *expressly* delegated to the United States in Congress assembled." Lacking was any bill of rights to limit the central government as the state bills limited the state governments.

On the other hand, the Constitution was federal in setting up a government that presupposed the existence of separate states and left wide powers to them. For instance, the states were to be represented as separate and equal entities in one of the two branches of the new legislature.

Within the allotted sphere of its powers, the new government was authorized to act directly upon the people of the United States. It would not have to act upon them solely through the member states, as the previous Confederation government, and indeed all confederation governments of the past, had done. Here, then, was something new and unique, something for which old terms were hardly adequate. It was a combination of two kinds of government, state and central, with each of them intended to be supreme within its respective sphere.

Next to the distinctive federal arrangement (the "division of powers"), the most striking feature of the new system was the complex organization and operation of the central government itself, with its checks and balances among the legislative, executive, and judicial branches (the "separation of powers").

This complicated structure resulted from accident—that is, from the compromising of contradictory views—as much as from deliberate planning. Nevertheless, the complexity was such as to give the Founding Fathers hope that no single group or combination of groups in the country could ever gain absolute and unchecked power. A government so divided against itself ought to frustrate tyranny from whatever source. When the Founding Fathers spoke of tyranny, they usually had in mind the rule of mobs and demagogues—the threat of such leaders as Daniel Shays.

## Federalists, Antifederalists

Since the delegates at Philadelphia had exceeded their instructions from Congress and the states, they had reason to doubt whether the Constitution would ever be ratified if they followed the procedures laid down in the Articles of Confederation, which required *all* of the state *legislatures* to approve alterations in the form of the government. So the convention changed the rules, specifying in the Constitution that the new government should go into effect among the ratifying states when only *nine* of the thirteen had ratified, and recommending to Congress that the Constitution be submitted to specially called state *conventions* rather than to the legislatures of the states.

The Congress in New York, completely overshadowed by the convention in Philadelphia, accepted the latter's work and submitted it to the states for their approval or disapproval. The state legislatures, again with the exception of Rhode Island, arranged for the election of delegates to ratifying conventions, and sooner or later each of these conventions got down to business. Meanwhile, from the fall of 1787 to the summer of 1788, the merits and demerits of the new Constitution were debated in the legislatures, in mass meetings, and in the columns of newspapers, as well as in the convention halls.

Since the idea of a strongly national government was thought to be unpopular, the advocates of the new Constitution chose to call themselves "Federalists" and to call their opponents "Antifederalists." These misnomers stuck, despite the insistence of opponents of ratification that they were "Federal Republicans," the true federalists of the time.

Among the Federalists were some of the most profound political philosophers of any period or place, including Hamilton, Madison, and Jay, who under the joint pseudonym "Publius" wrote a long series of newspaper essays expounding the meaning and virtues of the Constitution. Afterwards published in book form as *The Federalist,* these papers have been considered as the most authoritative of all constitutional commentaries and, indeed, as one of the greatest of all treatises on political science.

The opponents of ratification produced no comparable set of Antifederalist papers, yet these men too were able and sincere, and they made a vigorous case for themselves in their own speeches and newspaper propaganda. Necessarily, the Antifederalists resorted mainly to negative argument. The Constitution, they protested, was illegal — as indeed it was if judged by the Articles of Confederation, the existing fundamental law. The new government would increase taxes, obliterate the states, wield dictatorial powers, favor the "well-born" over the common people, and put an end to individual liberty, the Antifederalists added. Of all their specific criticisms the most compelling was this: the Constitution lacked a bill of rights.

For all the efforts of the Antifederalists, ratification proceeded during the winter of 1787–1788. Delaware, the first to act, did so unanimously, as did two others of the smallest states, New Jersey and Georgia. In the large states of Pennsylvania and Massachusetts the Antifederalists put up a determined struggle but lost in the final vote. By June 1788, when the New Hampshire convention at last made up its mind, nine of the states had ratified and thus had made it possible for the Constitution to go into effect among themselves.

A new government could hardly hope to succeed, however, without the participation of Virginia and New York, whose conventions remained closely divided. Before the end of the month Virginia and then New York consented to the Constitution by rather narrow votes. The New York convention yielded to expediency — even some of the most staunchly Antifederalist delegates feared that the state's commercial interests would suffer if, once the other states had got together under the "New Roof," New York were to remain outside. Massachusetts, Virginia, and New York all ratified on the assumption, though not on the express condition, that certain desired amendments would be added to the Constitution, above all a bill of rights. Deciding to wait and see what became of these hopes for amendment, the North Carolina convention adjourned without taking action. Rhode Island, for the time being, did not even call a convention to consider ratification.

## Filling in the Gaps

When the first elections under the Constitution were held, in the early months of 1789, the results showed that the new government was to be in the hands of its friends. Few if any of the newly elected congressmen and senators had been extreme Antifederalists; almost all had favored ratification, and many had served as delegates to the Philadelphia convention. The President-elect, George Washington, had presided at the convention; many who had favored ratification did so because they expected him to preside over the new government also. He received the votes of all the presidential electors whom the states, either by legislative action or by popular election, had named. John Adams, a firm Federalist, though not a member of the convention, received the next highest number of electoral votes and hence was to be Vice President.

By filling certain gaps in the Constitution, the first Congress served almost as a continuation of the constitutional convention. The work of the convention had been incomplete in various respects, especially in that it had omitted a bill of rights. Dozens of amendments intended to make up for this lack had been proposed in the state ratifying conventions, and Congress now undertook the task of sorting these, reducing them to a manageable number, and sending them to the states for ratification. Of the twelve sent out, ten were ratified, and these took effect in 1791. The first nine of them limited Congress by forbidding it to infringe upon certain basic rights, such as freedom of religion, of speech, and of the press, immunity from arbitrary arrest, and trial by jury. The Tenth Amendment, reserving to the states all powers except those specifically withheld from them or delegated to the federal government, bolstered state rights, and changed the emphasis of the Constitution from nationalism to federalism.

In regard to the structure of the federal courts, the Constitution had only this to say: "The judicial power of the United States shall be vested in one Supreme Court, and in such inferior courts as the Congress may from time to time ordain and establish." Thus the convention had left up to Congress the number of Supreme Court judges to be appointed and the kinds of lower courts to be organized. In the Judiciary Act of 1789 Congress provided for a Supreme Court of six members, with one chief justice and five associate justices; for thirteen district courts with one judge apiece; and for three circuit courts, each to consist of one of the district judges sitting with two of the Supreme Court justices. In the same act Congress gave the Supreme Court the power to make the final decision in cases involving the constitutionality of state laws. If the Constitution was in fact to be the "supreme law of the land," the various state courts could not be left to decide for themselves whether the state legislatures were violating that supreme law.

As for executive departments, the Constitution referred indirectly to them but did not specify what or how many they should be. The first Congress created three such departments—state, treasury, and war—and also the offices of attorney general and postmaster general.

In appointing department heads and other high officials, President Washington selected men who were qualified by character and experience, who were well disposed toward the Constitution (no Antifederalists), and who as a group would provide a balanced representation of the different sections of the country. To the office of secretary of the treasury he appointed Alexander Hamilton of New York, who had taken the lead in calling the constitutional convention and who, though only thirty-two, was an expert in public finance. For secretary of war he chose the Massachusetts Federalist, General Henry Knox. As attorney general he named Edmund Randolph of Virginia, sponsor of the plan upon which the Constitution had been based. He picked as secretary of state another Virginian, Thomas Jefferson, who had not opposed the Constitution though he had had nothing to do with its framing or adoption, having been away from the country as minister to France.

# Chapter 6.   FEDERALIST FOUNDATIONS

## Hamilton's Financial Plans

As President, George Washington thought it his duty to see that the laws of Congress, if constitutional, were faithfully carried out. A man of strong will, he was the master of his own administration, but (unlike later Presidents such as Andrew Jackson and Franklin D. Roosevelt) he did not conceive of himself as a popular leader who should find out the will of the people and then see that Congress enacted it into law. One of his department heads, Secretary of the Treasury Alexander Hamilton, provided the legislative leadership that Washington himself lacked.

Hamilton thought the new government could be strengthened and made to succeed if the support of the wealthy men of the country could be brought to it. And, believing that all men were motivated by self-interest, he assumed that the way to gain the support of the wealthy was to give them a stake in the success of the new government. He therefore planned a program of financial legislation which, among other things, was intended to cause the propertied classes to look to the federal government for profitable investments and for the protection and promotion of their property interests.

If men of means were to have faith in the government, then it must keep faith with them by paying its debts and establishing its credit on a sound basis. Therefore, first of all, Hamilton proposed that the existing public debt be "funded," or in other words that the miscellaneous, uncertain, depreciated certificates of indebtedness that the old Congress had issued during and since the Revolution be called in and exchanged for uniform, interest-bearing bonds, payable at definite dates. Next he recommended that the Revolutionary state debts be "assumed" or taken over by the United States, his object being to cause the state as well as the federal bondholders to look to the central government for eventual payment. His plan was not to pay off and thus eliminate the debt, either state or federal, but just the opposite: to create a large

and permanent public debt, new bonds being issued as old ones were paid off.

Hamilton also planned the establishment of a national bank. At the time, there were only a few banks in the country, located in Boston, Philadelphia, and New York. A new, national bank would serve several purposes. It would aid business by providing loans and currency—in the form of bank notes, which in those days were used instead of checks. It would aid the government by making a safe place available for the deposit of federal funds, by facilitating the collection of taxes and the disbursement of the government's expenditures, and by keeping up the price of government bonds through judicious bond purchases.

The funding and assumption of the debts, together with the payment of regular interest on them, would cost a great deal of money, and so Hamilton had to find adequate sources of revenue. He thought the government should depend mainly upon two kinds of taxes (in addition to the receipts to be anticipated from the sales of public land). One of these was an excise to be paid by distillers of alcoholic liquors. This tax would hit most heavily the whiskey distillers of the back country, especially in Pennsylvania, Virginia, and North Carolina. These were small farmers who converted part of their corn and rye crop into whiskey, so as to have a concentrated and valuable product that they could conveniently take to market by horseback or muleback over poor mountain roads.

The other tax upon which Hamilton relied was the tariff on imports. Such a tax would not only raise a revenue, but also protect and encourage American manufactures by raising the price of competing manufactured goods brought in from abroad. In the old Articles of Confederation, according to its defenders as well as its critics, the worst defect had been Congress' lack of power to levy customs duties. One of the first acts of the new Congress, in 1789, was the passage of a tariff law designed to foster industries while raising a revenue, but the average level of duties under this law was extremely low. Hamilton advocated a higher and more decidedly protective tariff. In his Report on Manufactures he glowingly set forth the advantages, as he saw them, of stimulating the growth of industry in the United States. Factories, he said, would make the nation more nearly self-sufficient in wartime, would increase prosperity by creating a home market for the produce of the farms, and would make possible the fuller utilization of all kinds of labor, including the labor of women and children, even those (to quote Hamilton himself) of "tender years."

## Enacting the Program

Between 1789 and 1792 Hamilton succeeded in persuading Congress to pass the necessary laws for erecting his financial system — but only after a bitter struggle with a rising opposition group.

His assumption bill ran into special difficulty. Its opponents had a very good case, for if the federal government took over the state debts, the people of one state would have to pay federal taxes for servicing the debts of other states, and some of these debts, such as that of Massachusetts, were much larger than others, such as that of Virginia. Naturally, Virginians did not think it fair for them to have to pay a share of the large Massachusetts debt, and their representatives in Congress balked at the assumption bill.

Finally the bill got the support of some of them and so managed to pass, but only because of a logrolling deal. The Virginians wanted the national capital to be permanently located near them in the South. After Jefferson's return from France, Hamilton appealed to him, and Jefferson held a dinner at which arrangements were made to barter Virginia votes for the assumption bill in return for Northern votes for a Southern location of the capital. In 1790 the capital was changed from New York back to Philadelphia for a ten-year period, and after that a new capital city was to be built on the banks of the Potomac River, on land to be selected by Washington himself.

When Hamilton's bank bill was introduced into Congress, Madison and others opposed it on the grounds that it was unconstitutional, and though a majority voted for it, President Washington himself had his doubts. He therefore asked his official advisers for written opinions on the subject. In Hamilton's opinion the establishment of a bank was a fitting exercise of the powers of Congress, though the Constitution nowhere explicitly gave Congress the right. But Jefferson, with the support of his fellow Virginian, Randolph, argued that the Constitution should be construed in a strict sense and that Congress should be allowed no powers not clearly given to it. Washington found Hamilton's case more convincing, and he signed the bank bill when it came to him. The Bank of the United States began operations in 1791, under a charter that granted it the right to continue in business for twenty years.

Once enacted, Hamilton's program worked as he had intended. The public credit quickly was restored; the bonds of the United States were soon selling at home and abroad at prices even above their par value.

At the same time, speculators got rich and corruption was rife. Many congressmen had bought up large amounts of the old certificates of indebtedness, and these men profited by their own legislation in funding the debt at par. Directly or indirectly, properly or improperly, thousands of wealthy merchants in the seaports also gained from the Hamilton program.

The mass of the people — the farmers scattered over the countryside — profited much less. While these people shared some of the benefit of national strength and prosperity, they bore most of the burden of paying for it. The financial program required taxes, and these came mostly from the farmers, who had to pay not only land taxes to their state and local governments but also the excise and, indirectly, the tariff to the federal government. The feeling grew that the Washington administration was not treating all the people fairly, and out of this feeling an organized political opposition arose.

## Rise of Political Parties

The Constitution made no reference to political parties, and the Founding Fathers, George Washington in particular, believed that such organizations were evil and should be avoided. Yet parties soon arose from a division between the followers of Hamilton and those of Madison and Jefferson.

Jefferson and Madison were such close collaborators that it is sometimes difficult to separate the contributions of the two. To describe the political philosophy of one is, in the main, to describe the political philosophy of both. Jefferson, himself a farmer, believed that farmers were God's chosen people and that an ideal republic would consist of sturdy citizens each tilling his own soil. Though an aristocrat by birth, his mother belonging to one of the first families of Virginia, the Randolphs, he had faith in the good intentions of such farmer-citizens and thought that, if properly educated, they could be trusted to govern themselves through the election of able and qualified men. But, in the 1790s, he feared city mobs as "sores upon the body politic." He then opposed the development of extensive manufactures because they would lead to the growth of cities packed with propertyless workers. While Hamilton emphasized the need for order and stability, Jefferson stressed the importance of individual freedom.

The two secretaries continued to work against each other, and each began to organize a following in Congress and in the country at large. Hamilton's followers came to be known as Federalists, Jefferson's as Republicans. Republicans and Federalists differed in their social philosophies as well as in their economic interests and their constitutional views. Their differences in social outlook are seen in their reactions to the progress of the revolution in France. When that revolution first began, as a rather mild movement in favor of constitutional monarchy and the rights of man, practically all Americans hailed it as a step in the right direction. But when the revolution went to radical extremes, with attacks on organized religion, the overthrow of the monarchy, and eventually the guillotining of the King and Queen, Americans adopted different views about the events in France, the Federalists denouncing and the Republicans applauding them. The Republicans believed that American interests would best be served by maintaining close relations with France, while Hamilton and the Federalists believed that friendship with Great Britain was essential for the success of the United States.

When the time came for the election of 1792, the Republicans had no candidate to put up against Washington. Jefferson as well as Hamilton urged him to run for a second term, and the President consented for the good of the country.

## Securing the Frontier

The Washington administration made the power of the federal government felt even on the farthest reaches of the frontier.

The federal authority was challenged when, in 1794, the farmers of western Pennsylvania refused to pay the whiskey excise and terrorized the would-be tax collectors, much as the colonists had done throughout America at the time of the Stamp Act. The so-called Whiskey Rebellion was not left to the authorities of Pennsylvania as Shays' Rebellion had been left to the authorities of Massachusetts. Urged on by Hamilton, Washington took drastic steps. Calling out the militia of three states, he raised an army of nearly 15,000, a larger force than he had commanded against the British during most of the Revolution, and he personally accompanied this army as far as the town of Bedford. At the approach of the militiamen, the farmers around Pittsburgh, where the rebellion centered, either ran for cover or stayed home and professed to be law-abiding citizens. The rebellion quickly collapsed.

While the whiskey rebels were intimidated into obedience, other frontiersmen were made loyal to the government by its acceptance of new states as members of the Union. First to be admitted were two of the original thirteen, North Carolina (1789) and Rhode Island (1790), both of which had ratified the Constitution when they found that a bill of rights was definitely to be added and that they could not conveniently go on as independent commonwealths. Then Vermont, which had had its own state government since the Revolution, was accepted as the fourteenth state (1791) after New York and New Hampshire finally agreed to give up their claims to sovereignty over the Green Mountain country. Next came Kentucky (1792) with the consent of Virginia, which previously had governed the Kentucky counties as its own. After North Carolina finally ceded its Western lands to the Union, these were given a territorial government similar to that of the Northwest Territory and after six years became the state of Tennessee (1796). With the admission of these frontier states, the schemes for separating Vermont, Kentucky, and Tennessee from the Union soon came to an end.

In the more remote areas of the Northwest and the Southwest, meanwhile, the government had to contend with the Indians and their foreign allies, British and Spanish, in order to get a firm grasp upon all the territory belonging to the United States. In 1790 President Washington tried to buy peace with the Southwestern Indians, but the Indians continued to accept subsidies from the Spaniards and to raid American settlements along the border. At last, in 1793–1794, the Tennesseans went on the warpath themselves, their militia invading the Indian country and making the Southwestern frontier safe.

In the Northwest the government pursued a policy of force against the Indians, even at some risk of becoming involved in hostilities with their protector and ally, Great Britain. Two expeditions failed before a third one finally succeeded in the conquest of the Ohio country. General "Mad Anthony" Wayne in the summer of 1794 met and decisively defeated the Indians in the Battle of Fallen Timbers. Next summer the Indians agreed in the Treaty of Greenville to abandon to the white men most of what afterwards became the state of Ohio.

Before the government could be sure of its hold upon the border areas, it had to bring to terms the foreign powers that persisted in exerting influence there — Great Britain and Spain. In its diplomacy the Washington administration, by taking advantage of the opportunities that arose from the accidents of international politics, managed to reassert American independence and redeem the West.

## Maintaining Neutrality

A crisis in foreign affairs faced the Washington administration when the French revolutionary government, after guillotining King Louis XVI, went to war in 1793 with Great Britain and her allies. Should the United States recognize the radical government of France by accepting a diplomatic representative from it? Was the United States obligated by the alliance of 1778 to go to war on the side of France? Washington decided to recognize the French government and to issue a proclamation announcing the determination of the United States to remain at peace. The proclamation (1793), though it did not mention the word "neutrality," was generally interpreted as a neutrality statement, which it actually was. Next year Congress passed a Neutrality Act, forbidding American citizens to participate in the war and prohibiting the use of American soil as a base of operations for either side.

The first challenge to American neutrality came from France. A newly arrived minister from that country, the youthful and brash Edmond Genêt, made plans for using American ports to outfit French warships, authorized American shipowners to serve as French privateers, and proposed to send a band of Americans on an overland expedition against the territory of Spain, which at the moment was an ally of Great Britain and an enemy of France. In all these steps Genêt brazenly disregarded American neutrality. At last Washington demanded that the French government recall him, but by that time Genêt's party, the Girondins, were out of power in France and the still more extreme Jacobins in control, so it would not have been safe for him to return. Generously the President granted him political asylum in the United States, and he settled down to live to a ripe old age with his American wife on a Long Island farm.

The second challenge, an even greater one, came from Great Britain. Early in 1794 the Royal Navy suddenly seized hundreds of American ships engaged in trade in the French West Indies. The pretext for these seizures was a British interpretation of international law — known as the Rule of 1756 — which held that a trade prohibited in peacetime (as American trade between France and the French overseas possessions had been) could not be legally opened in time of war. With peace thus endangered, Hamilton grew concerned, for war would mean an end to imports from England, and most of the revenue for maintaining his financial system came from duties on those imports.

## Jay's Treaty

To Hamilton and to other Federalists it seemed that this was no time for ordinary diplomacy. Jefferson had resigned in 1793 to devote himself to organizing a political opposition, and the State Department was now in the hands of an even more ardently pro-French Virginian, Edmund Randolph. By-passing the State Department, Washington named as a special commissioner to England the staunch New York Federalist, former Secretary for Foreign Affairs under the old Confederation and current Chief Justice of the Supreme Court, John Jay. Jay was instructed to secure damages for the recent spoliations, withdrawal of British forces from the frontier posts, and a satisfactory commercial treaty, without violating the terms of the existing treaty of amity and commerce with France, signed at the time of the alliance in 1778.

The treaty that Jay negotiated (1794) was a long and complex document, dealing with frontier posts, boundaries, debts, commerce, ship seizures, and neutral rights. It yielded more to Great Britain and obtained less for the United States than Jay had been authorized to give or instructed to get. When the terms were published in the United States, the treaty was denounced more than any treaty before or since, and Jay himself was burned in effigy in various parts of the country. The Republicans were unanimous in decrying it; they said it was a departure from neutrality, favoring Great Britain and unfair to France. Even some of the Federalists were outraged by its terms, those in the South objecting to its provision for the payment of the pre-Revolutionary debts. Opponents of the treaty went to extraordinary lengths to defeat it in the Senate, and French agents aided them and cheered them on. The American minister to France, James Monroe, and even the Secretary of State, Edmund Randolph, cooperated closely with the French in a desperate attempt to prevent ratification. Nevertheless, after amending the treaty a bit, the Senate gave its consent.

There was much to be said for Jay's Treaty, despite its very real shortcomings. By means of it the United States gained valuable time for continued peaceful development, obtained undisputed sovereignty over all the Northwest, and secured a reasonably satisfactory commercial agreement with the nation whose trade was most important. More than that, the treaty led immediately to a settlement of the worst of the outstanding differences with Spain.

In Madrid the Spanish foreign minister feared that the understanding between Great Britain and the United States might prove a prelude to joint operations between those two countries against Spain's possessions in North America. Spain was about to change sides in the European war, abandoning Great Britain for France, and it was therefore to Spain's interest to appease the

United States. The relentless pressure of American frontiersmen advancing toward the Southwest made it doubtful whether Spain could long hold her borderlands in any event. And so, when Thomas Pinckney arrived in Spain as a special negotiator, he had no difficulty in gaining practically everything that the United States had sought from the Spaniards for over a decade. Pinckney's Treaty (1795) recognized the right of Americans to navigate the Mississippi to its mouth and to deposit goods at New Orleans for reloading on ocean-going ships; fixed the northern boundary of Florida where Americans always had insisted it should be, along the thirty-first parallel; and bound the Spanish authorities to prevent the Indians in Florida from raiding across the border.

Thus, before Washington had completed his second term in office, the United States had freed itself from the encroachments of both Great Britain and Spain.

## Election of 1796

As the time approached for the election of 1796, some of the party friends of Washington urged him to run again. Already twice elected without a single vote cast against him in the electoral college, he could be counted upon to hold the Federalist party together and carry it to a third great victory. But Washington, weary of the burdens of the presidential office, disgusted with the partisan abuse that was being heaped upon him, longed to retire to his beloved home, Mount Vernon. Though he did not object to a third term in principle, he did not desire one for himself. To make his determination clear, he composed, with Hamilton's assistance, a long letter to the American people and had it published in a Philadelphia newspaper.

When Washington in this "Farewell Address" referred to the "insidious wiles of foreign influence," he was not writing merely for rhetorical effect. He had certain real evils in mind. Lately he had dismissed the Secretary of State, Edmund Randolph, and had recalled the minister to France, James Monroe, for working hand in hand with the French to defeat Jay's Treaty. The French were still interfering in American politics with the hope of defeating the Federalists in the forthcoming presidential election.

There was no doubt that Jefferson would be

the candidate of the Republicans. With Washington out of the running, there was some question as to who the Federalist candidate would be. Hamilton, the very personification of Federalism, was not "available" because his forthright views had aroused too many enemies. John Adams, who as Vice President was directly associated with none of the Federalist measures, finally got the nomination for President at a caucus of the Federalists in Congress. The Federalists elected a majority of their presidential electors, despite the electioneering tactics of the French government, whose efforts may have boomeranged and helped the Federalists. But when the electors balloted in the various states, some of the Adams men declined to vote for his running mate, Thomas Pinckney, so Pinckney received fewer votes than Jefferson. The next President was to be a Federalist, but the Vice President was to be a Republican!

By virtue of his diplomatic services during the Revolution, his writings as a conservative political philosopher, and his devotion to the public weal as he saw it, "Honest John" Adams ranks as one of the greatest American statesmen. Like most prominent members of the illustrious Adams family afterwards, however, he lacked the politician's touch essential for successful leadership in a republican society. Even Washington, remote and austere as he sometimes seems to have been, was fairly adept at conciliating factions and maintaining party harmony. Unwisely, the new President chose to continue Washington's department heads in office. Most of them were friends of Hamilton, and they looked to him for advice, though he held no official post.

## Quasi-War with France

As American relations with Great Britain and Spain improved in consequence of Jay's and Pinckney's treaties, relations with France, now under the government of the Directory, went from bad to worse. The French, asserting that they were applying the same principles of neutral rights as the United States and Great Britain had adopted in Jay's Treaty, continued to capture American ships on the high seas and, in many cases, to imprison the crews. The French declined to receive the new minister whom Adams sent to replace Monroe.

War seemed likely unless the Adams administration could settle the difficulties with France. Adams appointed a bipartisan commission of three to approach the Directory. In France, in 1797, the three Americans were met by three agents of the Directory's foreign minister, Prince Talleyrand, who had a reputation as the wizard of European diplomacy but who did not understand the psychology of Americans, even though he had lived for a time in the United States. Talleyrand's agents demanded a loan for France and a bribe for French officials before they would deal with Adams' commissioners.

When Adams received the commissioners' report, he sent a message to Congress in which he urged readiness for war, denounced the French for their insulting treatment of the United States, and vowed he would not appoint another minister to France until he knew the minister would be "received, respected and honored as the representative of a great, free, powerful and independent nation." The Republicans, doubting the President's charge that the United States had been insulted, asked for proof. Adams then turned the commissioners' report over to Congress, after deleting the names of the three Frenchmen and designating them only as Messrs. X., Y., and Z. When the report was published, the "X. Y. Z. Affair" provoked even more of a reaction than Adams had bargained for. It aroused the martial spirit of most Americans, made the Federalists more popular than ever as the party of patriotism, and led to a limited and undeclared war with France (1798–1800).

With the cooperation of Congress, which quickly passed the necessary laws, Adams cut off all trade with France, abrogated the treaties of 1778, and authorized public and private vessels of the United States to capture French armed ships on the high seas. Congress set up a Department of the Navy (1798) and appropriated money for the construction of warships. The new United States Navy soon gave a good account of itself. Its warships won a number of duels with French vessels of their own class and captured a total of eighty-five ships including armed merchantmen. Talleyrand finally began to see the wisdom of an accommodation with the Americans.

When, in 1800, Adams' new three-man commission arrived in France, Napoleon Bonaparte was in power as First Consul. The Americans requested that France terminate the treaties of 1778 and pay damages for seizures of American ships. Napoleon replied that, if the United States had any claim to damages, the claim must rest upon the treaties, and if the treaties were ended, the claim must be abandoned. Napoleon had his way. The Americans agreed to a new treaty that canceled the old ones, arranged for reciprocity in commerce, and ignored the question of damages. When Adams submitted this treaty to the Senate, the extreme Federalists raised so many objections that its final ratification was delayed until after he had left office. Nevertheless, the "quasi-war" had come to an honorable end, and the United States at last had freed itself from the entanglements and embarrassments of the "perpetual" alliance with France.

## Repression and Protest

The outbreak of hostilities in 1798 had given the Federalists an advantage over the political opposition, and in the congressional elections of that year they increased their majorities in both houses. Meanwhile their new-found power went to their heads. Some of them schemed to go on winning elections by passing laws to weaken and to silence the opposition. They had as an excuse the supposed necessity of protecting the nation from dangerous foreign influence in the midst of the undeclared war.

Since many Republican critics of the administration were foreigners by birth, especially Irish or French, the Federalists in Congress thought it desirable to limit the political rights of aliens and make it more difficult for them to become citizens of the United States. The Federalists struck at the civil liberties of both native Americans and the foreign-born in a series of laws commonly known as the Alien and Sedition Acts. These extended the residence requirement for naturalization from five to fourteen years, authorized the deportation of enemy aliens, and provided punishment for persons criticizing the government.

President Adams did not invoke the Alien Act nor deport any aliens, but this law together with the Naturalization Act doubtless had some effect in discouraging immigration and encouraging many foreigners already here to leave. The administration did enforce the Sedition Act, arresting about two dozen men and convicting ten of them.

The Republicans had no reason to look to the Supreme Court for protection of their civil rights. Indeed, the Court never yet had declared an act of Congress unconstitutional, and the Republicans denied that it had the power to do so. They believed, however, that the recent Federalist legislation, particularly the Sedition Act, was unconstitutional, for the First Amendment stated that Congress should pass no law abridging freedom of speech or of the press.

What agency of government should decide the question of constitutionality? The Republican leaders Jefferson and Madison concluded that the state legislatures should decide. They ably expressed their view in two sets of resolutions, one written (anonymously) by Jefferson and adopted by the Kentucky legislature (1798, 1799), and the other drafted by Madison and approved by the Virginia legislature (1798). These Kentucky and Virginia resolutions asserted the following doctrines. The federal government had been formed by a "compact" or contract among the states. It was a limited government, possessing only certain delegated powers. Whenever it exercised any additional and undelegated powers, its acts were "unauthoritative, void, and of no force." The parties to the contract, the states, must decide for themselves when and whether the central government exceeded its powers. And "nullification" by the states was the "rightful remedy" whenever the general government went too far. The resolutions urged all the states to join in declaring the Alien and Sedition Acts null and void and in requesting their repeal at the next session of Congress, but none of the others went along with Virginia and Kentucky.

## The Republicans Win

In the election of 1800 Thomas Jefferson and Aaron Burr, representing the alliance of Virginia and New York, were again the Republican candidates. Adams was running for reelection on the Federalist ticket.

During the nearly twelve years of Federalist rule, the party had created numerous political enemies in consequence of Hamilton's financial program, the suppression of the Whiskey Rebellion, Jay's Treaty, and the Alien and Sedition Acts. Denouncing these measures, and especially the last of them, the Republicans made state rights and constitutional liberties the main issues of their campaign in 1800. They pictured Adams as a tyrant and a man who wanted to be King. The Federalists, on the other hand, described Jefferson as a dangerous radical and his followers as wild men who, if they got into power, would bring on a reign of terror comparable to that of the French Revolution at its worst.

When the state electors cast their votes, Adams received a total of 65, but Jefferson got 73 and so did Burr. The election was not yet over: in accordance with the Constitution the decision between the two highest — between Burr and Jefferson — was up to the House of Representatives, with the delegation from each state casting a single vote.

Since the Federalists controlled a majority of the states' votes in the existing Congress, they had the privilege of deciding which of their opponents was to be the next President, though the Republicans, in making their nominations, had clearly intended for Jefferson to have the first place on their ticket. During the winter of 1800–1801 the House balloted again and again without mustering a majority for either candidate. Finally, only a few weeks before inauguration day, the tie was broken, and Jefferson was named as President, Burr as Vice President.

In addition to winning a majority of the presidential electors in 1800, the Republicans also won a majority of the seats in both houses of the next Congress. The only branch of the government left in Federalist hands was the judiciary, and Adams and his fellow partisans during his last months in office took steps to make their hold upon the courts secure.

By the Judiciary Act of 1801 the Federalists succeeded in greatly increasing the number of federal judgeships. To these newly created positions Adams proceeded to appoint deserving Federalists. It was said that he stayed up until midnight on his last day in office, March 3, 1801, in order to complete the signing of the judges' commissions, and so these officeholders were known as his "midnight appointments." Since federal judges held office for life — that is, with good behavior — Jefferson as the incoming President would be powerless to remove Adams' appointees. Or so the Federalists assumed.

# Chapter 7.   THE JEFFERSONIAN ERA

## Toward Cultural Independence

Having won political independence, the American people—or at least some of them—also aspired to a kind of cultural independence. More than that, they looked forward to a time when (as a "Poem on the Rising Glory of America" had foretold in 1772) their "happy land" would be the "seat of empire" and the "final stage" of civilization, with "glorious works of high invention and of wond'rous art." The United States, as Joel Barlow saw it in his *Vision of Columbus* (1787), was destined to be "the last and greatest theatre for the improvement of mankind."

The friends of learning advocated not merely education as such but a special kind of education, one that would fill the minds of youth with patriotic, republican thoughts. The Massachusetts geographer Jedidiah Morse, author of *Geography Made Easy* (1784), said the country must have its own textbooks so that the people would not be infected with the monarchical and aristocratic ideas of England. The Connecticut schoolmaster and lawyer Noah Webster likewise contended that the American schoolboy should be educated as a patriot. "As soon as he opens his lips," Webster wrote, "he should rehearse the history of his own country; he should lisp the praise of liberty, and of those illustrious heroes and statesmen who have wrought a revolution in her favor."

To foster a distinctive culture and unify the nation, Webster insisted upon a simplified and Americanized spelling—"honor" instead of "honour," for example. His *American Spelling Book* (1783), commonly known as the "blue-backed speller," eventually sold over 100 million copies to become the best-selling book (except for the Bible) in the entire history of American publishing. Webster also wrote grammars and other schoolbooks. His school dictionary (1806) was republished in many editions and eventually was much enlarged to form *An American Dictionary of the English Language* (1828). By means of his speller and his dictionary he succeeded in establishing a national standard of words and usages for the United States.

In their first constitutions, several of the states endorsed the principle of public education, but none actually required the establishment of free schools. A Massachusetts law of 1789 reaffirmed the colonial laws providing for the support of schools by the various towns. Jedidiah Morse observed later that the enforcement of the law was lax in many places. Even in Boston only seven public schools existed in 1790, and most of these were poorly housed; more than twice as many private schools were in operation.

At the outbreak of the Revolution there had been a total of nine colleges in all the colonies; in 1800 there were twenty-two in the various states, and the number continued steadily to increase thereafter. Whereas all but two of the colonial colleges were sectarian in origin and spirit, a majority of those founded during the first three decades of independence were non-denominational. Especially significant in foreshadowing the future pattern of higher education was the fact that five were state institutions: the universities of Georgia (1785), North Carolina (1789), Vermont (1791), Ohio (1804), and South Carolina (1805).

During the first decades of independence, the most widely read American writings—and some of the greatest ones (such as *The Federalist*)—were polemical and political, not esthetic. In pamphlets and newspapers the literate American followed the arguments about British colonial policy, the aims of the Revolution, the question of a new Constitution, and the party contests of the young republic. He became a "newspaper-reading animal," as an English visitor observed. This preoccupation with the news of the day drew attention away from literature of a more artistic and permanent kind.

## The Rights of Women

The scarcity of labor in the colonial economy created expanded opportunities for women in the marketplace as "helpmates" for their husbands, full-fledged owners of mercantile establishments (often in partnership with other women), plantation managers, and members of skilled trades. A widow was often able to carry on her husband's enterprise as a consequence of the informal training she had acquired. These accomplished women were aware of the potential of Revolutionary ideas, such as the natural rights philosophy of the Declaration of Independence, for enlarging the legal rights of women. Among them was Abigail Adams, the wife of John Adams, who during the Revolutionary era spent almost ten years alone as mistress of the Adams household, educator of the children, and manager of the family farm and business. "By the way," she wrote to her husband in 1776, "in the new code of laws which I suppose it will be necessary for you to make, I desire you would remember the ladies and be more generous and favorable to them than your ancestors. Do not put such unlimited power into the hands of the husbands." But Adams gently laughed off his wife's suggestion.

Women earned some consideration through their contributions to the Revolutionary cause. They joined willingly in sacrificing their comforts and boycotting British goods. Mercy Otis Warren, sister of James Otis and friend of Abigail Adams, rivaled her brother as a pamphleteer, composing satires and farces that ridiculed British pretensions. Afterward she wrote a history of the Revolution.

An outstanding American feminist of the time, along with Mrs. Adams and Mrs. Warren, was Judith Sargent Murray, who had shared the studies of her brother while he was preparing for Harvard and who, at the age of eighteen, had married a Massachusetts sea captain. In a 1779 essay Mrs. Murray argued that girls had minds as good as boys'. In a 1784 magazine article, the first of her works to be published, she maintained that education, by making young women self-confident and self-dependent, would keep them from rushing into early marriage for fear of spinsterhood or insecurity. Her trenchant writings on religion, politics, and manners and customs, as well as education, collected in three volumes under the title *The Gleaner* (1798), proved her an essayist at least equal to her leading male contemporaries, such as Noah Webster and Philip Freneau.

The women's cause received some support from a few prominent men, among them Benjamin Franklin, Benjamin Rush, and Thomas Paine. The immediate aim was not legal or political rights so much as educational opportunities that, some reformers hoped, would lead to eventual equality. However, the women's education recommended by Franklin was one that would simply equip future wives to be more effective custodians of their husband's property, more learned educators of their children, and better-informed helpmates. And women gained no rights in the Constitution of 1787.

The discussion of the place of women, in America and in the world, got added stimulus with the appearance of the English feminist Mary Wollstonecraft's provocative book *A Vindication of the Rights of Women* (1792). After reading this, Mrs. Murray rejoiced that "the Rights of Women" were beginning to be understood in the United States, and she predicted that girls then growing up would inaugurate "a new era in female history."

No such new era arrived in Mrs. Murray's lifetime (she died in 1820). In the young republic other women achieved individual success as writers. Susanna H. Rowson, for one, wrote a novel, *Charlotte: A Tale of Truth* (1791), that was to be the most popular of all American novels until the appearance sixty years later of another woman author's work, *Uncle Tom's Cabin*. With the passing of the Revolutionary generation, however, interest in the women's revolution declined, though it never disappeared.

## The Second Awakening

Americans of the young republic might have been patriotic enough but, from the point of view of many a religious leader, they were insufficiently pious. The religious excitement of the Great Awakening had passed, and sermons of the Revolutionary era lamented the "decay of vital piety," the "degeneracy of manners," and the luxurious growth of "vice."

Certainly large numbers of the people were turning away from familiar faiths. Many interested themselves in deism, the rational religion of Enlightenment philosophers, especially those in France. The deists believed in God but considered Him a rather remote being who had created the universe, not an intimate presence who was concerned with human individuals and their sins. Franklin, Jefferson, and others among the Founding Fathers held deistic views. Such views, at first confined to the well-educated, finally spread among the people at large. By 1800, books and articles attacking religious "superstitions" found eager readers all over the country.

While resisting the spread of free thought, the churches also had to deal with other problems. After the Declaration of Independence the groups with foreign ties had to reconsider their position, and even those without such ties faced the task of reorganizing on a national basis. As population moved westward, the churches had to follow the frontier if they were to grow with the country's growth. In responding to the challenges of the time, some denominations succeeded much better than others. New sects arose. The grim doctrines of Calvinism gave way to more optimistic faiths, and the religious pattern of the young republic became even more variegated than that of colonial America had been.

Along with the Baptists and the Presbyterians, the Methodists gained many converts in the Second Awakening, a new wave of revivalism that swept the country at the turn of the century. This revivalism had two distinct phases. It began among the Presbyterians in certain colleges of the East and South, reaching its height at Yale under the leadership of President Timothy Dwight (1797–1817). Then, with zealous graduates carrying the evangelical spirit to the West, it went to even greater extremes on the frontier. In 1800, in Kentucky, the Presbyterians held the first camp meeting, an outdoor revival that lasted several days. The Methodists soon took up the camp-meeting technique, and the circuit-rider Peter Cartwright won fame as the most effective soul-saver of all backwoods revivalists. The camp meeting was a Methodist "harvest time," as Bishop Francis Asbury said. It became increasingly popular, the bishop noting with satisfaction in 1811 that 400 camp meetings were to be held that year. Crowds of sinners as well as salvation seekers attended these open-air get-togethers, and the atmosphere sometimes was far from church-like. Many Presbyterians came to frown on the camp meeting. Even Cartwright deplored the worst outbreaks of frenzy, when men and women had fits, rolled in the dust, and lay twitching with the "holy jerks."

After 1800 the devil and the deists were on the run. Freethinkers by no means disappeared (the young Abraham Lincoln took up free thought in frontier Illinois), but they were put on the defensive. The great majority of Americans subscribed to some variant of revealed Christianity, though it usually was not quite the same as the predominant faith of their forefathers. The churches in the nineteenth century placed more emphasis on the New Testament and the saving grace of Jesus and less emphasis on the Old Testament and the stern decrees of Jehovah than those of the seventeenth or even the eighteenth century had done.

## Emerging Industrialism

While religious patterns were changing, so were industrial techniques. New modes of industrial organization and technology were developing, which were to have profound effects upon the future of the United States.

In part, the new organization and technology came from England, where the Industrial Revolution was beginning at the time the American Revolution occurred. The essence of the Industrial Revolution was simply this: more rapidly and extensively than ever before, power-driven machines were taking the place of hand-operated tools. To tend the machines, workers were brought together in factories or mills located at the sources of power. New factory towns arose, with a new class of dependent laborers and another of millowners or industrial capitalists. The new factory system was adapted most readily to the manufacture of cotton thread and cloth.

To protect England's superior position as a manufacturing nation, the British government tried to prevent the export of textile machinery and the emigration of skilled mechanics. Nevertheless, to take advantage of higher wages, a number of mechanics and millwrights made their way to the United States, the most important of them being Samuel Slater. In 1790, with the aid of American mechanics, Slater built a spinning mill for the Quaker merchant Moses Brown at Pawtucket, Rhode Island. Though a few inferior spinning mills already were in operation, Slater's work is generally considered as the beginning of the factory system in America.

In textiles and in some other manufactured

goods the young republic did not measure up to England. Americans generally produced the coarser kinds of yarn and cloth, and though they supplied their own needs in common metalware, they still imported the finer grades of cutlery and other metal products. Yet in certain respects American industry was neither imitative nor inferior, and some American inventors and engineers were equal to the greatest in the world. They were especially advanced in techniques of mass production that saved labor and thus helped American manufacturers compete with the English, who could employ workers more cheaply.

One of the most ingenious mechanics of his time was Oliver Evans, a Delaware farmer's son. Evans invented a card-making machine, constructed an automatic flour mill, improved upon the steam engine, and combined theory and practice in America's first textbook of mechanical engineering, *The Young Mill-Wright's and Miller's Guide* (1795). In his flour mill, which he put into operation the same year the constitutional convention met (1787), all the work was done by a variety of machines geared to the same water wheel. Only two men were needed. At one end of the mill a man emptied bags of wheat, and at the other end a man closed and rolled away barrels full of flour. Here was history's first continuous automatic production line, the beginning of automation.

Another pioneer in mass production was the Massachusetts-born, Yale-educated Eli Whitney, who was best known for the cotton gin. The rise of the textile industry in England and America created a tremendous demand for the cotton that planters had begun to grow in the American South. But the planters were faced with the problem of separating the seeds from the cotton fast enough to meet the demand. The planters were casting about for a machine or "gin" (that is, an engine) to do the job when Whitney, then serving as a tutor on the Georgia plantation of General Nathanael Greene's widow, created his famous invention in 1793. With it, one slave could clean cotton as fast as several could by hand. Soon cotton growing spread into the upland South, and within a decade the total crop increased eightfold. Slavery, which had become a dying institution with the decline of tobacco production, was now revived, expanded, and firmly fixed within the South.

In America as in England, though somewhat more slowly, the Industrial Revolution created new classes and class conflicts, hastened the growth of crowded manufacturing towns, and gave rise to troublesome political issues, such as the perennial issue of the protective tariff. But most importantly the Industrial Revolution provided the American people with dramatically more efficient means of production and enabled them to enjoy a sharp improvement in their standard of living.

## Transportation and Trade

Before the full potential of the Industrial Revolution could be realized in the United States, transportation had to be improved. What was needed was a system of roads and waterways that would connect all parts of the country and create a market extensive enough to justify production on a reasonably large scale. In the late eighteenth and early nineteenth centuries, goods still moved far more cheaply by water than by land. For the Atlantic seaports, ocean commerce with other continents was more easily carried on than overland trade with American settlements west of the Appalachian range.

When, in 1785, the *Empress of China* returned to New York from Canton, she brought back a cargo of silk and tea, which yielded a fabulous profit. Within five years Yankee ships were trading regularly with the Far East. Generally these ships carried various manufactured goods around Cape Horn to California, which the Spanish had begun to settle during the 1760s and 1770s. There New England merchants acquired hides and furs, and with these proceeded on across the Pacific, to barter them in China.

Not only in China but also in Europe and the Near East enterprising Yankees from Salem and other ports sought out every possible opportunity for commerce. These Yankees were aided by two acts of the new Congress (1789) giving preference in tariff rates and port duties to homeowned ships. American shipping was greatly stimulated (despite the loss of ships and cargoes seized by the belligerents) by the outbreak of European war in the 1790s. Neutral Yankee vessels took over most of the carrying trade between Europe and the European colonies in the Western Hemisphere. That trade stimulated a period of vigorous urban growth that continued until the War of 1812.

As early as 1793, the young republic had come to possess a merchant marine and a foreign trade larger than those of any other country except England. In proportion to its population, the United States had more ships and commerce than any other nation in the world.

Transportation and trade within the United States labored under handicaps, but improvements were steadily being made. In river transportation a new era began with the development of the steamboat. Oliver Evans' high-pressure engine, lighter and more efficient than James Watt's, made steam more feasible for powering boats as well as mill machinery and eventually the locomotive. The perfecting of the steamboat was chiefly the work of the inventor Robert Fulton and the promoter Robert R. Livingston. Their *Clermont,* equipped with paddle wheels and an English-built engine, voyaged up the Hudson in the summer of 1807, demonstrating the practicability of steam navigation even though taking 30 hours to go 150 miles.

Meanwhile, in land transportation, the turnpike era had begun. In 1792 a corporation constructed a toll road the sixty miles from Philadelphia to Lancaster, with a hard-packed surface of crushed rock. This venture proved so successful that similar turnpikes (so named from the kind of tollgate frequently used) were laid out from other cities to neighboring towns. Since the turnpikes were built and operated for private profit, construction costs had to be low enough and the prospective traffic heavy enough to assure an early and ample return. Therefore these roads, radiating from Eastern cities, ran for comparatively short distances and through rather thickly settled, highly productive, agricultural areas.

## Jefferson in Power

Washington City, the newly founded national capital, was only a raw and straggling village, the entire District of Columbia containing no more than 3,200 people. Its broad but unpaved avenues radiated from the uncompleted Capitol and the President's house in accordance with the elaborate plan of the French architect, P. C. L'Enfant. This small town provided a new focus for the growing nationalism of Americans, and it symbolized their grand hopes for the future of their country. President Adams and his wife

Abigail, sacrificing the comforts and attractions of Philadelphia, moved to Washington in 1800. And here President-elect Jefferson was inaugurated the following year.

Long afterwards Jefferson referred to his party's victory as "the revolution of 1800," but in his inaugural address of 1801, trying to sweeten the bitterness of the recent campaign, he emphasized the common principles of the two parties while restating the principles of his own. Noting that the country was separated by a wide ocean from the "devastating havoc" of the European war, he recommended a foreign policy of "peace, commerce, and honest friendship with all nations, entangling alliances with none" — much as George Washington had done in his Farewell Address. With respect to domestic affairs, Jefferson proposed a "wise and frugal government" that would leave men free to "regulate their own pursuits of industry." Yet he also favored the "encouragement of agriculture and of commerce as its handmaid."

From the outset Jefferson acted in a spirit of democratic simplicity, which was quite in keeping with the frontier-like character of the raw city of Washington, but which was very different from the ceremonial splendor of former Federalist administrations in the metropolis of Philadelphia.

Jefferson was a strong executive, but neither his principles nor his nature inclined him to dictate to Congress. To avoid even the semblance of dictation, and to indulge his distaste for public speaking, he decided not to deliver his messages to Congress in person as Presidents Washington and Adams had done. Instead, he submitted his messages in writing, thus setting a precedent which was followed for more than a century, until President Wilson revived the practice of addressing Congress in person. Yet Jefferson, as party leader, gave direction to his fellow partisans among the senators and representatives, by quiet and sometimes by rather devious means.

The Twelfth Amendment, added to the Constitution in 1804 before the election of that year, was intended to prevent another embarrassing tie vote like that of 1800. By implication the amendment recognized the function of political parties; it stipulated that the electors should vote for President and Vice President as separate and distinct candidates. Burr had no chance to run on the ticket with Jefferson a second time. In place of Burr, the congressional caucus of Republicans nominated his New York factional foe, George Clinton. The popular Jefferson carried even the New England states, except Connecticut, and was reelected by the overwhelming electoral majority of 162 to 14, while the Republican membership of both houses of Congress was increased.

During his second term Jefferson lost some of his popularity, and he had to deal with a revolt within the party ranks. His brilliant but erratic relative, John Randolph of Roanoke, the House leader, turned against him, accused him of acting like a Federalist instead of a state-rights Republican, and mustered a handful of anti-Jefferson factionalists who called themselves "Quids."

Randolph became a fanatic on the subject of the Yazoo land claims. These arose from the action of the Georgia legislature, which, before ceding its territorial rights to the federal government, had made and then canceled a grant of millions of acres along the Mississippi to the Yazoo Land Companies. Jefferson favored a compromise settlement that would have satisfied both the state of Georgia and the Yazoo investors, many of whom were Northern Republicans whose support he needed. But Randolph, insisting that the claims were fraudulent, charged the President and the President's friends with complicity in corruption.

Randolph had a special antipathy toward James Madison, whom he considered as one of the worst of the Yazoo men. He did all he could, which was not enough, to prevent Madison's nomination for the Presidency in 1808. Jefferson refused to consider a third term for himself, for he was opposed to it in principle, unlike Washington. Jefferson's refusal established a tradition against a third term for any President, a tradition that remained unbroken until Franklin D. Roosevelt was elected for a third time in 1940 (and then for a fourth time in 1944).

## Conflict with the Courts

The Federalists had used the courts as a means of strengthening their party and persecuting the opposition, or so it seemed to the Republicans, and soon after Jefferson's first inauguration his followers in Congress launched a counterattack against the Federalist-dominated judiciary.

They repealed the Naturalization Act, changing the residence period for citizenship of foreigners from fourteen to five years, and they allowed the hated Alien and Sedition Acts to expire. Then they repealed the Judiciary Act of 1801, abolishing the new judgeships that the Federalists had created and that President Adams had filled with his "midnight appointments."

In the debate on the Judiciary Act of 1801 the Federalists maintained that the Supreme Court had the power of reviewing acts of Congress and disallowing those that conflicted with the Constitution. The Constitution itself said nothing about such a power of judicial review, but Hamilton in one of *The Federalist* papers had argued that the Supreme Court should have the power, and the Court actually had exercised it as early as 1796, though upholding the law of Congress then in question. In 1803, in the case of *Marbury* v. *Madison,* the Court for the first time declared a congressional act, or part of one, unconstitutional. (Not for more than half a century, in the Dred Scott case of 1857, did the Court do so a second time.)

William Marbury, one of President Adams' "midnight appointments," had been named as a justice of the peace in the District of Columbia, but his commission, though duly signed and sealed, had not been delivered to him at the time Adams left the Presidency. Madison, as Jefferson's secretary of state, refused to hand over the commission, and so Marbury applied to the Supreme Court for an order (writ of mandamus) directing Madison to perform his official duty.

The Chief Justice of the United States was John Marshall, a leading Federalist and prominent lawyer of Virginia, whom President Adams had appointed in 1801. (For the remainder of Adams' term, Marshall had continued to serve also as secretary of state. It was he himself who, in that capacity, had neglected to see that Marbury's commission was delivered.) Marshall, as chief justice, did his best to give the government unity and strength.

In the case of *Marbury* v. *Madison,* Marshall decided that Marbury had a right to the commission but that the Court had no power to issue the order. True, the original Judiciary Act of 1789 had conferred such a power upon the Court, but, said Marshall, the powers of the Court had been defined in the Constitution itself, and Congress could not rightfully enlarge them. Thus, Marshall cleverly established a precedent of judicial review without placing the Court in the embarrassing position of having to enforce its ruling and thereby revealing its weakness.

While the case of *Marbury* v. *Madison* was still pending, President Jefferson prepared for a renewed assault on that Federalist stronghold, the judiciary. If he could not remove the most obnoxious of the judges directly, perhaps he could do so indirectly through the process of impeachment. Jefferson sent evidence to the House to show that one of the district judges, John Pickering of New Hampshire, was unfit for his position. The House accordingly impeached him, and the Senate, despite his obvious insanity, found him guilty of high crimes and misdemeanors. He was removed.

Later the Republicans went after bigger game, one of the justices of the Supreme Court itself. Justice Samuel Chase, a rabidly partisan Federalist, had applied the Sedition Act with seeming brutality and had delivered political speeches from the bench, insulting President Jefferson and denouncing the Jeffersonian doctrine of equal liberty and equal rights. A majority of the senators finally voted for conviction, but not the necessary two-thirds majority. Chase was acquitted.

## Dollars and Ships

According to the Republicans, the administrations of Washington and Adams had been extravagant. Yearly expenditures had risen so much that by 1800 they were almost three times as high as they had been in 1793, and the public debt also had grown, though not so fast, since revenues had increased considerably. A part of these revenues came from internal taxation, including the hated whiskey excise. In 1802 the Republicans in Congress abolished the whole system of internal taxes, leaving customs duties and land sales as practically the only sources of revenue. Despite the tax cut, the new administration was determined to reduce the public debt by economizing on federal expenses. Secretary of the Treasury Albert Gallatin proceeded to carry out a drastic retrenchment plan, scrimping as much as possible on expenditures for the ordinary operations of the government and effecting what Jefferson called a "chaste reformation" in

the army and the navy. The tiny army of 4,000 men was reduced to only 2,500. The navy was pared down from twenty-five ships in commission to seven, and the number of officers and men was cut accordingly.

But Jefferson was compelled to reverse his small-navy policy and build up the fleet because of trouble with pirates in the Mediterranean. For years the Barbary states of North Africa—Morocco, Algiers, Tunis, and Tripoli—had made piracy a national enterprise. They demanded protection money from all nations whose ships sailed the Mediterranean. "Tribute or war is the usual alternative of these Barbary pirates," he said. "Why not build a navy and decide on war?" The decision was not left to him. In 1801 the Pasha of Tripoli, dissatisfied with the American response to his extortionate demands, had the flagpole of the American consulate chopped down, that being his way of declaring war on the United States. Jefferson concluded that, as President, he had a constitutional right to defend the United States without a war declaration by Congress, and he sent a squadron to the relief of the ships already at the scene. In 1805 the Pasha, by threatening to kill captive Americans, compelled the United States to agree to a peace that ended the payment of tribute but exacted a large ransom ($60,000) for the release of the prisoners.

Though the war in Tripoli cost money, Secretary Gallatin pressed on with his plan for diminishing the public debt. He was aided by an unexpected increase in tariff revenues. By the time Jefferson left office, the debt had been cut almost in half (from $83 million to $45 million), despite the expenditure of $15 million to buy Louisiana from Napoleon Bonaparte.

## The Louisiana Purchase

In the year that Jefferson was elected President of the United States, Napoleon made himself dictator of France with the title of First Consul, and in the year that Jefferson was reelected, Napoleon assumed the name and authority of Emperor. These two men, the democrat and the dictator, had little in common, yet they were good friends in international politics until Napoleon's ambitions leaped from Europe to America and brought about an estrangement.

Jefferson began to reappraise Franco-American relations when he heard rumors of the secret retrocession of Louisiana from Spain to France. "It completely reverses all the political relations of the U.S.," he wrote to Minister Livingston (April 18, 1802). Always before, we had looked to France as our "natural friend." But there was on the earth "one single spot" the possessor of which was "our natural and habitual enemy." That spot was New Orleans, the outlet through which the produce of the fast-growing West was shipped to the markets of the world. If France should actually take and hold New Orleans, Jefferson said, then "we must marry ourselves to the British fleet and nation."

There was possibly a way out of the dilemma, and that was to purchase from Napoleon the port so indispensable to the United States. Jefferson sent a special envoy to work with the American minister, Robert R. Livingston, in persuading the French to sell. For this extraordinary mission he chose James Monroe, who was well remembered in France. While Monroe's coach was still rumbling on its way to Paris, Napoleon suddenly made up his mind to dispose of the entire Louisiana Territory. Napoleon then was expecting a renewal of the European war, and he feared that he would not be able to hold Louisiana if the British, with their superior naval power, should attempt to take it. He also realized that, quite apart from the British threat, there was danger from the United States: he could not prevent the Americans, who were pushing steadily into the Mississippi Valley, from sooner or later overrunning Louisiana.

Livingston and Monroe, after the latter's arrival in Paris, had to decide first of all whether they should even consider making a treaty for the purchase of the entire Louisiana Territory, since they had not been authorized by their government to do so. They dared not wait until they could get new instructions from home, for Napoleon in the meantime might change his mind as suddenly as he had made it up. They decided to go ahead, realizing that Jefferson could reject their treaty if he disapproved what they had done.

By the terms of the treaty (April 30, 1803), the United States was to pay 60 million francs directly to the French government and up to 20 million more to American citizens who held claims against France for ship seizures in the past—or a total of approximately $15 million. The United States was to incorporate the people of Louisiana into the Union and grant them as soon as possible the same rights and privileges as other citizens. This seemed to imply that the Louisiana inhabitants were to have the benefits of statehood in the near future. The boundaries were not defined, Louisiana being transferred to the United States simply with the "same extent" as when owned by France and earlier by Spain. When Livingston and Monroe appealed to Talleyrand for his opinion about the boundary, he merely replied: "You have made a noble bargain for yourselves, and I suppose you will make the most of it."

In Washington, the President was both pleased and embarrassed when he received the treaty. He was glad to get such a "noble bargain," but, according to his oft-repeated views on the Constitution, the United States lacked the constitutional power to accept the bargain. In the past he had always insisted that the federal government could rightfully exercise only those powers assigned to it in so many words, and nowhere did the Constitution say anything about the acquisition of new territory. Now he thought, at first, that an amendment should be adopted to give the government the specific right to buy additional land; he even went so far as to draft a suitable amendment. But his advisers cautioned him that ratification might be long delayed or possibly defeated, and they assured him that he already possessed all the constitutional power he needed: the President with the consent of the Senate obviously could make treaties, and the treaty-making power would justify the purchase of Louisiana. Years afterward (in 1828) the Supreme Court upheld this view, but Jefferson—strict constructionist that he had been—continued to have doubts about it. Finally he gave in, trusting, as he said, "that the good sense of our country will correct the evil of loose construction when it shall produce ill effects." Thus, by implication, he left the question of constitutional interpretation to public opinion, and he cut the ground from under his doctrine of state rights.

For the time being, Louisiana Territory was given a semimilitary government with officials appointed by the President; later it was organized on the general pattern of the Northwest Territory, with the assumption that it would be divided into states. The first of these was admitted to the Union as the state of Louisiana in 1812.

## Exploring the West

Meanwhile the geography of the far-flung territory was revealed by a series of explorations. Even before he became President, Jefferson, as a scientist, had been interested in finding out all he could about the nature and extent of the North American continent, and he had encouraged explorers interested in the Far West. After becoming President he renewed his efforts. In 1803, before Napoleon's offer to sell Louisiana, Jefferson planned an expedition that was to cross all the way to the Pacific Ocean and gather not only geographical facts but also information about the prospects for Indian trade. Congress having secretly provided the necessary funds, Jefferson named as leader of the expedition his private secretary and Virginia neighbor, the thirty-two-year-old Meriwether Lewis, who as a veteran of Indian wars was skilled in wilderness ways. Lewis chose as a colleague the twenty-eight-year-old William Clark, also an experienced frontiersman and Indian fighter.

Lewis and Clark, with a chosen company of four dozen hardy men, set up winter quarters in St. Louis at about the time the United States took formal possession of Louisiana. In the spring of 1804 they started up the Missouri River, and with the Shoshoni squaw Sacajawea as their guide, her papoose on her back, they eventually crossed the Rocky Mountains, descended the Snake and the Columbia rivers, and in the late autumn of 1805 encamped on the Pacific coast. In September 1806 they were back again in St. Louis, bringing with them carefully kept records of what they had observed along the way. No longer was the Far West a completely unknown country.

While Lewis and Clark were on their epic journey, Jefferson sent out other explorers to fill in the picture of the Louisiana Territory. The most important of these was Lieutenant Zebulon Montgomery Pike. In the fall of 1805, then only twenty-six, Pike led an expedition from St. Louis up the Mississippi River in search of its source, and though he did not find it, he learned a good deal about the upper Mississippi Valley. In the summer of 1806 Pike proceeded up the valley of the Arkansas and discovered, but failed in his attempt to climb, the peak that now bears his name. Then he turned southward into Mexico and ran into a Spanish army; he was compelled to surrender his maps and papers and return to the United States. His account of his Western travels left the impression that the land between the Missouri and the Rockies was a desert that American farmers could never cultivate and that ought to be left forever to the nomadic Indian tribes.

## The Burr Conspiracy

In the long run the Louisiana Purchase prepared the way for the growth of the United States as a great continental power. Immediately, however, the Purchase provoked reactions that threatened or seemed to threaten the very existence of the Union. From both the Northeast and the Southwest there soon arose rumors of secession plots.

Most of the American people heartily approved the acquisition of the new territory, as they indicated by their presidential votes in 1804, but some of the New England Federalists raged against it. Their feelings are understandable enough. Both their party and their section stood to lose in importance with the growth of the West. A group of the most extreme of these men, known as the Essex Junto, concluded that the only recourse for New England was to secede from the Union and form a separate "Northern Confederacy." They justified such action by means of state-rights arguments similar to those Jefferson had used only about five years earlier in opposition to the Alien and Sedition Acts.

If a Northern Confederacy were to have any hope for lasting success as a separate nation, it would have to include New York as well as New England, or so the prospective seceders believed. But the prominent New York Federalist Alexander Hamilton had no sympathy with the secessionist scheme. His New York Republican rival, Aaron Burr, agreed to run for governor with Federalist support in 1804. Rumor had it that he was implicated in the disunion plot and that, if elected, he would lead the state into secession along with New England. Hamilton accused Burr of plotting treason and cast slurs upon his personal character. Burr lost the election, then challenged Hamilton to a duel. And so the two men with their seconds met at Weehawken, New Jersey, across the Hudson River from New York City, on a July morning in 1804. Hamilton was mortally wounded; he died the next day.

Burr, indicted for murder in both New Jersey and New York, presided over the United States Senate the following winter and then, at the end of his term as Vice President, busied himself with mysterious affairs in the Southwest. Some people believed (and some historians still believe) that he intended to separate the Southwest from the Union and rule it as an empire of his own. His ultimate aim most probably was the conquest of Spanish territory beyond the boundaries of Louisiana rather than the division of the United States. In the fall of 1806 his armed followers started by boat down the Ohio River,

Burr himself joining them after they were well under way. Jefferson soon issued a proclamation calling for the arrest of Burr and his men as traitors. Eventually Burr was captured and brought to Richmond for trial.

Chief Justice Marshall, presiding over the case on circuit duty (1807–1808), applied quite literally the clause of the Constitution that says no one shall be convicted of treason except upon the testimony of at least two witnesses to the same "overt act." He excluded all evidence not bearing directly upon such an act, and so the jury had little choice but to acquit Burr, since not even one witness had actually seen him waging war against the United States or giving aid and comfort to its enemies. Though freed, Burr gained lasting notoriety as a traitor; after exiling himself abroad for a few years, he returned and lived long enough to hail the Texas revolution (1836) as the fruition of the same sort of movement that he had hoped to start.

# Chapter 8.  REASSERTIONS OF INDEPENDENCE

## Freedom of the Seas

In the early 1800s the warring nations of Europe found it impossible to take care of their own shipping needs. The merchant ships of France and Spain seldom ventured far upon the ocean, dominated as it was by the seapower of Great Britain, and the merchant marine of Britain herself was too busy in the waters of Europe and Asia to devote much attention to those of America. American shipowners prospered as, year after year, they engrossed a larger and larger proportion of the carrying trade between Europe and the West Indies. Farmers shared in the prosperity, for exports from the United States to the West Indies and Europe also increased prodigiously.

Powerless to invade the British Isles, Napoleon devised a scheme, known as the Continental System, which he hoped would bring the British to terms. If he could close the continent to their trade, he thought, they ultimately would have to give in. So, in a series of decrees beginning with those of Berlin (1806) and Milan (1807), he proclaimed that British ships and neutral ships touching at British ports were not to land their cargoes at any European port controlled by France or her allies.

The British government replied to Napoleon's decrees with a succession of orders-in-council. These announced an unusual kind of blockade of the European coast. The blockade was intended not to keep goods out of Napoleon's Europe but only to see that the goods were carried either in British vessels or in neutral vessels stopping at a British port and paying for a special license. Thus, while frustrating the Continental System, Britain would compel the neutrals to contribute toward financing her war effort, and she would limit the growth of her maritime rivals, above all the United States.

Caught between Napoleon's decrees and Britain's orders, American vessels sailing directly for Europe took the chance of capture by the British, and those going by way of a British port ran the risk of seizure by the French.

The British navy—with its floggings, its low pay, and its dirty and dangerous conditions on shipboard—was a "floating hell" to its sailors. They had to be impressed (forced) into the service and at every good opportunity they deserted, many of them joining the merchant marine of the United States and even its navy. To check this loss of vital manpower, the British claimed the right to stop and search American merchantmen, though not naval vessels, and reimpress deserters. They did not claim the right to take native-born Americans, but they did seize naturalized Americans born on British soil, for according to the laws of England a true-born subject could never give up his allegiance to the King: once an Englishman, always an Englishman. In actual practice the British often impressed native as well as naturalized Americans.

In the summer of 1807, in the *Chesapeake-Leopard* incident, the British went to more outrageous extremes than ever. The *Chesapeake* was a public and not a private vessel, a frigate of the United States navy and not an ordinary merchantman. Sailing from Norfolk, with several alleged deserters from the British navy among the crew, the *Chesapeake* was hailed by His Majesty's Ship *Leopard,* which had been lying in wait off Cape Henry, at the entrance to Chesapeake Bay. Commodore James Barron refused to allow the *Chesapeake* to be searched, and so the *Leopard* opened fire and compelled him, unprepared for action as he was, to strike his colors. A boarding party from the *Leopard* dragged four men off the American frigate.

This was an attack upon the United States, and most of the people cried for a war of revenge.

## "Peaceable Coercion"

Even at the height of the excitement over the *Chesapeake,* Jefferson made no preparations for a possible war. He and Madison believed that, if worse came to worst, the United States could bring Great Britain to terms, and France as well, through the use of economic pressure instead of military or naval force. Dependent as both nations were upon the Yankee carrying trade, they presumably would mend their ways if they were completely deprived of it.

Hence Jefferson hastily drafted an embargo bill, Madison revised it, and both the House and the Senate promptly enacted it into law. The embargo prohibited American ships from leaving this country for any port in the world. Throughout the United States—except in the frontier areas of Vermont and New York, which soon doubled their overland exports to Canada—the embargo brought on a serious depression. Though the Northeastern merchants disliked impressment, the orders-in-council, and Napoleon's decrees, they hated Jefferson's embargo much more. Previously, in spite of risks, they had kept up their business with excellent and even fabulous returns; now they lost money every day their ships idled at the wharves. Again, as at the time of the Louisiana Purchase, they concluded that Jefferson had violated the Constitution (as indeed he had—if judged by the principles he had advocated before becoming President).

A few days before going out of office, Jefferson approved a bill terminating his and Madison's first experiment with what he called "peaceable coercion." But Jefferson's succession by Madison meant no basic change in policy, and other experiments with measures short of war were soon to be tried.

Macon's Bill No. 2 (1810) freed commercial relations with the whole world, including Great Britain and France, but authorized the President to prohibit intercourse with either belligerent if it should continue its violations after the other had stopped. The freeing of American trade was more to the advantage of the British than the French, since it fitted in with the efforts of the former to pierce and weaken the Continental System. Napoleon had every incentive to induce the United States to reimpose the embargo against his enemy. He succeeded in doing so by means of a trick, the Cadore letter, which pretended to revoke the Berlin and Milan decrees as far as they interfered with American commerce. Madison accepted the Cadore letter as evidence of Napoleon's change of policy, even though the French continued to confiscate American ships. He announced that early in

1811, an embargo against Great Britain alone would automatically go into effect, in accordance with Macon's Bill, unless Britain meanwhile rescinded her orders-in-council.

In time the new embargo, though less well enforced than the earlier, all-inclusive one had been, hurt the economy of England enough to cause influential Englishmen to petition their government for repeal of the orders-in-council. Eventually the orders were repealed—too late to prevent war, even if they had been the only grievance giving rise to the martial spirit in the United States. But there were other grievances, namely, impressment and a border conflict between the British Empire and the expanding American frontier.

## Red Men and Redcoats

Receiving from Jefferson an appointment as governor of Indiana Territory, William Henry Harrison devoted himself to carrying out Jefferson's policy of Indian removal. According to the Jeffersonian program, the Indians must give up their claims to tribal lands and either convert themselves into settled farmers or migrate to the west of the Mississippi. Playing off one tribe against another, and using whatever tactics suited the occasion—threats, bribes, trickery—Harrison made treaty after treaty with the separate tribes of the Northwest. By 1807 the United States claimed treaty rights to eastern Michigan, southern Indiana, and most of Illinois. Meanwhile, in the Southwest, millions of acres were taken from other tribes in the states of Georgia and Tennessee and in Mississippi Territory. Having been forced off their traditional hunting grounds, the Indians throughout the Mississippi Valley seethed with discontent.

For years the British authorities in Canada had neglected their Indian friends across the border to the south. Then came the *Chesapeake* incident and the surge of anti-British feeling throughout the United States. Now the Canadian authorities, expecting war and an attempted invasion of Canada, began to renew friendship with the Indians and provide them with increased supplies. Thus the trouble on the sea over the question of impressment intensified the border conflict hundreds of miles inland.

Also intensifying this conflict was the rise of a

remarkable native leader, one of the most admirable and heroic in Indian history. Tecumseh, "The Shooting Star," chief of the Shawnees, aimed to unite all the tribes of the Mississippi Valley, resist the advance of white settlement, and recover the whole Northwest, making the Ohio River the boundary between the United States and the Indian country. He maintained that Harrison and others, by negotiating with individual tribes, had obtained no real title to land in the various treaties, since the land belonged to all the tribes and none of them could rightfully cede any of it without the consent of the rest.

In his plans for a united front, Tecumseh was aided by his brother, a one-eyed, epileptic medicine-man known as the Prophet. The Prophet, visiting the Great Spirit from time to time in trances, inspired a religious revival that spread through numerous tribes and helped bring them together. The Prophet's town, at the confluence of Tippecanoe Creek and the Wabash River, became the sacred place of the new religion as well as the headquarters of Tecumseh's confederacy. Leaving his brother there after instructing him to avoid war for the time being, Tecumseh journeyed down the Mississippi in 1811 to bring the Indians of the South into his alliance.

During Tecumseh's absence, Governor Harrison saw a chance to destroy the growing influence of the two Indian leaders. With 1,000 soldiers he camped near the Prophet's town, provoked an attack (November 7, 1811), and though suffering losses as heavy as those of the enemy, succeeded in driving off the Indians and burning the town. Tecumseh returned to find his confederacy shattered, yet there were still plenty of warriors eager for the warpath, and by the spring of 1812 they were busy with hatchet and scalping knife all along the frontier, from Michigan to Mississippi.

Westerners blamed Great Britain for the bloodshed along the border. Her agents in Canada encouraged Tecumseh, used the Prophet as a "vile instrument," as Harrison put it, and provided the guns and supplies that enabled the Indians to attack. To Harrison and most of the frontiersmen, there seemed only one way to make the West safe for Americans. That was to drive the British out of Canada and annex that province to the United States.

Three days before the Battle of Tippecanoe a new Congress met in Washington for the session of 1811–1812. Of the newly elected congressmen and senators, the great majority were warlike Republicans, and after the news of Tippecanoe they became more eager than ever for a showdown with the power that seemed to threaten both the security of the frontier and the freedom of the seas.

These "war hawks" got control of both the House and the Senate. As Speaker of the House, Henry Clay of Kentucky held a position of influence then second only to that of the President himself. Clay filled the committees with the friends of force, appointing John C. Calhoun of South Carolina to the crucial Committee on Foreign Affairs, and launched a drive toward war for the conquest of Canada.

While Congress debated, President Madison moved reluctantly toward the conclusion that war was necessary. In May 1812 the war faction took the lead in the caucus of Republican congressmen who renominated him for the Presidency, and on June 1 he sent his war message to Congress. The close vote on the declaration, 19 to 13 in the Senate and 79 to 49 in the House, showed how badly the American people were divided.

## The War of 1812

The conquest of Canada, supposedly a "mere matter of marching," as Jefferson himself put it, soon proved to be an exercise in frustration. A three-pronged invasion failed in 1812. While British seapower dominated the ocean, American fleets arose to control the Great Lakes. This made possible, at last, an invasion of Canada by way of Detroit. William Henry Harrison now pushed up the River Thames and won a victory (October 5, 1813), notable for the death of Tecumseh, whom the British had commissioned as a brigadier general. The Battle of the Thames resulted in no lasting occupation of Canadian soil, but it disheartened the Indians of the Northwest and eliminated the worst of the danger they had offered to the frontier.

While Harrison was harrying the tribes of the Northwest, another Indian fighter was striking an even harder blow at the Creeks in the Southwest. The Creeks, aroused by Tecumseh on his Southern visit, received supplies from the Spaniards in Florida. These Indians had fallen upon

Fort Mims, on the Alabama River just north of the Florida border, and had killed the frontier families taking shelter within its stockade. Andrew Jackson, Tennessee planter and militia general, turning from his plans for invading Florida, tracked down the Creeks. In the Battle of Horseshoe Bend (March 27, 1814) Jackson's men took frightful vengeance, slaughtering squaws and children along with warriors. Then Jackson went into Florida and seized the Spanish fort at Pensacola.

After the battles of the Thames and Horseshoe Bend, the Indians were of little use to the British. But, with the surrender of Napoleon in Europe, the British could send their veterans of the European war to dispose of the "dirty shirts," the unkempt Americans. In 1814 the British prepared to invade the United States by three approaches—Chesapeake Bay, Lake Champlain (the historic route of Burgoyne), and the mouth of the Mississippi.

The British marched into Washington (August 24, 1814), putting the government to flight. Then they deliberately burned the public buildings, including the White House. Leaving Washington in partial ruins, the invading army reembarked and proceeded up the bay, toward Baltimore. But Baltimore, guarded by Fort McHenry, was ready. From a distance the British bombarded the fort (September 12, 1814), then withdrew. Meanwhile the invasion force descending upon northern New York met defeat in the Battle of Plattsburg (September 11, 1814) and returned to Canada.

In December 1814, a formidable array of battle-hardened veterans, fresh from the Duke of Wellington's Peninsular campaign against the French in Spain, landed below New Orleans. On Christmas, Wellington's brother-in-law Sir Edward Pakenham arrived to take command. Neither he nor anyone else in America knew that a treaty of peace between the British and American governments had been signed in faraway Belgium the day before. Awaiting Pakenham's advance up the Mississippi was Andrew Jackson with a motley collection of Tennesseans, Kentuckians, Creoles, Negroes, and pirates drawn up behind breastworks. For all their drill and bravery, the redcoats advancing through the open (January 8, 1815) were no match for Jackson's well-protected men. Finally the British retreated, leaving behind 700 dead (including Pakenham himself), 1,400 wounded, and 500 other prisoners. Jackson's losses: 8 killed, 13 wounded.

## The Peace Settlement

With notable exceptions, such as the Battle of New Orleans, the military operations of the United States, 1812–1815, were rather badly bungled. This should cause little surprise. What is surprising is the fact that American arms succeeded as well as they did. After all, the government was woefully unprepared for the war at the outset and faced increasing popular opposition as the contest dragged on. The opposition centered in New England, and it went to remarkable extremes. Some of the Federalists there celebrated British victories, sabotaged their own country's war effort, and even plotted disunion and a separate peace.

On December 15, 1814, while the British were beginning their invasion by way of New Orleans, delegates from the New England states met in Hartford, Connecticut, to consider the grievances of their section against the Madison administration. The would-be seceders were overruled by the comparatively moderate men who were in the overwhelming majority at the Hartford Convention. The convention's report reasserted the right of nullification but only hinted at secession, observing that "the severance of the Union by one or more States, against the will of the rest, and especially in time of war, can be justified only by absolute necessity." But the report proposed seven essential amendments to the Constitution, presumably as the condition of New England's remaining in the Union. These amendments were intended to protect New England from the growing influence of the South and the West.

The Federalists, apparently in a strong bargaining position, assumed that the Republicans would have to give in to the Hartford Convention terms, since the government was in such dire extremity. Soon after the convention adjourned, however, the news of Jackson's smashing victory at New Orleans reached the cities of the Northeast. While most Americans rejoiced, the Federalists were plunged into gloom. A day or two later came tidings from abroad concerning the conclusion of a treaty of peace.

The Treaty of Ghent did not even mention the original war aims of eliminating impressment and acquiring Canada. It merely provided for peace on the basis of the status quo, which meant a return to things as they had been before the fighting began. Each of the belligerents was to restore its wartime conquests to the other. Four commissions with both American and British members were to be appointed to agree upon disputed or undetermined segments of the boundary between Canada and the United States.

The Treaty of Ghent was followed by other settlements that contributed to the improvement of Anglo-American relations. A separate commercial treaty (1815) gave Americans the right to trade freely with England and the British Empire except for the West Indies. The Rush-Bagot agreement (1817) provided for mutual disarmament on the Great Lakes. Gradually disarmament was extended to the land, and eventually (though not till 1872) the Canadian-American boundary became the longest "unguarded frontier" in the world.

## Banks, Tariffs, Roads

The War of 1812 led to chaos in shipping and banking, stimulated the growth of manufactures, and exposed dramatically the inadequacy of the existing transportation system. Hence arose the postwar issues of reestablishing the Bank of the United States, protecting the new industries, and providing a nationwide network of roads and waterways. On these issues the former war hawks Clay and Calhoun became the leading advocates of the national as opposed to the local or sectional point of view. The party of Jefferson now sponsored measures of a kind once championed by the party of Hamilton.

After the first Bank's charter expired (1811), a large number of state banks sprang up. These issued vast quantities of banknotes (promises to pay, which then served much the same purpose as bank checks were later to do) and did not always bother to keep a large enough reserve of gold or silver to redeem the notes on demand. The notes passed from hand to hand more or less as money, but their actual value depended upon the reputation of the bank that issued them, and the variety of issues was so confusing

as to make honest business difficult and counterfeiting easy.

Congress struck at the currency evil not by prohibiting state banknotes but by chartering a second Bank of the United States in 1816. Though its potentialities were not realized until the 1820s, this national bank possessed the power to control the state banks by presenting their notes from time to time and demanding payment either in cash or in its own notes, which were as good as gold. The state banks would have to stay on a specie-paying basis or risk being forced out of business. Beside contributing to monetary stability, the Bank's creation made it easier for the national government to finance its war debt since investors in the Bank were induced to purchase stock with government securities and since the Bank had to pay a "bonus" of $1.5 million in return for the charter.

Farmers, unable to get their produce out to the markets of the world, had suffered from the ruin of the carrying trade, but manufacturers prospered as foreign competition almost disappeared in consequence of the embargoes and the blockade. Much of the capital and labor formerly employed in commerce and shipbuilding was diverted to manufacturing. Goods were so scarce that, even with comparatively unskilled labor and poor management, new factories could be started with an assurance of quick profits.

As the war came to an end, the manufacturing prospects of the United States were suddenly dimmed. British ships swarmed alongside American wharves and began to unload their cargoes of manufactured goods at cut prices, even selling below cost. As Lord Brougham explained to Parliament, it was "well worth while to incur a loss upon the first exportation, in order, by the glut, to stifle in the cradle those rising manufactures in the United States, which war had forced into existence, contrary to the natural course of things."

The "infant industries" needed protection if they were to survive and grow strong enough to stand upon their own feet against foreign competition. So the friends of industry maintained, reviving the old arguments of Hamilton. In 1816 the protectionists brought about the passage of a tariff law with rates high enough to be definitely protective, especially on cotton cloth.

When Ohio was admitted as a state (1803) the federal government agreed that part of the proceeds from the sale of public lands there should be used for building roads. In 1807 Jefferson's Secretary of the Treasury, Albert Gallatin, proposed that a national road, financed partly by Ohio land sales, be built from the Potomac to the Ohio. Finally, in 1811, construction of the National Road began, at Cumberland, Maryland, on the Potomac. By 1818 this highway, with a crushed stone surface and massive stone bridges, was completed to Wheeling, Virginia, on the Ohio.

Despite the progress being made with steamboats and turnpikes, there remained serious gaps in the transportation network of the country, as experience during the War of 1812 had shown. Once the coastwise shipping had been cut off by the British blockade, the coastal roads became choked by the unaccustomed volume of north-south traffic. On the northern and western frontiers the military campaigns of the United States were frustrated partly by the absence of good roads.

With this wartime experience in mind, President Madison in 1815 called the attention of Congress to the "great importance of establishing throughout our country the roads and canals which can be best executed under the national authority," and he suggested that a constitutional amendment would resolve any doubts about the authority of Congress to provide for the construction of canals and roads. Representative Calhoun promptly espoused a bill by which the moneys due the government from the Bank of the United States – both the "bonus" and the government's profits from the 20 percent of the Bank's stock that it owned – would be devoted to internal improvements.

Congress passed the bonus bill, but President Madison, on his last day in office (March 3, 1817), returned it with his veto. While he approved its purpose, he still believed that a constitutional amendment was necessary.

## "Era of Good Feelings"

After 1800 the Presidency seemed to have become the special possession of Virginians, who passed it from one to another in unvarying sequence. After two terms in office Jefferson named his Secretary of State, James Madison, to succeed him, and after two more terms Madison secured the nomination of *his* Secretary of State,

James Monroe. Many in the North already were muttering against this succession of Virginians, the so-called "Virginia Dynasty," yet the Republicans had no difficulty in electing their candidate in the rather listless campaign of 1816.

Soon after his inauguration Monroe did what no other President since Washington had done: he made a goodwill tour through the country, eastward to New England, westward as far as Detroit. In New England, so recently the scene of rabid Federalist discontent, he was greeted everywhere with enthusiastic demonstrations. The *Columbian Centinel,* a Federalist newspaper of Boston, commenting on the "Presidential Jubilee" in that city, observed that an "era of good feelings" had arrived. This phrase soon became popular; it spread throughout the country, and eventually it came to be almost synonymous with the Presidency of Monroe.

There was a good deal of hidden irony in this phrase of 1817, for the "good feelings" did not last long, and the period over which Monroe presided turned into one of very bad feelings indeed. Yet he was reelected in 1820 with the nearest thing to a unanimous electoral vote that any presidential candidate, with the exception of George Washington, has ever had. Indeed, all but one of the electors cast their ballots for Monroe. The Federalists had not even bothered to put up an opposing candidate.

## Florida and the Far West

The first big problem facing John Quincy Adams as Secretary of State in the Monroe administration was that of Florida. Already the United States had annexed West Florida, but Spain still claimed the whole of the province, East and West, and actually held most of it, though with a grasp too feeble to stop the abuses against which Americans long had complained – the escape of slaves across the border in one direction, the marauding of Indians across it in the other. In 1817 Adams began negotiations with the Spanish minister, Don Luis de Onís, for acquiring all of Florida.

Andrew Jackson, in command of American troops along the Florida frontier, had orders from Secretary of War Calhoun to "adopt the necessary measures" to end the border troubles. Jackson also had an unofficial hint – or so he afterwards claimed – that the administration

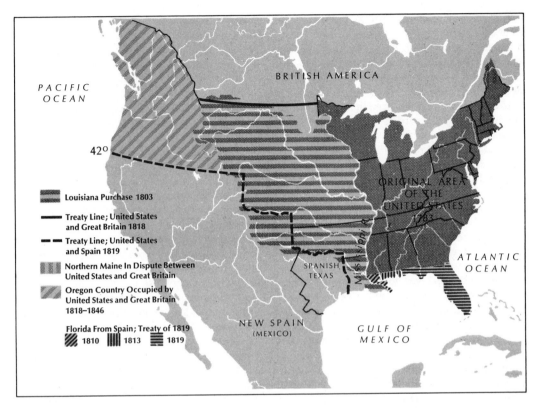

**PACIFIC OCEAN**

**BRITISH AMERICA**

42°

Louisiana Purchase 1803

Treaty Line; United States and Great Britain 1818

Treaty Line; United States and Spain 1819

Northern Maine In Dispute Between United States and Great Britain

Oregon Country Occupied by United States and Great Britain 1818–1846

Florida From Spain; Treaty of 1819
1810    1813    1819

**ORIGINAL AREA OF THE UNITED STATES** 1783

SPANISH TEXAS

**NEW SPAIN (MEXICO)**

**ATLANTIC OCEAN**

**GULF OF MEXICO**

**Boundary Settlements 1818–1819**

would not mind if he undertook a punitive expedition into Spanish territory. At any rate he invaded Florida, seized the Spanish forts at St. Marks and Pensacola, and ordered the hanging of two British subjects on the charge of supplying the Indians and inciting them to hostilities.

Jackson's raid demonstrated that the United States, if it tried, could easily take Florida by force. Unable to obtain British support, Spain had little choice but to come to terms. In the treaty of 1819 it was agreed that the King of Spain should cede "all the territories which belong to him situated to the eastward of the Mississippi and known by the name of East and West Florida." In return the United States assumed the claims of its citizens against the Spanish government to the amount of $5 million. The United States also gave up its claims to Texas, and Spain her claims to territory north of the forty-second parallel from the Rockies to the Pacific. Thus a line was drawn from the Gulf of Mexico northwestward across the continent delimiting the Spanish empire and transferring to

the United States the Spanish title to the West Coast north of California. Adams and Onís had concluded something more than a Florida agreement: it was a "transcontinental treaty."

At the time of his negotiations with Onís, Adams showed much more interest in the Far West than did most of his fellow countrymen. Few Americans were familiar with the Oregon coast except for New Englanders engaged in Pacific whaling or in the China trade. Only the fur traders and trappers knew intimately any of the land between the Missouri and the Pacific.

In 1819 and 1820, with instructions from the War Department to find the sources of the Red River, Major Stephen H. Long with nineteen soldiers ascended the Platte and South Platte rivers, discovered the peak named for him, and returned eastward by way of the Arkansas River, but failed to find the headwaters of the Red. "In regard to this extensive section of country between the Missouri River and the Rocky Mountains," Long said in his report, "we do not hesitate in giving the opinion that it is almost wholly unfit for cultivation, and of course uninhabitable by a people depending upon agriculture for their subsistence." On the published map of his expedition the Great Plains were marked as the "Great American Desert." Thus he gave increased currency to the idea earlier put forth by Pike that the farming frontier would run against a great natural barrier beyond the Missouri. Meanwhile the vacant lands to the east, between the Appalachians and the Mississippi, were rapidly being converted into plantations and farms.

## The Great Migration

One of the central themes of American history, for nearly three centuries after the founding of Jamestown, was the movement of population from the Atlantic coast to the interior and ultimately across the continent. This was no steady march, uniform along a broad front. It proceeded in irregular waves, following the lines of greatest attraction and least resistance, and accelerating in times of prosperity and peace. A sudden surge, greater than any preceding it, swept westward during the boom years that followed the War of 1812.

"Old America seems to be breaking up and moving westward," remarked an Englishman who joined the throng heading for the woodlands and prairies of the Old Northwest, particularly southern Ohio, Indiana, and Illinois. Some were Kentucky and Tennessee frontiersmen, restless spirits who had begun to feel crowded as their states became increasingly populous. Others were small farmers from the back country of Virginia and the Carolinas who fled the encroachment of slavery and the plantation system. Still others came from the middle states, New England, and foreign countries, but the great majority were Southerners. Whatever the starting point, the Ohio River was for most of the migrants the main route, the "grand track," until the completion of the Erie Canal in 1825.

To the Southwest moved people from Kentucky, from Tennessee, and from as far away as New England. Most numerous among the settlers on the Southern frontier, however, were farmers and planters from the South Atlantic states, especially from the piedmont of Georgia and the Carolinas. Their motive for migrating was, in a word, cotton. With the spread of cotton cultivation throughout the uplands of the older

South, the soil there lost much of its natural fertility from repeated croppings, or washed away as torrential rains gullied the hillsides. Seeking fresh soil with a climate suitable for cotton, the planters naturally looked to the Southwest, around the end of the Appalachian range, where there stretched a broad zone within which cotton could thrive. Included in this zone was the Black Belt of central Alabama and Mississippi, a prairie with a fabulously productive soil of rotted limestone.

Though by 1819 settlers already were pushing beyond the Mississippi, much of the area to the east of the river, around the Great Lakes and along the Gulf of Mexico, was yet to be occupied. Despite the gaps in settlement, the population of the Mississippi Valley had increased far more rapidly than that of the nation as a whole. The census of 1810 indicated that only one American in seven lived to the west of the Appalachian Mountains; the census of 1820, almost one in four. During the immediate postwar years four new states were created in this region — Indiana (1816), Mississippi (1817), Illinois (1818), and Alabama (1819). Meanwhile Missouri had grown populous enough for statehood. For the time being, however, the westward movement was slowed down by the onset of the depression following the Panic of 1819.

Rising prices for farm products had stimulated a land boom in the United States, particularly in the West. After the war the government land offices did a bigger business than ever before; not for twenty years were they to do as good a business again. Neither the settlers nor the speculators needed hard cash to buy government land: they could borrow from the state banks and pay the government with banknotes. And, under the law of 1800, they could buy on credit, with a down payment of one-fourth and the rest in three yearly installments.

In 1819 the United States Bank suddenly began to tighten up. It called in loans and foreclosed mortgages, acquiring thousands of acres of mortgaged land in the West. It gathered up state banknotes and presented them to the state banks for payment in cash. Having little money on hand, many of these banks closed their doors. Most of the rest soon had to follow suit, for they were beset by depositors with notes to be cashed. A financial panic was on.

Six years of depression followed. Prices rapidly fell. With the prices of farm products so low,

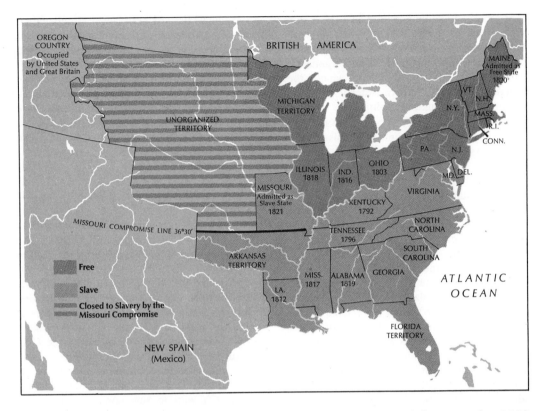

The Missouri Compromise 1820

those settlers buying land on credit could not hope to keep up their payments. Some stood to lose everything – their land, their improvements on it, their homes. They demanded relief from their congressmen, and Congress responded with the land law of 1820 and the relief act of 1821. By the new land law the credit system was abolished but the minimum price was lowered from $2.00 (as set in 1796) to $1.25 and the minimum tract from 160 (as set in 1800) to 80 acres. Hereafter a purchaser would have to buy his farm outright, but he could get one for as little as $100. The relief act allowed a previous buyer to pay off his debt at the reduced price, to accept the reduced acreage and apply the payments to it, and to have an extension of time in meeting his installments.

## The Missouri Compromise

When Missouri applied for admission as a state, slavery already was well established there. Rep-

resentative James Tallmadge, Jr., of New York, moved to amend the enabling bill so as to prohibit the further introduction of slaves into Missouri and to provide for the gradual emancipation of those already there. This Tallmadge amendment provoked a controversy that was to rage for the next two years.

Though the issue arose suddenly, waking and terrifying Thomas Jefferson like "a fire bell in the night," as he said, sectional jealousies that produced it had been accumulating for a long time. Already the concept of a balance of power between the Northern and Southern states was well developed. From the beginning, partly by chance and partly by design, new states had come into the Union more or less in pairs, one from the North, another from the South. With the admission of Alabama in 1819, the Union contained an equal number of free and slave states, eleven of each. Thus the free and slave states were evenly balanced in the Senate, though the free states with their more rapidly growing population had a majority in the House.

If Missouri should be admitted as a slave state, the existing sectional balance would be upset. Northerners, in particular the Federalists, never tired in their denunciations of the Virginia Dynasty and the three-fifths clause which, they charged, gave the Southern states a disproportionate weight in national politics.

The Missouri question soon was complicated by the application of Maine for admission as a state. Massachusetts had consented to the separation of the northern part of the Commonwealth but only on the condition that Maine be granted statehood before March 4, 1820. The Speaker of the House, Henry Clay, informed Northerners that if they refused to consent to Missouri's becoming a slave state Southerners would deny the application of Maine.

A way out of the impasse opened when the Senate combined the Maine and Missouri bills, without prohibiting slavery in Missouri. Then, to make the package more acceptable to the House, Senator Jesse B. Thomas of Illinois proposed an amendment prohibiting slavery in all the rest of the Louisiana Purchase territory north of the southern boundary of Missouri (latitude 36° 30'). The Senate adopted the Thomas amendment, and Speaker Clay undertook to guide the amended Maine-Missouri bill through the House. Eventually, after the measure had been broken up into three separate bills, he succeeded.

The first Missouri Compromise (1820) did not end the dispute; a second compromise was necessary. In 1820 Maine was actually admitted as a state, but Missouri was only authorized to form a constitution and a government. When the Missouri constitution was completed, it contained a clause forbidding free Negroes or mulattoes to enter the state. Several of the existing states, denying the right of citizenship to "free persons of color," already had laws against their immigration. Other states, among them New York, recognized colored persons as citizens. According to the federal Constitution, "The citizens of each State shall be entitled to all privileges and immunities of citizens in the several States." This meant that a citizen of such a state as New York, whether he was white or black, was entitled to all the privileges of a citizen of Missouri, including of course the privilege of traveling or residing in the state. The anti-Negro clause was clearly unconstitutional, and a majority in the House of Representatives threatened

to exclude Missouri until it was eliminated. Finally Clay offered a resolution that Missouri should be admitted to the Union on the condition that the clause should never be construed in such a way as to deny to any citizen of any state the privileges and immunities to which he was entitled under the Constitution of the United States. In the circumstances, this resolution was meaningless, yet it made possible the admission of Missouri as a state in 1821.

## Marshall and the Court

John Marshall remained as chief justice for almost thirty-five years, from 1801 to 1835. During these years Republican Presidents filled vacancies with Republican justices, one after another, and yet Marshall continued to carry a majority with him in most of the Court's decisions. He was a man of practical and penetrating mind, of persuasive and winning personality, and of strong will. The members of the Court boarded together, without their families, during the winter months when the Court was in session, and Marshall had abundant opportunity to bring his talents to bear upon his younger associates. He not only influenced their ways of thinking; he also molded the development of the Constitution itself. The net effect of the hundreds of opinions delivered by the Marshall Court was to strengthen the judicial branch at the expense of the other two branches of the government; increase the power of the United States and lessen that of the states themselves; and advance the interests of the propertied classes, especially those engaged in commerce.

For example, in *McCulloch* v. *Maryland* (1819), Marshall confirmed the "implied powers" of Congress by upholding the constitutionality of the Bank of the United States. The Bank, with headquarters in Philadelphia and branches in various cities throughout the country, had become so unpopular that several of the states tried to drive the branches out of business by outright prohibition or by prohibitory taxes. Maryland, for one, laid a heavy tax on the Baltimore branch of the Bank. This case presented two constitutional questions to the Supreme Court: could Congress charter a bank and, if so, could one of the states thus tax it? As one of the Bank's attorneys, Daniel Webster first repeated the arguments used originally by Hamilton to prove that the establishment of such an institution came within the "necessary and proper" clause. Then, to dispose of the tax issue, Webster added an ingenious argument of his own. The power to tax, he said, involved a "power to destroy," and if the states could tax the Bank at all, they could tax it to death. But the Bank with its branches was an agency of the federal government: no state could take an action tending to destroy the United States itself. Marshall adopted Webster's words in deciding for the Bank.

The case of *Gibbons* v. *Ogden* (1824) brought up the question of the powers of Congress, as against the powers of the states, in regulating interstate commerce. The state of New York had granted Robert Fulton's and Robert Livingston's steamboat company the exclusive right to carry passengers on the Hudson River to New York City. From this monopoly Aaron Ogden obtained the business of navigation across the river between New York and New Jersey. Thomas Gibbons, with a license granted under an act of Congress, went into competition with Ogden, who brought suit against him and was sustained by the New York courts. When Gibbons appealed to the Supreme Court, the justices faced the twofold question whether "commerce" included navigation and whether Congress alone or Congress and the states together could regulate interstate commerce. Marshall replied that "commerce" was a broad term embracing navigation as well as the buying and selling of goods. Though he did not exactly say that the states had no authority whatever regarding interstate commerce, he asserted that the power of Congress in regard thereto was "complete in itself" and might be "exercised to its utmost extent." He concluded that the state-granted monopoly was void.

For some time Virginia Republicans like Thomas Jefferson and John Taylor of Caroline (a Virginia county) had protested against the views of their fellow Virginian John Marshall. In *Construction Construed and Constitutions Vindicated* (1820) Taylor argued that Marshall and his colleagues were not merely interpreting but were actually changing the nature of the Constitution, which should properly be changed only by the amending process, requiring the approval of three-fourths of the states. In Congress some critics of the Court, mostly from the South and the West, proposed various means (none of

which was adopted) of curbing what they called judicial tyranny.

## Origin of the Monroe Doctrine

To most people in the United States, South and Central America had been "dark continents" before the War of 1812. Suddenly they emerged into the light, and Americans looking southward beheld a gigantic spectacle: the Spanish empire struggling in its death throes, a whole continent in revolt, new nations in the making with a future no man could foresee.

Already a profitable trade had developed between the ports of the United States and those of the Rio de la Plata in South America, of Chile, and above all of Cuba, with flour and other staples being exported in return for sugar and coins. Presumably the trade would increase much faster once the United States had established regular diplomatic and commercial relations with the countries in revolt.

Secretary Adams and President Monroe hesitated to take the risky step of recognition unless Great Britain would agree to do so at the same time. In 1818 and 1819 the United States made two bids for British cooperation, and both were rejected. Finally, in 1822, President Monroe informed Congress that five nations—La Plata (Argentina), Chile, Peru, Colombia, and Mexico—were ready for recognition, and he requested an appropriation for sending ministers to them. This was a bold stroke: the United States was going ahead alone as the first country to recognize the new governments, in defiance of the rest of the world.

In 1823 President Monroe stood forth as an even bolder champion of America against Europe. Presenting to Congress his annual message on the state of the Union, he announced a policy which afterwards—though not for thirty years—was to be known as the "Monroe Doctrine." One phase of this policy had to do with the relationship of Europe to America. "The American continents," Monroe declared, ". . . are henceforth not to be considered as subjects for future colonization by any European powers." Furthermore, "we should consider any attempt on their part to extend their system to any portion of this hemisphere as dangerous to our peace and safety." And we should consider any "interposition" against the sovereignty of existing American nations as an unfriendly act. A second aspect of the President's pronouncement had to do with the relationship of the United States to Europe. "Our policy in regard to Europe," said Monroe, ". . . is not to interfere in the internal concerns of any of its powers."

How did the President happen to make these statements at the time he did? After Napoleon's defeat the powers of Europe including Russia combined in a "concert" to uphold the principle of "legitimacy" in government and to prevent the overthrow of existing regimes from within or without. In 1823, after assisting in the suppression of other revolts in Europe, the European allies including Russia authorized France to intervene in Spain to restore the Bourbon dynasty that revolutionists had overthrown. Some observers in England and the Americas wondered whether the allies next would back France in an attempt to retake by force the lost Spanish empire in America.

Besides the vague threat Russia offered to Latin American independence, there were other causes of friction between her and the United States. Russia owned Alaska, and Russian fur traders ranged as far south as California. In 1821 the Tsar issued a ukase (imperial order) requiring foreign ships to keep approximately one hundred miles from the Northwest coast above the 51st parallel. This order perturbed Adams not only because it interfered with the activities of American fur traders and whalers in the North Pacific but also because it implied a Russian territorial claim that would enlarge the area of Russian America.

In the minds of most Americans, certainly in the mind of their Secretary of State, Great Britain also seemed a serious threat to American interests. Adams was much concerned about supposed British designs upon Cuba. Yet he was pleased to see the rift that had developed between Great Britain and the concert of Europe. He was willing to cooperate with her, but only to the extent that her policies and his own coincided in regard to this hemisphere.

These policies did not exactly coincide, however, as was shown in 1818 and 1819 by the British rejection of the American overtures for joint recognition of Latin American independence, and as was shown again in 1823 by the American reaction to a British proposal for a joint statement in opposition to European intervention in Latin America. The American minister in London was ready to go ahead on one condition—that Great Britain agree to recognize the Latin American nations as the United States already had done. When the British declined to promise recognition, he wrote home for instructions.

Adams did not like the joint statement that had been proposed. It included a pledge by Great Britain and the United States that neither of the two would seek further territory in this hemisphere, and he did not wish to stop this country from future territorial acquisitions. Besides, he thought it would be more honorable for the American government to speak out on its own instead of following along like a "cockboat in the wake of the British man-of-war."

In issuing his challenge to Europe, Monroe had in mind the domestic situation as well as the international scene. At home the people were bogged down in a business depression, divided by sectional politics, and apathetic toward the rather lackluster administration of Monroe. In the rumors of European aggression against this hemisphere lay an opportunity for him to arouse and unite the people with an appeal to national pride.

**SELECTED READINGS**    On the Confederation period and the movement for a stronger government, see the following: Merrill Jensen, *The New Nation: A History of the United States During the Confederation, 1781–1789\** (1950); M. L. Starkey, *A Little Rebellion* (1955), concerning the Shays uprising; G. S. Wood, *The Creation of the American Republic, 1776–1787* (1969); E. S. Morgan, *The Birth of the Republic, 1763–89\** (1956); Max Farrand, *The Framing of the Constitution of the United States\** (1913); Clinton Rossiter, *The Grand Convention* (1966); J. T. Main, *The Anti-Federalists: Critics of the Constitution, 1781–1788* (1961), and *Political Parties Before the Constitution* (1972); R. A. Rutland, *The Ordeal of the Constitution: The Antifederalists and the Ratification Struggle of 1787–1788* (1966); and J. E. Cooke (ed.), *The Federalist\** (1961).

General accounts of the Federalist regime are J. C. Miller, *The Federalist Era, 1789–1801\** (1960), and Leonard White, *The Federalists\** (1948). The beginnings of the political parties are described in Joseph Charles, *The Origins of the American Party System\** (1956), and W. N. Chambers, *Political Parties in a New Nation: The American Experience, 1776–1809\** (1963). Two books dealing with political rights and their repression are J. M. Smith, *Freedom's Fetters: The Alien and Sedition Laws and American Civil Liberties* (1956), and J. C. Miller, *Crisis in Freedom: The Alien and Sedition Acts\** (1951). Diplomacy is the subject of S. F. Bemis, *Jay's Treaty\** (1923) and *Pinckney's Treaty\** (1926); Alexander De Conde, *The Quasi-War: Politics and Diplomacy of the Undeclared War with France, 1797–1801* (1966); and Bradford Perkins, *The First Rapprochement: England and the United States, 1795–1805* (1955). Relevant biographies include D. S. Freeman, *George Washington* (7 vols., 1948–1957); Gilbert Chinard, *Honest John Adams\** (1933); and J. C. Miller, *Alexander Hamilton: Portrait in Paradox* (1959).

Aspects of life in the young republic are treated in R. B. Nye, *The Cultural Life of the New Nation, 1776–1830\** (1960); C. M. Green, *Eli Whitney and the Birth of American Technology\** (1956); C. F. Ware, *The Early New England Cotton Manufacture* (1931); J. T. Flexner, *Steamboats Come True* (1944); and W. D. Jordan, *White Over Black: American Attitudes toward the Negro, 1550–1812\** (1969).

On the Jefferson administration, see N. E. Cunningham, Jr., *The Jeffersonian Republicans in Power: Party Operations, 1801–1809* (1963); Morton Borden, *Parties and Politics in the Early Republic, 1789–1815\** (1967); M. D. Peterson, *The Jeffersonian Image in the American Mind\** (1960); Adrienne Koch, *The Philosophy of Thomas Jefferson\** (1943) and *Jefferson and Madison: The Great Collaboration* (1950); A. P. Whitaker, *The Mississippi Question, 1795–1803* (1934); John Bakeless, *Lewis and Clark, Partners in Discovery\** (1947); Nathan Schachner, *Aaron Burr\** (1937), a sympathetic biography; T. P. Abernethy, *The Burr Conspiracy* (1954), an unfriendly account; and Dumas Malone, *Jefferson and His Time* (3 vols., 1948–1962).

The following deal with the second war with England: Bradford Perkins, *Prologue to War: England and the United States, 1805–1812* (1961); Reginald Horsman, *The Causes of the War of 1812\** (1962); and H. L. Coles, *The War of 1812\** (1965). Aspects of the postwar period form the subject of George Dangerfield, *The Era of Good Feelings\** (1952); F. J. Turner, *The Rise of the New West\** (1906); and R. M. Robbins, *Our Landed Heritage: The Public Domain\** (1942). Relevant biographies include C. M. Wiltse, *John C. Calhoun: Nationalist, 1782–1828* (1944); Glenn Tucker, *Tecumseh: Vision of Glory* (1956); and S. F. Bemis, *John Quincy Adams and the Foundations of American Foreign Policy* (1949). Other important works are Glover Moore, *The Missouri Controversy, 1819–1821* (1953); R. K. Faulkner, *The Jurisprudence of John Marshall* (1968); A. P. Whitaker, *The United States and the Independence of Latin America, 1800–1830\** (1941); and Dexter Perkins, *The Monroe Doctrine, 1823–1826* (1927).

\* Titles available in paperback.

# PART THREE

# Sectionalism Contends with Nationalism as the Country Expands

Between the War of 1812 and the Civil War, Americans acquired a strong material basis for national unity. Capitalists, engineers, and laborers advanced toward a solution of the transportation problem by building canals and eventually railroads to link coastal cities with the interior, the East with the West, the North with the South. Telegraph lines connected all parts of the country. Merchants widened the scope of their activities until business came to be conducted on a scale more nearly nationwide than ever before. With the continued growth of industry, some workers began to show at least faint signs of self-consciousness as members of a distinct class, with common interests transcending those of their separate localities. The people as a whole, benefiting from the new developments in transportation, communication, and manufacturing, were able to raise their living standards while steadily increasing in numbers.

Some of the population increase was due to immigration from Europe. On the one hand, the immigrants stimulated a sense of nationalism, both because of their attachment to their new homeland as a whole (they had no inherited loyalty to any of the particular states) and because of the anti-foreigner and self-consciously "American" feeling they aroused on the part of many natives. On the other hand, the arrivals from abroad contributed to social differentiation between North and South, since they did not distribute themselves evenly throughout the country but settled in much the larger numbers in the free states.

Sectionalism—the rivalry of one part of the country against another—had its origins early in American history. Even in colonial times there were three great areas (New England, the middle colonies, and the South) that developed characteristics different enough to set them apart as distinct sections. As the country grew after independence, the composition of the sections changed, and sectional feelings were intensified. By the 1840s three sections that could be distinguished were the Northeast, the Northwest, and the South. These were in the process of being reduced to two, the North and the South.

In each section a particular economic activity predominated, laying the basis for enhanced sectionalism. In the Northeast industry and overseas commerce prevailed; in the Northwest most of the people were small farmers; in the South, where also the small farmers were the most numerous group, they yielded to the large planters, who exercised a controlling influence. In this section slavery persisted and, indeed, was expanding. Slavery provided the most striking difference between the South and the Northeast, where slavery had disappeared, and between the South and the Northwest, where the Northwest Ordinance had prohibited it from the beginning.

The rise of industry not only intensified sectionalism but also raised questions about the future of democracy itself. So it seemed to Alexis de Tocqueville, a twenty-six-year-old French nobleman who visited the United States in 1831–1832 and wrote a two-volume study of *Democracy in America* (1835–1840). Tocqueville feared that, with the continued growth of factories, there might eventually arise a large group of dependent workingmen and a small group of new aristocrats, an industrial plutocracy. For "at the very moment at which the science of manufactures lowers the class of workmen, it raises the class of masters." With this prospect of widening class differences, some Americans wondered about the wisdom of extending political rights to larger and larger numbers. President Andrew Jackson and his followers, however, generally encouraged the common man's participation in politics.

To most Americans, progress was a profound faith. As invention followed invention, they were confirmed in the belief that they lived in a wondrous age of increasing ease and plenty. Some assumed that improvement in material things led automatically to improvement in government and society as well. Others came to the conclusion that active effort would be needed to keep social improvement abreast of technological advance.

These progress-minded Americans were convinced that their country led the rest of the world in moral as well as material development. They sprang to the defense whenever foreigners criticized American ways, as foreigners often did. The Americans themselves, however, readily found fault with conditions in their own country when these conditions seemed to hinder the perfecting of society and man. There resulted a tumultuous and many-sided movement for social reform. From the reformers' point of view, one social evil came to stand out above all others. That was the plight of the Americans of African descent, most of whom were slaves and the rest of whom were less than wholly free. Eventually the reform drive concentrated its main force on a single goal, the elimination of slavery. The reform spirit—a "freedom's ferment"—had never stirred the South so much as it had the North, and with the development of an anti-slavery crusade white Southerners rallied to the defense of their "peculiar institution." Thus the nation began increasingly to divide on moral as well as economic and political grounds.

In the time of President James K. Polk the egalitarian spirit of Jacksonian Democracy broadened into a nationalistic demand for military conquest. Expansion was "Manifest Destiny," a phrase coined by a Democratic party journalist who, in 1845, prophesied "the fulfillment of our manifest destiny to overspread the continent allotted by Providence for the free development of our yearly multiplying millions." In other words, the United States had a divine mission to take the whole of North America, by force if necessary, and thus make room for its own rapidly growing people while carrying the blessings of democracy to less favored peoples who happened to occupy attractive lands nearby. Not all Americans agreed with that, nor did the expansionists themselves try to obtain the whole of the North American continent. Yet by 1848 the United States had expanded to the Pacific Coast, attaining essentially the size and shape that it still has (so far as the forty-eight contiguous states are concerned).

Expansionism rose from nationalism and would strengthen it after the Civil War. But the immediate result was to endanger national unity, for expansion provoked and aggravated sectional conflict.

# Chapter 9. TOWARD A NATIONAL ECONOMY

## Population Growth

During the whole of American history, three trends of population were fairly obvious: rapid increase, migration to the West, and movement to towns and cities.

Americans continued to multiply almost as fast as in the colonial period. The population still doubled every twenty-five years or so, even though the nation's birth rate began to decline by 1810. The total figure, lower than 4 million in 1790, rose to about 17 million in 1840, and then, fueled by accelerating immigration, to more than 31 million in 1860. The United States was growing much more rapidly in population than the British Isles or Europe: by 1860 it had gone ahead of the United Kingdom and had nearly overtaken Germany and France.

The West (including both Northwest and Southwest) continued to grow much more rapidly than the rest of the country. By 1830 more than a fourth of the American people lived to the west of the Appalachians; by 1850, nearly a half. Some of the seaboard states suffered serious losses of manpower and womanpower, not to mention the personal property that departing migrants took away. Year after year the Carolinas gave up nearly as much in human resources as they gained by natural increase; their populations remained almost stationary. The same was true of Vermont and New Hampshire. Many a village in these two states was completely depopulated, its houses and barns left to rot, as its people scattered over the country in search of an easier life than the granite hills afforded.

Not all the migrating villagers and farmers sought the unsettled frontier: some moved instead to increasingly crowded population centers. Urban places (considered as communities of 2,500 or more) grew faster than the nation as a whole, and in the 1820s their growth rate was accelerated. While the vast majority of Americans continued to reside in the open country or in small towns, the number of city dwellers increased remarkably. In 1790 one person in twenty lived in a community of 2,500 or more; in 1840, one in ten.

The rise of New York City was phenomenal. By 1810 it had surpassed Philadelphia, which earlier had replaced Boston as the largest city in America. New York steadily increased its lead in both population and trade. Its growth was based on the possession of a superior natural harbor and on several historical developments after the War of 1812. After the war the British chose New York as the chief place to "dump" their manufactured goods and thus helped make it an import center. State laws, which were liberal with regard to auction sales, encouraged inland merchants to do their buying in New York. The first packet line, with regularly scheduled monthly sailings between England and the United States, made New York its American terminus (1816) and hence a more important center of overseas commerce than ever. The Erie Canal (completed in 1825) gave the city unrivaled access to the interior. And New York's sheer size and concentration of population gave it advantages as a commercial center.

## Rising Immigration

Immigration accounted for little of the population growth before the 1840s. Then the floodgates opened. From 1840 to 1850 over 1.5 million Europeans moved to America; in the last years of the decade the average number arriving yearly was almost 300,000. Of the 23 million people in the United States in 1850, 2,210,000 were foreign-born; of these almost 1 million were Irish and over 500,000 were German. Special reasons explained the prevalence of immigrants from Ireland and Germany: widespread unemployment produced by the dislocations of the Industrial Revolution; famines resulting from the failure of the potato and other crops; dislike of English rule by the Irish; and the collapse of the liberal revolutions of 1848 in Germany. The great majority of the Irish settled in the Eastern cities where they swelled the ranks of unskilled labor. But they never outnumbered the native-born in the labor population of Eastern cities. Most of the Germans, having a little more money than the Irish, who had practically none, moved on to the Northwest, where they tended to become farmers or went into business in the Western towns.

The number of immigrants who came in the fifties exceeded even that of the previous decade, reaching an estimated aggregate of over 2.5 million. As before, the overwhelming majority of the newcomers hailed from Ireland and Germany. Other nationalities represented in the immigrant tide were Englishmen, Frenchmen, Italians, Scandinavians, Poles, and Hollanders. Most of the foreigners collected in the urban centers of the Northern states.

Few immigrants settled in the South. Only 500,000 lived in the slave states in 1860, and a third of these were concentrated in Missouri; of the Southern cities, only New Orleans contained a large number of foreign-born residents. Immigrants avoided the South partly because of the climate, partly because most of them were opposed to slavery or feared the competition of slave labor, and also because the bulk of them landed at Northern ports and from these points gravitated easily to areas in the North that attracted them.

In some cities and states the foreign vote assumed pivotal importance. Existing laws in many states permitted aliens to vote if they had been in the country for a year and had declared intention to seek citizenship. Particularly in the large cities, the politicians courted the immigrant voters with material favors, including outright money payments, and in some places it became common to buy votes in blocks.

## The Nativist Movement

The presence of huge numbers of aliens occasioned the first important organized nativist movement in American history. While some natives recognized the contribution that the newcomers were making to the cultural and material development of their adopted land, many others disliked their ways and feared their influence. These critics contended that many of the immigrants were mentally and physically defec-

tive, that they created slums, and that they corrupted politics by selling their votes. Laborers complained that the aliens, willing to work for low wages, were stealing their jobs. Protestants, impressed by the aptitude that the Catholic Irish demonstrated for politics, believed, or affected to believe, that the Church of Rome was attaining an undue power in American government. Many Americans of older stock were honestly concerned that the immigrants would not assimilate into national life or would inject new and radical philosophies into national thought.

In 1834 an anti-Catholic mob set fire to a convent in Charlestown, Massachusetts, and the next year Samuel F. B. Morse (who is better remembered as a portrait painter and as the inventor of the telegraph) published his *Foreign Conspiracy*, which served thereafter as a textbook for nativists crusading against what they imagined was a popish plot to gain control of the United States. Still, the federal government did nothing to check immigration, and shipowners, employers, and some of the states took measures to encourage it.

Out of the tensions and prejudices emerged a number of secret societies to combat the "alien menace." Originating in the East and later spreading to the West and South, these groups combined in 1850 to form the Supreme Order of the Star-Spangled Banner. Included in the official program of the order were opposition to Catholics or aliens holding public office and support of stricter naturalization laws and literacy tests for voting. When members were asked to define their platform, they replied, because of the secrecy rule, "I know nothing," and hence were dubbed "Know-Nothings."

Soon the leaders, deciding to seek their objectives by political methods, formed the so-called American party. In the East the new organization scored an immediate and astonishing success in the elections of 1854, casting a large vote in Pennsylvania and New York and winning control of the state government in Massachusetts. Elsewhere the progress of the Know-Nothings was more modest and tempered by local conditions. Western members of the party, because of the presence of many German voters in the area, found it expedient to proclaim that they were not opposed to naturalized Protestants. In the South, where Catholics were few, the leaders disavowed any religious bias, and

Catholics participated in the movement. The party's spectacular growth would soon be interrupted by the rise of the larger issue of slavery.

## The Canal Age

Despite the road improvements of the turnpike era (1790–1830) Americans continued as in colonial times to depend wherever possible on water routes for travel and transportation. The larger rivers, especially the Mississippi and the Ohio, became increasingly useful as steamboats grew in number and improved in design.

New waterways were needed, particularly to link Eastern cities with Northwestern farmers who had to rely upon poor East-West roads or the Mississippi for long-distance commerce. However, sectional jealousies and constitutional scruples stood in the way of action by the federal government, and necessary expenditures were too great for private enterprise. If extensive canals were to be dug, the job would be up to the various states.

New York was the first to act. It had the natural advantage of a comparatively level route between the Hudson River and Lake Erie, through the only break in the entire Appalachian chain. Yet the engineering tasks were imposing. The distance was more than 350 miles, and there were ridges to cross and a wilderness of woods and swamps to penetrate. The Erie Canal, begun in 1817 and completed in 1825, was by far the greatest construction job that Americans ever had undertaken. It quickly proved a financial success as well. The prosperity of the Erie encouraged the state to enlarge its canal system by building several branches.

The range of the New York canal system was still further extended when the states of Ohio and Indiana, inspired by the success of the Erie Canal, provided water connections between Lake Erie and the Ohio River. In 1825 Ohio began the building of two canals, one between Portsmouth and Cleveland and the other between Cincinnati and Toledo, both of which were in use by 1833. In 1832 Indiana started the construction of a canal that was to connect Evansville with the Cincinnati-Toledo route. These canals made it possible to ship or to travel by inland waterways all the way from New York to New Orleans, though several changes between canal, lake, and river craft would be nec-

essary. By way of the Great Lakes it was possible to go by water from New York to Chicago. After the opening of the Erie Canal, shipping on the Great Lakes by sail and steam rapidly increased.

Rival cities along the Atlantic seaboard took alarm at the prospect of New York's acquiring so vast a hinterland, largely at their expense. If they were to hold their own, they too must find ways of tapping the Western market. Boston, remote from the West, her way to the Hudson River impeded by the Berkshire Hills, seemed out of the running, at least so far as a canal was concerned. Philadelphia and Baltimore, though they had the still more formidable Allegheny Mountains to contend with, did not give up without an effort at canal building.

For none of these rivals of New York did canals provide a satisfactory way to the West. Some cities, however, saw their opportunity in a different and newer means of transportation. Before the canal age had reached its height, the era of the railroad already was beginning.

## Development of Railroads

By 1804 both English and American inventors had experimented with steam engines for propelling land vehicles as well as boats. In 1820 John Stevens ran a locomotive and cars around a circular track on his New Jersey estate. Finally, in 1825, the Stockton and Darlington Railroad in England began to operate with steam power over a short length of track and to carry general traffic.

This news quickly aroused the interest of American businessmen, especially in those seaboard cities that sought better communications with the West. First to organize a railroad company was a group of New Yorkers, who in 1826 obtained a charter for the Mohawk and Hudson and five years later began running trains the sixteen miles between Schenectady and Albany. First to begin actual operations was the Baltimore and Ohio. The only living signer of the Declaration of Independence, Charles Carroll of Carrollton, dug a spadeful of earth in the ceremonies to start the work on July 4, 1828, and a thirteen-mile stretch opened for business in 1830. In that same year the Charleston and Hamburg ran trains over a segment of its track in South Carolina; when this line was completed, in 1833, it was the longest in the world (136 miles). By 1836 a total of more than 1,000 miles of track had been laid in eleven states.

From the outset railroads and canals were bitter competitors. For a time the Chesapeake and Ohio Canal Company blocked the advance of the Baltimore and Ohio Railroad through the narrow gorge of the upper Potomac, and the state of New York prohibited railroads from hauling freight in competition with the Erie Canal and its branches. These restrictions and the slow pace of railroad building meant that canals carried twice as much tonnage as railroads even as late as 1852. But railroads had the advantages of speed and year-round operation (canals closed down for the winter freeze) and could be located almost anywhere, regardless of terrain and the availability of water. These assets, combined with a slight price advantage, produced a victory for railroads during the 1850s. By the end of the decade, they took most of the nation's passenger traffic and carried more freight than the canals.

There was a speed-up of construction in the forties, and by the end of the decade the total mileage had risen to 9,021. The amount of trackage tripled between 1850 and 1860. The Northeast had the most efficient system, with twice as much trackage per square mile of land as the West and four times as much as the South. Railroads were reaching even west of the Mississippi, which at several points was spanned by iron bridges. Several independent lines furnished a continuous connection between the Ohio River and New Orleans.

A new feature in railroad development — and one that would profoundly affect the nature of sectional alignments — was the trend toward the consolidation of short lines into trunk lines. By 1853 four roads had surmounted the Appalachian barrier to connect the Northeast with the Northwest. Chicago became the rail center of the country, served by fifteen lines and over a hundred trains daily. The appearance of the great trunk lines tended to divert traffic from the water routes — the Erie Canal and the Mississippi River. By lessening the dependence of the West upon the Mississippi, the railroads helped to weaken the connection between the Northwest and the South. By binding more closely the East and West, they prepared the way for a coalition of those sections.

Capital to finance the railroad boom came from various sources. Most came from private parties: some of it was provided by American investors, and large amounts were borrowed abroad. Substantial aid was provided by local governmental units eager to have a road to serve their needs. This support took the form of loans, stock subscriptions, subsidies, and donations of land for rights of way. The railroads also obtained assistance from the federal government in the shape of public land grants. In 1850 Senator Stephen A. Douglas and other railroad-minded politicians persuaded Congress to grant lands to the state of Illinois to aid the Illinois Central, then building toward the Gulf of Mexico; Illinois was to transfer the land to the Central as it carried its construction forward. Other states and their railroad promoters demanded the same privileges, and by 1860 Congress had allotted over 30 million acres to eleven states.

The operation of railroads was facilitated by the magnetic telegraph, the lines of which were extended along the tracks to connect one station with another.

## The New Journalism

Culminating several years of experimentation with an electric (magnetic) telegraph, Samuel F. B. Morse in 1844 transmitted from Baltimore to Washington the news of James K. Polk's nomination for the Presidency. The Morse telegraph seemed, because of the relatively low cost of constructing wire systems, the ideal answer to the problems of long-distance communication. By 1860 over 50,000 miles of wire connected most parts of the country, and a year later the Pacific telegraph, with 3,595 miles of wire, was open between New York and San Francisco. Nearly all of the independent lines had been absorbed into one organization, the Western Union Telegraph Company.

American enthusiasm for wire communication was not limited to the confines of the nation. Cyrus W. Field, a New York businessman, conceived the project of laying an Atlantic cable between Newfoundland and Ireland. With financial aid from associates and encouragement from the British and American governments, he completed a cable in 1858. Messages between Great Britain and the United States were exchanged, and man seemed to have accomplished another conquest of distance. But within a few weeks the cable went dead, nor could Field, who continued to believe in his idea, get it to work again. (After the Civil War, Field returned to his labors, and in 1866 succeeded in laying a permanent cable.)

In 1846 Richard Hoe invented the steam cylinder rotary press, making it possible to print newspapers at a much faster rate and a much lower cost. The development of the telegraph, together with the introduction of the rotary press, made possible much speedier collection and distribution of news than ever before. In 1846 the Associated Press was organized for the purpose of cooperative news gathering by wire; no longer did publishers have to depend on exchanges of newspapers for out-of-town reports.

Other changes in journalism also occurred. Originally Washington had been the national news center, and the papers published there had been government or party organs that filled their columns with dull documents and speeches. With the advent of the telegraph and the railroad and with the government's assumption of the function of public printing, the center of news transmission shifted to New York. A new type of newspaper appeared, one that was more attuned to the spirit and the needs of the new America. Although newspapers continued to concentrate on politics, they came to report more human interest stories and to record the most recent news, the happenings of yesterday.

In one respect, the new journalism helped to feed the fires of sectional discord. The rapid reporting of detailed information regarding differences between the sections prompted men to anger more quickly and more often than otherwise would have been the case. But viewed in a longer perspective, the revolution in news was a unifying factor in American life. As one historian of journalism (L. M. Starr) has pointed out the ultimate result of the news revolution was to endow the American people with that mystic sense of common destiny that is conveyed only by news of great events being reported everywhere simultaneously and soon after their occurrence.

## The World of Business

Industrial growth was greatest in the states of the Northeast. Of the approximately 140,000 manufacturing establishments in the country in 1860, 74,000 were located in this section; they represented well over half the total national investment in manufactures, and the annual value of their products was two-thirds of the national figure. Of the 1,311,000 workers in the entire country, about 938,000 were employed in the mills and factories of New England and the middle states.

Even the most highly developed industries still showed qualities of immaturity and were still far away from the production levels they would attain after 1865. The cotton manufacturers, for example, concentrated on producing goods of coarse grade, making little attempt to turn out fine items, which continued to be imported from England. A similar situation existed in the woolens industry, which because of a short American supply of raw wool could not even meet the domestic demand for coarse goods. As yet, American industry, which exported very little, was unable to satisfy fully the wants of American consumers. Manufacturers tended to specialize in the simple processing of abundant American agricultural products.

Technical advances in American industry owed much to American inventors. The patent records reveal the growth of Yankee ingenuity. In 1830 the number of inventions patented was 544; in 1850 the figure rose to 993; and in 1860 it stood at 4,778. In 1839 Charles Goodyear, a New England hardware merchant, discovered a method of vulcanizing rubber; his process had been put to 500 uses by 1860, and the rubber industry was firmly established. In 1846 Elias Howe of Massachusetts constructed a sewing machine, upon which improvements were soon made by Isaac Singer. The Howe-Singer machine was soon employed in manufacturing ready-to-wear clothing. A little later, during the Civil War, it would supply the Northern troops with uniforms.

Despite technical advances and increasingly large factories, the organization of industry underwent little change. Almost all industries were owned by individuals or partnerships operating on a small scale. In manufacturing giant firms would arise only after the Civil War. However, there already were great business figures in other areas of economic life, particularly commerce. The North's wealthiest individuals were the merchant capitalists who not only dispatched fleets of trading vessels to the South, the West Indies, the newly independent nations of

Latin America, Europe, and the Orient, but also invested in manufacturing, bought and sold urban real estate, and built far-flung western railroads. Increasingly, these businessmen organized corporations. Corporations had the advantage of combining the resources of a large number of shareholders, but their development was retarded by restrictive laws. Incorporation had been considered a distinct privilege, with a special act of the legislature required to grant a corporate charter. By the 1830s the states were beginning to pass general incorporation laws that tended to lend incorporation the status of a right. According to these laws, any group meeting certain minimal requirements could secure a charter merely by paying a fee. Moreover, the laws began to grant the privilege of limited liability, which meant that the individual stockholder was liable only to the extent of losing the value of his stock should the corporation fail.

## Workers and Unions

In response to the needs of industry a considerable class of wage earners finally began to form. Its members came mostly from the marginal farms of the East (those farms unable to compete with the fertile fields of the West) and somewhat later from the British Isles and Europe.

In the textile mills two different methods of labor recruitment were used. One of these, which prevailed in the middle states and parts of New England, brought whole families to the mill. Father, mother, and children, even those no more than four or five years old, worked together in tending the looms. The second, the Waltham or Lowell system, which was common in Massachusetts, enlisted young women in their late teens and early twenties. These unmarried girls went from farms to factories to work for only a few years and then returned with their savings. They did not form a permanent working class.

Much worse off were the construction gangs who performed the heavy, unskilled work on turnpikes, railroads, and canals. A large and growing number of these men were Irish immigrants. They received low pay and, since their work was seasonal and uncertain, did not make enough in a year to maintain a family at what was generally considered a decent living standard; many of them lived in the most unhealthful

of shanties. After about 1840 Irish men and women began to be employed in textile mills. As these newcomers replaced the native farm girls, working conditions deteriorated somewhat. Piece rates were paid instead of a daily wage; these and other devices were used to speed up production and use the labor force more efficiently.

Neither ditchdiggers nor mill hands, however, were the first to organize and act collectively to improve the conditions of their work. Skilled artisans formed the earliest labor unions and arranged the first strikes (shortly before 1800). From the 1790s on, the printers and cordwainers took the lead. The cordwainers — makers of high-quality boots and shoes, each man fashioning his entire product — suffered from the competition of manufacturers who put out work to be performed in separate tasks. These artisans sensed a loss of security and status with the development of mass-production methods, and so did members of other skilled trades, such as carpenters, joiners, masons, plasterers, hatters, and shipbuilders. In cities like Philadelphia, Baltimore, Boston, and New York, the skilled workers of each craft formed societies for mutual aid. During the 1820s and 1830s the craft societies began to combine on a city-wide basis and set up central organizations known as trade unions. Since, with the widening of the market, workers of one city competed with those at a distance, the next step was to federate the trade unions or to establish craft unions of national scope. In 1834 delegates from six cities founded the National Trades' Union, and in 1836 the printers and the cordwainers set up their own national craft unions.

This labor movement soon collapsed. Labor leaders struggled against the handicap of hostile laws and hostile courts. By the common law, as interpreted by judges in the industrial states, a combination among workers was viewed as, in itself, an illegal conspiracy. But adverse court decisions did not halt, though they handicapped, the rising unions. The death blow came from the Panic of 1837 and the ensuing depression, but the most serious flaw in this first labor movement was its reliance on workers whose skills were obsolete.

Workers attempted, with little success, to persuade state legislatures to pass laws setting a maximum workday. New Hampshire, in 1847, enacted a statute providing that no person be required to work more than ten hours in one day unless he agreed to an "express contract" calling for greater time; in the following year Pennsylvania adopted a similar law for the textile and paper industries. These measures were largely inoperative because many employers forced prospective employees to sign agreements for longer hours. Three states — Massachusetts, New Hampshire, and Pennsylvania — passed laws regulating child labor, but the statutes merely forbade the employment of minors for more than ten hours in a day without the consent of their parents. Probably the greatest legal victory achieved by labor was in a judicial case in Massachusetts. The supreme court of that state, in *Commonwealth* v. *Hunt* (1842), declared that unions were lawful organizations and that the strike was a lawful weapon. Other state courts gradually accepted the principles of the Massachusetts decision.

But labor did not recover, before 1860, the ground it had lost in the lean depression years. In the 1850s the first signs of the modern labor movement appeared. Several national craft unions were formed by such groups as machinists, hat workers, printers, molders, stone cutters, and a few others. These were organizations of skilled factory workers, but they represented only a tiny minority of labor. The mass of laborers remained unorganized.

## The Land of Farms

There was some industry in the Northwest, more than in the South, and in the two decades before the Civil War the section experienced a steady industrial growth. The most important industrial products were farm machines, flour, meats, distilled whiskey, and leather and wooden goods. But the West predominantly was a land of family farms and small farmers. The average size of Western farms was 200 acres, and the great majority of the farmers owned their own land.

Of the Northwest's total farm output, by far the greatest part was disposed of in the Northeast; only the surplus remaining after domestic needs were satisfied was exported abroad. The well-being of Western farmers, then, was in part sustained by Eastern purchasing power. Eastern industry, in turn, found an augmenting market for its products in the prospering West.

Between the two sections there was being forged a fundamental economic relationship that was profitable to both.

To meet the increasing demands for its products, the Northwest had to expand its productive capacities. The presence of large blocks of still unoccupied land made it possible to enlarge the area under cultivation during the 1840s. By 1850 the growing Western population had settled the prairie regions east of the Mississippi and was pushing beyond the river. Stimulated to greater production by rising prices and conscious of the richness of his soil, the average Western farmer engaged in wasteful, exploitative methods of farming that often resulted in rapid soil depletion.

More efficient grain drills, harrows, mowers, and hay rakes were placed in wide use. The cast-iron plow, devised earlier, continued to be popular because its parts could be replaced when broken. An even better implement appeared in 1847 when John Deere established at Moline, Illinois, a factory to manufacture plows with steel moldboards, which were more durable than those made of iron and were also self-scouring.

Two new machines heralded a coming revolution in grain production. The most important was the automatic reaper, invented by Cyrus H. McCormick of Virginia. The reaper, taking the place of sickle, cradle, and hand labor, enabled a crew of six or seven men to harvest in a day as much wheat (or any other small grain) as fifteen men could harvest using the older methods. McCormick, who had patented his device in 1834, established in 1847 a factory at Chicago in the heart of the grain belt. By 1850 he was turning out 3,000 reapers a year; by 1860, over 100,000 were in use on Western farms. Almost as helpful an aid to the grain grower was the thresher, which appeared in large numbers after 1840. Before that time, grain was flailed out by hand (seven bushels a day was a good average) or trodden out by farm animals (twenty bushels a day on the average). The threshing machines could thresh twenty-five bushels or more in an hour.

## King Cotton's Country

The Southern agricultural system was organized around the great staples: tobacco, rice, sugar, and above all cotton. These were the section's money crops, but they did not constitute by any means its only forms of agricultural effort. General or diversified farming was carried on in many areas, notably in the Shenandoah Valley of Virginia and the Bluegrass region of central Kentucky. Most planters produced on the plantation the foodstuffs needed by the family and the slaves. On some large plantations, more acres were planted in corn than in cotton, and in 1850 half the corn crop of the country was raised in the South.

The Cotton Kingdom stretched from North Carolina to Texas. From 1 million bales in 1830, cotton production steadily increased until it reached 4 million bales in 1860. In that year Southern cotton brought $191 million in the European markets and constituted almost two-thirds of the total export trade of the United States. (By way of contrast, the annual value of the rice crop was $2 million.) No wonder that Southerners said smugly, "Cotton is King."

Like the farmers of the Northwest, those of the South employed methods that exhausted the soil. They gave little attention to crop rotation, the use of fertilizers, or deep plowing. Like other Americans, they considered it easier to migrate to new lands than to restore old ones. Still, there were agricultural societies and journals in the South, as in the other sections, and there were dedicated individuals who labored to improve farm techniques. Such a man was the famous Edmund Ruffin of Virginia, advocate of fertilization, rotation, and deep plowing. The author of a work on calcareous manures and the founder of the excellent *Farmers' Register,* Ruffin was one of the best agricultural experts in the country during the 1850s. Through his efforts and those of others, some progress in checking soil depletion was made in the older states.

Was slavery profitable? On the whole, the planters made profits that compared very favorably with those earned elsewhere in the economy. As a consequence of the high profits earned from cotton production, the largest planters were among the nation's wealthiest men. But their numbers were small. Only one family in four owned slaves, and a still smaller proportion owned large numbers of them. The comparatively few wealthy planters nevertheless represented the social ideal of the South. With their broad acres, imposing mansions, and numerous black servants, the planter class was the one to which all others paid deference and dreamed of becoming rich enough to join. Ordinary farmers — those who owned a few slaves apiece and the much larger number who owned none at all — lived lives of rude plenty. Most of them owned their land. Occupying the lowest position in white society was the degraded group of "poor whites," who in 1850 totaled perhaps half a million. They tended to either subsist on unproductive land or work for little more than starvation wages.

Villages and cities were comparatively few, and the urban society correspondingly small. It included some businessmen, the proprietors of flour, textile, iron, and other mills, especially in Virginia, the Carolinas, and Georgia. The Tredegar Iron Works in Richmond compared favorably with the best iron mills in the Northeast. More important than the budding manufacturers were the merchants, particularly the brokers or factors who marketed the planters' crops. These men, in cities such as New Orleans, Charleston, Mobile, and Savannah, acted as selling and purchasing agents and frequently as bankers for the planter, providing him with money or goods on credit. Many of the businessmen and also the professional men were themselves slaveowners, and they identified with the planter class.

# Chapter 10.  JACKSONIAN DEMOCRACY

## More and More Voters

When Ohio and other new states in the West joined the Union, they adopted constitutions that gave the vote to all adult white males and allowed all voters the right to hold public office. Thus the new states set an example for the older ones. These older states became concerned about the loss of their population to the West, and they began slowly and haltingly to grant additional political rights to their people so as to encourage them to stay at home. Even before the War of 1812 a few of the Eastern states permitted white men to vote whether or not they owned property or paid a tax. After 1815 the states began to revise their constitutions by calling conventions that served as grand committees of the people to draw up new documents and submit them for public approval. Eventually all the states (some of them not till after the Civil War) changed their constitutions in the direction of increased democracy.

Progress was peaceful, except in Rhode Island. There the constitution was the old colonial charter, little changed, and it disqualified as voters more than half the adult males of the state. Thomas L. Dorr and his suffragist followers, despairing of reform by legal processes, held a convention of their own, drew up a new constitution, and tried to set up an administration with Dorr as governor. When the existing state government began to imprison his followers, he led a band of his men in an attack upon the Providence arsenal (1842). The Dorr Rebellion was quickly put down, yet it hastened the reforms that came afterward in Rhode Island.

With few exceptions, free Negroes could not vote anywhere in the South, nor could they vote in most of the Northern states. Pennsylvania at one time allowed Negro suffrage but eventually (1838) amended the constitution so as to prohibit it. Several other states did the same. In North and South, women continued to be denied the vote, regardless of the amount of property they might own. Everywhere the ballot was open, not secret, and often it was cast as a spoken vote rather than a written one. The lack of secrecy meant that voters could be, and sometimes were, bribed or intimidated.

In most of the states there was at first no popular vote for President. As late as 1800, the legislature chose presidential electors in ten of the states, and the people in only six. The trend was toward popular election, however, and after 1828 the legislature made the choice in only one state, South Carolina. There the people had no chance to vote in presidential elections until after the Civil War.

Despite the persisting limitations, the number of voters increased far more rapidly than did the population as a whole. In the presidential election of 1824 fewer than twenty-seven in one hundred adult white males voted (though previously, in some of the states, more than fifty had done so). In the election of 1828 the proportion rose to about fifty-five in one hundred—more than twice the figure for 1824—and in the elections of 1832 and 1836 the proportion remained approximately the same as in 1828. Then, in 1840, people flocked to the polls as never before, seventy-eight in one hundred white men casting their ballots. The multiplication of voters was due only in part to the widening of the electorate. It was due in greater measure to a heightening of interest in politics and a strengthening of party organization. Citizens were aroused, and those who in former times had seldom bothered with elections now came out to vote.

Not only did the number of voters increase; so did the number of elective offices in the states. The first state constitutions had provided for the appointment of high state officials by the governor or by the legislature. The newer constitutions put the election of these officials, including judges in some cases, into the hands of the people. Supposedly the people thus were to have increased control over government. Actually, with authority so divided and diffused, it was harder than ever for the people to locate and hold to account the officials responsible for particular policies.

Political parties became more important as both the electorate and the elections grew in number and complexity. Parties were necessary for bringing together voters of diverse interests and providing common goals so that the will of the people could express itself in a united and meaningful way. Parties were also necessary to give central direction to governments made up of independently elected officials. Hence, as the states became more democratic, political organizations within them became more tightly knit. Political machines and party bosses appeared in states like New York and Pennsylvania which had large and heterogeneous electorates with a variety of conflicting interests. In New York and Pennsylvania the spoils system was introduced before it was transplanted to the federal government. State jobs were awarded to loyal workers of the victorious party, and job-seeking came to be the motive that held together and inspirited the core of the party membership.

## "Corrupt Bargain!"

From 1796 to 1816, presidential candidates had been nominated by caucuses of the members of each of the two parties in Congress. In 1820, when the Federalists declined to oppose his candidacy, Monroe ran as the Republican nominee without the necessity of a caucus nomination. If the caucus system were revived and followed in 1824, this would mean that the nominee of the Republicans in Congress would run unopposed, as Monroe had done. Several men aspired to the Presidency, however, and they and their followers were unwilling to let a small group of congressmen and senators determine which one was to win the prize.

In 1824 "King Caucus" was overthrown. Fewer than a third of the Republicans in Congress bothered to attend the gathering that went through the motions of nominating a candidate (William H. Crawford) and he found the caucus nomination as much a handicap as a help in the campaign. The rest of the candidates—John Quincy Adams, Andrew Jackson, and Henry Clay—received nominations from state legislatures and endorsements from irregular mass meetings throughout the country.

In those states where the people chose the presidential electors, Jackson led all the rest at the polls. In the electoral college also he came out ahead, with 99 votes to Adams' 84, Crawford's 41, and Clay's 37. He lacked the necessary majority, however. So, in accordance with the Twelfth Amendment, the final decision was left to the House of Representatives, which was to choose among the three candidates with the highest electoral vote.

If Clay, in 1825, could not be President, he could at least be President-maker, and perhaps he could lay the ground for his own election later on. As speaker, he was in a strategic position for influencing the decision of the House of Representatives. In deciding among the three leading candidates, the House was to vote by states, the delegation from each state casting one vote. Clay, as the winner of the recent election in Kentucky, Ohio, and Missouri, could swing the congressional delegations of those three states at least. Finally Clay gave his support to Adams, and the House elected him.

The Jacksonians were angry enough at this, but they became far angrier when the new President made known his appointments. Clay was to be the secretary of state! The State Department being the well-established route to the Presidency, Adams thus appeared to be naming Clay as his own successor. The two must have agreed to make each other President—Adams now, Clay next—or so the Jacksonians exclaimed, and they pretended to be horrified by this "corrupt bargain." Very likely there had been some sort of understanding, and though there was nothing improper in it, it proved to be politically unwise for both Adams and Clay.

Soon after Adams' inauguration as President, Jackson resigned from the Senate to accept a renomination for the Presidency from the Tennessee legislature and to begin a three-year campaign for election in 1828. Politics now overshadowed everything else. Throughout his term in the White House, Adams and his policies were to be thoroughly frustrated by the political bitterness arising from the "corrupt bargain."

## The Second President Adams

The career of John Quincy Adams divides naturally into three parts. In the first part, as befitted the son of John Adams, he made a brilliant record in diplomacy, serving as the American minister in one foreign capital after another and then as one of the most successful of all secretaries of state. In the second phase of his career, as President (1825–1829), he endured four ineffectual years that amounted to a mere interlude between the periods of his greatness. In the third, as a congressman from Massachusetts, he served his constituents and the nation with high distinction, gaining fame as "Old Man Eloquent," the foremost congressional champion of free speech. His frustration in the White House shows that the Presidency demands more than exceptional ability and high-mindedness, for John Quincy Adams possessed both. The Presidency also requires political skill and political luck, and these he did not have.

In his inaugural address and in his first message to Congress he boldly stated a broad conception of the powers and duties of the federal government. He recommended "laws promoting the improvement of agriculture, commerce, and manufactures, the cultivation of the mechanic and of the elegant arts, the advancement of literature, and the progress of the sciences, ornamental and profound." He had no chance of getting an appropriation from Congress to improve the minds of his countrymen. The most he could get was a few million dollars for improving rivers and harbors and for extending the National Road westward from Wheeling. This amount was more than Congress had appropriated for internal improvements under all his predecessors together, but it was far less than he hoped for.

Adams was worsted also in a contest with the state of Georgia. That state attempted to remove the remaining Creek and Cherokee Indians so as to gain additional soil for cotton planters. The Creeks, however, had a treaty with the United States (1791) that guaranteed them the possession of the land they occupied. A new treaty (1825) ceded the land to the state, but Adams refused to enforce this treaty, believing that it had been obtained by fraud. The Georgia governor defied the President of the United States and went ahead with plans for Indian removal. At last the Creeks agreed to still another treaty (1827) in which they yielded their claims. Adams' stand had been honorable but unpopular. Southerners condemned him for encroaching upon state rights, and Westerners as well as Southerners disapproved of his interfering with efforts to get rid of the Indians.

Southerners again denounced the administration and its supporters on account of the tariff of 1828. The bill of 1828 contained high duties not only on woolens but also on a number of other items, such as flax, hemp, iron, lead, molasses, and raw wool. Thus it displeased New England manufacturers, for it would raise the cost of their raw materials as well as the price of their manufactured goods. A story arose that the bill had taken its shape from a Jacksonian plot to embarrass New Englanders and discredit Adams. The bill related to "manufacturers of no sort or kind

but the manufacture of a President of the United States," John Randolph said. Supposedly it was intended to put Adams in a dilemma that would lose him friends whether he signed or vetoed it. While some politicians did see the measure as an electioneering device, others intended it seriously as a means of benefiting the farmers and manufacturers of the middle states and the West.

When the bill was considered item by item, Southerners voted against reductions in the hope that some of its outrageous duties would so antagonize New Englanders that they would help defeat it. But when it came to a final test, the bill got enough New England votes to pass. Adams signed it. The Southerners, whose tactics had backfired, cursed it as the "tariff of abominations."

## The Comman Man's President

By 1828, the Republican party having split completely, there were again two parties in the campaign—the Adamsites, who called themselves National Republicans, and the Jacksonians, who took the name of Democratic Republicans. Adams himself once had been a Federalist, and most of the old Federalists joined his party, though some became followers of Jackson.

Issues figured little in the campaign of 1828, though much was said about the "corrupt bargain" and something was said about the "tariff of abominations." Regarding the tariff, Adams was on record, having signed the abominations bill, but nobody knew exactly where Jackson stood. More was made of personalities than of policies, and there was far worse mudslinging than ever before. Indeed, one would have thought that two criminals were running for the highest office in the land. Though the majority voted for Jackson, a large minority (44 per cent) favored Adams, who received all but one of the electoral votes from New England.

Though the new President was no democratic philosopher like Jefferson, he nevertheless held certain democratic convictions, notably that government should offer "equal protection and equal benefits" to all the people. His enemies denied that he ever really championed the people's cause, but they could not deny that he became a living symbol of democracy or that, far more than any of his predecessors, he gave a sense of participation in government to the common man.

As President, Jackson promptly set about to "reform" the personnel procedures of the federal government. For a generation, ever since the downfall of the Federalists in 1800, there had been no complete party turnover in Washington. Officeholders accordingly stayed on year after year and election after election, many of them growing gray and some of them growing corrupt in office. "Office is considered as a species of property," Jackson told Congress, "and government rather as a means of promoting individual interests than as an instrument created solely for the service of the people." He believed that official duties could be made "so plain and simple that men of intelligence may readily qualify themselves for their performance." According to him, offices belonged to the people, not to the entrenched officeholders. Or, as one of his henchmen, William L. Marcy of New York, more cynically put it, "To the victors belong the spoils."

A corollary to the spoils system was the doctrine of rotation in office. Since ordinary men ("of intelligence") presumably were fit or could easily be fitted for government service, and since loyal members of the victorious party deserved government jobs, a particular position should not be held too long by any one person but should be passed around, or rotated, among several deserving applicants.

Eventually the Jacksonians adopted another instrument of democratic politics — the national nominating convention — which was originated by the earliest of the third parties in American history, the Anti-Masonic party. This party was a response to widespread resentment against the secret and exclusive, hence supposedly undemocratic, Society of Freemasons. Feeling rose to new heights when, in 1826, a man named William Morgan mysteriously disappeared from his home in Batavia, New York. Since Morgan had been about to publish a book purporting to expose the secrets of freemasonry, his friends believed that vengeful Masons had done away with him. The excitement spread, and politicians in New York, Pennsylvania, and several other states seized upon it to organize a party with popular appeal. The party was anti-Jackson as well as anti-Mason, Jackson being a high-ranking member of the lodge. In 1831 the Anti-Masons held a national convention in Harrisburg, Pennsylvania, to nominate a candidate for the next year's presidential campaign.

# The Nullification Theory

President Jackson had taken office with no clearly announced program to carry out. His followers — who soon began to call themselves simply Democrats — had interests so diverse that a statement of definite aims would have alienated many of the party at the outset. This is not to say that Jackson himself was lacking in convictions. Far from it. Besides believing in government by and for the common man, he stood for strong presidential leadership and, while respecting what he considered the legitimate rights of the states, he was devoted to the national Union. He did not hesitate to assert his principles when South Carolina tried to put into effect the nullification (or interposition) theory of John C. Calhoun.

Vice President in John Quincy Adams' administration, Calhoun in 1828 was running as the vice-presidential candidate on the Jackson ticket. And he could look forward to the Presidency itself after a term or two for Jackson — if all went well.

But the tariff question placed Calhoun in a dilemma. Once he had been a forthright protectionist, coming out strongly for the tariff of 1816, but since that time many South Carolinians had changed their minds on the subject, and so had he. Carolina cotton planters were disturbed because their plantations were less profitable than it seemed they should have been. The whole state appeared to be stagnating, its population remaining almost stationary, its countryside showing signs of ruin and decay. One reason was the depletion of the South Carolina soil, which could not compete with the newly opened, fertile lands of the Southwest. But the Carolinians blamed their trouble on quite another cause — the tariff, in particular the "tariff of abominations," the law of 1828. They reasoned correctly that protective duties raised the prices of the things they had to buy, whether they bought them at home or from abroad, and lowered the price of the cotton they sold, most of which was exported.

Quietly Calhoun worked out a theory to justify state action in resisting the tariff law. He intended for this action, if and when it became necessary, to be strictly legal and constitutional, not revolutionary. So he had to find a basis for his plan in the Constitution itself. He believed he was following the lines laid down by Madison and Jefferson in their Virginia and Kentucky resolutions of 1798–1799. Indeed, his reasoning was quite similar to theirs, but he carried it farther than they had done, and he provided a definite procedure for state action, which they had not. If Congress enacted a law of doubtful constitutionality—say, a protective tariff—a state could "interpose" to frustrate the law. That is, the people of the state could hold a convention, and if (through their elected delegates) they decided that Congress had gone too far, they could declare the federal law null and void within their state. In that state the law would remain inoperative until three-fourths of the whole number of states should ratify an amendment to the Constitution specifically assigning Congress the power in question. And if the other states should ever get around to doing this, the nullifying state would then submit—or it could secede. The legislature of South Carolina published Calhoun's first statement of his theory, anonymously, in a document entitled *The South Carolina Exposition and Protest* (1828).

## "Our Federal Union"

After the Jackson-Calhoun ticket had won its victory at the polls, Calhoun realized he had a powerful rival for Jackson's favor in the person of Martin Van Buren. Van Buren, the "Red Fox," resigned the governorship of New York and went to Washington when Jackson called him to head the new cabinet as secretary of state. This cabinet was not intended to form a council of advisers: Jackson did not even call cabinet meetings. Instead, he relied on an unofficial circle of political cronies who came to be known as the "Kitchen Cabinet." Soon to be the most important of all was Van Buren, a member of both the official and the unofficial group, who offered to Jackson an aptitude for political management that had been finely honed in tumultuous New York politics.

Eventually Jackson picked Van Buren for the presidential succession and marked Calhoun as the worst of foes. The final break came when Jackson learned the inside story of a Monroe cabinet meeting years earlier. At the time of Jackson's Florida raid (1817) and for a long time afterward he supposed that Calhoun, as Monroe's secretary of war, had stood up for him when others in the administration proposed to

punish him for his action. The truth, as Calhoun's enemies at last convinced Jackson, was quite otherwise.

If there had been only personal differences between Jackson and Calhoun, their parting would have been less significant than it actually was. But there were also differences of principle, which were dramatically revealed in consequence of a great debate on the nature of the Constitution.

The Webster-Hayne debate, in January 1830, grew out of a Senate discussion of public lands, a discussion provoked when a senator from Connecticut suggested that all land sales and surveys be discontinued for the time being. Robert Y. Hayne of South Carolina argued against the proposal. He and other Southerners hoped to get Western support for their drive to lower the tariff, and at the moment they were willing to grant abundant and cheap lands to the Westerners in exchange for such support. He hinted that the South and the West might well combine in self-defense against the Northeast.

Daniel Webster, now a senator from Massachusetts, once had been a state-rights and anti-tariff man but, like Calhoun, only in reverse, he had changed his position with the changing interests of his section. The day after Hayne's speech he took the floor in an effort to head off the threatened rapprochement of the West and the South and thus to protect the interests of New England, including the tariff interest.

Webster challenged Hayne to meet him, not on the original grounds of the public lands and the tariff, but on the issue of state rights versus national power, an issue that could be made to seem one of treason versus patriotism. And in due time Hayne, coached by Calhoun, came back with a flashing defense of the nullification theory. It took Webster two afternoons to deliver what schoolboys were afterward to know as the second reply to Hayne. "I go for the Constitution as it is, and for the Union as it is," he declaimed. "It is, Sir, the people's Constitution, the people's government, made for the people, made by the people, and answerable to the people." And he meant one people, the whole nation. He concluded with the ringing appeal: "Liberty *and* Union, now and for ever, one and inseparable!"

Calhoun's followers were sure that Hayne had the better of the argument. The important question at the moment, however, was what Pres-

## JACKSONIAN DEMOCRACY

Many of the early biographers of Andrew Jackson and historians of the Jackson period were upper middle-class Easterners who sympathized with his opponents, the Whigs. These unfriendly, Whiggish authors described him as a "barbarian" whose election was a "mistake" and whose policies on the whole were "deplorable." Such views prevailed until the end of the nineteenth century.

Then a new generation of scholars, nearly all of them from the West or the South, began to rewrite history in a manner highly favorable to Jackson. They saw him as a true democrat who, much like the progressives of their own time, strove to make government responsive to the will of the people rather than the desires of the special interests. The most influential of the newer historians, Frederick Jackson Turner, in his famous essay "The Significance of the Frontier in American History" (1893) and in later writings, maintained that Jacksonian Democracy had originated in the "frontier democratic society" of the West. Turner's "frontier interpretation" soon became predominant, though one authority on early Tennessee politics (Thomas P. Abernethy) insisted that Jackson actually had been a frontier aristocrat and had opposed the democratic trend in his own state.

In recent years historians have emphasized social classes rather than geographical sections in seeking to explain Jackson and his program, but they have disagreed about which class he represented. Arthur M. Schlesinger, Jr., contended in *The Age of Jackson* (1945) that Jacksonian Democracy was an effort "to control the power of the capitalistic groups, mainly Eastern, for the benefit of noncapitalist groups, farmers and laboring men, East, West, and South." Critics of Schlesinger, however, argued that Jackson was antilabor rather than prolabor and that he really reflected the interests of the rising businessmen. In *Banks and Politics in America from the Revolution to the Civil War* (1957) Bray Hammond described the Jacksonian cause as "one of enterpriser against capitalist, of banker against regulation, and of Wall Street against Chestnut" — that is, of New York City bankers against the Philadelphia-based Bank of the United States.

Disagreeing with both Hammond and Schlesinger and also with earlier historians such as Turner, Lee Benson maintained that the very term "Jacksonian Democracy" had "obscured rather than illuminated" our understanding of the period. In *The Concept of Jacksonian Democracy: New York as a Test Case* (1961) Benson showed that, at least in the state of New York, both the Jackson and the anti-Jackson parties included the same kinds of big as well as small businessmen in addition to farmers and city workers and that politicians on both sides made use of similar "agrarian" rhetoric. According to Benson, the democratic movement was much broader than the Democratic party. Therefore, he suggested, we could take a step toward clarification by "discarding the old caption for period" and substituting "the Age of Egalitarianism" for "the Age of Jackson."

ident Jackson thought and what side, if any, he would take. An answer soon was given at a Democratic banquet that was supposed to honor Thomas Jefferson as the founder of the party. When Jackson's turn came to give a toast, he stood up, looked sternly at Calhoun, and declared: "Our *Federal* Union — *It must be preserved!*"

## Removing the Indians

Jackson's pro-Union and antinullification feelings did not mean that he was opposed to state rights as such. On the contrary, as he had declared in his inaugural address, he believed in none but "constitutional" undertakings by the federal government. During his administration he readily vetoed laws that he thought exceeded the powers originally granted to Congress by the states; in fact, he used the veto more freely than any President before him. And he stood up for state rights when Georgia defied the Supreme Court in dealing with the Indians within its borders.

As an old Indian-fighter, Jackson was no lover of the red man, and he desired to continue and expedite the program, which Jefferson had begun, of moving all the tribes to territory west of the Mississippi. The land between the Missouri and the Rockies, according to such explorers as Lewis and Clark and Stephen H. Long, was supposed to be a vast desert, unfit for white habitation. Why not leave that land for the Indians? By the Indian Removal Act of 1830 Congress proposed to exchange tribal lands within the states for new homes in the West, and by the Indian Intercourse Act of 1834 Congress marked off an Indian country and provided for a string of forts to keep the Indians inside it and the whites outside. Meanwhile the President saw that treaties, nearly a hundred in all, were negotiated with the various tribes and that reluctant tribesmen along with their women and children were moved west, with the prodding of the army.

In the process of Indian removal there was much tragedy and a certain amount of violence. When (in 1832) Chief Black Hawk with a thousand of his hungry Sac and Fox followers — men, women, and children — recrossed the Mississippi into Illinois to grow corn, the frontiersmen feared an invasion. Militiamen and regular troops soon drove the unfortunate Indians into Wisconsin and then slaughtered most of them as they tried to escape down the Wisconsin River. In Florida a war began when Chief Osceola led an uprising of his tribesmen (including runaway Negroes), who refused to move west in accordance with a treaty of 1833, and the fighting lasted off and on for several years. Jackson sent troops to Florida, but the Seminoles with their Negro associates were masters of guerrilla warfare in the jungly Everglades. Even after Osceola had been treacherously captured under a flag of truce and had died in prison, the red and black rebels continued to resist.

Unlike the Sacs and Foxes or the Seminoles, the Cherokees in Georgia had a written language of their own (invented by Sequoyah in 1821) and followed a settled way of life as farmers. Yet the state of Georgia, after getting rid of the Creeks, was eager to remove the Cherokees also and open their millions of fertile acres to white occupation. In 1827 these Indians adopted a constitution and declared their independence as the Cherokee Nation. Promptly the Georgia legislature extended its laws over them and directed the seizure of their territory. Hiring a prominent lawyer, the Cherokees appealed to the Supreme Court. In the case of *Cherokee Nation* v. *Georgia* (1831) Chief Justice Marshall gave the majority opinion that the Indians were "domestic dependent nations" and had a right to the land they occupied until they voluntarily ceded it to the United States. In another case, *Worcester* v. *Georgia* (1832), Marshall and the Court held that the Cherokee Nation was a definite political community with territory over which the laws of Georgia had no force and into which Georgians could not enter without permission.

President Jackson did not sympathize with the Cherokees as President Adams had done with the Creeks. Jackson's attitude is well expressed in the comment attributed to him: "John Marshall has made his decision; now let him enforce it." The decision was never enforced.

In 1835 a few of the Cherokees were induced to sign a treaty giving up the nation's Georgia land in return for $5 million and a reservation in Indian Territory (Oklahoma). The great majority of the 17,000 Cherokees were unwilling to leave their homes, so Jackson sent an army of 7,000 men under General Winfield Scott to drive them westward at bayonet point. About a thousand fled across the state line to North Carolina, where eventually the federal government provided a reservation for them. Most of the rest made the long, forced trek to the West, beginning in midwinter 1838. Several thousand perished before reaching their undesired destination. The survivors were never to forget the hard march to Indian Territory. They called it "The Trail Where They Cried," the trail of tears.

## South Carolina Interposes

After waiting four years for Congress to undo the "tariff of abominations," the South Carolina followers of Calhoun lost all patience when Congress denied them any real relief in the tariff of 1832. Calhoun had come out openly for nullification, elaborated the doctrine further, and induced the extremists to adopt it as their remedy. The legislature now called for the election of delegates to a state convention. The convention adopted an ordinance of nullification that declared null and void the tariffs of 1828 and 1832 and forbade the collection of duties within the state. The legislature then passed laws to enforce the ordinance and make preparations for military defense. Needing a strong man to take command at home, and another to present the South Carolina case ably in Washington, the nullifiers arranged for Hayne to become governor and for Calhoun to replace Hayne as senator. So Calhoun resigned as Vice President.

Unofficially President Jackson threatened to hang Calhoun. Officially he proclaimed that nullification was treason and its adherents traitors. He also took steps to strengthen the federal forts in South Carolina, ordering General Winfield Scott and a warship and several revenue cutters to Charleston. When Congress met, the President asked for specific authority with which to handle the crisis. His followers introduced a "force bill" authorizing him to use the army and navy to see that acts of Congress were obeyed.

At the moment Calhoun was in a predicament. South Carolina, standing alone, itself divided, could not hope to prevail if a showdown with the federal government should come. If the nullifiers meekly yielded, however, they would lose face and their leader would be politically ruined. Calhoun was saved by the timely intervention of the Great Pacificator, Henry Clay. Newly elected to the Senate, Clay in consultation with Calhoun devised a compromise scheme by which the tariff would be lowered year after year, reaching in 1842 approximately the same level as in 1816. Finally Clay's compromise and the force bill were passed on the same day (March 1, 1833).

Though Calhoun and his followers, having brought about tariff reduction, claimed a victory for nullification, the system had not worked out in the way its sponsors had intended. Calhoun had learned a lesson: no state could assert and maintain its rights by independent action. Thereafter, while continuing to talk of state rights and nullification, he devoted himself to building up a sense of Southern solidarity so that, when another trial should come, the whole section might be prepared to act as a unit in resisting federal authority.

## The Bank War

The Bank of the United States, with its headquarters in Philadelphia and its branches in twenty-nine other cities, did a tremendous business in general banking. Its services were important to the national economy because of the credit it provided for profit-making enterprises (particularly in the West), because of its banknotes that circulated throughout the country as a dependable medium of exchange, and because of the restraining effect that its policies had upon the less well-managed banks chartered by the various states.

Nicholas Biddle, president of the Bank from 1823 on, had done much to put the company on a sound and prosperous basis. A banker, not a politician, he had no desire to mix in politics. But he finally concluded it was necessary to do so in self-defense when, with the encouragement of Jackson, popular opposition to the Bank rose to a threatening pitch.

Opposition came from two very different groups. The first, consisting largely of state bankers and their friends, objected to the Bank of the United States because it competed with state banks and restrained the state banks from issuing notes as freely as some of them would have liked, through its policy of collecting such notes and presenting them for payment in cash. These critics of the Bank desired more paper money (that is, banknotes circulating as money), not less, and could be categorized as "soft money" people. The second set of critics, the "hard-money" people, had the opposite complaint. Believing in coin as the only safe currency, these people condemned all banks of issue—all banks issuing banknotes—whether charter by the states, as all but one of them were, or by the federal government, as the Bank alone was.

To preserve the institution, Biddle began to

grant banking favors to influential men in the hope of winning them to his side. At first he sought to cultivate Jackson's friends, with some success in a few instances. Then he turned more and more to Jackson's opponents. He extended loans on easy terms to several prominent newspaper editors, to a number of important state politicians, and to more than fifty congressmen and senators. In particular, he relied upon Senators Clay and Webster, the latter of whom was connected with the Bank in various ways — as legal counsel, director of the Boston branch, frequent and heavy borrower, and Biddle's personal friend.

Clay, Webster, and other advisers persuaded Biddle to apply to Congress for a recharter bill in 1832, four years ahead of the expiration date. After investigating the Bank and its business, Congress passed the recharter bill. At once Jackson vetoed it, sending it back to Congress with a stirring message in which he denounced the Bank as unconstitutional, undemocratic, and un-American. The veto stood, for the Bank's friends in Congress failed to obtain the two-thirds majority necessary for overriding it. And so the Bank question emerged as the paramount issue of the coming election, just as Clay had fondly hoped it would. In 1832 Clay ran as the unanimous choice of the National Republicans, who had held a nominating convention in Baltimore late in the previous year.

Jackson took his decisive reelection as a sign that the people endorsed his views on the Bank of the United States. As soon as the nullification crisis had been disposed of, he determined to strike a blow at this banking "monster," this dangerous money power, as he saw it. He could not put an end to the Bank before the expiration of its charter, but at least he could lessen its power by seeing to the removal of the government's deposits. The government opened accounts with a number of state banks, depositing its incoming receipts with them. Jackson's enemies called them his "pet banks."

Biddle soon struck back. He felt that the loss of government deposits, amounting to several millions, made it necessary for him to call in loans and raise interest rates, since the government deposits had served as the basis for much of the Bank's credit. He realized that, by making borrowing more difficult, he was bound to hurt business and cause unemployment, but he consoled himself with the belief that a short depression would help to bring about a recharter of the Bank.

The banker finally carried his contraction of credit too far to suit his own friends among the anti-Jackson businessmen of the Northeast. To appease the business community he at last reversed himself and began to grant credit in abundance and on reasonable terms. The "Bank War" was over, and Jackson had won it. But, with the passing of the Bank of the United States (in 1836), the country lost a valuable financial institution.

## Whigs Against Democrats

During the bank war the opponents of Jackson not only formally censured him in the Senate but also denounced him throughout the country for his allegedly high-handed and arbitrary actions. His opponents often referred to him as a tyrant, "King Andrew I," and they began to call themselves "Whigs," after the party which in England stood traditionally for limiting the power of the King.

The Whig party, organized in time for the congressional elections of 1834 and the presidential election of 1836, was an aggregation of dissimilar groups. It included the National Republicans who had opposed Jackson in 1828 (some of these were old Federalists, others former Jeffersonian Republicans), and it also included many people who had supported Jackson in 1828 but had turned against him afterward. Some of the Whigs, as in Virginia, were really state-rights Democrats who had broken with the President when he threatened to use force against a sister state, South Carolina. On the whole the new party was strongest among the merchants and manufacturers of the Northeast, the wealthier planters of the South, and the farmers most eager for internal improvements in the West. But the party as a rule did not appeal very strongly to the mass of voters. Throughout its existence of twenty years or so the party was able to win only two presidential elections (1840 and 1848), both of them with military heroes as its candidates.

Jackson and his party, in the course of his two presidential terms, developed a fairly definite and coherent political philosophy. The Jacksonians believed in laissez faire. That is, they believed that the government should let economic activities pretty much alone. They proposed the elimination of governmental favors to private enterprise, the destruction of government-granted monopolies and other corporate privileges. Then in theory the people through free and fair competition would be able to take care of themselves, each prospering in accordance with his own labor and skill. The worst of poverty and of social inequality would thus be done away with when the government ceased to help the rich and hinder the poor. While the Democrats did not advocate social revolution, the more radical of them (known as "Loco Focos") maintained that revolutionary violence might unfortunately appear unless economic inequalities were removed.

Webster, the leading Whig philosopher, stoutly denied the contentions of the radical Democrats. If there was any revolutionary discontent among the American people, he charged, it was due to the policies of the Jackson administration and the clamor of Democratic agitators. He maintained that the people had common interests rather than conflicting ones, at least so long as the government pursued the correct policies. He believed that a wise and active federal government, by stimulating and regulating economic activity through a national banking system, a protective tariff, and expenditures for internal improvements, could assure the economic well-being of all the people and thereby harmonize the interests of every section and class.

As the presidential election of 1836 approached, the Democrats had the advantages of patronage, Jackson's prestige, and a superior party organization. Jackson, not desiring a third term for himself, was able to choose the President to succeed him. The Democratic convention readily nominated his favorite, Van Buren.

The Whigs in 1836 could boast no such unity and discipline. Indeed, they could not even agree upon a single candidate. Their strategy, master-minded by Biddle, was to run several candidates, each of them supposedly strong in part of the country. Webster was the man for New England, and Hugh Lawson White of Tennessee was to seek the votes of the South. The former Indian fighter and hero of the War of 1812 from Ohio, William Henry Harrison, was counted upon in the middle states and the West.

The three Whigs proved to be no match for the one Democrat.

## Van Buren and Hard Times

At the time of the election of 1836 a nationwide boom was reaching its height. Land as usual was a favorite investment, especially the land sold by the federal government. Land sales were the government's largest source of revenue, but customs duties under the compromise tariff of 1833 added considerably to total income. The government received more money than it paid out. Steadily the national debt was reduced, as Jackson insisted it should be, and finally from 1835 to 1837 the government for the first and only time in its history was out of debt. Not only that: there was also a large and growing surplus in the federal treasury. The question for Congress and the administration was how to get rid of the treasury surplus.

In 1836 Congress passed and Jackson signed a distribution act providing that the surplus accumulated by the end of the year (estimated at $40 million) be paid to the states in four quarterly installments as a loan without security or interest, each state getting a share proportional to its representation in Congress. No one seriously expected the "loan" to be repaid. As the states began to receive their shares they promptly spent the money, mainly to encourage the construction of highways, railroads, and canals. The distribution of the surplus thus gave further stimulus to the boom. At the same time the withdrawal of federal funds strained the "pet banks," for they had to call in a large part of their own loans in order to make the transfer of funds to the state governments.

Though money continued to pour into the treasury from the land offices, most of it was money of dubious value. The government was selling good land and was receiving in return a miscellaneous collection of state banknotes, none of them worth any more than the credit of the issuing bank. Jackson finally decided to act. He issued his Specie Circular (1836) announcing that in the future only hard money or the notes of specie-paying banks would be accepted in payment for public lands.

President Van Buren had been in office less than three months when the Panic of 1837 broke. The ensuing depression, while mild by twentieth-century standards, was the worst the American people ever had experienced and lasted for about five years.

The distribution of the treasury surplus, by weakening the pet banks, helped to bring on the crash. So did Jackson's Specie Circular, which started a general run on the banks as land buyers rushed to get cash in return for banknotes to make land-office payments. Distribution of the surplus and the Specie Circular only precipitated the depression, however; they did not cause it. While the Bank of the United States, if continued, could have lessened the overexpansion of credit, a period of financial stringency doubtless would have come anyhow. For the depression was international, affecting England and Western Europe as well as the United States.

The modern concept that government can successfully fight depressions, and has an obligation to do so, simply did not exist in President Van Buren's time. Consequently Van Buren recommended no significant antidepression measure, except for the borrowing of $10 million to meet expenses during the emergency. However, Van Buren did favor the development of an economic program that would please the dominant farmer-labor segment of his party. Accordingly, he urged Congress to reduce the price of public lands and to pass a general preemption bill giving settlers the right to buy 160 acres at a set minimum price before land in any particular area was opened for public sale. These programs failed in Congress, but Van Buren was able to satisfy his urban followers through his presidential order that established a ten-hour work day on all federal projects. For the first time in the nation's history the government had taken direct action to aid the rising labor class.

The most important measure in the President's program, and the most controversial, was his proposal for a new fiscal system. With the Bank of the United States destroyed and with Jackson's expedient of "pet banks" discredited, some kind of new sytem was urgently needed. Van Buren's fiscal ideas demonstrate both his mental ingenuity and his sincere devotion to Democratic principles. The plan he suggested, known as the "Independent Treasury" or "Subtreasury" system, was simplicity itself. Government funds would be placed in an independent treasury at Washington and in subtreasuries in specified cities throughout the country. Whenever the government had to pay out money, its own agents would handle the funds. No bank or banks would have the government's money or name to use as a basis for loans. The government and the banks would be "divorced." Not until 1840, the last year of Van Buren's Presidency, did the administration succeed in driving the measure through both houses of Congress.

## The Log Cabin Campaign

As the campaign year of 1840 approached, the Whigs scented victory. The depression still gripped the country, and the Democrats, the party in power, could be blamed for it. The veteran Whig leader Henry Clay expected the nomination, but the party bosses decided otherwise. Clay had too definite a record; he had been defeated too many times; he had too many enemies. Passing him over, the Whig convention nominated William Henry Harrison of Ohio, and for Vice President, John Tyler of Virginia. The Democrats renominated Van Buren.

The campaign of 1840 set a new pattern in American politics. It introduced the circus-carnival atmosphere that would mark presidential elections for years in the future and that would awe or amuse European beholders — vast meetings, shouting parades, party badges and other insignia, and campaign songs.

Throughout the campaign the eager Whigs were on the offensive. They depicted themselves as the party of the people and the party that could save the nation from depression. They said Van Buren was an aristocrat who used cologne, drank champagne, and engaged in other undemocratic and un-American practices. A Democratic newspaper unwisely sneered that Harrison was a simple soul who would be glad to retire to a log cabin if provided with a pension and plenty of hard cider. In a country where many people lived or had lived in log cabins, this was almost handing the election to the Whigs, and they took the cue. Yes, their candidate was a simple man of the people, they proclaimed, and he loved log cabins and cider (actually he was a man of substance and lived in a large and well-appointed house).

Thereafter the log cabin was an established symbol at every Whig meeting, and hard cider an established beverage. Hundreds of Whig orators bragged that they had been born in log cabins or apologized for having been brought into the world in more sumptuous edifices. Thousands of Whig auditors listened to these effusions and happily chanted the songs that turned every Whig gathering into a frenzy of enthusiasm: "Tippecanoe and Tyler too" and "Van, Van is a used-up man." Against such techniques and the lingering effects of the depression the Democrats could not avail.

# Chapter 11. FREEDOM'S FERMENT

## Democracy and Civilization

"In the four quarters of the globe, who reads an American book? or goes to an American play? or looks at an American picture or statue?" So asked the English wit Sydney Smith in the *Edinburgh Review* (1820), and he assumed that the answer was obvious—nobody. Like him, many cultivated Europeans believed that the American democracy was a cultural vacuum.

On the whole, British travelers in the United States confirmed Smith's impression of American culture. To them the typical Yankee seemed filthy, rude, ignorant, quarrelsome, boastful, and greedy, as well as sickly and sallow. The Southerner seemed even worse, tyrannical and brutal, a beater of slaves. North, South, and West, the American male according to the British visitors was an inveterate tobacco chewer and spitter, with an aim that was none too good.

Quite different was the attitude of the young French visitor Alexis de Tocqueville, who welcomed political equality as the way of the future for France and the world. Even though he disapproved of much that he saw, he sought to understand American behavior, not to denounce it. Like the British observers, he concluded that Americans were backward in respect to science, literature, and the arts, but he did not blame their backwardness on democracy. He wrote: "Their strictly Puritanical origin—their exclusively commercial habits—even the country they inhabit, which seems to divert their minds from the pursuit of science, literature and the arts—the proximity of Europe, which allows them to neglect these pursuits without relapsing into barbarism—a thousand special causes, of which I have only been able to point out the most important—have singularly concurred to fix the mind of the American upon purely practical objects."

Colonial attitudes persisted in America so far as things of the mind were concerned. Seldom was an American author appreciated at home until he had been praised by critics abroad, and sometimes not even then. Despite the rise of book publishing in several American cities, especially in New York, the great majority of books published and sold were written, as before, by English authors. The romantic novels of Charles Dickens and Sir Walter Scott were as much the rage in the United States as in the British Isles. Scott was a special favorite among Southerners, who often applied Scott's word "Southron" to themselves, and who viewed their own section as the contemporary land of chivalry and romance.

As in the Revolutionary era, the question of literary independence continued to draw much discussion from American writers. "The more we receive from other countries, the greater the need of an original literature," said William Ellery Channing (1830). And Ralph Waldo Emerson, in his notable Phi Beta Kappa address at Harvard (1837), urged scholars, philosophers, and men of letters to do all they could toward developing a self-reliant nationhood. But James Russell Lowell said (1849), "It may not be our destiny to produce a great literature."

Foreign critics were too severe and native commentators too modest in their appraisals of American letters. In retrospect the period from the 1820s to the 1850s has seemed, indeed, a kind of golden age of literature in the United States. It was the time of Washington Irving, James Fenimore Cooper, Herman Melville, and Walt Whitman (all New Yorkers); Edgar Allan Poe (a Southerner by affirmation though not by birth); and Ralph Waldo Emerson, Henry David Thoreau, and Nathaniel Hawthorne (New Englanders). All these writers contributed to world literature: sooner or later they won lasting renown abroad as well as at home. Besides them, a number of others gained the esteem at least of their own countrymen and their own generation.

New York had become the literary capital of the nation after 1820. Then during the 1840s New York, as a center of authorship, was largely eclipsed by New England, if not by the one village of Concord, Massachusetts. Why there should have been such a literary "flowering" in New England is hard to explain. Of course, there was a long tradition of literacy and scholarship in the region. Ships returning from exotic ports throughout the world, including the Far East, brought in stimulating ideas along with profitable cargoes. Travelers, among them students attending German universities, returned with the stimulus of European romanticism. And the rise of industry altered society and the countryside, unsettling old habits and beliefs and, perhaps, provoking the imagination.

Americans were more noted for applied science than for scientific theory. Nevertheless, from observation and experiment, some of them made significant contributions to scientific knowledge. At Harvard the zoologist and geologist Louis Agassiz and the botanist Asa Gray not only taught but also carried on important research in their respective fields. Through his studies of plant distribution Gray assisted the English scholar Charles Darwin in formulating the theory of evolution. When Darwin's epoch-making book *On the Origin of Species* appeared (1859), Gray endorsed and Agassiz rejected the idea that plants and animals, instead of remaining unchanged since God created them, had developed through a process of natural selection.

The South did not produce a literature or a body of scientific findings to compare with those of the Northeast. The planters, the class that might have patronized a Southern literature, considered oratory and statesmanship to be much more significant activities. And much of the creative energy of the South was channeled into the defense of slavery. Under criticism from the outside, the section felt a compulsion to glorify its image of itself and to enforce conformity to that image. Freedom of thought, which was largely accepted in the North and which Jefferson and other former Southern leaders had said was necessary in a good society, was stifled in the South.

## Spirit of Social Reform

"In no country in the world has the principle of association been more successfully used, or more unsparingly applied to a multitude of different objects, than in America," Tocqueville observed. "Societies are formed to resist enemies which are exclusively of a moral nature, and to diminish the vice of intemperance: in the United States associations are established to promote public order, commerce, industry, morality, and religion; for there is no end which the human will, seconded by the collective exertions of individuals, despairs of attaining."

This reform spirit derived from a variety of sources, religious and rational, domestic and foreign. The Christian doctrine of human worth, the Revolutionary philosophy of the equality of man—these were part of the general background. More immediately, the rise of industrialism in the British Isles and Western Europe as well as the United States produced social dislocations and suffering but at the same time gave promise of a more abundant life for all. No doubt, with some people, a determination to improve human welfare was stimulated by the contrast between what actually was and what apparently might be. The humanitarian stirrings of the time were to be found in many lands at once, and most conspicuously in those countries that were being most rapidly industrialized.

Emerson's philosophy of transcendentalism contributed to the reform spirit. Emerson evolved the doctrine of the Oversoul or spiritual essence from which all things derived, including the soul of man. Since all humanity shared in this essential Being, this all-in-all, there existed a very real brotherhood of mankind. And since the Oversoul was good there could be no such thing, in the last analysis, as evil. This philosophy, for all its obscurities and inconsistencies, had practical consequences for its believers. It made them optimistic. It taught them that they were potentially divine and could increase their divinity by identifying themselves more and more fully with the Oversoul, with Being, with Truth. It led them to believe in the perfectibility of man.

Still more important as a call to reform were the preachings of the revivalist Charles G. Finney, who was at first a Presbyterian and later a Congregationalist. In upstate New York and in Ohio, beginning in the 1820s, Finney delivered many a memorable sermon on the dangers of damnation and the possibilities of salvation— through good works as well as faith. "The church," he maintained, "must take right ground on the subject of Temperance, and Moral Reform, and all the subjects of practical morality which come up for decision from time to time." Not all the churches did so, and some reformers (known as "come-outers") left the fold and even turned against organized religion, denouncing it as a bulwark to the status quo.

The reform spirit was far more prevalent among Whigs than among Democrats. Though it affected some of the latter too, it cannot be considered as essentially an extension of Jacksonian

Democracy. The Jacksonians advocated political and economic reforms, such as the widening of the suffrage and the destruction of monopoly, but were far from unanimous in supporting social reforms, such as the abolition of slavery. Nor can the reform spirit be viewed as an outgrowth of the labor movement, except in certain cases, notably the drive for free public schools. Most reform leaders disbelieved in unions, opposed strikes, and were indifferent to the plight of the unemployed. William Lloyd Garrison, the abolitionist, denounced labor agitators for trying "to inflame the minds of our working classes against the more opulent, and to persuade men that they are contemned and oppressed by a wealthy aristocracy." A few of the "more opulent," such as the merchants Arthur and Lewis Tappan of New York and Amos and Abbott Lawrence of Boston, contributed vast sums to finance various reforms. This is not to say, however, that big business in general was favorable to the reform movement. More often than not, reform was resisted by both the laborer and the capitalist. It was essentially a middle-class movement, receiving its greatest support from the reasonably well-to-do farmers, shopkeepers, and professional people of the Northeast and the Northwest.

## Advancing Education

As of 1830 no state could yet boast a general system of free public education in the modern sense — with full tax support, compulsory attendance, and enforced maintenance of schools — though Massachusetts, as in earlier times, came fairly close to it. A very high proportion of American children had the benefit of the three R's, but most of them still got their learning from church schools, proprietary institutions, private tutors, or members of their own families.

Then, during the 1830s, a widespread demand for state-supported primary education arose. This demand came from reformers who feared the consequences of allowing every man to vote, including in many cases even the newly arrived immigrant, without making public provision for his literacy at least. The demand came also from workingmen who hoped that book learning would enable their children to rise in the world. Opposition was forthcoming, however, from taxpayers (especially childless ones) who objected to paying for the education of other people's families, and from Lutherans, Roman Catholics, and other religious groups who already supported their own church schools and did not wish to be taxed for public education besides.

Educational reformers made considerable headway against such opposition in several of the states. The greatest of these leaders was Horace Mann, the first secretary of the Massachusetts board of education, which was established in 1837. He reorganized the state's school system, lengthened the school year (to six months), doubled teachers' salaries, enriched the curriculum, improved teacher training and teaching methods, and promoted the employment of young women, arguing that they were well educated and required only modest salaries.

By the 1850s the principle of tax-supported elementary schools was accepted in all the states, and all of them were making at least a start toward putting the principle into practice. Still, there were vast differences in the quantity and quality of public schools from place to place, the poorest performances and the lowest literacy rates being found in the newly settled areas of the West and in the more sparsely populated parts of the South. In the country as a whole, only a small proportion of children of school age were actually going to school — one white child out of every seven in the South and one out of every six elsewhere (1860). American society did not significantly increase the share of its resources devoted to education until the 1880s.

The principle of state support was applied later to secondary than to elementary schools. By 1860 there were 22 tax-supported "free academies" in New York, more than 100 public high schools in Massachusetts, and a total of about 300 such institutions in the nation as a whole. At the same time there were approximately 6,000 private academies. Most of them were open to boys only, a few were coeducational, and a growing number were female seminaries.

While the private academies were multiplying, so were the private colleges, though at a slower rate, about eighty being founded between 1830 and 1850. Almost all of these were denominational colleges, with close church connections, and their chief though not their only purpose was to prepare a learned clergy.

None of these institutions admitted women until, in 1837, Oberlin accepted four girls as regular students and thus became the first coeducational college. Some outsiders feared that coeducation was a rash experiment approximating free love, but the Oberlin authorities were confident that "the mutual influence of the sexes upon each other is decidedly happy in the cultivation of both mind & manners." Only a few other institutions copied Oberlin's example before the Civil War. Interest in higher education for women generally led to the creation of women's colleges. The first to have a curriculum equivalent to those of men's colleges was Mount Holyoke, founded by Mary Lyon in 1837.

The idea of state support for higher education had to contend against the prevailing concept of private, denominational control. Besides the older states with public universities, the newer states of Indiana, Michigan, Kentucky, Missouri, Mississippi, Iowa, Wisconsin, Minnesota, and Louisiana committed themselves to the support of higher learning before the Civil War. None of these state institutions, whether old or new, was a true university in the European sense of an institution devoted to high-level, graduate training.

## Remedying Society's Ills

While many reformers hoped to make possible a better life by creating opportunities through education or by eliminating specific social evils, some of the more advanced thinkers aspired to start afresh and remake society by founding ideal, cooperative communities. America still seemed a spacious and unencumbered country where models of a perfect society could be set up with a good chance to succeed. Presumably success would lead to imitation, until communities free of crime, poverty, and other evils would cover the land. Among the dozens of experimental communities were New Harmony, founded in Indiana by the philanthropic Scottish millowner Robert Owen; Brook Farm, an association of intellectuals, near Boston; and the Oneida Community in upstate New York, where the followers of John Humphrey Noyes carried out his unorthodox sexual theories, including the planned mating of old men with young women and vice versa, supposedly in the interest of eugenics.

From the 1820s on, the states one by one abolished imprisonment for debt, and some of them greatly improved their handling of the criminal and the insane. In the 1830s several states ended public hangings and began to hold executions within the privacy of prison walls, and later a few states did away with capital punishment entirely. The Boston schoolmistress, Dorothea Dix, shocked by her chance visit to the Cambridge jail (1841), devoted her life to securing the establishment of insane asylums in Massachusetts and other states.

In looking for causes of insanity, pauperism, and crime, many reformers concluded that these evils could be traced largely to strong drink. An organized temperance movement had begun with the formation of local societies in New England, and in 1826 the American Society for the Promotion of Temperance appeared as a coordinating agency for the various groups. As the temperance forces grew and spread over the country, the crusaders diverged, some advocating total abstinence and others seeing no harm in wine or beer; some favoring prohibition laws and others relying on the individual conscience. Massachusetts and other states experimented with legislation for local option, allowing communities to regulate or prohibit liquor sales, and Maine passed a statewide prohibition law in 1851.

## Improving Woman's Lot

Whatever the social handicaps that beset man as man, those that a woman had to face in early nineteenth-century America were considerably worse. Legally she remained an inferior. According to both common and statute law, a husband still had almost absolute authority over the person and property of his wife: what was his was his, and what was hers was his also. Though women worked hard in household and mill, they could not look forward to skilled factory jobs or careers in medicine, the ministry, politics, or law. By custom they were forbidden to speak in public to a mixed audience, lest they "unsex" themselves and lose their feminine charm. As long as women kept their expected place, men in America generally treated them with great deference—with much greater deference, foreign travelers noted, than men in Europe did.

Women took an active and often a leading part in the various reform movements, but most of the male reformers tried to confine the women to a subordinate role, though some husbands gave them every encouragement, a few even going so far as to omit the word "obey" from the wedding ceremony. When, in 1840, a world antislavery convention met in London, the men in charge refused to allow women delegates to participate. One of the rejected American delegates was Lucretia Mott, the happily married wife of a Massachusetts sea captain and eventually the mother of six children. Another was Elizabeth Cady Stanton, an abolitionist's wife, who had set out to prove herself the equal of any man after her father, on the death of his only son, had said to her: "Oh, my daughter, I wish you were a boy." The rebuff in London helped to convince Mrs. Mott and Mrs. Stanton that their first duty, as reformers, was to raise the status of women. Finally they called a women's rights convention, which met in Seneca Falls, New York, in 1848. This convention adopted resolutions (patterned on the Declaration of Independence) to the effect that all men *and women* are created equal and endowed with certain inalienable rights.

While the feminists failed to obtain the right to vote or hold office, they made noticeable gains before the Civil War. As early as 1839, Mississippi had recognized the right of married women to control their own property, and during the next two decades several other states, including New York (1848), did the same. Meanwhile a number of women from well-to-do and well-educated families, in addition to Mrs. Mott and Mrs. Stanton, broke the barriers that had kept women from professional and public careers. For example, Dr. Elizabeth Blackwell, born in England, gained acceptance and fame as a physician. Her sister-in-law Antoinette Brown Blackwell became the first ordained woman minister (Congregational and Unitarian) in the United States. Another sister-in-law, Lucy Stone, who was determined to "call no man master," kept her maiden name with her husband's approval. A graduate of Oberlin College, where she was not allowed to take part in public speaking, she rose to be one of the country's most popular and successful lecturers. Emma Willard, founder of the Troy Female Seminary (1821), and Catharine Beecher, founder of the Hartford Female Seminary (1823), made great contributions to progressive education, especially for young women.

## The Negro in the North

In the 1850s there were more than 4 million black Americans, of whom about 95 percent were confined to the South. That left nearly a quarter of a million of them living in the North. These people were concentrated mainly in the cities, about 22,000 in Philadelphia and about 12,000 in New York. Many were fugitives from slavery.

The Northern Negro faced severe handicaps in even managing to exist. He had little or no political influence: he could vote only in New England (not including Connecticut), and in New York only if he owned a certain amount of property, which was not required of white voters. In most places he was excluded from the public schools that whites attended. He faced the constant danger of being attacked by white mobs or kidnapped by slave dealers and sold, or resold, into slavery. Usually he had no choice but to take a low-paid job as a domestic servant or unskilled laborer. Seafaring offered him one of his best opportunities; in the 1850s, when the American merchant marine was at its height, nearly half the sailors in it were blacks.

In the early 1800s a Massachusetts free Negro, Paul Cuffe, tried to begin a back-to-Africa movement so as to give his people a new life in their ancestral homeland. Cuffe had spent $4,000 on the project, without success, when he died in 1817. That same year a group of prominent white Virginians organized the American Colonization Society to "colonize" freed slaves in Africa. Some Northern Negroes feared this was a scheme to get rid of them, and James Forten, a prosperous Negro businessman, called a mass meeting of Philadelphia blacks to object to it. Many well-meaning Northern whites favored it as a step toward emancipation; they thought it would encourage slaveowners to free at least some of their slaves. The American Colonization Society received private contributions and appropriations from Congress and the Virginia and Maryland legislatures to carry on the work. Though shipping out of the country fewer Negroes in a decade than were being born in it each month, the society succeeded in founding and governing on the west coast of Africa the colony of Liberia, which it converted into an independent black republic in 1846.

Meanwhile, in Massachusetts, a new note of black militancy had been struck. David Walker, born free in North Carolina, made his living by selling secondhand clothes in Boston. There, in 1829, he published a pamphlet entitled *Walker's Appeal . . . to the Colored Citizens*. In it he ridiculed the "Christian" pretensions of the slaveholders and urged slaves to cut their masters' throats. "Kill, or be killed!"

A number of other black critics of slavery, most of them less bitterly outspoken than Walker, appeared in the North. The greatest of all — and one of the most electrifying orators of his time, black or white — was Frederick Douglass. Born a slave in Maryland, Douglass ran off to Massachusetts in 1838, made a name for himself as an antislavery leader, and lectured for two years in England, where he was lionized. (More than a dozen other black abolitionists also visited the British Isles and made a strong impression there.) After returning to the United States in 1847, Douglass purchased his freedom from his Maryland owner and founded an antislavery newspaper, the *North Star,* in Rochester, New York.

As early as 1830, black abolitionists had held their first national convention. They were ready to cooperate with white reformers when some of these launched an aggressive antislavery movement.

## The White Abolitionists

During the 1820s the most active white crusader against slavery was the New Jersey Quaker Benjamin Lundy, who published the leading antislavery newspaper of the time, the *Genius of Universal Emancipation,* in Baltimore. Lundy used moderate language and advocated a mild and gradual program.

In 1831 his helper, the young Massachusetts-born printer William Lloyd Garrison, sounded a much more strident note when he presented the first issue of his own weekly, *The Liberator,* in Boston. From the outset Garrison condemned the thought of gradual, compensated emancipation and demanded immediate abolition, without reimbursement for slaveholders. He denounced the American Colonization Society as no emancipationist agency but the reverse, a group whose real aim was to strengthen slavery by ridding the country of Negroes already free. He got support from free Negroes, who bought most of the subscriptions to *The Liberator.* Despite his strong language, he was no advocate of slave rebellions, and he criticized *Walker's Appeal* as a "most injudicious publication."

Under the leadership of Garrison the New England Antislavery Society was founded in 1832 and the American Antislavery Society the following year. But he shocked many friends of freedom, including Frederick Douglass, by the extremes to which he went. He opposed the government, characterizing the Constitution as "a covenant with death and an agreement with hell," and he opposed the churches on the grounds that they were bulwarks of slavery. In 1840 he split the American Antislavery Society by insisting upon the right of women to participate fully in its activities, even to speak before audiences that included men as well as women.

By that time there were in existence nearly 2,000 local societies with a total of almost 200,000 members. These societies remained alive, active, and growing after the disruption of the national organization.

Another outstanding leader, busy in New York and the Northwest, was Theodore Weld. Converted to reform by Charles G. Finney's preaching, Weld worked within the churches, especially the Presbyterian and Congregational. He married Angelina Grimké, a South Carolina planter's daughter who, with a sister, had turned against slavery. With the aid of his wife, Weld compiled an overwhelming factual indictment of the institution in the book *American Slavery As It Is: Testimony of a Thousand Witnesses* (1839).

## The Campaign for Liberation

Most of the active members of organized societies were "abolitionists" in the sense that they favored immediate abolition. But this did not mean precisely what it seemed to mean. The abolitionists aimed at what they called "immediate abolition gradually accomplished." That is, they hoped to bring about a sudden and not a gradual end to slavery, but they did not expect to achieve this for some time. At first, they counted on "moral suasion": they were going to appeal to the conscience of the slaveholder and convince him that slaveholding was a sin.

Later they turned more and more to political action, seeking to induce the Northern states and the federal government to aid the cause where possible. They helped runaway slaves find refuge in the North or in Canada, though in doing so they did not set up any such highly organized system as the term "Underground

Railroad" implies. After the Supreme Court (in *Prigg* v. *Pennsylvania, 1842*) held that the states need not aid in enforcing the federal fugitive-slave law of 1793, abolitionists secured the passage of "personal liberty laws" in several of the Northern states. These laws forbade state officials to assist in the capture and return of runaways. Above all, the antislavery societies petitioned Congress to abolish slavery in places where the federal government had jurisdiction—in the territories and the District of Columbia—and to prohibit the interstate slave trade. Only a very few of the abolitionists supposed that Congress constitutionally could interfere with a "domestic" institution like slavery with the Southern states themselves.

While the abolitionists engaged in pressure politics, they never formed a political party with an abolition platform. In 1840 the Liberty party was launched, with the Kentucky antislavery leader James G. Birney as its presidential candidate, but this party and its successors did not campaign for outright abolition: they stood for "free soil," that is, for keeping slavery out of the territories. Some free-soilers were friends of the slave; others were Negrophobes who cared nothing about slavery but desired to make the West a white man's country. Garrison said free-soil-ism was really "white-man-ism."

The real friends of the Negro were quite aware that, to be consistent, they would have to help the free as well as the enslaved, since so-called freedom was "but an empty name—but the debasing mockery of true freedom." Garrison assured his "free colored brethren" that the attainment of equal rights for them was "a leading object." He and other abolitionists did try to open new opportunities for them. They had little success in appealing to employers to hire additional Negroes and give them training as apprentices. But the reformers made other rather modest gains. They established schools for Negroes (by 1837 there were a hundred young white women teaching black children in Ohio) and even colleges (Wilberforce in Ohio, Avery in Pennsylvania). They opened Oberlin College to black students. They brought about the desegregation of all Massachusetts public schools in 1855, six years after Charles Sumner had argued in a Boston lawsuit (as opponents of segregation elsewhere were to do a century later) that, no matter how good the facilities provided for Negro pupils, "the separate school is not equivalent." The reformers also secured the repeal of Massachusetts and Ohio laws requiring separate Negro cars on railroads.

The abolitionists might have accomplished more reforms in the North had it not been for the widespread anti-Negro if not proslavery feeling there. Prejudice was reinforced by the desire of many Northern businessmen to keep on good terms with Southern customers or suppliers, and by the fear on the part of wage-earning Northern whites that Negroes, if freed and given equal opportunities, would be dangerous competitors for jobs. The antislavery movement provoked much hostility in the North, especially during the early years. When Prudence Crandall undertook to admit Negro girls to her private school in Connecticut, local citizens had her arrested and threw filth into her well, forcing her to close the school. A mob burned the Philadelphia abolitionists' "temple of liberty" and started a bloody race riot (1834). Another mob seized Garrison on the streets of Boston and threatened to hang him, and a member of still another group shot and killed the antislavery editor Elijah Lovejoy in Alton, Illinois (1837). Throughout the North antislavery lecturers, risking their health if not their lives, time and again were attacked with rotten eggs or stones.

In the South the reaction was far stronger, and if no abolitionists were killed there, it was only because (from the 1830s on) very few of them dared even venture into that part of the country.

## The "Peculiar Institution"

Slavery was an institution established by law and regulated in detail by law. The slave codes of the Southern states forbade a slave to hold property, to leave his master's premises without permission, to be out after dark, to congregate with other slaves except at church, to carry firearms, to strike a white man even in self-defense. The codes prohibited teaching a slave to read or write, and denied the right of a slave to testify in court against a white person. They contained no provisions to legalize slave marriages or divorces. Any person showing a strain of African ancestry was presumed to be a slave unless he could prove otherwise. If an owner killed a slave while punishing him, the act was not considered a crime.

Even though the price of slaves had been driven up by the closing of the trans-Atlantic

slave trade in 1808, the profits earned from own-
ing slaves were high. The master had an economic interest in taking reasonably good care of
his slaves. He was likely to use hired labor,
when available, for the most unhealthful or dangerous tasks. A traveler in Louisiana noted, for
example, that Irishmen were employed to clear
malarial swamps and to handle cotton bales at
the bottom of chutes extending from the river
bluff down to a boat landing. If an Irishman
died of disease or was killed in an accident, the
master could hire another for a dollar a day or
less. But he would be out perhaps a thousand
dollars or more if he lost a prime field hand. Still,
a cruel master might forget his pocketbook in the
heat of momentary anger. And slaves were often
left to the discipline of an overseer, who had no
pecuniary stake in their well-being; he was paid
in proportion to the amount of work he could get
out of them.

Household servants had a somewhat easier
life than field hands. On a small plantation the
same persons might serve in both capacities, but
on a large one there would be a separate staff of
nursemaids, housemaids, cooks, butlers, coach-
men, and the like. These people lived close to
the master and his family, eating the leftovers
from the family table, and in some cases even
sleeping in the "big house." Between the blacks
and whites of such a household, there might develop an affectionate, almost familial relationship. And, indeed, some house slaves bore a
striking resemblance to their masters.

Slavery in the cities differed significantly from
slavery in the country. On the more or less
isolated plantation the slaves were kept apart
from free Negroes and lower-class whites. The
master, his family, and his overseers maintained
a fairly direct and effective control. A deep and
unbridgeable chasm yawned between slavery
and freedom. In the city, however, the master
often could not supervise his slaves closely and
at the same time use them profitably. Even if
they slept at night in carefully watched backyard
barracks, they went about by day on errands of
various kinds. Others were hired out, and after
hours they fended for themselves, neither the
owner nor the employer caring to look after
them. Thus the urban slaves gained numerous
opportunities to mingle with free Negroes and
with whites, including fair-complexioned prosti-
tutes. A line between slavery and freedom remained, but it became less and less distinct.

The domestic slave trade, while essential to
the growth and prosperity of the whole system,
was one of the least defensible aspects of it. Not
only did the trade dehumanize all who were involved in it; it also separated children from
parents, and parents from one another. Even in
the case of a kindly master who had kept families together, they might be broken up in the
division of his estate after his death. Planters
condoned the trade and eased their consciences
by holding the traders in contempt and assigning
them a low social position—except those who
invested their profits in plantations (like Nathan
Bedford Forrest, a slave trader and then a
planter and eventually a war hero of the Confederacy).

The foreign slave trade was as bad or worse.
Though federal law had prohibited the importation of slaves from 1808 on, they continued to be
smuggled in as late as the 1850s. The numbers
were small and the Southern commercial conventions, which met annually to consider means
of making the South economically independent,
began to discuss the legal reopening of the trade.
"If it is right to buy slaves in Virginia and carry
them to New Orleans," William L. Yancey of
Alabama asked his fellow delegates at the 1858
meeting, "why is it not right to buy them in
Cuba, Brazil, or Africa and carry them there?"
The convention that year voted to recommend
the repeal of all laws against slave imports. Only
the delegates from the states of the upper South,
which profited from the domestic trade, opposed
the opening of foreign competition.

## The Slave's Response

By the 1850s few slaves in the United States
could do more than dimly recall the lore of their
ancestors in Africa. The Africans had developed
a variety of complex cultures, but much of the
tribal custom and language was lost in the
disruptive transition to slavery. The slaves no
longer possessed a tribal or cultural identity of a
kind that would help them to offset the deper-
sonalizing effects of slavery. They were left to
respond to their lot, individually, as best they
could, and they responded in a variety of ways.
Some, especially among favored domestic servants, identified with the master and accepted
their subservient position with little difficulty,
perhaps with real contentment. Others learned
to adjust to necessity by acting out, in the white

man's presence, the expected role of shuffling, grinning, head-scratching deference. Still others could never quite bring themselves to either acceptance or accommodation. They harbored an unquenchable spirit of rebelliousness, and from the frustration it brought them they sometimes developed personality disorders (signs of these were seen in newspaper advertisements for runaways who were described as having a stutter or a "downcast look" or other behavioral quirks).

For the vast majority, there was no way out of their predicament. A few were allowed to earn money with which they managed to buy their own and their families' freedom. Some had the good luck to be set free by their master's will after his death – like the more than 400 slaves belonging to John Randolph of Roanoke (1833). From the 1830s on, however, state laws made it more and more difficult, and in some cases practically impossible, for an owner to manumit his slaves. The laws, when permitting manumission, often required the removal of the freed slaves from the state. The masters objected to the very presence of free Negroes, who set a disturbing example for the slaves and provided cover for escaping slaves.

By 1860 there nevertheless were about 250,000 free Negroes in the slaveholding states, more than half of them in Virginia and Maryland. A few, as in the North, attained wealth and prominence. A few themselves owned slaves, usually relatives whom they had bought in order to assure their ultimate emancipation. Most lived in abject poverty, even worse than in the North. Law or custom closed many occupations to them, forbade them to assemble without white supervision, and placed numerous other restraints upon them. They were only quasi-free, and yet they had all the burdens of freedom, including the obligation of paying taxes.

Great as were the hardships of freedom, Negroes generally preferred them to the hardships of slavery. Occasionally slaves sought freedom through flight. They might succeed in hiding out for a time, but the chance of escaping to the North or to Canada was exceedingly slim except for those who lived fairly close to the free-state border and who got help from free Negroes and friendly whites on the so-called Underground Railroad. For fugitives from the deep South, the hazards of distance and geographical ignorance, of white patrols and bloodhounds, were hard if not impossible to overcome, especially since every Negro at large was presumed to be a runaway slave unless he carried documentary proof to the contrary.

The discontented slave could express his feelings through individual acts of resistance. He might be deliberately careless with his master's property, losing or breaking tools, setting fire to houses or barns. He might make himself useless by cutting off his fingers or even commiting suicide. Or, despite the terrible consequences, he might turn upon the master and kill him.

The idea of combining with other blacks, rising up, and overthrowing the masters occurred to slaves and free Negroes from time to time. In 1800 Gabriel Prosser gathered a thousand rebellious slaves outside Richmond, but two blacks gave the plot away, and the Virginia militia were called out in time to head it off. Gabriel and thirty-five others were executed. In 1822 the Charleston free Negro Denmark Vesey and his followers – rumored to total 9,000 – made preparations for revolt, but again the word leaked out and retribution followed. In 1831 Nat Turner, a slave preacher, led a band of Negroes who armed themselves with guns and axes and, on a summer night, went from house to house in Southampton County, Virginia. They slaughtered sixty white men, women, and children before being overpowered by state and federal troops. More than a hundred Negroes were put to death in the aftermath. Nat Turner's was the only actual slave insurrection in the nineteenth-century South, but slave conspiracies and threats of renewed violence continued throughout the section as long as slavery lasted.

## The Proslavery Reaction

By the 1830s slavery was being threatened from three directions – from the slaves themselves, from Northern abolitionists, and from Southern slaveless farmers. There were still antislavery societies in the South, and as late as 1827 there had been a larger number than in the North. They were most numerous in the border slave states, where a few antislavery men, notably Cassius M. Clay of Kentucky, kept up their campaign through the 1850s. Between 1829 and 1832 a Virginia constitutional convention and then the state legislature, responding to demands from non-slaveholders in the western part of the state, seriously considered ending slavery through compensated emancipation but were

## THE SLAVE'S RESPONSE TO SLAVERY

For many years after its publication in 1918, Ulrich B. Phillips' *American Negro Slavery* was accepted as the standard authority on the subject. Phillips assumed (as defenders of slavery had done before the Civil War) that the typical plantation Negro was lazy, childlike, irresponsible, contented, and submissive—all because of his African racial make-up. Further, Phillips believed that the American Negro kept little if any of his African cultural inheritance.

Eventually strong dissenters appeared. In *The Myth of the Negro Past* (1941) the white anthropologist Melville J. Herskovits emphasized the number of "Africanisms" that survived through slavery times. In *American Negro Slave Revolts* (1943) the historian Herbert Aptheker claimed to have discovered "approximately two hundred and fifty revolts and conspiracies in the history of American Negro slavery" and concluded that "discontent and rebelliousness" were "characteristic of American Negro slaves." In *The Peculiar Institution* (1956) Kenneth M. Stampp viewed the black slaves as "ordinary human beings" who reacted to slavery in a variety of ways, much as white people would have done in the same circumstances.

Then, in 1959, Stanley M. Elkins provoked continuing controversy with his *Slavery: A Problem in American Institutional and Intellectual Life.* Elkins agreed with Phillips that the typical slave had a "Sambo" personality but accounted for it in terms of the psychological shock of enslavement and the enforced "adjustment to absolute power" in the hands of the master. In the process the slaves lost the tribal or cultural identity that might have helped them to maintain their personal independence. Slave rebels, such as Denmark Vesey and Nat Turner, stand out because they were, in Elkins' words, "so exceptional" and "so few."

Recently several historians have taken issue with Elkins by pointing to aspects of slave culture that provided slaves with a sense of independence. John Blassingame, in *The Slave Community* (1973), found that American-born slaves were able to retain their ancestors' culture, largely through the slave family, which enabled its members to "cooperate with other blacks" and maintain their self-esteem. Eugene D. Genovese, in *Roll, Jordan, Roll: The World the Slaves Made* (1974), also found strength in the slave family but emphasized the development of the slaves' religion as "the organizing center of their resistance within accommodation." Genovese concluded that it "strengthened their love for each other and their pride in being black people."

On the basis of an elaborate quantitative study, Robert W. Fogel and Stanley L. Engerman concluded, in *Time on the Cross: The Economics of American Negro Slavery* (1974), that planters themselves, out of self-interest, encouraged stable family relationships and provided slaves with a standard of living comparable with that of free people. Moreover, they found the slaves to have been neither lazy nor rebellious types but extremely productive workers. But their findings encountered immediate criticism, led by historian Herbert G. Gutman, in *Slavery and the Numbers Game: A Critique of "Time on the Cross"* (1975), and a group of economists, in *Reckoning with Slavery* (1976). While agreeing that slaves developed a supportive culture and displayed real achievement, they stressed the low standard of living of the slaves, the obstacles slaves faced in maintaining a stable family life, and the violence used by planters to maintain order.

discouraged by the tremendous expense it would have required.

Meanwhile the news of the Turner insurrection terrified whites in Virginia and all over the South. They had always been uneasy, always mindful of the horrors of the successful slave uprising in Santo Domingo (in the 1790s). Now they were reminded of their insecurity, and they were especially horrified because there had been long trusted house servants among Nat's followers who, axe in hand, had suddenly confronted their masters' sleeping families. Who among the blacks could the whites really depend upon? Many of the master class now blamed Garrison and the abolitionists for the slaves' defection. Planters were determined to make slavery secure against all dangers.

While the Southern states strengthened their slave codes, controlling the movement of slaves and prohibiting their being taught to read, Southern leaders proceeded to elaborate an intellectual defense of slavery. According to the proslavery argument it was good for the slave because he was an inferior creature who needed the master's guidance and who was better off—better fed, clothed, and housed, and more secure—than the Northern factory worker. It was good for Southern society because it was the only way two races so different as the black and the white could live together in peace. It was good for the nation as a whole because the entire Southern economy depended on it, and the prosperity of the nation depended on the prosperity of the South. It was good in itself because the Bible sanctioned it—did not the Hebrews of the Old Testament own bondsmen, and did not the New Testament apostle Paul advise, "Servants, obey your masters"? These and other arguments convinced most Southerners, even those (the great majority) who owned no slaves and had no direct interest in the peculiar institution.

While spreading proslavery propaganda, Southern leaders tried to silence the advocates of freedom. In 1835 a mob destroyed sacks containing abolition literature in the Charleston post office, and thereafter Southern postmasters generally refused to deliver antislavery mail. Southern state legislatures passed resolutions demanding that Northern states suppress the "incendiary" agitation of the abolitionists. In Congress, Southern representatives with the cooperation of Northerners secured the adoption of the "gag rule" (1836) according to which antislavery petitions were automatically laid on the table without being read.

As a champion of freedom of speech and petition, John Quincy Adams led a struggle against the gag rule, finally (1844) securing its repeal. Throughout the North many people who were not abolitionists began to feel that civil liberties were endangered in the entire country, not just the South. These people were inclined to sympathize with the abolitionist as a martyr for freedom in the broadest sense. They came to suspect that there really existed, as the abolitionist claimed, a kind of "Slave Power Conspiracy" to destroy the liberties of the country as a whole. Thus the majority of Northerners, though not usually for love of the Negro, eventually came to sympathize in varying degrees with the antislavery cause, while an even larger and more determined majority of Southerners rallied to the defense of the peculiar institution, thereby laying the foundation for a "solid South."

# Chapter 12.　MANIFEST DESTINY

## Frustration of the Whigs

The Whigs found themselves divided and frustrated despite their overwhelming victory in the "log cabin" campaign of 1840, which had brought into office their appealing ticket of "Tippecanoe and Tyler too."

"Old Tippecanoe," William Henry Harrison, was never to have a chance to demonstrate what sort of President he would have made. Though he seemed to be in good health, he was sixty-eight years old in 1841, and the strain of the campaign and the inauguration and the pressing demands of his office-seeking supporters were apparently too much for him. He contracted a cold which turned into pneumonia, and he died on April 4, 1841, exactly one month after he had been inaugurated—the first President to die in office. In his brief presidential tenure he had looked for advice to the accepted leaders of the party, particularly to Clay and Webster. Webster became secretary of state, and four of Clay's friends went into the cabinet. Clay and Webster had expected to guide the old soldier through the political jungle.

Vice President John Tyler, though some contended he was merely the second officer acting as the first, immediately assumed the title as well as the powers of the Presidency. For the time being, he kept Harrison's cabinet. A member of an aristocratic Virginia family, Tyler had left the Democratic party in protest against Jackson's overly equalitarian program and imperious methods. One reason the Whigs had put him on the ticket with Harrison was the hope that he would attract the votes of similar conservative former Democrats. Nevertheless, Clay apparently had the impression that the new President would support a national bank and other Whig projects, but Tyler soon broke with Clay.

A part of Clay's program was enacted without causing serious division in the party. With near unanimity the Whigs passed a measure, which Tyler signed, abolishing the Independent Treasury system. They also agreed on a bill, the Tariff of 1842, which raised the rates to approximately the same level as in 1832. Tyler accepted this bill, too, but with no great show of enthusiasm.

Part of the Whig legislative program made a bid for the approval of Western settlers and farmers. The frontier was continuing its steady expansion. Arkansas became a state in 1836, Michigan in 1837, and Florida in 1845. The greatest rush of settlers was into the future states of Wisconsin, Iowa, and Minnesota. To attract Western voters the Whig leadership put through the Preemption Act of 1841, which made it possible for a "squatter" on public land to claim 160 acres before they were offered for sale and to pay for them later at $1.25 an acre. This "log cabin bill" was hailed by the Whigs as a relief measure for sufferers from the depression and as a proof of their party's devotion to the welfare of the common man.

The Whig leadership was committed to restoring a financial system similar to the Bank of the United States. But Tyler desired a kind of "state-rights national bank," one that would confine its operations to the District of Columbia and establish branches in the states only with their consent. He twice vetoed bills for setting up what the Whigs tried to disguise as a "Fiscal Corporation."

Lacking a sufficient majority to override the veto, the Whigs fumed with rage at the President, who added to their anger by vetoing a number of internal improvement bills. In an unprecedented action, a conference of congressional Whigs read Tyler out of the party. All the cabinet members resigned except Webster, who had some diplomatic business with Great Britian that he wished to settle. To fill their places, the President appointed five men of his own stripe — former Democrats.

A portentous new political alignment was taking shape. Tyler and a small band of conservative Southern Whigs who followed him were getting ready to rejoin the Democrats. When the office of secretary of state became vacant in 1844, Tyler appointed John C. Calhoun—who had left the Democratic party in the 1830s and had since rejoined it. Into the common man's party of Jackson and Van Buren came a group of men who had aristocratic ideas about government, who thought that government had an obligation to protect and even expand the institution of slavery, and who believed in state rights with a single-minded, almost fanatical devotion.

## Webster's Diplomacy

Starting in the late 1830s a series of incidents brought Great Britain and the United States once again close to war. In 1837 rebellion broke out in the eastern provinces of Canada, and many Americans applauded the rebels and furnished them with material aid. The rebels chartered a small American steamship, the *Caroline,* to carry supplies across the Niagara River from New York. One night while the ship was moored at a wharf on the American side, the Canadian authorities sent over a force that took possession of the *Caroline* and burned her; in the melee one American was killed. Excitement flared on both sides of the border.

While the *Caroline* affair simmered, the troublesome issue of the Maine boundary came up. As defined by the Treaty of 1783, this line was impossible to locate. Previous attempts to fix it by mutual agreement and by arbitration had failed. In 1838 Americans and Canadians, mostly lumberjacks, began to move into the Aroostook River region in the disputed area. A head-smashing brawl between the two parties — the "Aroostook War" — threatened more trouble between England and America.

In an attempt to stamp out the African slave trade, Great Britain was asking for the right to search American merchant ships suspected of carrying black cargoes. Since the American government, sensitive on the matter of search, had always refused the British request, slavers of other nations frequently sought to avoid capture by hoisting the American flag. Complicating the issue was the domestic slave trade, in which slaves were carried by sea from one American port to another. Sometimes the ships in this trade were blown off their course to the British West Indies, where the authorities, acting under English law, freed the slaves. In 1841 an American brig, the *Creole,* sailed from Virginia for New Orleans with over a hundred slaves aboard. En route the slaves mutinied, took possession of the ship, and took it to the Bahamas. Here British officials declared the bondsmen

free. Although Webster protested, England refused to return the slaves. Many Americans, especially Southerners, were infuriated.

At this critical juncture a new government came to power in Great Britain, one that was more disposed to conciliate the United States and to settle the outstanding differences between the two countries. The new ministry sent to America an emissary, Lord Ashburton, to negotiate an agreement on the Maine boundary and other matters. Ashburton liked Americans, and Webster admired the English. To avoid war, both were willing to compromise. The result of their deliberations was the Webster-Ashburton Treaty of August 9, 1842.

By the terms of this arrangement, the United States received about seven-twelfths of the disputed area, which was about as much as it could expect. Minor rectifications in the boundary were made in the Lake Champlain area and from Lake Superior to the Lake of the Woods. The boundary was now established as far west as the Rocky Mountains. Other issues disposed of were the extradition of criminals and the slave trade. Seven crimes were listed for which the United States and Canada would extradite accused citizens of the other country. It was agreed that both Great Britian and the United States would maintain naval squadrons off the African coast, the American ships being charged with chasing slavers using the American flag.

Through exchanges of notes that were not part of the treaty, Webster and Ashburton also eased the memory of the *Caroline* and *Creole* affairs. Ashburton expressed "regret" for the raid on the *Caroline,* and he pledged that in the future there would be no "officious interference" with American ships forced by "violence or accident" to enter British ports — presumably meaning there would be no repetition of the *Creole* episode.

Webster used secret funds to inspire newspaper propaganda favorable to his arrangements with Ashburton, and the treaty proved quite popular. War talk was forgotten for the time being, as Anglo-American relations suddenly looked better than they had for many years.

## Election of Polk

In 1844 Henry Clay expected to be the Whig candidate, and Van Buren the Democratic nominee. Both wanted to avoid taking a stand on the annexation of Texas, because a stand, no matter on which side, was certain to lose some votes. Consequently, they issued separate statements, so similar in tone as to indicate previous consultation between the authors. They both favored annexation, but only with the consent of Mexico. Since this consent was most unlikely to be forthcoming, the statements had little or no meaning.

Clay's action did not harm his candidacy. The Whig convention nominated him unanimously, although the platform discreetly omitted any reference to Texas. But Van Buren had destroyed his chances with the Democrats, particularly with those from the South, who were enraged by his equivocal stand on annexation. The Democratic convention threw him aside, and nominated James K. Polk, a champion of expansion. The platform caught the prevailing mood in its key resolution: "that the re-occupation of Oregon and the re-annexation of Texas at the earliest practicable period are great American measures." The words "*re*-occupation" and "*re*-annexation" were intended to imply that, in taking Oregon and Texas, the United States would only be confirming its claim to territories that had already belonged to it. By combining Oregon and Texas, the Democrats hoped to appeal to both Northern and Southern expansionists.

Too late Clay realized that he had muffed the expansion issue. In mid-campaign he announced that under certain circumstances he might be for the acquisition of Texas. His tardy straddling probably cost him more votes than it gained. Polk carried the election by 170 electoral votes to 105, though his popular majority was less than 40,000. The Liberty party, running James G. Birney a second time, polled 62,000 votes (as compared with 7,000 in 1840), most of which were cast by Whigs who turned against Clay.

"Who is James K. Polk?" the Whigs had sarcastically asked during the campaign. Actually, he was not so obscure as all that. Born in North Carolina, he had moved, when in his mid-twenties, to Tennessee, thus following the pattern of the man who became his political mentor, Andrew Jackson. Elected to the national House of Representatives, he held his seat for fourteen consecutive years, serving for four of them as speaker. He was thin, worn, even grim-looking, and his public manners comported with his appearance. But he had a good mind, he worked hard at his job, and above all he had an iron, implacable will. Probably no other President entered office with so clearly defined a program and accomplished so much of it as did Polk.

## Partitioning of Oregon

The ownership of Oregon had long been in dispute, but its boundaries were clearly defined —on the north the latitude line of 54° 40′, on the east the crest of the Rocky Mountains, on the south the 42nd parallel, and on the west the Pacific Ocean. Included in its half-million square miles were the present states of Oregon, Washington, and Idaho, parts of Montana and Wyoming, and half of British Columbia.

At various times in the past the Oregon country had been claimed by Spain, Russia, France, England, and the United States. By the 1820s only the last two nations remained in contention. The others had withdrawn and surrendered their rights to Britian or to the United States or to both. The American and British claims were equally valid—or invalid. Both countries could assert title on the basis of the activities of their explorers, maritime traders, and fur traders. The English had one solid advantage: they were in actual possession of a part of the area. In 1821 the powerful British fur trading organization, the Hudson's Bay Company, established a post at Fort Vancouver, north of the Columbia River.

Several times the English government proposed the Columbia as a suitable line of division. The United States, also showing a desire to compromise, countered by suggesting the 49th parallel. This difference in official views prevented a settlement of the Oregon question in the treaty of 1818. Unable to agree on a demarcation line, the diplomats of the two powers agreed that the citizens of each should have equal access to Oregon for ten years. This arrangement, called joint occupation, was renewed in 1827 for an indefinite period, with either nation empowered to end it on a year's notice.

The first real American interest in Oregon came as a result of the activities of missionaries, both Protestant and Catholic. All the American missionaries located their posts south of the Columbia River, mostly in the fertile Willamette Valley. They described their work in reports and

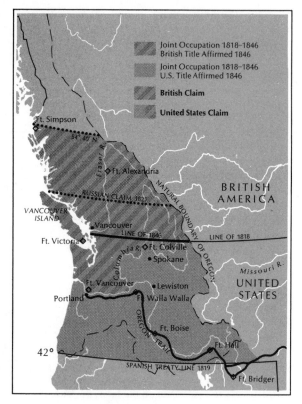

**American Expansion in Oregon**

ington rejected Polk's offer without referring it to London. Abruptly Polk took a more militant attitude. Saying America should look John Bull "straight in the eye" and hinting at war, he asserted claim to all of Oregon. Though there was loose talk of war on both sides of the Atlantic, neither nation really wished to resort to force. The British government now offered to divide Oregon at the 49th parallel—that is, to accept Polk's original proposal. In the 1846 treaty the United States secured the larger and better part of the Oregon country and certainly all that it could have reasonably expected to get.

## Annexation of Texas

Southwest of the United States stretched the northern provinces of Mexico—Texas, New Mexico, and Upper California—once parts of Spain's colonial empire in North America but, since 1822, states in the independent republic of Mexico. Under Spanish rule the provinces had been subject to only the lightest supervision from the government of the vice-royalty in Mexico, and only a few thousand white men had settled in them. The same conditions prevailed under the republic, which lacked the power, the population, and the economic incentive to govern and settle such distant areas. At one time the United States had advanced a claim to Texas as a part of the Louisiana Purchase, but had renounced the claim in 1819. Twice thereafter, however, in the presidencies of John Quincy Adams and Jackson, the United States had offered to buy Texas, only to meet with indignant Mexican refusals.

The Mexican government invited the inevitable in Texas. In the early 1820s it encouraged American immigration by offering land grants to men like Stephen Austin who promised to colonize the land, swear loyalty to Mexico, and abandon Protestantism. Probably the motive of the government was to build up the economy of Texas, and hence its tax revenues, by increasing the population with foreigners, but the experiment was to result in the loss of Texas to the United States. Thousands of Americans, attracted by reports of the rich soil in Texas, took advantage of Mexico's welcome. The great majority, by the very fact of geography, came from the Southern states, sometimes bringing with them slaves, although slavery was forbidden in

letters that were published in influential religious journals and widely reprinted in secular newspapers. These reports dwelt as much on the rich soil and lovely climate of Oregon as on the spiritual condition of the Indians.

Beginning in 1841, thousands of pioneers set out for Oregon. Amazed observers remarked upon the "Oregon fever." Two thousand miles in length, the Oregon Trail penetrated Indian country and crossed mountains and semidesert regions. To the emigrants, traveling in caravans of covered wagons and accompanied by huge herds of cattle, it presented enormous problems in transportation. The average period required for the journey was from May to November. Some never lived to complete it. But the great majority got through. By 1845, 5,000 Americans were living south of the Columbia—and demanding that their government take possession of Oregon.

When Polk assumed office, he was willing to compromise—to effect a division on the line of the 49th parallel. The British minister in Wash-

Mexico after 1829. By 1835 approximately 35,000 Americans were living in Texas, which was ten times the number of native Mexicans there.

Almost from the beginning there was friction between the settlers and both the Mexicans and the Mexican government. The Americans failed to appreciate the gentility of Spanish culture and blamed the illiteracy of the Mexican peasants on racial inferiority; they were convinced that their life style was in every way superior to that of the original Mexicans and believed that it was their mission to bring progress to a backward society. By the 1830s the numerically and financially dominant settlers had relegated the native Mexicans to inferior status.

Finally the Mexican government, realizing that its power over Texas was being challenged by the settlers and recognizing the plight of the native Mexicans, moved to exert control. A new law reduced the powers of the various states of the republic, a measure that the Texans took to be aimed specifically at them; another law threatened to prohibit slavery after 1842; and when protesting in Mexico City Stephen Austin found himself thrown in jail. In 1836 the Texans proclaimed their independence.

The Mexican dictator Santa Anna advanced into Texas with a large army. Even with the aid of volunteers, money, and supplies from private groups in the United States, the Texans were having difficulty in organizing a resistance. Their garrison at the Alamo mission in San Antonio was exterminated; another at Goliad suffered substantially the same fate when the Mexicans murdered most of the force after it surrendered. But General Sam Houston, emerging as the national hero of Texas, kept a small army together, and at the battle of San Jacinto (April 21, 1836, near present-day Houston) he defeated the Mexican army, killing more than 600 Mexican soldiers in retaliation, and taking Santa Anna prisoner. Although the Mexican government refused to recognize the captured dictator's vague promises to withdraw Mexican authority from Texas and limited fighting continued into the early 1840s, Texas had won its independence.

The new republic desired to join the United States and through its president, Sam Houston, asked for recognition, to be followed by annexation. Though President Jackson favored annexation, he proceeded cautiously.

Abolitionism was beginning to make its influence felt in politics. Many Northerners expressed a conviction that it would be immoral to extend the dominion of slavery. Others were opposed to incorporating a region that would add to Southern votes in Congress and in the electoral college. Jackson feared that annexation might cause an ugly sectional controversy and bring on a war with Mexico. He did not, therefore, propose annexation and did not even extend recognition to Texas until just before he left office in 1837. His successor, Van Buren, also refrained, for similar reasons, from pressing the issue.

Refused by the United States, Texas sought recognition, support, and money in Europe. Her leaders talked about creating a vast southwestern nation, stretching to the Pacific, which would be a rival to the United States. It was the kind of talk that Europe, particularly England, was charmed to hear. An independent Texas would be a counterbalance to the United States and a barrier to further American expansion; it would supply cotton for European industry and provide a market for European exports. England and France hastened to recognize Texas and to conclude trade treaties with her. The English government played with the idea of guaranteeing Texan independence. Meanwhile, by 1846, the population of Texas grew to 142,000.

President Tyler, eager to increase Southern power and worried about Texas becoming a British protectorate, persuaded Texas to apply again, and Secretary of State Calhoun submitted an annexation treaty to the Senate in April 1844. Unfortunately for Texas, Calhoun presented annexation as if its only purpose were to extend and protect slavery. The treaty was soundly defeated.

President Tyler, who remained in office until March 1845, viewed the election returns of 1844 as a mandate to carry annexation through. He proposed to Congress that Texas be annexed by a joint resolution of both houses, a device that would get around the necessity of obtaining a two-thirds majority in the Senate for a treaty. In February 1845, Congress voted to admit Texas to the Union. It became a state in December 1845.

Promptly, the Mexican government broke off diplomatic relations with the United States. To make matters worse, a dispute over Texas' boundary with Mexico now developed. The

Texans claimed that the Rio Grande constituted the western and southern border, an assertion that would place much of what is now New Mexico in Texas. Mexico, while not formally conceding the loss of Texas, replied that the border had always been the Nueces River and pointed out that Texans had not settled between the Nueces and the Rio Grande. Polk recognized the Texan claim, and in the summer of 1845 he sent a small army under General Zachary Taylor to the Nueces line and massed a naval force in the Gulf to protect Texas, he said, against the Mexicans.

## Lands Beyond Texas

New Mexico, another of Mexico's frontier provinces, supported a scanty population on a semi-primitive economy. Its small metropolis and trade center, Santa Fe, was 300 miles from the most northern settlements in Mexico. Under Spanish rule the New Mexicans had to export their few products over 1,000 miles to Mexico City and Vera Cruz and from these economic centers import their meager supply of finished goods. When Mexico achieved independence from Spain, she let it be known that traders from the United States would be welcome in New Mexico.

An American wagoned a load of merchandise to Santa Fe in 1821 and sold it at a high profit. Out of his success arose the famous and colorful "Santa Fe trade." Every year traders with a stock of manufactured goods gathered at Independence, Missouri, and traveled in an organized caravan over the Santa Fe Trail, more than 800 miles long. The merchants brought back gold, silver, furs, and mules. The Santa Fe trade opened up another route to the West and pointed another direction for expansion.

Even more distant from Mexico City and even freer from Mexican supervision was the third of the northern provinces, California. In this vast, rich region lived perhaps 100,000 Indians and 3,000 Mexicans, descendants of Spanish colonists, who engaged in agricultural pursuits, chiefly ranching, lived lives of primitive plenty, and carried on a skimpy trade with the outside world.

The first Americans to enter California were maritime traders and captains of ships engaged in whaling or in harvesting sea otters for their furs. Following them came merchants, who established stores, imported merchandise, and conducted a profitable trade in furs, hides, and tallow with the Mexicans and Indians. Thomas O. Larkin, who set up business in Monterey in 1832, soon attained the status of a leading citizen. Although Larkin maintained close and friendly relations with the Mexican authorities, he secretly longed for the day when California would become an American possession. In 1844–1845 he accepted an appointment as United States consul, with instructions to arouse sentiment among the Californians for annexation.

As reports spread of the rich soil and mild climate, immigrants began to enter California from the east by land. These were pioneering farmers, men of the type who were penetrating Texas and Oregon in search of greener pastures. By 1845 there were 700 Americans in California, most of them concentrated in the valley of the Sacramento River and thus removed from the centers of Mexican power on the coast.

President Polk feared that Great Britain wanted to acquire or dominate California as well as Texas — a suspicion that was given credence by the activities of British diplomatic agents in the province. His dreams of expansion went beyond the Democratic platform. He was determined to acquire for his country New Mexico and California and possibly other parts of northern Mexico.

At the same time that he sent Taylor to the Nueces, Polk also sent secret instructions to the commander of the Pacific naval squadron to seize the California ports if he heard that Mexico had declared war. A little later Consul Larkin was informed that, if people wanted to revolt and join the United States, they would be received as brethren. Still later an exploring expedition led by Captain John C. Frémont, of the army's corps of topographical engineers, entered California. The Mexican authorities, alarmed by the size of the party and its military aspects, ordered Frémont to leave. He complied, but moved only over the Oregon border.

## "American Blood"

After preparing measures that looked like war, Polk resolved on a last effort to achieve his objectives by diplomacy. He dispatched to Mexico

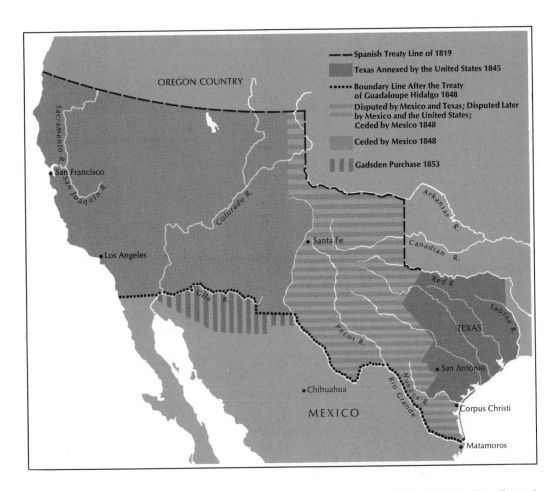

**American Expansion into the Southwest**

a special minister, John Slidell, a Louisiana politician, with instructions to settle with American money all the questions in dispute between the two nations. If Mexico would acknowledge the Rio Grande boundary for Texas, the United States would assume the damage claims, amounting to several millions, which Americans held against Mexico. If she would cede New Mexico, the United States would pay $5 million. And for California, the United States would pay up to $25 million. Slidell soon notified his government that his mission had failed. Immediately after receiving Slidell's information, on January 13, 1846, Polk ordered Taylor's army to move across the Nueces to the Rio Grande.

If Polk was hoping for trouble, he was disappointed for months. Finally, in May, he decided to ask Congress to declare war on the grounds that Mexico had refused to honor its financial

obligations and had insulted the United States by rejecting the Slidell mission. While Polk was working on a war message, the news arrived from Taylor that Mexican troops had crossed the Rio Grande and attacked a unit of American soldiers. Polk now revised his message. He declared: "Mexico has passed the boundary of the United States . . . and shed American blood upon the American soil" — "war exists by the act of Mexico herself." Congress accepted Polk's interpretation of events and on May 13, 1846, declared war by votes of 40 to 2 in the Senate and 174 to 14 in the House.

Although Congress had accepted war with near-unanimity, there was more opposition than appeared on the surface. Opposition increased and intensified as the war continued and costs and casualties came home to the people. The Whigs in Congress supported the military appropriation bills, but they became ever bolder and more bitter in denouncing "Mr. Polk's war" as aggressive in origin and objectives.

## War with Mexico

In the opening phases of the war President Polk assumed the planning of grand strategy, a practice that he continued almost to the end of the war. His basic idea was to seize key areas on the Mexican frontier and then force the Mexicans to make peace on American terms. Accordingly, he ordered Taylor to cross the Rio Grande and occupy northeastern Mexico, taking as his first objective the city of Monterrey. Taylor, "Old Rough and Ready," attacked Monterrey in September 1846 and took it, but at the price of agreeing to let the garrison evacuate without pursuit.

Two other offensives planned by Polk were aimed at New Mexico and California. In the summer of 1846 a small army under Colonel Stephen W. Kearny made the long march to Santa Fe and occupied the town with no opposition. Then he proceeded with a few hundred troopers to California to take charge of operations there. In California a combined revolt and war was being staged by the settlers, Frémont's exploring party, and the American navy. With some difficulty, Kearny brought the disparate American elements under his command, and by the autumn of 1846 completed the conquest of California.

In addition to northeastern Mexico, the United States now had possession of the two provinces for which it had gone to war. In a sense, the objectives of the war had been achieved. The only trouble was that Mexico refused to recognize realities; she would not agree to a peace and cede the desired territory. At this point Polk turned to General Winfield Scott, the commanding general of the army and its finest soldier, for help. Together Polk and Scott devised a plan to force the Mexicans to accept peace. From Vera Cruz, on the Gulf coast, Scott would move west along the National Highway to Mexico City.

While Scott was assembling his army off the coast, General Santa Anna, again in power as Mexican dictator, decided to take advantage of the division of American forces by marching northward and crushing Taylor and then return-

ing to deal with Scott. With an army much larger than Taylor's, Santa Anna attacked the Americans at Buena Vista (February 1847). Santa Anna could not break the American line and had to return to defend Mexico City.

In the meantime Scott had taken Vera Cruz by siege and was moving inland, in one of the most brilliant campaigns in American military annals. With an army than never numbered more than 14,000, he advanced 260 miles into enemy territory, conserved the lives of his soldiers by using flanking movements instead of frontal assaults, and finally achieved his objective without losing a battle. At Cerro Gordo, in the mountains, he inflicted a smashing reverse on the Mexicans. He met no further resistance until he was within a few miles of Mexico City. After capturing the fortress of Chapultepec in a hard fight, the Americans occupied the enemy capital. A new Mexican government came into power, one that recognized the fact of defeat and that was willing to make a peace treaty.

Polk, in his growing anxiety to get the war finished, had sent with the invading army a presidential agent who was authorized to negotiate an agreement. On February 2, 1848, the agent concluded the Treaty of Guadalupe Hidalgo. Mexico agreed to cede California and New Mexico and to acknowledge the Rio Grande boundary of Texas. In return, the United States contracted to assume the claims of its citizens against Mexico and to pay $15 million to Mexico.

## Settlers in the Far West

When the war ended, a portion of the territory acquired from Mexico was already settled by Americans who, ironically, had left their country because they were unhappy there. These people were adherents of a religious sect formally known as the "Church of Jesus Christ of Latter Day Saints" and more commonly known as Mormons. The Mormon faith, one of the numerous new religions that flowered in America in the 1820s and 1830s, had originated in western New York. The Mormons believed in a tightly knit and disciplined community life directed by the church elders. Seeking a more congenial environment, under the leadership of their prophet, Joseph Smith, they moved to Ohio, then to Missouri, and finally to Nauvoo, Illinois. Everywhere they met with resentment, largely caused by their economic and commu-

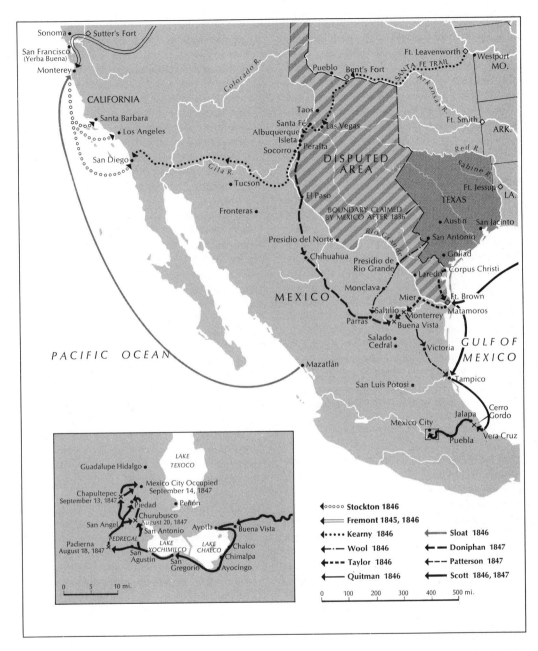

**The Mexican War**

nity organization. At Nauvoo they particularly outraged the opinions of their neighbors by introducing polygamy. Their troubles came to a climax when a mob lynched Smith.

Smith's successor, Brigham Young, now decided that if the Mormons were to escape further persecution they would have to move outside the United States. In 1846 almost the entire Mormon community left Nauvoo. Their destination, picked out by Young, was the Great Salt Lake basin in Utah, so arid that no other people would have the courage to live there. By 1850 over 11,000 people were settled in and around the Mormon metropolis of Salt Lake City. With the aid of irrigation they made the desert bloom. They established thriving industries, and they built up a profitable trade with emigrants on the way to California.

In January 1848, gold was accidentally discovered in the Sacramento Valley in California. As word of the strike spread, inhabitants of California and the whole Far West, fired by hopes of becoming immediate millionaires, stampeded to the area to stake out claims. By the end of summer the news had reached the Eastern states and Europe. Then the gold rush really started. From the United States and all the world, thousands of "Forty-Niners" poured into California. Those who left from the older states could choose between three routes of travel: overland by covered wagon, inexpensive but involving a long journey over the Great Plains and across the Rockies; by ship around Cape Horn, quicker but more expensive; or the dangerous, difficult shortcut across the Isthmus of Panama. By all three routes, disdaining hunger, thirst, disease, and even death, the seekers after gold came—more than 80,000 of them in 1849. By the end of that year, California had a population of approximately 100,000, more than enough to entitle her to statehood.

## Wartime and Postwar Politics

In domestic politics President Polk was as aggressive—and successful—as he was in foreign policy. At his insistence Congress reestablished the Independent Treasury system, thus pleasing all sections of the Democratic party and redeeming one of its platform promises. Again at his demand, Congress fulfilled another platform pledge by lowering the tariff. The Tariff of 1846 reduced the average rates enough to delight the South, but it could not have been passed without the votes of Northwestern Democrats.

Naturally, the Westerners expected something in return, and specifically they expected Southern support for internal improvements. Two internal improvements bills passed Congress, but Polk, who sincerely believed that the national government had no legal power to finance such projects, vetoed both of them. The Westerners were disappointed and angered.

Before Polk left office, a much more dangerous issue emerged. In August 1846, while the

war was in progress, he had asked Congress to provide him with $2 million that he could use to purchase peace with Mexico. When the appropriation was introduced in the House, David Wilmot of Pennsylvania, an antislavery Democrat from a high-tariff state, moved an amendment that slavery should be prohibited in any territory secured from Mexico. The so-called Wilmot Proviso passed the House, but failed in the Senate. It would be called up again and be debated and voted on for years.

Diametrically opposed to the Wilmot Proviso was the formula of the Southern extremists. They contended that the states jointly owned the territories and that the citizens of each state possessed equal rights in them, including the right to move to them with their property, particularly slave property. According to this view, Congress, which was the only agent for the joint owners, had no power to prohibit the movement of slavery into the public domain or to regulate it in any way except by extending protection. Neither could a territorial legislature, which was a creature of Congress, take any action to ban slavery.

Two compromise plans were presented. One, which numbered President Polk among its advocates, proposed to run the Missouri Compromise line of 36° 30′ through the new territories to the Pacific coast, banning slavery north of the line and permitting it south. The other, first prominently espoused by Lewis Cass, Democratic senator from Michigan, was originally called "squatter sovereignty." Later, when taken up by Stephen A. Douglas, an Illinois senator of the same party, it was given the more dignified title of "popular sovereignty." According to this formula, the question of slavery in each territory should be left to the people there, acting through the medium of their territorial legislature.

Congress and the country debated the various formulas, but at the end of Polk's administration no decision had been reached. No territorial government had been provided for California or New Mexico (New Mexico included most of present New Mexico and Arizona, all of Utah and Nevada, and parts of Colorado and Wyoming). Even the organization of Oregon, so far north that obviously slavery would never enter it, was held up by the controversy. Southern members of Congress, hoping to gain some advantage in the regions farther south, blocked a territorial bill for Oregon until August 1848, when a free-soil government was finally authorized.

The debate was partially stilled by the presidential campaign of 1848. Both the Democrats and the Whigs tried to avoid definite and provocative references to the slavery question. The Democrats nominated as their candidate Lewis Cass of Michigan, an elderly, honest, dull wheel horse of the party. Although the platform was purposely vague, it was capable of being interpreted as an endorsement of squatter sovereignty. The Whigs adopted no platform and presented as their candidate a military hero with no political record—General Zachary Taylor of Louisiana.

Ardent abolitionists and even moderates who merely opposed the expansion of slavery found it difficult to swallow either Cass or Taylor. The situation was ripe for the appearance of a third party. The potential sources for such a group were the existing Liberty party and the antislavery members of the old organizations. Late in the campaign, third-party promoters held a national convention, adopted a platform endorsing the Wilmot Proviso, free homesteads, and a higher tariff, and nominated former President Van Buren for the Presidency. Thus was launched the Free-Soil party.

Taylor won a narrow victory. Though Van Buren failed to carry a single state, he polled an impressive 291,000 votes, and the Free-Soilers elected ten members to Congress. It is probable that Van Buren pulled enough Democratic votes away from Cass, particularly in New York, to throw the election to Taylor.

**SELECTED READINGS**

General accounts of economic development are W. E. Brownlee, *Dynamics of Ascent: A History of the American Economy* (1974), and D. C. North, *The Economic Growth of the United States, 1790–1860\** (1961). Labor is treated in Norman Ware, *The Industrial Worker, 1840–1860* (1924), and overseas commerce in S. E. Morison, *The Maritime History of Massachusetts, 1783–1860\** (1921). On transportation and communication, see G. R. Taylor, *The Transportation Revolution, 1815–1860* (1951); R. E. Shaw, *Erie Water West: A History of the Erie Canal, 1792–1854* (1966); J. F. Stover, *American Railroads\** (1961); and R. L. Thompson, *Wiring a Continent* (1947), on the spread of the telegraph. Aspects of urban development are seen in R. G. Albion, *The Rise of New York Port, 1815–1860* (1939), and R. C. Wade, *The Urban Frontier: The Rise of Western Cities, 1790–1830\** (1959). Immigration and nativism are discussed in M. L. Hansen, *The Atlantic Migration, 1607–1860\** (1940); Oscar Handlin, *Boston's Immigrants\** (1941); and P. Taylor, *The Distant Magnet\** (1971).

On Jacksonian politics and democratic trends, see the following: Alexis de Tocqueville, *Democracy in America\** (2 vols., 1945); R. P. McCormick, *The Second American Party System: Party Formation in the Jacksonian Era* (1966); S. F. Bemis, *John Quincy Adams and the Union* (1956); G. G. Van Deusen, *The Jacksonian Era, 1828–1848\** (1959); and A. M. Schlesinger, Jr., *The Age of Jackson\** (1945). See also Lee Benson, *The Concept of Jacksonian Democracy: New York as a Test Case\** (1961), and Edward Pessen, *Jacksonian America* (1970). Indian policy is treated in F. P. Prucha, *American Indian Policy in the Formative Years* (1962), and Grant Foreman, *Indian Removal: The Emigration of the Five Civilized Tribes* (1923); nullification in W. W. Freehling, *Prelude to Civil War: The Nullification Controversy in South Carolina, 1810–1836* (1966), and R. N. Current, *John C. Calhoun\** (1963); and the "bank war" in Bray Hammond, *Banks and Politics in America from the Revolution to the Civil War* (1957); and Peter Temin, *The Jacksonian Economy\** (1969). Whig politics are seen in R. N. Current, *Daniel Webster and the Rise of National Conservatism\** (1955); G. G. Van Deusen, *The Life of Henry Clay\** (1937); and R. G. Gunderson, *The Log Cabin Campaign* (1957).

On cultural trends and the reform spirit, see A. F. Tyler, *Freedom's Ferment: Phases of American Social History to 1860\** (1940); A. A. Ekirch, *The Idea of Progress in America, 1815–1860* (1944); A. M. Schlesinger, *The American as Reformer* (1950); Van Wyck Brooks, *The Flowering of New England, 1815–1865\** (1936); and Carl Bode, *The Anatomy of American Popular Culture, 1840–1861* (1959). The following deal with abolitionist activity: L. F. Litwack, *North of Slavery: The Negro in the Free States, 1790–1860* (1961); Benjamin Quarles, *Black Abolitionists* (1969); Louis Filler, *The Crusade Against Slavery, 1830–1860\** (1960); G. H. Barnes, *The Antislavery Impulse, 1830–1844\** (1933); Bertram Wyatt-Brown, *Lewis Tappan and the Evangelical War Against Slavery* (1969); and R. B. Nye, *William Lloyd Garrison and the Humanitarian Reformers\** (1955). Slavery is the subject of U. B. Phillips, *American Negro Slavery\** (1918); K. M. Stampp, *The Peculiar Institution: Slavery in the Ante-Bellum South\** (1956); S. M. Elkins, *Slavery: A Problem in American Institutional and Intellectual Life\** (1959); A. H. Conrad and J. R. Meyer, *The Economics of Slavery* (1964); E. D. Genovese, *The Political Economy of Slavery\** (1965) and *Roll, Jordan, Roll* (1974); R. W. Fogel and S. L. Engerman, *Time on the Cross, The Economics of American Negro Slavery\** (1974); Herbert G. Gutman; *Slavery and the Numbers Game: A Critique of "Time on the Cross"\** (1975); and Paul A. David *et al., Reckoning with Slavery\** (1976).

On expansion, see the following: R. A. Billington, *The Far Western Frontier, 1830–1860\** (1956); N. A. Graebner, *Empire on the Pacific* (1955); A. K. Weinberg, *Manifest Destiny\** (1935); Bernard De Voto, *The Year of Decision, 1846\** (1943); W. C. Binkley, *The Texas Revolution* (1952); W. J. Ghent, *The Road to Oregon* (1929); Nels Anderson, *Desert Saints: The Mormon Frontier in Utah\** (1942); A. H. Bill, *Rehearsal for Conflict: The War with Mexico, 1846–1848* (1947); O. A. Singletary, *The Mexican War\** (1960); and Frederick Merk, *Slavery and the Annexation of Texas* (1972).

\* Titles available in paperback.

# PART FOUR

# North and South Separate, Fight, and Rejoin, while the Slaves Gain Partial Freedom

George Washington on leaving the Presidency had cautioned his fellow citizens that it might "disturb our Union" if political parties should ever be organized on a geographical basis—Eastern against Western or Northern against Southern—"whence designing men may endeavour to excite a belief that there is a real difference of local interests and views." He explained: "One of the expedients of a party to acquire influence, within particular districts, is to misrepresent the opinions and aims of other districts."

From the beginning the parties had been national, not sectional. From the 1830s on, Whigs from North and South cooperated against Democrats from North and South. Partisan loyalties cut across geographical lines and served as bonds of national union. Then, during the 1850s, the Whig party disintegrated. In the North it was replaced by a new party, the Republican, which had no members in the South. For a while the Democratic party continued to have a nationwide membership, but the party was weakened by sectional strains, and in 1860 it split into Northern and Southern wings. The time was at hand against which George Washington had warned.

No doubt some of the politicians of each section had misrepresented the "opinions and aims" of the other. Still, the sectionalization of parties was due not merely to the influence of "designing men" but also to a "real difference of local interests and views." The breaking of the bonds of union and of the Union itself could hardly have occurred without real and substantial causes—the rise of opposition to slavery on moral grounds, the rapid industrialization of the North, and the westward movement of population. The political disputes that led to national disruption centered on the question of future slavery in the West, not present slavery in the South, but that was largely due to the nature of the American Constitution. Opponents of slavery could hardly contend that the Constitution gave the federal government power to abolish it in the states where it already existed. These people did maintain—though defenders of slavery denied—that the federal government could, and should, prevent its spread to new territories.

After the new Northern party had won a presidential election, the Southern states seceded, and war came. From the seceders' point of view, it was a war for Southern independence. Afterwards (but not at the time) Southerners were to call it "the War between the States," thus implying that secession and resistance to federal authority had been legitimate, constitutional exercises of state rights. Yet the Southerners both during and after the fighting were proud to call themselves "rebels," and from the Northern view they were certainly engaging in rebellion as well as war. The official name that the Union government gave the conflict was "the War of the Rebellion."

This was the first great military experience of the American people. Compared to it the earlier wars—the one with Mexico, the War of 1812, even the Revolutionary struggle itself—were minor and episodic. It has been called the first of modern wars. It involved masses of men and new kinds of technology: railroads and railroad artillery, the telegraph, armored ships, balloons, the Gatling gun (precursor of the machine gun), repeating rifles, trenches, wire entanglements, water and land mines (including what were then called "infernal machines" and would now be known as "booby traps"), torpedo boats, even submarines. It compelled both sides to concentrate a high proportion of their resources on the pursuit of total victory. More than most wars, this one settled some things and settled them permanently. It brought about the destruction of slavery and the preservation of the Union. But it did not settle the question of the precise relationship of the states to the Union or of the blacks to the whites.

When Americans of a later generation looked back on the 1860s and 1870s, it seemed to many of them that there had been a sharp break between the Civil War and the ensuing period of Reconstruction. The war itself, for all its suffering and sacrifice, was remembered on the whole as an ennobling experience, one of high purpose and gallantry on both sides. The postwar years, by contrast, appeared to have been a time of low, unscrupulous politics, a time when vengeful men among the victors disgraced the country while unnecessarily delaying a real, heartfelt reunion of the North and the South.

That view contains elements of historical reality, but it misses an essential truth about the troubled postwar period. The struggle over Reconstruction was, in part, a continuation of the Civil War. It was a struggle, as the war had been, that involved (among other things) the question of both state rights and human rights. The victory for Union and emancipation had not been completely won on the battlefield. In the postwar years an effort was made to confirm the supremacy of the national government over the Southern states and to assure the benefits of freedom to the millions of emancipated slaves. This effort, provoking resistance as it did, had the effect of keeping the country psychologically divided.

The struggle over Reconstruction ended in the Compromise of 1877. This arrangement, a combination of "reunion and reaction," brought the sections together at the expense of the black people. The federal government gave up the attempt to enforce the Negro's rights and left the Southern states in the hands of conservative whites. Yet two great charters of human liberty still stood as documents of the Reconstruction era—the Fourteenth and Fifteenth amendments to the federal Constitution—which had been intended to assure citizenship and the suffrage to the former slaves. For the time being, these documents were disregarded, but a day was to come, several decades later, when they would provide the legal basis for a renewed drive to bring true freedom and equality to all Americans.

# Chapter 13.   THE ROAD TO DISUNION

## Taylor and the Territories

Zachary Taylor was the first man to be elected President with no previous political training or experience. He was also the first professional soldier to sit in the White House. Although he came from the South and was a slaveholder, Taylor was a Southerner only in a technical sense. From his long years in the army he had acquired a national outlook and an attachment to the concept of nationalism.

He had to face immediately the problem of providing civil government for the area annexed from Mexico, which was being administered by military officials who were responsible to the President. The old soldier had a penchant for simple solutions, and a ready answer came to him—statehood for these territories. Statehood would not only provide civil government but prevent a controversy over slavery in the territories, because it was universally conceded that a territory on becoming a state could do whatever it wanted about slavery. Therefore, after assuming office in March 1849, he encouraged California and also New Mexico to frame constitutions and apply for statehood.

California needed no prodding; by October the Californians had prepared and ratified a constitution in which slavery was prohibited. Without waiting for congressional approval of their work, as required by law, they elected a state government and representatives to Congress. New Mexico, with a smaller population and less pressing governmental problems, moved more slowly, but prepared to call a constitutional convention. When Congress assembled in December 1849, Taylor proudly described his efforts, and recommended that California be admitted as a free state and that New Mexico, when she was ready, be permitted to come in with complete freedom to decide the status of slavery.

Immediately it became apparent that Congress was not going to accept the President's program. For one reason, the legislative branch felt a natural jealousy of the power of the execu-tive, a feeling that had been increasing since Jackson's time; many legislators believed Taylor should have consulted Congress before acting.

Simultaneously a number of side issues emerged to worsen the situation. One of them arose out of the demand of the antislavery forces that slavery be abolished in the District of Columbia, a demand that was angrily resisted by Southerners. Another concerned the "personal liberty" laws enacted by many Northern states, laws that forbade their courts and police officers to assist in the return of fugitive slaves. In retaliation, some Southerners were calling for a stringent *national* fugitive slave law.

A third issue related to the boundary between Texas and New Mexico. Texas claimed the portion of New Mexico east of the Rio Grande, although the national government had assigned this region to New Mexico. Texans resented this action and also the government's refusal to assume the Texas war debt. Southern extremists supported the pretensions of Texas, while their fellows in the North upheld New Mexico.

Finally, there was the fear felt by the South at the prospect of two new free states being added to the Northern majority. In the structure of the national government the South retained an equal voice only in the Senate. The number of free and slave states was equal in 1849; there were fifteen of each. But now the admission of California would upset the balance and deprive the South of its last constitutional protection—and New Mexico, Oregon, and Utah were yet to come!

Responsible Southern leaders declared that if California was to be admitted, and if slavery was to be prohibited in the territories, the time had come for the South to secede from the Union. At the suggestion of Mississippi, a call went out for a Southern-rights convention to meet in June 1850 at Nashville, Tennessee, to consider whether the South should resort to secession. In the North excitement ran equally high. Every Northern state legislature but one adopted resolutions demanding that slavery be barred from the territories; public meetings all through the

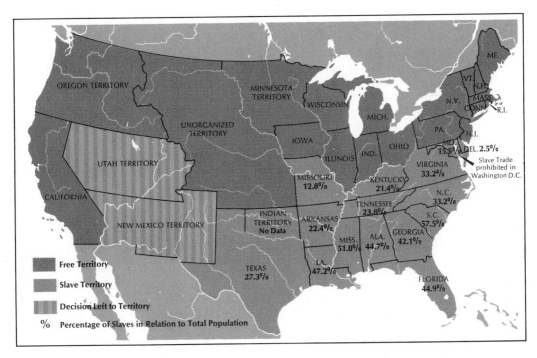

**Slave and Free Territory   1850**

free states called for the Wilmot Proviso and the abolition of slavery in the District of Columbia.

## The Compromise of 1850

As the crisis worsened, moderate men in Congress naturally turned their thoughts to the framing of a compromise that would satisfy both sections and restore tranquility, and for a leader they turned to Henry Clay, the venerable Kentuckian. Clay believed that no compromise would have any significant or lasting effects unless it settled all the issues in dispute between the sections. Accordingly, he took a number of separate measures which had been proposed by various members of both parties and combined them into one set of resolutions which on January 29, 1850, he presented to the Senate. His proposals were as follows: (a) that California be admitted as a free state; (b) that, in the rest of the Mexican cession, territorial governments be formed without restrictions as to slavery; (c) that Texas yield in her boundary dispute with New Mexico and be compensated by the federal government's taking over her public debt; (d)

that the slave trade, but not slavery itself, be abolished in the District of Columbia; and (e) that a new and more effective fugitive-slave law be passed.

These resolutions started a debate which raged for months in Congress and throughout the country. Clay himself opened the oratorical tournament with a defense of his measures and a plea to North and South to be mutually conciliatory and forebearing.

Early in March, John C. Calhoun, who had less than a month to live, presented the views of the Southern extremists. Too ill and weak to speak, he sat grimly in his seat while a colleague read his speech. Almost ignoring Clay's proposals, he devoted his argument to what to him was the larger and the only subject—the minority South—and he asked more for his section than could be given. The North must admit that the South possessed equal rights in the territories, must agree to observe the laws concerning fugitive slaves, must cease attacking slavery, and must accept an amendment to the Constitution guaranteeing a balance of power between the sections.

After Calhoun came the third of the elder statesmen, Daniel Webster. His "Seventh of

March address" was probably the greatest forensic effort of his long oratorical career. Although he still nourished White House ambitions, he now sought to calm angry passions and to rally Northern moderates to support of compromise, even at the risk of alienating the strong antislavery sentiment of his native New England.

Other speakers now entered the debate. Some recommended popular sovereignty; others advocated extending the Missouri Compromise line. Of particular import were the views of the Northern extremists, voiced by the New York Whig William H. Seward. There was a higher law than the Constitution, Seward proclaimed, the law of God, which required men to oppose slavery.

After most of the speeches had been made, Clay's resolutions were referred to a special committee, headed by Clay, which was to frame them into acceptable laws and report back to the Senate. When the bills were introduced, popular sentiment in all sections was slowly swinging in favor of some kind of compromise. The country was entering upon a period of prosperity, and conservative economic interests everywhere wanted to terminate the sectional dispute and concentrate the attention of the nation upon internal expansion. Even in the South excitement seemed to be abating. The Nashville convention met in June, and after adopting some tame resolutions adjourned to await final action by Congress.

For a time, however, it seemed that Congress was not going to act. One reason was the opposition of Taylor. The President persisted in his stand that the admission of California, and possibly New Mexico, must come first and alone; after that, it might be possible to discuss other measures. In the meantime, if the South wanted to try anything like secession, "Old Zack" was ready to use force against his native section and to lead the armed forces in person.

On July 9, President Taylor suddenly died, the victim of a violent stomach disorder following an attack of heat prostration. He was succeeded by the Vice President, Millard Fillmore of New York. The new chief executive was a practical politician who understood the importance of compromise in statecraft. At once he ranged himself on the side of the advocates of adjustment, using his powers of persuasion and patronage to swing Northern Whigs into line. At about the same time, Clay, exhausted by his labors, temporarily left Congress, and Stephen A. Douglas took over the leadership of the compromise forces. Discarding the Kentuckian's all-or-nothing strategy, Douglas broke up the various measures reported by Clay's committee, and presented them one by one. By mid-September the series of measures had been enacted by both houses of Congress and signed by the President.

It was one thing to pass the Compromise through Congress and another to persuade the country to accept it. In the North the task of winning popular acceptance was easier than in the South. The only provision that really gagged Northern opinion was the Fugitive Slave Act. By this measure, a Negro accused of being a runaway was denied trial by jury and the right to testify in his own behalf. His status was to be decided by a federal judge or by a special commissioner appointed by the federal circuit courts. He could be remanded to slavery on the bare evidence of an affidavit presented by the man who claimed to be his owner.

The advocates of the Compromise in the South had to fight hard to carry the day. The adjourned session of the Nashville convention met in November 1850 (with only about a third of the original delegates present) and condemned the Compromise. Eventually, the South brought itself to accept the Compromise, but only after much agonizing, and then only conditionally. Several states declared that if in the future Southern rights were denied, the section would have to consider secession.

## Renewed Agitation

At their national convention in 1852 the Democrats adopted a platform pledging their devotion to the Compromise of 1850 and their opposition to all attempts to renew the agitation of the slavery question. Not so unanimous when it came to choosing a candidate, they wrangled through forty-nine ballots, with no one of the leading contenders — Cass, Douglas, or James Buchanan of Pennsylvania — being able to secure a two-thirds majority. Finally, the prize went to one of the more obscure aspirants, Franklin Pierce of New Hampshire. The Whigs likewise endorsed the Compromise but in much milder terms and over the opposition of many antislavery, or

"Conscience," Whigs. Instead of nominating a man connected with the Compromise, they named General Winfield Scott, whose views were unknown and whose support by Northern delegates made him suspect to Southerners. Only the Free Soilers, with John P. Hale of New Hampshire as their candidate, repudiated the Compromise.

Probably because they had taken the strongest stand in its favor, the Democrats won at the polls. Pierce carried twenty-seven states and Scott four, and the Democrats got 254 electoral votes to the Whigs' 42—the largest majority that any candidate had attained since Monroe's victory in 1820. The Free Soilers received only about half the number of votes they had polled in 1848.

When Franklin Pierce was inaugurated in 1853, he was, at the age of forty-nine, the youngest man up to that time to become President. Amiable and charming, he had been selected as the Democratic nominee largely for reasons of party harmony. In his short political career he had upheld few opinions and made few enemies. He was to make many enemies as President.

The Compromise did not dissolve the abolitionist organizations nor stop their crusade to convince the Northern masses that slavery was a sin. In the 1850s the abolitionists intensified their efforts and found a growing audience.

The most powerful, the most telling document in the abolitionist propaganda attack was a novel, *Uncle Tom's Cabin,* written by Harriet Beecher Stowe and published in 1852. Mrs. Stowe belonged to a famous New England ministerial family (her father and her seven brothers were preachers), and she had married a minister. For several years she had lived in Cincinnati, and from there had made several forays into Kentucky to view slavery and plantation life. Her novel, written after she and her husband had left Cincinnati for Maine, was an indictment of slavery although not of the slaveholders; her purpose was to show that the slave system had a brutalizing effect on all who were connected with it.

The book had a terrific impact on the Northern mind. Other abolitionists had attacked slavery in the abstract or as an evil institution, but Mrs. Stowe assailed it in terms of human personalities. In such a form, her message appealed to emotions and sympathies as nothing had done

before, and it inspired other similar novels. The book sold over 300,000 copies in its year of publication. Dramatized, it reached other thousands who attended the play.

Northern hostility to the new Fugitive Slave Act was intensified when Southerners appeared in the Northern states to pursue fugitives or to claim as slaves Negroes who had been living for years in Northern communities. Mobs attempted to impede enforcement of the law. In 1851 a crowd in Boston took from a federal marshal a runaway named Shadrach and sent him on his way to Canada. Later there were similar rescues or rescue attempts in other places throughout the North.

These displays of violence alarmed the South, and so did the new personal-liberty laws passed by several Northern legislatures. The frank purpose of the statutes was to nullify the Fugitive Slave Act. They interposed state power between the accused fugitive and the federal authority. In Wisconsin and Massachusetts, state courts were instructed to issue writs of habeas corpus (requiring an appearance before a judge) against any person detaining a fugitive and to grant the fugitive a judicial hearing in which the burden of proof was placed on the pursuer. The supreme court of Wisconsin, in the case of *Ableman* v. *Booth* (1857), declared the national law void. When the Supreme Court of the nation decided against the state, the Wisconsin court ignored the decision. Thus legal and judicial barriers were being thrown in the way of the one provision of the Compromise that the South considered a positive victory, and Southerners were deeply angered.

## "Young America"

In Europe the great liberal and nationalist revolutions of 1848 were running their course, some succeeding, others petering out in failure. A vision of a republican Europe, with governments to be based on the model of the United States, stirred the American imagination. A group of Democrats started a "Young America" movement with vague ideas of aiding revolutionaries abroad. These adventurous, romantic Democrats also aimed to promote American commerce in the Pacific and elsewhere and to extend the sweep of Manifest Destiny with new acquisitions in this hemisphere. Other politicians in both parties caught the "Young America" spirit, and it influenced the foreign policies of both the Fillmore and the Pierce administrations. At first these aggressive policies abroad were intended to offset the divisive, sectional feelings at home. Before long, however, the interest in additional territories complicated the relations between the sections as well as the relations between the United States and foreign governments.

Showing concern for Pacific commerce, the Fillmore administration sent out an expedition under Commodore Matthew C. Perry to open trade relations with Japan, which for two centuries had been a hermit nation. Perry touched at Japan in 1853 and reappeared there the following year with an impressive display of naval might. He obtained a treaty opening two ports and providing for the residence of an American consul in one of them. The first consul, Townsend Harris, after years of patient labor, secured a new treaty (1858) with additional trading rights.

The Fillmore administration was cautious about American schemes for taking Cuba, the rich "pearl of the Antilles," which Polk once had tried to purchase from Spain. Later a Venezuelan adventurer, General Narciso López, proposed to conquer the island with a force of American volunteers and present it to the United States. On his third attempt, in 1851, López landed in Cuba with about 400 men, mostly Americans, but ran into a much stronger army of Spaniards. They defeated and captured him and most of his followers, then executed him and more than fifty others.

The Pierce administration, though more aggressive than its predecessor, was frustrated in its expansionist hopes because of sectional jealousies. Schemes to get new slave territories aroused opposition in the North, and the acquisition of lands unsuited to slavery was unpopular in the South. Though the kingdom of Hawaii agreed to join the United States (1854), the annexation treaty had no chance for Senate approval, since it contained a clause prohibiting slavery.

The old idea of adding Canada to the United States had never died out among Americans, and it was beginning to appeal to more and more Canadians. Some of them saw a union as the only way out of their economic difficulties. As a result of British free-trade policy (after 1846) and the American tariff, Canadians had lost much of their export trade. Annexation would open the American market to them. To deal with Canada's economic problem, and to settle a revived quarrel over American fishing rights along the Newfoundland and Labrador coasts, the British government sent Lord Elgin on a special mission to Washington in 1854. Lord Elgin and Secretary of State William L. Marcy negotiated a treaty specifying fishing rights and providing for tariff reciprocity. Canada was to accept certain American commodities, and the United States certain Canadian commodities, duty free. Thus Canadians, without annexation, would have access to American markets. The Elgin Treaty was promptly ratified. A Vermont senator explained that many of his fellow senators, those from the South, had been in a hurry to head off the union movement.

Meanwhile the Pierce administration had made all too clear its determination to obtain Cuba. In 1854 Secretary Marcy instructed the minister to Spain, Pierre Soulé of Louisiana, to make a new offer to buy the island. If this was refused he was to try to "detach" Cuba from Spain. Soulé was plotting with Spanish revolutionaries to overthrow the Spanish monarchy when he received new instructions: he was to consult with the ministers to England and France, James Buchanan and John Y. Mason. The three embodied their recommendations in a diplomatic dispatch that shortly found its way into the newspapers and became notorious as the Ostend Manifesto. This remarkable document stated that if Spain should persist in refusing to sell Cuba, and if disturbances there should threaten American security, the United States would be justified in "wresting" the island from Spain.

Antislavery Northerners now charged the administration with violating the spirit of the Compromise of 1850. They said that Pierce, acting as the tool of the South, was conspiring to bring in a new slave state even at the risk of war with Spain and other European powers.

## The Kansas-Nebraska Act

By the 1850s the line of frontier settlement had reached the great bend of the Missouri. Beyond the western boundaries of Minnesota, Iowa, and Missouri stretched the vast expanse of plains earlier called the Great American Desert and designated as an Indian reserve. Now it was known that large sections of this region were suited to farming, and in the Northwest people were saying that the national government should open the area to settlement and provide it with a railroad.

The idea of a transcontinental railroad had been discussed in and out of Congress for years and found wide approval in principle. Disagreement arose when people talked about the eastern terminus of the road and its specific route. Several cities pressed their claims, but the leading contenders were Chicago, St. Louis, Memphis, and New Orleans. The transcontinental railroad, like nearly everything else in the fifties, became entangled in sectionalism. People talked about a "southern road" or a "northern road."

One argument against a southern route had been removed through the foresight of Secretary of War Jefferson Davis. Surveys had indicated that a road from a southern terminus would probably have to pass through an area south of the Gila River, in Mexican territory. At Davis' suggestion, Pierce appointed James Gadsden, a Southern railroad builder, to negotiate with Mexico for the sale of this region. Gadsden persuaded the Mexican government to dispose of a strip of land that today comprises a part of Arizona and New Mexico, the so-called Gadsden Purchase (1853), which cost the United States $10 million.

The leading advocate of a northern route was Senator Stephen A. Douglas, and his interest influenced him to introduce in Congress a fateful legislative act, one that accomplished the final destruction of the truce of 1850. As a Senator from Illinois and a resident of Chicago and, above all, as the acknowledged leader of the Northwestern Democrats, Douglas naturally wanted the transcontinental railroad for his own city and section. He realized too the potency of the principal argument urged against the northern route: that west of the Mississippi it would run largely through unsettled Indian country. Hence in January 1854 he introduced a bill to organize a huge new territory, to be known as Nebraska, west of Iowa and Missouri.

Douglas seemed to realize that his bill would encounter the opposition of the South, partly because it would prepare the way for a new free state, the proposed territory being in the Louisiana Purchase area north of the 36° 30′ line of the Missouri Compromise and hence closed to slavery. In an effort to make the measure acceptable to Southerners, Douglas inserted a provision that the status of slavery in the territory would be determined by the territorial legislature, that is, by popular sovereignty. The concession was not enough to satisfy extreme Southern Democrats, particularly those from Missouri who feared that their state would be surrounded by free territory. They demanded more, and Douglas had to give more to get their support. He agreed to a clause specifically repealing the territorial section of the Missouri Compromise and to a provision creating two territories, Nebraska and Kansas, instead of one. Presumably the latter, because of its more southern location, would become a slave state. In its final form the measure was known as the Kansas-Nebraska Act.

Douglas induced President Pierce to endorse his bill, and so it became an offical Democratic measure. But even with the backing of the administration, it encountered stiff opposition and did not become a law until May 1854. Nearly all the Southern members of Congress, whether Whigs or Democrats, supported the bill, and nearly all the Northern Whigs opposed it. The Northern Democrats split, with half of their votes in the House going for the act and half against it.

Probably no other piece of legislation in congressional history produced as many immediate, sweeping, and ominous changes as the Kansas-Nebraska Act. It destroyed the Whig party in the South except in the border states. At the same time, as many Southern Whigs became Democrats, it increased Southern influence in the Democratic party. It destroyed the popular basis of Whiggery in the North, with the result that by 1856 the national Whig party had disappeared and a conservative influence in American politics had been removed. It divided the Northern Democrats and drove many of them from the party. Most important of all, it called into being a new party that was frankly sectional in composition and creed.

Men in both the major parties who opposed Douglas' bill took to calling themselves Anti-Nebraska Democrats and Anti-Nebraska Whigs. In their anger at the South they were in a mood to defend their opinions by forming a new party. And in 1854 this took form—the Republican party. Originating in a series of spontaneous popular meetings throughout the Northwest, the Republican movement soon spread to the East. In the elections of 1854 the Republicans, often acting in concert with the Know-Nothings, elected a majority to the House and won control of a number of Northern state governments. For the moment the new party was a one-idea organization: its only platform was opposition to the expansion of slavery into the territories. Composed mainly of former Whigs and Free Soilers but including also a substantial number of former Democrats, it represented in large part the democratic idealism of the North. But it contained, in addition, Northern power groups who felt that the South — the champion of a low tariff, the enemy of homesteads and internal improvements — was blocking their legitimate economic aspirations.

## "Bleeding Kansas"

The pulsing popular excitement aroused in the North by the Kansas-Nebraska Act was sustained by events occurring during the next two years in Kansas. Almost immediately settlers moved into this territory. Many of them came to Kansas simply to make homes. But there were some who came for the specific purpose of engaging in a struggle over ideologies. They were dedicated men who were determined to make Kansas free — or slave. Those who came from the North were encouraged by press and pulpit and the powerful organs of abolitionist propaganda; often they received financial help from antislavery organizations. Those who came from the South were stimulated by similar influences of a Southern nature; often they received financial contributions from the communities they had left.

In the spring of 1855 elections were held for a territorial legislature. Thousands of Missourians, some traveling in armed bands, moved into Kansas and voted. Although there were probably only some 1,500 legal votes in the territory, over 6,000 votes were counted. With such conditions prevailing, the proslavery forces elected a majority to the legislature, which proceeded immediately to enact a series of laws legalizing slavery. The outraged free-staters, convinced that they could not get a fair deal from the Pierce administration, resolved on extralegal action. Without asking permission from Congress or the territorial governor, they elected delegates to a constitutional convention which met at Topeka and adopted a constitution excluding slavery. They then chose a governor and legislature, and petitioned Congress for statehood. Pierce stigmatized their movement as

unlawful and declared that the government would support the proslavery territorial legislature.

A few months later a proslavery federal marshal assembled a huge posse, consisting mostly of Missourians, to arrest the free-state leaders in Lawrence. The posse not only made the arrests but sacked the town. Retribution came immediately. Among the more extreme antislavery men was a fierce, fanatical old man named John Brown who considered himself an instrument of God's will to destroy slavery. Estimating that five antislavery men had been murdered, he decided that it was his sacred duty to take revenge. He gathered six followers, and in one night murdered five proslavery settlers (the "Pottawatomie massacre"). The result was to touch off civil war in Kansas — irregular, guerrilla war conducted by armed bands, some of them more interested in land claims or loot than in ideologies. People all over the country talked about "Bleeding Kansas."

In May 1856 Charles Sumner of Massachusetts arose in the Senate to discuss affairs in the strife-torn territory. He entitled his speech "The Crime against Kansas." Sincere, doctrinaire, Sumner embodied the extreme element of the political antislavery movement. In his address he fiercely denounced the Pierce administration, the South, and slavery; and he singled out for particular attention as a champion of slavery Senator Andrew P. Butler of South Carolina.

Particularly enraged by the attack was Butler's nephew, Preston Brooks, a member of the House from South Carolina. He resolved to punish Sumner by a method approved by the Southern code — by publicly and physically chastising the Senator. Approaching Sumner at his desk when the Senate was not in session, he proceeded to beat his kinsman's traducer with a cane until Sumner fell to the floor in bloody unconsciousness. The injured Senator stayed out of the Senate four years, and during his absence his state refused to elect a successor. Brooks, censured by the House, resigned and stood for reelection. He was returned by an almost unanimous vote.

The violence in Congress, like that in Kansas, was a symbol. It showed that Americans were becoming so agitated by their differences that they could not settle them by the normal political processes of debate and the ballot.

## Buchanan and Sectional Politics

The presidential campaign of 1856 got under way with the country convulsed by the Brooks assault and the continuing violence in Kansas. The Democrats adopted a platform that endorsed the Kansas-Nebraska Act and defended popular sovereignty. The leaders wanted a candidate who had not made many enemies and who was not closely associated with the explosive question of "Bleeding Kansas." So the nomination went to James Buchanan of Pennsylvania, a reliable party stalwart who had been minister to England and hence had been safely out of the country during the recent troubles.

The Republicans, engaging in their first presidential contest, faced the campaign with confidence. They denounced the Kansas-Nebraska Act and the expansion of slavery but also approved a program of internal improvements, thus beginning to combine the idealism of antislavery with the economic aspirations of the North. Just as eager as the Democrats to present a safe candidate, the Republicans nominated John C. Frémont, who had made a national reputation as an explorer of the Far West, and who had no political record and hence was highly available.

The American, or Know-Nothing, party was beginning to break apart on the inevitable rock of sectionalism. At its convention, many Northern delegates withdrew because the platform was not sufficiently firm in opposing the expansion of slavery. The remaining delegates nominated ex-President Millard Fillmore. His candidacy was endorsed by the sad remnant of another party, the few remaining Whigs who could not bring themselves to support either Buchanan or Frémont.

The results of the election seemed to indicate that the prevailing mood of the country was conservative. Buchanan carried all the slave states except Maryland (whose eight votes went to Fillmore) and five Northern states (Illinois, Indiana, New Jersey, Pennsylvania, and California). Frémont won the other eleven Northern states, and he received a large minority vote in the five states carried by Buchanan. In fact, his popular vote was only 400,000 less than Buchanan's.

James Buchanan had been in politics and in public office almost continuously since he was twenty-three years old. At the time of his inauguration he was nearly sixty-six, the oldest President, with the exception of Harrison, that the country has had. Undoubtedly his age and general physical infirmity had something to do with the indecision he often displayed. He seemed to be obsessed by one idea — to meet every crisis by giving the South what it wanted.

In the year Buchanan took office, a financial panic struck the American economy, but the following depression, instead of drawing the nation closer together in a sense of common misfortune, sharpened sectional differences. The South was not hit as hard as the North. The result was to confirm the opinion of Southern leaders that their economic system was superior to that of the free states; and, smarting under previous Northern criticisms of Southern society, they loudly boasted to the North of their superiority.

In the North the impact of the depression had the effect of strengthening the sectional Republican party. Distressed economic groups — manufacturers and farmers — came to believe that the depression had been caused by unsound policies forced upon the government by Southern-controlled Democratic administrations. They thought that prosperity could be restored by a program embracing such items as a high tariff (the tariff was lowered again in 1857), a homestead act, and internal improvements — all measures to which the South was opposed. Northern resentment at what seemed to be Southern restraint of the nation's economic future was one important reason why the Democrats lost their majority in the House in the election of 1858.

## The Dred Scott Case

Two days after Buchanan was inaugurated, the Supreme Court of the United States projected itself into the sectional controversy with its decision in the case of *Dred Scott v. Sanford.*

Dred Scott was a Missouri slave, once the property of an army surgeon, who on his military pilgrimages had carried him to Illinois, a free state, and to Minnesota Territory, where slavery was forbidden by the Missouri Compromise. Eventually both the owner and the slave returned to Missouri, where the surgeon died. Scott was persuaded by some abolitionists to bring suit in the Missouri courts for his freedom on the ground that residence in a free territory made him a free man. The state supreme court decided against him, but meanwhile the officer's widow had married an abolitionist. Her brother, J. F. A. Sanford, a New Yorker, became executor of her estate. Since Sanford was a citizen of another state, Scott's lawyers were able to get his case into the federal courts with the claim that the suit lay between citizens of different states. Regardless of the final decision, Scott would be freed, as his abolitionist owners would not keep him a slave. The case was intended to secure a federal decision on the status of slavery in the territories.

Of the nine justices, seven were Democrats (five of them from the South), one was a Whig, and one was a Republican. Chief Justice Taney, in the majority opinion, announced two important principles. First, the Chief Justice declared that Scott was not a citizen of Missouri and hence could not bring a suit in the federal courts. Second, Scott's residence in territory north of the Missouri Compromise line had not made him free. Slaves were property, said Taney, and the Fifth Amendment prohibited Congress from taking property without "due process of law." Consequently, Congress possessed no authority to pass a law depriving persons of their slave property in the territories. The Missouri Compromise, therefore, had always been null and void.

Few judicial opinions have stirred as much popular excitement as this one. Southerners were elated: the highest tribunal in the land had invested with legal sanction the extreme Southern argument. Republicans denounced the decision as a partisan opinion by a partisan body. As for settling the status of slavery in the territories, that section of the opinion was an *obiter dictum* and had no legal justification. Boldly the Republicans announced that when they secured control of the national government they would reverse the decision – by altering the personnel of the Court.

## Kansas Again

President Buchanan, who had known in advance the nature of the Dred Scott decision (having been tipped off by two of the Justices), had said in his inaugural address that he hoped the forthcoming opinion would end the agitation over slavery in the territories. With equal blindness, he decided that the best solution for the Kansas troubles was to force the admission of that territory as a slave state.

The existing proslavery territorial legislature called an election for delegates to a constitutional convention. The free-state people refused to participate. As a result, the proslavery forces won control of the convention, which met in 1857 at Lecompton and framed a constitution establishing slavery. When an election for a new territorial legislature was called, the antislavery groups turned out to vote and won a majority. Promptly the legislature moved to submit the Lecompton constitution to the voters. The document was rejected by more than 10,000 votes. The picture in Kansas was now clear enough. The majority of the people did not want to see slavery established. Unfortunately Buchanan could not see, or did not want to see, the true picture. He urged Congress to admit Kansas under the Lecompton constitution, and he tried to force the party to back his proposal. Douglas and other Western Democrats refused to accept this perversion of popular sovereignty. Openly breaking with the administration, Douglas denounced the Lecompton proposition. And although Buchanan's plan passed the Senate, Western Democrats helped to block it in the House. Partly to avert further division in the party, a compromise measure, the English bill, was offered (1858) and passed. It provided that the Lecompton constitution should be submitted to the people of Kansas for a third time. If the document was approved, Kansas was to be admitted and given a federal land grant; if it was disapproved, statehood would be postponed until the population reached 93,600, the legal minimum for a representative in Congress. Again, and for the last time, the Kansas voters decisively rejected the Lecompton constitution. Not until the closing months of Buchanan's administration, in 1861, when a number of Southern states had withdrawn from the Union, would Kansas enter the Union – as a free state.

## Lincoln Against Douglas

The congressional elections of 1858 were unusually hard fought. The contest that excited the widest public attention was the senatorial election in Illinois. There Stephen A. Douglas, the most prominent Northern Democrat, was a candidate for reelection, and he was fighting for his political life. He faced a Republican opponent who was an exceptionally able campaigner, Abraham Lincoln.

Lincoln had been the leading Whig in Illinois. After the passage of the Kansas-Nebraska Act he had, after some hesitation, joined the new party, and he was now the leading Republican in his state. But because he was not as well known as Douglas, Lincoln challenged the Senator to a series of seven joint debates. Douglas accepted, and the two candidates argued their cases before huge crowds in every congressional district in the state. The Lincoln-Douglas debates, as the oratorical jousts came to be known, were widely reported by the nation's press, and before their termination the Republican who had dared to challenge the "Little Giant" was a man of national prominence.

Douglas devoted his principal efforts to defending popular sovereignty and attacking the Republicans. Popular sovereignty was a democratic way of settling the slavery issue in the territories, he said. Although his formula would keep slavery out of the territories, he did not seem to think it was important to call the institution wrong.

Lincoln, for his part, wanted not only to bar slavery from the territories but also to call it wrong. If slavery was prevented from expanding into the territories, he claimed, it would eventually die a natural death.

In the debate at Freeport, Lincoln asked Douglas a question which made this meeting historically the most significant of all the debates. His query was: Can the people of a territory exclude slavery from its limits prior to the formation of a state constitution? Or in other words, is popular sovereignty still a legal formula despite the Dred Scott decision? The question was a trap, for no matter how Douglas answered it, he would lose something. If he disavowed popular sovereignty he would undoubtedly be defeated for reelection and his political career would be ended. But if he reaffirmed his formula, Southern Democrats would be offended, the party split deepened, and his chances of securing the Democratic nomination in 1860 damaged if not destroyed.

Boldly Douglas met the issue. The people of a territory, he said, could, by lawful means, shut out slavery prior to the formation of a state constitution. Slavery could not exist a day without the support of "local police regulations": that is, without territorial laws supporting slave ownership. The mere failure of a legislature to enact such laws would have the practical effect of keeping slaveholders out. Thus a territory could

still exclude slavery. Douglas' reply became known as the Freeport Doctrine or, in the South, as the Freeport Heresy. It satisfied his followers sufficiently to win him a return to the Senate, but throughout the North it aroused little enthusiasm.

The elections went heavily against the Democrats, who lost ground in almost every Northern state. The administration retained control of the Senate but lost its majority in the House, where the Republicans gained a plurality. The rise of Republican strength was another frightening manifestation to the South.

## John Brown's Raid

But more frightening was an event occurring in 1859. John Brown, the grim fanatic of the Pottawatomie killings, now made a spectacular appearance on the national scene. Still convinced that he was God's instrument to destroy slavery, he decided to transfer his activities from Kansas to the South itself. With encouragement and financial aid from certain Eastern abolitionists, he devised a wild scheme to liberate the slaves. His plan was to seize a mountain fortress in Virginia from which he could make raids to free slaves; he would organize his freedmen, whom he intended to arm, into a Negro state within the South, and eventually he would force the South to concede emancipation. Because he needed guns, Brown fixed on Harpers Ferry, where a United States arsenal was located, as his base of operations. In October, at the head of eighteen followers, he descended on the town and captured the arsenal. Almost immediately he was attacked by citizens and local militia companies, who were shortly reinforced by a detachment of United States marines sent to the scene by the national government. With ten of his men killed, Brown had to surrender. He was promptly tried in a Virginia court for treason against the state, found guilty, and sentenced to death by hanging. Six of his followers met a similar fate.

Probably no single event had as much influence as the Brown raid in convincing Southerners that the welfare of their section was unsafe in the Union. Despite all the eulogies of slavery they penned, one great fear always secretly gnawed at their hearts: the possibility of a general slave insurrection. But now it seemed that such an uprising might be encouraged by men in the North, specifically by Republicans.

# Chapter 14.  THE NATION DIVIDED

## The Great Decision of 1860

The election of 1860, judged by its consequences, was the most momentous in our history.

As the Democrats gathered in convention at Charleston, South Carolina, in April, most of the Southern delegates came with the determination to adopt a platform providing for federal protection of slavery in the territories. The Western Democrats were angered at the rule-or-ruin attitude of the Southerners, but hoped to negotiate a face-saving statement on slavery that would hold the party together. They vaguely endorsed popular sovereignty and proposed that all questions involving slavery in the territories be left up to the Supreme Court. When the convention adopted the Western platform, the delegations from eight Lower South states withdrew from the hall. The remaining delegates then proceeded to the selection of a candidate. Stephen A. Douglas led on every ballot, but he could not muster the two-thirds majority (of the original number of delegates) required by party rules. Finally the managers adjourned the convention to meet again in Baltimore in June. At Baltimore most of the Southerners reappeared, only to walk out again. The rest of the Southerners had assembled at Richmond. The rump convention at Baltimore nominated Douglas. The Southern bolters at Baltimore and the men in Richmond nominated John C. Breckinridge of Kentucky. There were now two Democratic candidates in the field, and, although Douglas had supporters in the South and Breckinridge in the North, one was the nominee of the Northern Democrats and the other of the Southern Democrats.

The Republicans held their convention in Chicago in May. The party managers were determined that the party, in both its platform and its candidate, should appear to the voters as representing conservatism, stability, and moderation. No longer was the Republican party a one-idea organization composed of crusaders against slavery. It now embraced, or hoped to embrace, every major interest group in the North that believed that the South, the champion of slavery, was blocking its legitimate economic aspirations.

The platform endorsed such measures as a high tariff, internal improvements, a homestead bill, and a Pacific railroad to be built with federal financial assistance. On the slavery issue, the Republicans affirmed the right of each state to control its own institutions. But they also denied the authority of Congress or of a territorial legislature to legalize slavery in the territories.

The leading contender for the nomination was William H. Seward, whose very prominence and long record hurt his availability. Passing him and other aspirants over, the convention nominated on the third ballot Abraham Lincoln – who was prominent enough to be respectable but obscure enough to have few foes, and who was radical enough to please the antislavery faction in the party but conservative enough to satisfy the ex-Whigs.

Still a fourth party entered the lists – the Constitutional Union party. Although posing as a new organization, it was really the last surviving remnant of the oldest conservative tradition in the country; its leaders were elder statesmen, and most of its members were former Whigs. Meeting in Baltimore in May, this party nominated John Bell of Tennessee and Edward Everett of Massachusetts. Its platform declared for the Constitution, the Union, and enforcement of the laws.

In the November election Lincoln won a majority of the electoral votes and the Presidency, though only about two-fifths of the popular votes. The Republicans had elected a President, but they had failed to secure a majority in Congress; and of course they did not have the Supreme Court.

## The Secession of the South

During the campaign various Southern leaders had threatened that if the Republicans won the election the South would secede from the Union. Southern threats of secession had been voiced at intervals since 1850, without any action following, and Northerners had come to believe they were intended as bluffs. This time, however, the threats were serious.

The South believed that secession was a legal process. Sovereign states could leave the Union they had entered. But the process had to be a solemn one—the voters of a state elected a convention which had the power to take the state out of the Union.

South Carolina, long the hotbed of Southern separatism, led off the secession parade, its convention taking the state out of the Union on December 20, 1860, by a unanimous vote. It was followed quickly by six other states—Mississippi, Florida, Alabama, Georgia, Louisiana, and Texas. And in February 1861 representatives of the seceded states met at Montgomery, Alabama, and formed a new, Southern nation—the Confederate States of America.

Northern opinion was puzzled by secession, and the indecision was reflected in the thinking of President Buchanan. In his message to Congress of December 1860 he denied the right of a state to secede; but he added that he did not think the federal government possessed the power to coerce a state back into the Union. He intended to avoid a collision of arms and to maintain the symbolic authority of the national government until his successor could take office.

As the various states seceded, they took possession of federal property within their boundaries, but they lacked the strength to seize certain offshore forts, notably Fort Sumter in the harbor of Charleston, South Carolina, and Fort Pickens in the harbor of Pensacola, Florida. South Carolina, aggressively "independent," sent commissioners to Washington to ask for the surrender of Sumter, garrisoned by a small force under Major Robert Anderson. Buchanan, fearful though he was of provoking a clash, refused to yield the fort.

Buchanan also recommended to Congress that it frame compromise measures to hold the Union together. The Senate and the House appointed committees to study plans of adjustment. Outside Congress, representatives from twenty-one states met in a Peace Convention at Washington to try to shape a compromise. None of the compromise efforts succeeded. The one that came closest to adoption was offered by the Senate committee, the Crittenden Compromise. But it foundered on the issue that destroyed the others. The contending parties could agree on several questions, such as a constitutional amendment guaranteeing the permanence of slavery—but on the question of slavery in the territories they split apart.

And so nothing had been resolved when Abraham Lincoln was inaugurated President on March 4, 1861. In his inaugural address he laid down the following basic principles: the Union was older than the Constitution, no state could of its own volition leave the Union, the ordinances of secession were illegal, the acts of violence to support secession were insurrectionary or revolutionary. He declared that he meant to execute the laws in all the states and to "hold, occupy, and possess" the federal property in the seceded states (Forts Sumter and Pickens).

Lincoln soon found an opportunity to apply his policy in the case of Fort Sumter. Major Anderson was running short of supplies; unless he received fresh provisions the fort would have to be evacuated. After much deliberation Lincoln decided to dispatch to the fort a naval relief expedition. His move placed the Confederates in a dilemma. If they permitted the expedition to land, they would be bowing tamely to federal authority. But the only alternative was to reduce the fort before the ships arrived—in short, to invoke war. The government in Montgomery ordered General P. G. T. Beauregard, in charge of Confederate forces at Charleston, to demand Anderson's surrender and, if the demand was refused, to reduce the fort. Beauregard made the demand and Anderson rejected it. The Confederates then bombarded the fort for two days, April 12–13, 1861. On April 14 Anderson surrendered.

War had come. Lincoln moved to increase the army and called on the states to furnish troops to restore the Union. Now four more slave states seceded and joined the Confederacy: Virginia (April 17); Arkansas (May 6); Tennessee (May 7); and North Carolina (May 20). The mountain counties in northwestern Virginia refused to accept the decision of their state, established their own "loyal" government, and in 1863 secured admission to the Union as the new state of West Virginia. The four remaining slave states, Maryland, Delaware, Kentucky, and Missouri, cast their lot with the Union. Lincoln kept a keen watch on their actions, and in two, Maryland and Missouri, helped to ensure their decision by employing military force.

## War Potential, North and South

In the war the North had a larger manpower reservoir from which to draw its armed forces. In the North, or the United States, were twenty-three states with a population of approximately 22,000,000. In the South, or the Confederate States, were eleven states with a population of some 9,000,000. Of these, approximately 3,500,000 were slaves, leaving a white population of something under 6,000,000.

The Northern economy was vastly superior to that of the South, and especially in industrial production. Eighty percent of the factories of the country were concentrated in the North. Thus the Northern system, once it became geared to war production, could produce all the goods needed by its armies and civilian population. The Southern system, although it was expanded during the war, was unable to meet military and particularly civilian needs. Its failure in this respect was one reason why Southern morale dropped badly after 1863.

The transportation system of the North was superior to that of the South. The North had more and better inland water transport (steamboats, barges), more surfaced roads, and more wagons and animals. The North had approximately 20,000 miles of railroads, while the South, containing at least as large a land area, had only 10,000 miles. The trackage figures, however, do not tell the whole story of Southern inferiority. There were important gaps between key points in the South, which meant that supplies had to be detoured long distances or carried between railheads by wagons. As the war wore on, the Confederate railroad system steadily deteriorated, and by the last year and a half of the struggle it had almost collapsed. The great weapon of sea power was also in the hands of the North.

The material factors give the impression that the South had absolutely no chance to win the war. Actually, these odds were not so great as they appear at first glance. The South, for the most part, fought on the defensive in its own country and commanded interior lines. The Northern invaders had to maintain long lines of communication, to supply themselves in areas where transportation was defective, and to garrison occupied regions. Furthermore, the North had to do more than capture the enemy capital or defeat enemy armies. It had to convince the

Southern civilian population that the war was hopeless by seizing and holding most of the Confederacy. The South was fighting for something very concrete, very easy for its people to understand. It simply wanted to be independent, to be let alone; it had no aggressive designs on the North. If the South could have convinced the North that it could not be conquered or that the result would not be worth the sacrifices, it might, even after 1863, have won its independence.

## The North's Economic Program

For Northern industry and agriculture the wartime years were a period of significant legislative gains. The Republicans represented Northern industry and agriculture, and, now that the war had removed Southern opposition, they proceeded to put into effect the kind of program their supporters expected.

The Homestead Act (1862) and the Morrill Land Grant Act (1862) were measures the West had long sought. The first provided that any citizen, or any alien who had declared his intention to become a citizen, could register claim to a quarter section of public land (160 acres), and, after giving proof that he had lived on it for five years, receive title on payment of a small fee. The Morrill Law provided federal aid for the promotion of agricultural education and, in turn, agricultural productivity. By its terms each state was to receive 30,000 acres of public land for each of its congressional representatives, the proceeds from the donation to be used for education in agriculture, engineering, and military science.

Industry scored its first gain a few days before President Buchanan left office. Congress passed the Morrill Tariff Act, which provided a moderate increase in duties, bringing the rates up to approximately what they had been before 1846. Later measures enacted in 1862 and 1864 were frankly protective. By the end of the war the average of duties was 47 percent, the highest in the nation's history, and more than double the prewar rate.

Other legislative victories for business were achieved in connection with railroads and immigration. Two laws (1862, 1864) created two federal corporations: the Union Pacific Railroad Company, which was to build westward from Omaha, and the Central Pacific,

# THE CAUSES OF THE CIVIL WAR

**Where Historians Disagree**

On the causation of the Civil War, historians' views have changed with changing times, thus illustrating the fact that history reflects the period *in* which it is written as well as the period *about* which it is written. In the 1890s, when the United States was emerging as a world power, the Civil War seemed to have been concerned with fundamental issues, for it had not only destroyed slavery but also preserved the Union, thus making possible the nation's rise to greatness. Such was the implied theme of the leading authority of the time, James Ford Rhodes. In his *History of the United States from the Compromise of 1850* . . . (7 vols., 1893–1900) Rhodes saw the war as originating in the conflict between Northern opponents and Southern defenders of slavery.

This view prevailed until the 1920s, when Charles and Mary Beard challenged it in *The Rise of American Civilization* (2 vols., 1927). The Beards believed that in politics the most powerful of human motivations were economic. Like many of their contemporaries among the intellectuals, these authors were disillusioned with the efforts of progressives to curb business monopolies. The Beards maintained that the basic causes of the Civil War were economic. According to them, the war arose out of a clash between Northern industrialists and Southern planters, each group seeking to control the federal government in its own interest, and both groups using arguments about slavery and state rights only as smoke screens. The Beards had doubts about the results of the "Second American Revolution," as they called the war, for it brought on the evils associated with the rise of big business.

In the 1930s the Beardian interpretation began to be superseded by the views of the "revisionists." While these men were writing, the American revulsion against war was at its height. The recent war to "end war" and "make the world safe for democracy" had obviously done neither, and American participation in it seemed now like a great mistake. The Civil War, too, had been unfortunate and useless according to the revisionists, such as Avery Craven and James G. Randall, who blamed it on the fanaticism and political ineptitude of a "blundering generation."

After World War II, which appeared to have saved democracy from the threat of Hitlerism, historians took a new look at the Civil War and concluded, once again, that it had been necessary and worthwhile. Arthur Schlesinger, Jr., explained that violence was sometimes indispensable for clearing away obstacles to social progress and that slavery had been such an obstacle. Allan Nevins, beginning a multivolume restudy of the period 1850–1877 in *The Ordeal of the Union* and *The Emergence of Lincoln* (4 vols., 1947–1950), characterized the Civil War as "a war over slavery *and* the future position of the Negro race in North America." As the civil rights movement gained momentum in the 1950s and 1960s, historians gave more and more attention to slavery and race relations as central issues in the sectional conflict of the 1850s and 1860s. Eugene Genovese, for one, saw the war as growing out of the Southern planters' efforts to protect and expand the slave system.

which was to build eastward from California. The government would aid the companies by donating public lands and advancing government loans. Immigration from Europe fell off in the first years of the war, and the decrease, coupled with the military demands for manpower, threatened to cause a labor shortage. President Lincoln and business leaders asked Congress for governmental encouragement of immigration. In 1864 Congress passed a contract labor law authorizing employers to import laborers and collect the costs of transportation from future wages. Over 700,000 immigrants entered the country during the war years.

Perhaps the most important measure affecting the business-financial community was the National Bank Act, enacted in 1863 and amended in 1864. The act created the National Banking System, which lasted without serious modification until 1913. Its architects thought of it as a law that would provide a badly needed national banknote currency; at the outbreak of the war 1,500 banks chartered by twenty-nine states were empowered to issue notes. Furthermore, the new system would enable the government to market its bonds more cheaply, and thus aid the financing of the war.

The act spelled out a process by which a "banking association" (an existing state bank or a newly formed corporation) could secure a federal charter of incorporation and become a National Bank. Each association was required to possess a minimum amount of capital and to invest one-third of its capital in government securities, thereby supporting the war effort. Upon depositing the securities with the national treasury, it would receive, and could issue as banknotes, United States Treasury notes up to 90 percent of the current value of the bonds. Various clauses in the law provided for federal supervision and inspection of the banks. When many of the state banks, disliking the regulatory features, held aloof from the new system, Congress (in 1865) placed a tax on all state banknotes. This action forced state notes out of existence, induced many state banks to seek federal charters, and made the nation's currency more uniform. By the end of the war the system numbered 11,582 National Banks that were circulating notes amounting to over $200,000,000.

The North financed the war from three principal sources: taxation, loans, and paper money issues. From taxes, including the tariff, the government received approximately $667,000,000; loans, including treasury notes, accounted for $2,600,000,000; and $45,000,000 of paper currency ("greenbacks") was issued.

Not until 1862, when mounting war expenses forced the country to face realities, did Congress pass an adequate war tax bill. Then it enacted the Internal Revenue Act, which placed sales taxes on practically all goods and introduced (in 1861) the nation's first income tax, a duty of 3 percent on incomes above $800. Later (in 1862 and 1865) the rates were increased to 5 percent on incomes between $600 and $5,000, and to 10 percent on incomes above the latter figure.

The greenbacks, because they bore no interest, were not supported by a specie reserve, and depended for redemption on the good faith of the government, fluctuated in value. In 1864 a greenback dollar, in relation to a gold dollar, was worth only 39 cents, and even at the close of the war its value had advanced to but 67 cents.

## Raising the Union Armies

Congress, the only agency authorized by the Constitution to raise armies, was not in session when hostilities started. Lincoln met the crisis with bold decision. He called for 42,000 volunteers for national service for three years and authorized an increase of 23,000 in the regular army. When Congress met in July 1861, it legalized the President's acts and, at his recommendation, provided for enlisting 500,000 volunteers to serve for three years. All in all, the government of the North, despite some minor bungling, adopted a sound military policy from the beginning. It acted to raise a large force (numbers were on the side of the North), and it avoided the mistake of short-term enlistments.

At first the volunteering system brought in enough men to fill the armies. But soon the initial enthusiasm waned, and men came forward to enlist in diminishing numbers. Even the generous cash bounties held out to prospective volunteers by the Federal government and by the states were insufficient lures. Finally, in March 1863, Congress enacted the first national draft law in American history (the South had employed conscription almost a year earlier). Few exemptions were permitted: only high national and state officials, preachers, and men who were the sole support of a dependent family. But a drafted man could escape service by hiring a substitute to go in his place or by paying the government a fee of $300. Eventually this cash commutation was repealed.

The purpose of the draft law was to spur enlistments by threatening to invoke conscription. Each state was divided into enrollment districts, and at announced intervals was assigned a quota of men to be raised. If a state, by bounties or other means, could fill the quota, it escaped the draft completely. Although the draft directly inducted only 46,000 men, it stimulated enlistments er.ormously. The Federal armies increased steadily in size, reaching a maximum number in 1865. The number of enlistments was 2,900,000, but this figure includes many who enlisted several times or served short terms. A reasonably accurate estimate is that 1,500,000 served for three years (as contrasted with 900,000 in the Confederate forces).

The casualty rate was tremendous. This was due to two factors, one military and the other medical. The weapons employed in the war — rifles and artillery with a faster rate of fire and a longer range than those used in previous wars — gave armies a vastly increased firepower. In many battles the proportion of men killed and wounded ranged from 20 to 32 percent. Medical knowledge and practice had improved greatly by 1861, and further progress would be registered during the war. But much remained to be discovered, particularly about the care of wounds, sanitation, and diet, and more men died of disease than of bullets.

## Northern Politics, to 1862

When Lincoln first came to Washington, he was almost universally considered a small-time prairie politician, unfit for his job. He strengthened this impression by his unpretentious air. Actually, he was well aware of his great abilities and of his superiority over other Northern leaders. His supreme confidence in himself was demonstrated by his choice of a cabinet. Representing every faction of the Republican party and every segment of Northern opinion, it was an extraordinary assemblage of advisers and a difficult set of prima donnas to manage. Three of the secretaries, William H. Seward (State), Salmon P. Chase (Treasury), and Edwin M. Stanton (War), were able men who thought they could dominate Lincoln — but in the end were dominated by him.

Lincoln's confidence in his inner strength was revealed by his bold exercise of the war powers of his office. In order to accomplish his purposes, he was ready to violate parts of the Constitution, explaining that he would not lose the whole by being afraid to disregard a part. In this spirit he called for troops to repress the rebellion

(an act equivalent to a declaration of war), illegally increased the size of the regular army, and proclaimed a naval blockade of the South. It is a curious and significant fact that Lincoln and other Northern leaders, heading an established government, exhibited more revolutionary zeal and even ruthlessness than the new and revolutionary government they were opposing.

Opposition to the war came from two sources: from Southern sympathizers in the Union slave states and from the peace wing of the Democratic party. War Democrats were willing to support the war and even to accept offices from the administration. Peace Democrats or, as their enemies called them, "Copperheads," feared that agriculture and the West were being subordinated to industry and the East and that state rights were going down before nationalism. Simply stated, their war policy was as follows: to call a truce in the fighting, invite the South to attend a national convention, and amend the Constitution to preserve state rights. On the whole, the Peace Democrats were unionists, in that they did not favor a division of the country. But some of them were willing to countenance Southern independence.

To deal with opponents of the war, Lincoln resorted to military arrests. He suspended the right of habeas corpus, so that an alleged offender could be arrested and held without trial or, if tried, had to appear before a military court. At first Lincoln denied the civil process only in specified areas, but in 1862 he proclaimed that all persons who discouraged enlistments or engaged in disloyal practices would come under martial law. In all, over 13,000 persons were arrested and imprisoned for varying periods. The most prominent Copperhead in the country, Clement L. Vallandigham of Ohio, was seized by military authorities, although not at Lincoln's instigation, and later exiled to the Confederacy. (After the war, in 1866, the Supreme Court held, in *Ex parte Milligan*, that military trials in areas where the civil courts were capable of functioning were illegal.)

There were factions too in the dominant Republican party — the Radicals and the Conservatives. On most questions, including economic matters, they were in fundamental agreement, but they differed on the disposition to be made of slavery. The Radicals wanted to seize the opportunity of the war to strike slavery down — abolish it suddenly and violently. The Conservatives, who were also antislavery, wanted to accomplish the same result in a different way — easily and gradually. Lincoln, who tended to be a Conservative, made several notable although unsuccessful attempts to persuade the loyal slave states to agree to a program of compensated gradual emancipation. He feared, at first, that the introduction of abolition as a war aim would divide Northern opinion and alienate the border slave states.

## Emancipation

As the war demanded more sacrifices of the North, public opinion inevitably became more antislavery — and more Radical. In July 1862 Congress enacted the second Confiscation Act, which was in essence a bold attempt to accomplish emancipation by legislative action. The principal provisions were as follows: it declared the property of persons supporting the "rebellion" subject to forfeiture to the United States government; it declared free the slaves of persons aiding and supporting the insurrection; and it authorized the President to employ Negroes, including freed slaves, as soldiers. Although the measure was a "paper" edict so far as immediate concrete results were concerned, it marked a turning point in the war. The country had come to accept emancipation as an aim of the war.

The signs were not lost on the astute master of politics in the White House. Lincoln saw that in order to achieve his larger purpose of saving the Union he would have to yield his lesser goal of preventing the sudden destruction of slavery. To preserve the nation he had to have the support of his own party and particularly of the Radicals. And if a majority of the Northern people wanted slavery destroyed, he could not afford to divide popular opinion by opposing their will. In July 1862 he decided to take the leadership of the antislavery impulse away from the Radicals by putting himself at the head of it.

On September 22, 1862, after the battle of Antietam, the President issued his preliminary Emancipation Proclamation, and on the first day of 1863 his final Emancipation Proclamation. This document declared forever free the slaves in designated areas of the Confederacy. Excepted from the edict was the whole state of Tennessee, most of which was under Union control, and western Virginia and southern Louisiana, which were occupied by Federal troops. Presumably these areas were omitted because they were not enemy territory and hence were not subject to the President's war powers. For a similar reason the Proclamation did not apply to the border slave states.

The Proclamation freed immediately but few slaves. But it indicated that henceforth there was to be a war for the emancipation of the slaves as well as for preservation of the Union. Eventually as Federal armies occupied large areas of the South, the Proclamation became a practical reality, and hundreds of thousands of slaves were freed by its operation. Equally important in the process of emancipation was the induction of many former slaves into the armed forces: some 186,000 served as soldiers, sailors, and laborers, thereby making a substantial contribution to the freeing of their race. Furthermore, the impulse to abolition, which the Proclamation symbolized, increased in intensity throughout the country. The final and inevitable action was taken early in 1865 when Congress approved the Thirteenth Amendment (ratified by the required number of states several months after the war closed), which freed all slaves everywhere and abolished slavery as an institution.

Early in the war, and particularly after the election of 1862, in which the Republicans suffered heavy losses, the party leaders proceeded to form a broad coalition of all groups who supported the war, trying particularly to attract the War Democrats. The new organization, which was composed of a Republican core with a fringe of War Democrats, was known as the Union party. It encountered its major political test in the presidential election of 1864, which was the first national election held in the midst of a great war.

When the Union convention met in June, it nominated Lincoln, with the chilly assent of the Radicals, and, for Vice President, Andrew Johnson of Tennessee, a War Democrat who had refused to follow his state into secession. In August the Democratic convention nominated George B. McClellan, a former Union general whose opposition to emancipation made him an object of hatred to all good Radicals. The peace faction got a plank into the platform denouncing the war as a failure and calling for a truce to be followed by an invitation to the South to enter a national convention. Although Mc-

Clellan repudiated the plank, the Democrats stood before the country as the peace party. At the same time several Northern military victories, particularly the capture of Atlanta, Georgia, early in September, rejuvenated Northern morale and gave promise of Republican success in November.

The outcome of the election was a smashing electoral triumph for Lincoln, who got 212 votes to McClellan's 21 and carried every state except Kentucky, New Jersey, and Delaware. Lincoln's popular majority, however, was uncomfortably small.

## The Confederate Government

Although the first seven Southern states to secede had left the Union as individual sovereignties, they had no intention of maintaining separate political existences. It was understood from the first that they would come together in a common confederation to which, they hoped, the states of the Upper South would eventually adhere. Accordingly, representatives of the seceded states assembled at Montgomery, Alabama, early in February 1861 to create a Southern nation. Montgomery, "the cradle of the Confederacy," was the capital of the new nation until after Virginia seceded. Then the government moved to Richmond, partly out of deference to Virginia, partly because Richmond was one of the few Southern cities large enough to house the government.

There was significance in the name of the Southern government: it was a confederation of sovereign states, not a federation of united ones. State sovereignty was expressly recognized in the constitution. Interestingly enough, proposals to insert the right of a state to secede failed of adoption; the right was implied but never mentioned. In structure, the Confederate government was an almost exact duplicate of the model which Southerners had just discarded.

As President the Montgomery convention elected Jefferson Davis of Mississippi, and as Vice President, Alexander H. Stephens of Georgia. Davis had been a firm but not extreme advocate of Southern rights in the former Union; he was a moderate but not an extreme secessionist. Stephens had been the chief among those who had contended that secession was unnecessary.

Although Davis was intelligent and honest, he showed grave defects as a war leader. First, he spent too much time on routine items, on what one observer called "little trash." He was a good administrator who loved to administer; he was his own Secretary of War but he rarely rose above the secretarial level. Second, Davis failed to grasp the all-important fact that the Confederacy was not an established, recognized nation but a revolution. He proceeded on the basis that the Confederacy was a legal and permanent organization that could fight a war in the normal fashion of older countries. Whereas the situation demanded that the South act with ruthless efficiency, Davis assumed that it should observe every constitutional punctilio. Lincoln, without clear constitutional sanction, suspended habeas corpus; Davis asked his Congress to let him suspend it and received only partial permission.

The Confederate cabinet was a body of shifting personnel displaying, at best, only average ability. Davis selected the first incumbents almost entirely on a geographical basis: he wanted to include a representative from each state except his own Mississippi. This practice resulted, in some cases, in a man's being named to one post when he was better fitted for another that had to be allotted to an individual whose state would not otherwise be represented.

The personnel of the cabinet changed rapidly and frequently. There were three secretaries of state, two secretaries of the treasury, four attorney generals, and five secretaries of war. Not a man in the cabinet ever dared to oppose the will of the President.

## Southern Money and Men

The men seeking to devise measures for financing the Confederacy's war effort, Treasury Secretary Christopher G. Memminger and the congressional leaders, had to reckon with a number of hard facts. Southern banking houses, except in New Orleans, were fewer and smaller than those of the North. Because excess capital in the South was usually invested in slaves and land, the sum of liquid assets on deposit in banks or in individual hands was relatively small. The only specie possessed by the government was that seized in United States mints located in the South.

The Confederate Congress, like its counterpart in the North, was reluctant to enact rigorous wartime taxes. In 1861 the legislators provided for a direct tax on property to be levied through the medium of the states. If a state preferred, it could meet its quota by paying as a state. Most of the states, instead of taxing their people, assumed the tax, which they paid by issuing bonds or their own notes. This first tax measure produced a disappointing return of only $18 million. Moving more boldly in 1863, Congress passed a bill which included license levies and an income tax. A unique feature was "the tax in kind." Every farmer and planter had to contribute one-tenth of his produce to the government. Although Congress later raised the rates in the internal revenue measure and enacted other taxes, the revenue realized from taxation was relatively small. The Confederacy raised only about 1 per cent of its total income in taxes.

The bond record of the Confederacy was little better than its tax program. Congress authorized a $100 million loan to be paid in specie, paper money, or produce. The expectation was that the bulk of the proceeds would be in the form of products—"the loan in kind." The loan was subscribed, partly in paper currency and mostly in produce or pledges of produce. But many of the pledges were not redeemed, and often the promised products were destroyed by the enemy. The Confederacy also attempted to borrow money in Europe by pledging cotton stored in the South for future delivery, but secured little from this source.

Since ready revenue was needed and since cash was scarce, the government resorted in 1861 to the issuance of paper money and treasury notes. Once it started, it could not stop. By 1864 the staggering total of one billion dollars had been issued. In addition, states and cities issued their own notes. The inevitable result was to depreciate the value of the money. Prices skyrocketed to astronomical heights. Some sample figures for 1863–1864 are as follows: flour, $300 a barrel; broadcloth, $125 a yard; chickens, $35 a pair; beef, $5 a pound; men's shoes, $125 a pair. Many people, particularly those who lived in towns or who had fixed incomes, could not pay these prices. They did without, and lost some of their will to victory.

Like the United States, the Confederate States first raised armies by calling for volunteers. By the latter part of 1861 volunteering had dropped off badly. As the year 1862 opened, the Confederacy was threatened by a manpower crisis.

The government met the situation boldly. At Davis' recommendation, Congress in April enacted the First Conscription Act, which declared that all able-bodied white males between the ages of eighteen and thirty-five were liable to military service for three years. A man who was drafted could escape his summons if he furnished a substitute to go in his place. The prices for substitutes eventually went up to as high as $10,000 in Confederate currency. The purpose of this provision was to exempt men in charge of agricultural and industrial production, but to people who could not afford substitutes it seemed like special privilege to the rich. It was repealed late in 1863 after arousing bitter class discontent.

The first draft act and later measures provided for other exemptions, mostly on an occupational basis. The laws erred in excusing men who were not doing any vital services and in permitting too many group exemptions. The provision most bitterly criticized was that exempting one white man on each plantation with twenty or more slaves. Angrily denounced as the "twenty-nigger law," it caused ordinary men to say: "It's a rich man's war but a poor man's fight."

In September 1862 Congress adopted a second conscription measure, which raised the upper age limit to forty-five. At the end of the year, an estimated 500,000 soldiers were in the Confederate armies. Thereafter conscription provided fewer and fewer men, and the armed forces steadily decreased in size.

As 1864 opened, the situation was critical. In a desperate move, Congress lowered the age limits for drafted men to seventeen and raised them to fifty, reaching out, it was said, toward the cradle and the grave. Few men were obtained. War weariness and the certainty of defeat were making their influence felt. In 1864–1865 there were 100,000 desertions. On the army rolls 200,000 names were carried, but at the end probably only 100,000 were in service. In a frantic final attempt to raise men, Congress in 1865 authorized the drafting of 300,000 slaves. The war ended before this incongruous experiment could be tried out.

## Confederate Politics

Only in the mountain areas of the South did organized opposition to the war exist. The mass of the people were united in support of the war. But they became bitterly divided on how it should be conducted.

The great dividing force was, ironically enough, the principle of state rights. State rights had become a cult with Southerners, to the point that they reacted against any sort of central control, even to controls necessary to win the war. If there was an organized faction of opposition to the government, it was that group of quixotic men who counted Vice President Stephens as their leader and who are usually known as the state-rights party. They had one simple, basic idea. They believed first in state sovereignty and then in the Confederacy. They wanted the Confederacy to win its independence, but they would not agree to sacrificing one iota of state sovereignty to achieve that goal. If victory had to be gained at the expense of state rights, they preferred defeat.

The state-righters fought every attempt of the government to impose centralized controls. They concentrated their fire against two powers that the central government sought to exercise: the suspension of habeas corpus, and conscription.

Recalcitrant governors, like Joseph Brown of Georgia and Zebulon M. Vance of North Carolina, contending that the central government had no right to draft troops, tried in every way to obstruct the enforcement of conscription. Their chief weapon was certifying state militia troops as exempt. In the spring of 1862 an estimated 100,000 men throughout the South were held in state service. In Georgia in 1864 more men between eighteen and forty-five were at home than had gone into the army since 1861. Unwittingly, the state-righters helped to bring about the Confederacy's defeat.

# Chapter 15.  THE CIVIL WAR

## The Commanders in Chief

It was the responsibility of the President as commander in chief of the army and navy — of Abraham Lincoln for the Union and Jefferson Davis for the Confederacy — to see to the making and carrying out of an overall strategy for winning the war. Lincoln, a civilian all his life, had had no military education and no military experience except for a brief militia interlude. Yet he became a great war President, and a great commander in chief, superior to Davis, who was a trained soldier. By the power of his mind, Lincoln made himself a fine strategist, often showing keener insight than his generals. He recognized that numbers and matériel were on his side, and immediately he moved to mobilize the maximum strength of Northern resources. He urged his generals to keep up a constant pressure on the whole defensive line of the Confederacy until a weak spot was found, and a breakthrough could be made. At an early date he realized that his armies ought to seek the destruction of the Confederate armies rather than the occupation of Southern territory.

During the first three years of the war, Lincoln performed many of the functions that in a modern command system would be done by the chief of the general staff or the joint chiefs of staff. He formulated policy, devised strategic plans, and even directed tactical movements. Some of his decisions were wise, some wrong, but the general effect of his so-called "interfering" with the military machine was fortunate for the North.

In the command system arrived at in 1864, Ulysses S. Grant, who had emerged as the North's greatest general, was named general in chief. Charged with directing the movements of all Union armies, Grant, because he disliked the political atmosphere of Washington, established his headquarters with the Army of the Potomac but did not technically become commander of that army. As director of the armies, Grant proved to be the man for whom Lincoln had been searching. He possessed in superb degree the ability to think of the war in overall terms

and to devise strategy for the war as a whole. Because Lincoln trusted Grant, he gave the general a relatively free hand.

Southern command arrangements consisted mainly of President Davis. The Confederacy failed to achieve a modern command system. Early in 1862 Davis assigned General Robert E. Lee to duty at Richmond, where, "under the direction of the President," he was "charged" with the conduct of the Confederate armies. Despite the fine words, this meant only that Lee, who had a brilliant military mind, was to act as Davis' adviser, furnishing counsel when called on.

## The Role of Sea Power

The Union had the advantage of overwhelmingly preponderant sea power, and President Lincoln made the most of it. It served two main functions. One was to enforce the blockade of the Southern coast that he proclaimed at the start of the war (April 19, 1861). The other was to assist the Union armies in combined land-and-water operations.

In the Western theater of war, the vast region between the Appalachian Mountains and the Mississippi River, the larger rivers were navigable by vessels of considerable size. The Union navy helped the armies to conquer this area by transporting supplies and troops for them and joining them in attacking Confederate strong points. In defending themselves against the Union gunboats on the rivers, the Confederates had to depend mainly on land fortifications because of their lack of naval power. These fixed defenses proved no match for the mobile land-and-water forces of the Union.

At first, the blockade was too large a task for the Union navy. Even after the navy had grown to its maximum size, it was unable to seal off completely the long shoreline of the Confederacy. Though ocean-going ships were kept away, small blockade runners continued to carry goods into and out of some of the Southern ports. Gradually the Federal forces tightened the blockade by occupying stretches of the coast and seizing one port after another, the last remaining important one (Wilmington, North Carolina) early in 1865. Fewer and fewer blockade runners got through, and the blockade increasingly hurt the South.

In bold and ingenious attempts to break the blockade, the Confederates introduced some new weapons, among them an ironclad warship. They constructed this by plating with iron a former United States frigate, the *Merrimack,* which the Yankees had scuttled in Norfolk harbor when Virginia seceded. On March 8, 1862, the *Merrimack* steamed out from Norfolk to attack the blockading squadron of wooden ships in Hampton Roads. She destroyed two of the ships and scattered the rest. Jubilation reigned in Richmond, and consternation in Washington. But the federal government had already placed orders for the construction of several ironclads of its own, which had been designed by John Ericsson. One of these, the *Monitor,* arrived at Hampton Roads on the night of March 8. When the *Merrimack* emerged on the following day to hunt for more victims, the *Monitor* met her and engaged her in the first battle between ironclad ships. Neither vessel was able to penetrate the other's armor, but the *Monitor* put an end to the depredations of the *Merrimack.*

The Confederates later experimented with other new kinds of craft in the effort to pierce the blockade. One of these was a torpedo boat, which carried the torpedo (mine) on a long pole projecting out in front. Another was a small, cigar-shaped, hand-powered submarine. In 1864, in Charleston harbor, such a submarine, pulling its mine behind it on a cable, dived under a blockading vessel, exploded the mine against the hull, and then was dragged to the bottom by the sinking ship. For the first time in the history of warfare, a submarine had made a successful strike. This and other ingenious efforts, however, fell far short of breaking or even weakening the blockade.

To weaken it, the Confederates had meanwhile decided to build or buy fast ships to prey on the Northern merchant marine on the high seas. The hope was that the Union would detach ships from the blockade to pursue the commerce raiders. The Confederates also hoped to get, from abroad, a specially built "ram" with which to smash the wooden blockading ships. As a result of these efforts, the naval war became an important element of the general war and signifi-cantly affected the relations of the Union and the Confederacy with the powers of Europe.

## Europe and the Disunited States

In the relationship of Europe to the Civil War, the key nations were Great Britain and France. These two had acted together against Russia in the Crimean War and were united by an entente, one of the understandings of which was that questions concerning the United States fell within the sphere of British influence. Napoleon III, therefore, would not act in American affairs without the concurrence of Britain. Russia, the third power of Europe, was, like the United States, an up-and-coming nation that thought its aspirations were being blocked by England. Feeling a community of interest with democratic America, autocratic Russia openly expressed sympathy for the Northern cause.

In the minds of Southern leaders, cotton was their best diplomatic weapon. Their analysis was as follows: the textile industry was basic to the economies of England and France, which depended on the South for the bulk of their cotton supply; deprived of Southern cotton, these countries would face economic collapse. Therefore they would have to intervene on the side of the Confederacy.

But this diplomacy based on King Cotton never worked as its champions envisioned. In 1861 English manufacturers had a surplus of cotton on hand. The immediate effect of the blockade was to enable the textile operators to dispose of their remaining finished goods at high prices. Thereafter the supply became increasingly short, and many mills were forced to close. Both England and France, however, managed to avoid a complete shutdown of their textile industries by importing supplies from new sources, notably Egypt and India.

No European nation extended diplomatic recognition to the Confederacy. Though several times England and France considered offering mediation, they never moved to intervene in the war. Neither could afford to do so unless the Confederacy seemed on the point of winning, and the South never attained a prospect of certain victory.

Immediately after the outbreak of hostilities, Great Britian issued a proclamation of neutrality, thus attributing to the Confederacy the status of a belligerent. France and other nations followed suit. Although the Northern government, which officially insisted that the war was not a war but a domestic insurrection, furiously resented England's action, the British government had proceeded in conformity with accepted rules of neutrality and in accordance with the realities of the situation. The United States was fighting a *war,* a fact that Lincoln himself had recognized in his proclamation establishing a blockade. Thereafter three crises or near-crises between England and the United States developed, any one of which could have resulted in war between the two countries.

The first crisis, and the most dangerous one — the so-called *Trent* affair — occurred late in 1861. The Confederate commissioners to England and France, James M. Mason and John Slidell, had slipped through the then ineffective blockade to Havana, Cuba, where they boarded an English steamer, the *Trent,* for England. Hovering in Cuban waters was an American frigate, the *San Jacinto,* commanded by Captain Charles Wilkes, an impetuous officer who knew that the Southern diplomats were on the *Trent.* Acting without authorization from his government, Wilkes stopped the British vessel, arrested the commissioners, and bore them off in triumph to Boston. The British government drafted a demand for the release of the prisoners, reparation, and an apology. Lincoln and Seward, well aware that war with England would be suicidal, spun out the negotiations until American opinion had cooled off, then returned the commissioners with an indirect apology.

The second issue — the case of the Confederate commerce destroyers — generated a long-lasting diplomatic problem. Lacking the resources to construct the vessels, the Confederacy contracted to have them built and equipped in British shipyards. Six cruisers, of which the most famous were the *Alabama,* the *Florida,* and the *Shenandoah,* were sold to the Confederacy. The British government knew what was going on, but winked at the practice. The United States protested that it was in violation of the laws of neutrality.

The third incident — the affair of the Laird rams — could have developed into a crisis, but did not because the British government suddenly decided to mend its ways. In 1863 the Confederacy placed an order with the Laird shipyards for two powerful ironclads with pointed prows for ramming and sinking Union vessels and thus breaking the blockade. The British government acted to detain the rams and to prevent the Confederacy from obtaining any other ships.

If Napoleon III had had his way, France and England would have intervened at an early date. Unable to persuade Britain to act, he had to content himself with expressing sympathy for the Southern cause and permitting the Confederates to order commerce destroyers from French shipyards. The Emperor's primary motive for desiring an independent South was his ambition to establish French colonial power in the Western hemisphere: a divided America could not block his plans. He seized the opportunity of the war to set up a French-dominated empire in Mexico.

Napoleon's Mexican venture was a clear violation of the Monroe Doctrine, perhaps the greatest one that had ever occurred. The United States viewed it in such a light, but for fear of provoking France into recognizing the Confederacy, it could do no more than register a protest. Only after the Civil War was ended did the United States feel strong enough to put pressure on France to get out of Mexico.

## The Opening Battles   1861

Since the powers of Europe refrained from direct intervention in the war, the two contestants in America were left to fight it out on their own.

The year 1861 witnessed several small battles that accomplished large results and one big battle that had no important outcome. The small engagements occurred in Missouri and in western Virginia, the mountainous region that shortly would become the state of West Virginia.

In Missouri, which had its own internal war, the Union forces were able to hold most of the state. Into western Virginia came a Federal force that had been assembled in Ohio under the command of George B. McClellan. Crossing the Ohio River, the invaders succeeded by the end of the year in "liberating" the mountain people.

The one big battle of the year was fought in Virginia in the area between the two capitals. Just south of Washington was a Federal army of over 30,000 under the command of General Irvin McDowell. Opposing it was a Confederate army of over 20,000 under P. G. T. Beauregard based at Manassas in northern Virginia about thirty miles southwest of Washington; and there were other Confederate troops in the Shenandoah Valley, commanded by Joseph E. Johnston.

In mid-July McDowell marched his inexperienced troops toward Manassas, his movement well advertised to the Confederates by Northern newspapers and Southern spies. Beauregard retired behind Bull Run, a small stream north of Manassas, and called on the government to order Johnston to join him. Most of Johnston's army reached Beauregard the day before the battle, making the Northern and Southern armies approximately equal in size, each numbering something over 30,000.

The Battle of Bull Run, or Manassas (July 21), might be summarized by saying that Beauregard never got his offensive into motion and that McDowell's attack almost succeeded. The Confederates stopped a last strong Union assault. Beauregard then ordered a counterattack. As the Confederates slashed forward, a sudden wave of panic struck through the Union troops, wearied after hours of hot, hard fighting and demoralized by the abrupt change of events. They gave way and crossed Bull Run in a rout. Unable to get them in hand north of the stream, McDowell had to order a retreat to Washington.

The Confederates, as disorganized by victory as the Federals were by defeat, and lacking supplies and transport, were in no condition to undertake a forward movement. Lincoln replaced McDowell with General McClellan, the victor of the fighting in western Virginia, and took measures to increase the army. Both sides girded themselves for real war.

## The Western Theater 1862

The first decisive operations in 1862 were in the Western theater. Here the Federals were trying to secure control of the Mississippi line by moving on the river itself or parallel to it. Most of their offensives were combined land-and-naval operations. To achieve their objective, the Federals advanced on the Mississippi from the north and south, moving down from Kentucky and up from the Gulf of Mexico toward New Orleans.

In April a Union squadron of ironclads and wooden vessels forced the civil authorities to surrender the city. For the rest of the war the Federals held New Orleans and the southern part of Louisiana. They closed off the mouth of the great river to Confederate trade, grasped the South's largest city and greatest banking center, and secured a base for future operations.

A fatal weakness marked the Confederate line in Kentucky. The center, through which flowed the Tennessee and Cumberland rivers, was thrown back (southward) from the flanks, and was defended by two forts, Henry on the Tennessee and Donelson on the Cumberland. The forts had been built when Kentucky was trying to maintain a position of neutrality, and were located just over the Tennessee line. If the Federals, with the aid of naval power, could pierce the center, they would be between the two Confederate flanks and in position to destroy either.

This was exactly what the Federals did in February. Grant proceeded to attack Fort Henry, whose defenders, awed by the ironclad river boats accompanying the Union army, surrendered with almost no resistance (February 6). Grant then marched to Donelson while his naval auxiliary moved to the Cumberland River. At Donelson the Confederates put up a scrap, but eventually the garrison of 20,000 had to capitulate (February 16). Grant had inflicted a near-disaster on the Confederacy. As a result of his movement, the Confederates were forced out of Kentucky and had to yield half of Tennessee.

Grant, with about 40,000 troops, now advanced up the Tennessee (southward). The immediate objective was to destroy Confederate railroad communications in the Corinth, Mississippi, area. Grant debarked his army at Pittsburg Landing, about thirty miles from Corinth. The battle that ensued (April 6–7) is usually known as Shiloh. The Confederates caught Grant by surprise, and by the end of the first day's fighting drove him back to the river, but here the attack was halted. The next day Grant, reinforced by 25,000 fresh troops, went over to the offensive, and regained his original lines. Shiloh turned out to be an extremely narrow Union victory. The Federals eventually seized Corinth and the railroads of which it was the hub. By early June they had occupied the river line down as far as Memphis.

The Confederates held approximately the eastern half of Tennessee. They hoped to recover the rest of the state and, if possible, carry the war back to Kentucky. When Confederate

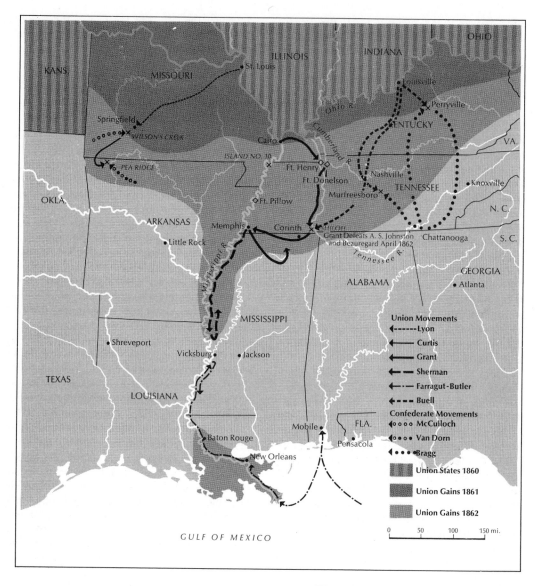

**The War in the West   1861–1862**

General Braxton Bragg moved from Tennessee into Kentucky, Union General Don Carlos Buell followed him. The two armies met in the indecisive Battle of Perryville (October 8), and Bragg returned to Tennessee.

## The Virginia Front   1862

In the Eastern theater in 1862 Union operations were directed by young George B. McClellan,

commander of the Army of the Potomac and the most controversial general of the war. McClellan was a superb trainer of men but lacked the fighting instinct, necessary in a great captain, to commit his men to decisive battle.

During the winter of 1861–1862 McClellan had remained inactive, training his army of 150,000 men near Washington. He finally settled on a plan of operations for the spring campaign. Instead of striking for Richmond by moving southward from Washington, he would have the navy transport his army to Fort Monroe on the Virginia coast in the region between the York and James rivers known as the Peninsula. Late in March McClellan started putting his troops on transports to begin his Peninsula campaign.

The Confederate high command (Davis and Lee) had misgivings about General Joseph E. Johnston's strategy of drawing McClellan closer to Richmond before fighting and they were worried by the possibility that reinforcements might join McClellan. To prevent this, the commander of the Confederate forces in the Shenandoah Valley, Thomas J. ("Stonewall") Jackson, was directed to move northward, giving the impression that he meant to cross the Potomac. Partly to defend the approaches to Washington and partly to trap Jackson, Lincoln rushed forces to the Valley. Jackson slipped back to safety before the various Union forces could converge on him.

While these events were unfolding in the Valley, Johnston at last attacked McClellan at Fair Oaks or Seven Pines (May 31–June 1). The attack failed to budge McClellan, and Johnston was so seriously wounded that he had to relinquish the command. To replace him Davis named the man who would lead the Army of Northern Virginia for the rest of the war, Robert E. Lee.

Lee, a brilliant field commander, realized that the Confederacy could not win its independence merely by repelling offensives. He decided to call Jackson from the Valley, bringing his total numbers up to 85,000 (as compared to McClellan's 100,000), mass his forces, and attack. The operation that followed, which involved several engagements, is known as the Battle of the Seven Days (June 25–July 1). It did not proceed as Lee expected. He drove back McClellan, who headed southward. Lee followed, trying desperately to destroy the Federals, but McClellan extricated his army, even inflicting a bloody repulse on Lee at Malvern Hill. He reached Harrison's Landing on the James, where with naval support, he was safe from any attack Lee could launch.

At Harrison's Landing the Federal army was only twenty-five miles from Richmond, and it had a secure line of water communications. But Lincoln, instead of replacing McClellan with a more aggressive commander, decided to evacuate the army to northern Virginia where it would

be combined with a smaller force under John Pope—to begin a new operation on the Washington-to-Richmond "overland" route.

As the Army of the Potomac left the Peninsula by water, Lee, understanding what was happening, moved his army northward with the purpose of striking Pope before he was joined by McClellan. Pope, who was rash where McClellan was timid, attacked the Confederates in the Second Battle of Manassas or Bull Run (August 29–30). Lee easily halted the assault, and in a powerful counterstroke swept Pope from the field. The beaten Federals retired to the Washington defenses, where Lincoln relieved Pope and placed all the troops around the city under McClellan's command.

Lee gave the Federals no respite. Early in September he went over to the offensive, invading western Maryland. With some misgivings, Lincoln let McClellan go to meet Lee. Lee had time to pull most of his army together behind Antietam Creek near the town of Sharpsburg. Here, on September 17, McClellan, with 87,000 men, threw a series of powerful attacks at Lee's 50,000. McClellan might have won with one more assault. But his caution asserted itself, and he called off the battle. Lee retired to Virginia, and after an interval of reorganization McClellan followed. Lincoln, disgusted by McClellan's failure to exploit his victory, removed him from command in November.

As McClellan's successor Lincoln appointed Ambrose E. Burnside, a modest mediocrity. Burnside thought that the government desired him to fight, and fight he would. He planned to drive at Richmond by crossing the Rappahannock at Fredericksburg, the strongest defensive point on that river. On December 13 he flung his army at Lee's defenses in a hopeless, bloody attack. At the end of a day of bitter failure and after suffering 12,000 casualties, he withdrew to the north side of the Rappahannock. Soon he was relieved at his own request.

## Year of Decision 1863

As 1863 opened, the Union army in the East was commanded by Burnside's successor, Joseph Hooker—"Fighting Joe," as the newspapers called him. His army, which numbered 120,000, fell back to a defensive position at

Chancellorsville in the desolate area of scrub trees and brush known in Virginia as the Wilderness. Here Lee came up to attack him.

The Battle of Chancellorsville (May 1–5) was one of Lee's most brilliant exploits. With an army of only 60,000 (part of his force had been detached for other service), he took great but justified risks. He divided his army and sent Jackson to hit the Union right, which was exposed, while he struck from in front. Again Lee had won, but he had lost his ablest lieutenant. Jackson, wounded in the fighting, died soon afterward.

While the Federals were failing in the East, a different story was unfolding in the West. U. S. Grant was driving at Vicksburg, the most strongly fortified Confederate point on the Mississippi River. Afer failing to storm the strong works, he settled down to a siege, which endured for six weeks, Vicksburg capitulating on July 4.

At last the Federals had achieved one of their principal strategic aims; they had gained control of the Mississippi line. The Confederacy was split into two parts, and the trans-Mississippi area was isolated from the main section. A great turning point in the war had been reached.

When the siege of Vicksburg began, the Confederate high command in Richmond was dismayed at the prospect of losing the great river fortress. Various plans to relieve the city were discussed, the principal one being a proposal to send part of Lee's army to Tennessee, possibly with Lee himself in command, to launch an offensive. But Lee put forward a counterscheme: he would invade Pennsylvania. If he could win a victory on Northern soil, he said, great results would follow. The North might abandon the war, England and France might intervene, and the pressure on Vicksburg and other fronts would be broken. The government assented, and in June Lee started his movement, swinging his army west toward the Valley and then north through Maryland into Pennsylvania.

As Lee advanced, Hooker moved back to confront him, marching parallel to the line of Lee's route. But Hooker evidently had been unnerved by his experience at Chancellorsville. He seemed to be looking for a chance to escape his responsibility, and he soon found an excuse to ask to be relieved. To replace him Lincoln appointed an army corps commander, George G. Meade, a solid if unimaginative soldier. Meade

followed Lee, and approached what might be called the strategic rear of the Confederate army in southern Pennsylvania. Lee, who had not expected the Federals to move so rapidly, was astounded when he learned of their nearness. With his army marching in three columns, he was in a dangerous position; hurriedly he had to concentrate his forces. Meade, realizing that Lee in enemy country had to attack or retreat, selected a strong defensive site at the little town of Gettysburg, a road hub in the region, and Lee, seeking contact with the Federals, moved toward the same spot. Here on July 1–3 was fought the most celebrated battle of the war.

Lee finally withdrew his shattered forces to Virginia. Meade made but a feeble pursuit. Although he had thrown away an opportunity to end the war, Gettysburg was another turning point. The total Confederate losses in the campaign were close to 25,000. Never again would Lee feel strong enough to fight offensively.

A third turning point against the Confederacy was reached in Tennessee. In the autumn Union General William S. Rosecrans moved toward Chattanooga. Bragg evacuated the town. Rosecrans rashly plunged over the Georgia line in pursuit, where Bragg, reinforced by troops from Lee's army, was lying in wait. Rosecrans barely got his scattered forces in hand before Bragg delivered his crushing assault at Chickamauga (September 19–20). The beaten Union army fell back into the Chattanooga defenses.

Bragg eventually occupied the heights south of Chattanooga. Mounting batteries on these points, he commanded the roads leading into the city and virtually shut off its supplies. Grant was named departmental commander of the West. Immediately he came with part of his own army to the relief of the beleaguered city. At the Battle of Chattanooga (November 23–25) the Federals hurled Bragg from his lines on Missionary Ridge and Lookout Mountain and back into northern Georgia. They then proceeded to occupy most of east Tennessee.

From the Chattanooga base the Federals were in position to split the Confederacy again—what was left of it. Chattanooga deserves to be ranked with Vicksburg and Gettysburg as a decisive Union victory. After 1863 the Confederacy had no chance on any front to win its independence by a military decision. Now it could hope to triumph only by exhausting the Northern will to fight.

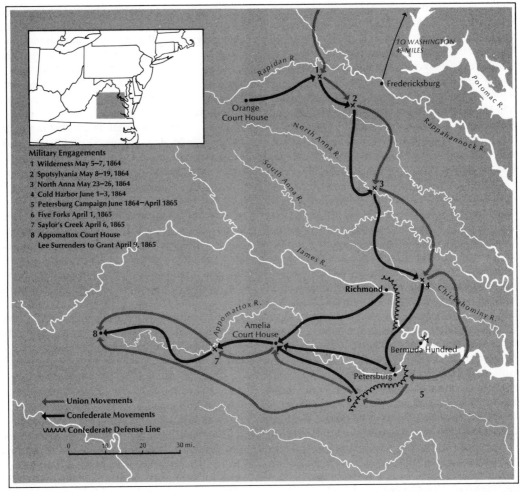

**Military Engagements**

1 Wilderness May 5–7, 1864
2 Spotsylvania May 8–19, 1864
3 North Anna May 23–26, 1864
4 Cold Harbor June 1–3, 1864
5 Petersburg Campaign June 1864–April 1865
6 Five Forks April 1, 1865
7 Saylor's Creek April 6, 1865
8 Appomattox Court House
  Lee Surrenders to Grant April 9, 1865

Union Movements
Confederate Movements
Confederate Defense Line

0    10    20    30 mi.

**Virginia Campaigns**

## The Ending   1864–1865

Grant's plans for 1864 called for two great offensives. The Army of the Potomac, commanded by Meade but accompanied and directed by Grant, was to seek to bring Lee to decisive battle in northern Virginia. From near Chattanooga the Western army, commanded by William T. Sherman, was to advance into northern Georgia, destroy the Confederate army, now commanded by Joseph E. Johnston, and wreck the economic resources of Atlanta.

From its position in northern Virginia the Army of the Potomac, 115,000 strong, crossed the Rappahannock and Rapidan rivers, and plunged into the Wilderness area. Grant's plan

was to envelop Lee's right and force him to a showdown battle. Lee, whose army numbered about 75,000 at the beginning of the campaign, was determined to avoid a showdown unless he saw a chance to deal a decisive blow. In the battles of the Wilderness (May 5–7), Spotsylvania Court House (May 8–19), and Cold Harbor (June 1–3), Grant pressed stubbornly on toward Richmond, at tremendous human cost. In a month of fighting he lost a total of 55,000 men — killed, wounded, and captured — and Lee lost 31,000.

Now Grant had to alter his strategy. If he remained where he was, Lee would retire into the Richmond defenses to stand a siege, something Grant wanted to avoid. Masking his movements from his adversary, Grant moved southward across the James heading for Petersburg, directly south of Richmond. Petersburg was the hub of all the railroads feeding into the capital; if Grant could secure it, he could force Lee to come into the open to fight for his communications. He almost succeeded, but finally had to resort to a siege. He dug in, and so did Lee. The trench lines of the two armies stretched for miles above and below Petersburg. Always Grant strove to extend his left around Lee's right so as to get on the railroads that were the lifeline of the Southern army. It would be nine months before he reached his objective.

Meanwhile Sherman, with an army of over 90,000, moved toward Atlanta against Johnston's army, which numbered 60,000 at the beginning. Johnston's plan was to delay Sherman, to fight for time, and not to commit his forces unless the conditions were exceptionally favorable. As Sherman was approaching Atlanta, President Davis replaced Johnston with John B. Hood. Combative by nature, Hood threw two successive attacks at Sherman, both of which failed. The Union army occupied Atlanta on September 2.

Sherman had not destroyed the enemy army. Eager to strike deeper into Georgia, he sent 30,000 of his army to Tennessee under George H. Thomas, and prepared to move for Savannah on the coast. At the same time Hood decided to invade Tennessee, hoping to force Sherman to follow him. Despite disastrous losses at Franklin, Tennessee (November 30), Hood moved on northward and took up a position outside Nashville. In the Battle of Nashville (December 15–16) Thomas drove Hood from the field. As the Confederates retreated toward Mississippi, they were harried by the most merciless cavalry pursuit of the war. Only a few units reached Mississippi intact. The Confederate Army of Tennessee had, in effect, ceased to exist.

In the meantime Sherman was marching almost unopposed across Georgia, inaugurating a new kind of warfare. He was the prophet of modern total war—war against the civilian population of the enemy, war intended to break the enemy people's will to resist. His army marched on a sixty-mile front, destroying property and supplies that might be used by the Confederate forces and committing many individual depredations as well. By December 20 Sherman was at Savannah.

Sherman then turned into South Carolina, still facing slight opposition and still ripping up enemy property. When he advanced into North Carolina, the Confederate government got together an army of 30,000 under Johnston to oppose him, but this small force could do little more than delay his march.

In April 1865, Grant finally passed a part of his army around Lee's right to the vital railroads. The Confederates evacuated Petersburg and Richmond, and Lee moved westward with his army, now shrunk to about 25,000. His one forlorn hope was to reach a rail line to North Carolina and unite with Johnston. But the pursuing Federal army barred his escape route. At last he realized that further fighting was hopeless, and on April 9 he met Grant at Appomattox and surrendered the Army of Northern Virginia. In North Carolina Joe Johnston reached the same conclusion, and on April 18 he surrendered to Sherman near Durham. Jefferson Davis, defiant to the last and unable to recognize defeat, fled southward, and was captured in Georgia. The war was soon over.

## The War's Aftermath

In the North, the postwar years were prosperous, but Northerners who visited the South were appalled when they gazed upon the desolation left in the wake of the war—gutted towns, wrecked plantations, neglected fields, collapsed bridges, and ruined railroads. Much of the personal property of Southerners had been lost with the lost cause. Confederate bonds and currency were now worthless, and capital that had been invested in them was gone forever. And with the emancipation of the slaves, slave owners would be deprived of property worth an estimated $2 billion. There was little to cheer the thousands of Confederate soldiers who were drifting back to their homes—258,000 never returned and other thousands went back wounded or sick.

If conditions were bad for Southern whites, they were generally worse for Southern blacks—the 4 million who were emerging from the bondage that had held them and their ancestors for two and a half centuries. Many of these people, too, had seen service of one kind or another during the war. Some had served as body servants for Confederate officers or as teamsters and laborers for the Confederate armies. Tens of thousands had fought as combat troops in the Union ranks, and more than 38,000 had given their lives for the Union cause.

As the war ended, freedom appeared to be on the way, but its arrival was uncertain. The Thirteenth Amendment, which would make slavery unconstitutional, had yet to be ratified by the requisite number of states (it had passed Congress on February 1, 1865, and was to be proclaimed in effect on December 18, 1865). On many plantations the blacks were still being detained and forced to work. Most planters agreed with a former Confederate leader who was saying (in June 1865) that slavery had been "the best system of labor that could be devised for the Negro race" and that the wise thing to do now would be to "provide a substitute for it."

To get away from their old masters, thousands of Negroes continued to leave the plantations. Old and young, many of them feeble and ill, they trudged to the nearest town or city or they roamed the countryside, camping at night on the bare ground. Few had any possessions except the rags on their backs. Somehow they managed to stay alive.

What the Negroes wanted was, first of all, to be assured of their freedom—to feel it, to exercise it, and to know it was not going to be taken from them. Next, they needed immediately relief from the threat of starvation. Then, looking ahead, they desired land, farms of their own, a bit of economic independence. A few of the freed slaves had already settled on abandoned plantations, notably on the Sea Islands along the South Carolina coast and on land in Mississippi that had belonged to the Davis family. The Negroes also longed for schooling for their children if not for themselves. In some places, above all in New Orleans, there were well educated and highly cultured communities of blacks who had been free for generations. But education was a rare and precious thing to the new freedmen, most of whom were as illiterate as the slave codes had intended them to be. Finally, a number of the Negroes were beginning to demand political rights. "The only salvation for us besides the power of the Government is in the *possession of the ballot*," a convention of black people of Virginia resolved in the summer of 1865. "All we ask is an *equal chance*."

The federal government, besides keeping troops (many of them black) in the South to preserve order and protect the Negroes, was doing something to assist them in the transition from slavery to freedom. Congress had set up (in March 1865) the Bureau of Freedmen, Refugees, and Abandoned Lands as an agency of the army. This Freedmen's Bureau was empowered to provide food, transportation, assistance in getting jobs and fair wages, and schools for former slaves, and also to settle them on abandoned or confiscated lands. Cooperating with the bureau, especially in its educational work, were missionaries and teachers who had been sent to the South by Freedmen's Aid Societies and other private and church groups in the North.

## Reconstruction: The Issues

The word "Reconstruction," as contemporaries used it, referred to the process by which peace was to be made, that is, the process by which the states of the defeated Confederacy were to be brought back to their former places in the Union.

A quick and easy restoration of the Union would be to the advantage of the former Confederates and the Democratic party North and South. The Southern Democrats could expect to rejoin the Northern Democrats and get control of both Congress and the Presidency. The consequences of an easy peace, by the same token, could be disastrous for the Republican party. The outlook was disturbing for Northern businessmen who during the war had obtained favors from the federal government—a high tariff, railroad subsidies, the national banking system —which might be ended once the Democrats were back in power. For the Negroes emerging from slavery, a quick restoration of the Southern states would be catastrophic. The master class, which had dominated the state governments before and during the war, would continue to do so. The Negroes then could expect to be kept in a position that, at best, would be somewhere between slavery and freedom.

The Radical Republicans, directed by leaders like Thaddeus Stevens of Pennsylvania and Charles Sumner of Massachusetts, stood for a hard peace; they urged that the civil and military chieftains of the late Confederacy be subjected to severe punishment, that large numbers of Southern whites be disfranchised, and that the property of rich Southerners who had aided the

Confederacy be confiscated and distributed among the freedmen. From the first, some Radicals favored granting suffrage to the former slaves, as a matter of right or as a means of creating a Republican electorate in the South. Other Radicals agreed with them, but hesitated to state a position for fear of public opinion — few of the Northern states permitted Negroes to vote.

Democrats and Conservative Republicans, claiming that secession was illegal, contended that the seceded states had never legally been out of the Union, were still in it, and had all the rights of states. The Radicals, the uncompromising nationalists of the war, now insisted that the Southern states had in fact withdrawn from the nation and had therefore forfeited their rights. Sumner argued that by seceding they had committed "state suicide," and Stevens bluntly referred to them as "conquered provinces." On the other hand, Southerners who had fought to uphold the right of secession now demanded all the privileges they had previously enjoyed in the Union they had tried to dissolve.

## Lincoln's Plan

The process of Reconstruction was put into motion while the war was still going on, and the first plan was presented by President Lincoln. He believed there were a considerable number of actual or potential Unionists in the South. These people, most of them former Whigs, could possibly be encouraged to rejoin the old Whigs of the North and thus strengthen the Republican party, once the Union had been restored. More immediately, these men could serve as the nucleus for setting up new and loyal states in the South and thereby hastening reunion. All along, Lincoln was concerned with principle as well as politics: the principle of the inviolability of the Union. He wanted to restore the American experiment in democracy as soon as possible. The question of whether the defeated states were in or out of the Union he dismissed as a "merely pernicious abstraction." They were only out of their proper, practical relationship to the Union, he said, and they should be restored to that relationship as soon as possible.

Specifically, Lincoln's plan, which he announced to the public in a proclamation of December 1863, offered a general amnesty to all who would take an oath pledging future loyalty to the government. Temporarily excluded from the right to swear the oath were high civil and military officials of the Confederacy. Whenever in any state 10 percent of the number of voters in 1860 took the oath, they could proceed to set up a state government. The oath required acceptance of the wartime acts and proclamations of Congress and the President concerning slavery. Instead of demanding outright abolition (the Thirteenth Amendment had not yet been passed, and the postwar effect of the Emancipation Proclamation was uncertain, since it was a war measure), Lincoln told Southern leaders that he hoped they would provide for permanent freedom. He also urged them to give the ballot to at least a few Negroes — to those who were educated, owned property, and had served in the Union army. In three Southern states — Louisiana, Arkansas, and Tennessee — loyal governments were reestablished under the Lincoln formula in 1864.

The Radical Republicans were angered and astonished at the mildness of Lincoln's program, and they were able to induce Congress to repudiate his governments. Representatives from the Lincoln states were not admitted to Congress, and the electoral votes of those states were not counted in the election of 1864.

The Radicals prepared and passed (in July 1864) the Wade-David Bill, which was far more drastic than the Lincoln plan. This bill would have required a majority — instead of Lincoln's 10 percent — to take an oath of future loyalty. It would have disfranchised all who could not swear an additional "iron-clad oath" that they had never willingly borne arms against the United States. And it would have compelled the newly formed states to abolish slavery.

The Wade-Davis Bill was passed a few days before Congress adjourned, which enabled Lincoln to dispose of it with a pocket veto. His action enraged the authors of the measure, Benjamin F. Wade and Henry Winter Davis, who issued a blistering denunciation of the veto, the Wade-Davis Manifesto, warning the President not to interfere with the powers of Congress to control Reconstruction. Lincoln could not ignore the bitterness and the strength of the Radical opposition. Practical as always, he realized that he would have to accept some of the objections of the Radicals. He began to move toward a new approach to Reconstruction, possibly one that would have included greater benefits for the freedmen.

What plan he would have come up with nobody can say. On April 14, 1865, a crazed actor, John Wilkes Booth, under the delusion that he was helping the South, shot the President in a Washington theater. Lincoln died early the following morning, and because of the circumstances of his death—the heroic leader, the Great Emancipator struck down in the hour of victory by an assassin—he achieved immediate martyrdom. In the wild excitement of the hour, it was widely assumed that Booth had been instigated to his mad act by leaders of the South, and the Radicals played on this theme with reckless charges implicating high Confederates.

## Johnson and "Restoration"

The conservative leadership in the controversy over Reconstruction fell upon Lincoln's successor, Andrew Johnson. Of all the men who accidentally inherited the Presidency, Johnson was undoubtedly the most unfortunate. A Southerner and former slaveholder, he became President as the bloody war against the South was drawing to a close. A Democrat before he had been placed on the Union ticket with Lincoln in 1864, he became the head of a Republican administration at a time when partisan passions, held in some restraint during the war, were about to rule the government.

Johnson revealed his plan of Reconstruction —or "Restoration," as he preferred to call it— soon after he took office, and he proceeded to execute it during the summer of 1865 when Congress was not in session. He recognized as legal organizations the Lincoln governments in Louisiana, Arkansas, Tennessee, and Virginia and applied a new formula to the eight states of the late Confederacy that had not come under the Lincoln plan.

Like his predecessor, Johnson assumed that the seceded states were still in the Union, and he announced his design in a proclamation of amnesty that extended pardon for the past conduct to all who would take an oath of allegiance. Denied the privilege of taking the oath until they received individual pardons from the President were high-ranking Confederate officials and also men with land worth $20,000 or more; Johnson excluded a larger number of leaders than Lincoln had. For each state the President appointed a provisional governor who was to invite the qualified voters to elect delegates to a constitutional convention. As conditions of readmittance, the state had to revoke the ordinance of secession, abolish slavery and ratify the Thirteenth Amendment, and repudiate the Confederate and state war debts.

By the end of 1865 all the seceded states had been reconstructed and were ready to resume their places in the Union—if Congress chose to recognize them when it met in December.

# Chapter 16. RADICAL RECONSTRUCTION

## Congress Takes Over

When Congress met in December 1865, it denied admission to the senators and representatives from the states that President Johnson had "restored." The Radical leaders explained that the Southerners should be excluded until Congress knew more about conditions in the South. Congress must first be assured that the former Confederates had accepted the results of the war and that Southern Negroes and loyal whites were safe. Accordingly, Congress set up the Joint Committee on Reconstruction to investigate opinions in the South and to advise Congress in laying down a Reconstruction policy.

During the next few months the Radicals, though disagreeing among themselves, advanced toward a more severe program than their first plan, the Wade-Davis Bill of 1864. The Radicals gained the support of moderate Republicans because of Johnson's intransigent attitude. Johnson insisted that Congress had no right even to consider a policy for the South until his own plan had been accepted and the Southern congressmen and senators had been admitted.

Northern opinion was aroused by the so-called Black Codes, which the Southern legislatures adopted during the sessions of 1865–1866. These measures were the South's solution to the problem of the free Negro laborer, and they were also the South's substitute for slavery as a white-supremacy device. They all authorized local officials to apprehend unemployed Negroes, fine them for vagrancy, and hire them out to private employers to satisfy the fine. Some of the codes tried to force Negroes to work on the plantations by forbidding them to own or lease farms or to take other jobs except as domestic servants.

An appropriate agency for offsetting the Black Codes was the Freedmen's Bureau, but its scheduled year of existence was about to end. It had been losing some of its original functions. With the passing of the immediate postwar emergency, there was decreasing need for the bureau's relief activities. And President Johnson had been pardoning so many former rebels—thus restoring to them their confiscated plantations—that there was less and less land available for resettling former slaves.

In February 1866 Congress passed a bill to prolong the life of the bureau and to widen its powers by authorizing special courts for settling labor disputes. Thus the bureau could set aside work agreements that might be forced upon Negroes under the Black Codes. Johnson vetoed the bill, denouncing it as unconstitutional.

In April Congress again struck at the Black Codes by passing the Civil Rights Bill, which made United States citizens of Negroes and empowered the federal government to intervene in state affairs when necessary for protecting the rights of citizens. Johnson vetoed this bill, too. With moderates and Radicals acting together, Congress had the necessary two-thirds majority, and it promptly overrode the veto. Then, Congress repassed the Freedmen's Bureau Bill and overcame another veto.

The Joint Committee on Reconstruction submitted to Congress in April a proposed amendment to the Constitution, the Fourteenth, which constituted the second Radical plan of Reconstruction, and which was sent to the states for approval in the early summer. Section 1 of the amendment declared that all persons born or naturalized in the United States were citizens of the United States and of the state of their residence. This clause, which set up for the first time a national definition of citizenship, was followed by a statement that no state could abridge the rights of citizens of the United States or deprive any person of life, liberty, or property without due process of law or deny to any person within its jurisdiction the equal protection of the laws. Section 2 provided that if a state denied that suffrage to any of its adult male inhabitants, its representation in the House of Representatives and the Electoral College should suffer a proportionate reduction. Section 3 disqualified from any state or federal office persons who had previously taken an oath to support the Constitution and later had aided the Confederacy — until Congress by a two-thirds vote of each house should remove their disability. Johnson himself advised Southerners to defeat the amendment. Only Tennessee, of the former Confederate states, ratified it, thus winning readmittance. The other ten, joined by Kentucky and Delaware, voted it down. The amendment thus failed to receive the required approval of three-fourths of the states and was defeated — but only temporarily.

Public acceptance of the Radical program was strikingly manifested in the elections of 1866. This was essentially a contest for popular support between Johnson and the Radicals. The Radicals could point to recent events in the South — bloody race riots in which Negroes were the victims — as further evidence of the inadequacy of Johnson's policy. Johnson did his own cause no good by the intemperate, brawling speeches he made on a stumping tour from Washington to Chicago and back. The voters returned to Congress an overwhelming majority of Republicans, most of them of the Radical variety.

## The Congressional Plan of 1867

After compromising differences among themselves and with the Moderates, the Radicals formulated their third plan of Reconstruction in three bills that passed Congress in the early months of 1867. All three were vetoed by Johnson and repassed.

This plan was based squarely on the principle that the seceded states had lost their political identity. The Lincoln-Johnson governments were declared to have no legal standing, and the ten seceded states (Tennessee was now out of the Reconstruction process) were combined into five military districts. Each district was to be put in the charge of a military commander, supported by troops, who was to prepare his provinces for readmission as states. To this end, he was to have made a registration of voters, which was to include all adult Negro males and white males who were not disqualified for participation in rebellion. The whites who were excluded were those coming under the disability of the Fourteenth Amendment; but each voter had to swear a complicated loyalty oath, and the registrars were empowered to reject white men on

the suspicion that they were not acting in good faith.

After the registration was completed in each province, the commanding general was to call on the voters to elect a convention to prepare a new state constitution that had to provide for Negro suffrage. If this document were ratified by the voters, elections for a state government could be held. Finally, if Congress approved the constitution, if the state legislature ratified the Fourteenth Amendment, and if this amendment were adopted by the required number of states and became a part of the Constitution — then the state was to be restored to the Union.

By 1868 six of the former Confederate states — Arkansas, North Carolina, South Carolina, Louisiana, Alabama, and Florida — had complied with the process of restoration outlined in the Reconstruction Acts and were readmitted to the Union. Delaying tactics by the whites held up the return of Mississippi, Virginia, Georgia, and Texas until 1870. These four laggard states had to meet an additional requirement, which with the existing requirements constituted the fourth and final congressional plan of Reconstruction. They had to ratify another constitutional amendment, the Fifteenth, which forbade the states and the federal government to deny the suffrage to any citizen on account of "race, color, or previous condition of servitude."

The great majority of the Northern states still denied the suffrage to Negroes at the time when the Reconstruction Acts granted it to Negroes in the Southern states. Attempts to give the vote to Northern blacks by amending the state constitutions had met with practically no success. Hence an amendment to the federal Constitution seemed necessary. Its sponsors were motivated by both idealistic and practical considerations. They would be consistent in extending to the Negro in the North a right they had already given to him elsewhere. At the same time they would be putting into the Constitution, where it would be safe from congressional repeal, the basis of Republican strength in the South. They were also concerned with the party's future in the North. In several of the Northern states the Negro vote, though small, would be large enough to decide close elections in favor of the Republicans.

A number of the Northern and border states refused to approve the Fifteenth Amendment, and it was adopted only with the support of the four Southern states that had to ratify it in order to be readmitted to the Union. In the case of both the Fourteenth and Fifteenth amendments, the Southern states were deemed capable of ratifying even while they were not otherwise recognized as states and had no representation in Congress.

## The President Impeached

To curb the President, Congress passed the Tenure of Office Act (1867), which forbade him to remove civil officials, including members of his cabinet, without the consent of the Senate. Its principal purpose was to protect the job of Secretary of War Edwin M. Stanton, who was cooperating with the Radicals in his command of military units in the South.

Early in 1867 the Radicals began searching for evidence that Johnson had comitted crimes or misdemeanors in office, the only legal grounds for impeachment, but they could find nothing upon which to base charges. Then he gave them a plausible reason for action by deliberately violating the Tenure of Office Act. He suspended and then dismissed Secretary of War Stanton.

In the House of Representatives the elated Radicals framed and presented to the Senate eleven charges against the President. The first nine accusations dealt with the violation of the Tenure of Office Act. The tenth and eleventh charged Johnson with making speeches calculated to bring Congress into disrespect and of not faithfully enforcing the various Reconstruction Acts. In the trial before the Senate (March 25 to May 26, 1868) Johnson's lawyers maintained that he was justified in technically violating a law in order to force a test case and that the measure did not apply to Stanton anyway: it gave tenure to cabinet members for the term of the President by whom they had been appointed, and Stanton had been appointed by Lincoln. The House managers of the impeachment stressed the theme that Johnson had opposed the will of Congress. They implied that in doing so he was guilty of crimes and misdemeanors. They brought terrific pressure upon all the Republican senators, but seven Republicans joined the twelve Democrats to vote for acquittal. On three of the charges the vote was identical, 35 to 19, one short of the required two-thirds majority. Thereupon the Radicals called off the proceedings.

## The Reconstructed States

In the ten states of the South that were reorganized under the congressional plan, approximately one-fourth of the white men were at first excluded from voting or holding office. The voter registration of 1867 enrolled a total of 703,000 black and 627,000 white voters. The Negro voters constituted a majority in half the states — Alabama, Florida, South Carolina, Mississippi, and Louisiana — though only in the last three of these states did the blacks outnumber the whites in the population as a whole. However, once new constitutions had been made and new governments launched, most of these permitted nearly all whites to vote (though for several years the Fourteenth Amendment continued to keep the leading ex-Confederates from holding office). This meant that in most of the Southern states the Republicans could maintain control only with the support of a great many Southern whites.

These Southern white Republicans, whom their opponents derisively called "scalawags," consisted in part of former Whigs who, after the break-up of the Whig organization in the 1850s, had acted with the Southern Democrats but had never felt completely at home with them. Some of the scalawag leaders were wealthy (or once wealthy) planters or businessmen. Such men, having long controlled the Negroes as slaves, expected to control them also as voters. Many other Southern whites who joined the Republican party were farmers living in areas where slavery had been unimportant or nonexistent. These men, many of whom had been wartime Unionists, favored the Republican program of internal improvements, which would help them get their crops to market.

White men from the North also served as Republican leaders in the South. Opponents of Reconstruction referred to them as "carpetbaggers," thus giving the impression that they were penniless adventurers who had arrived with all their possessions in a carpetbag (a then common kind of valise covered with carpeting material) in order to take advantage of the Negro vote for their own power and profit. In fact, the majority of the so-called carpetbaggers were veterans of the Union army who had looked upon the South as a new frontier, more promising than the West, and at the war's end had settled in it as hopeful planters or business or professional men.

## THE NATURE OF RECONSTRUCTION

**Where Historians Disagree**

Historical writing on Reconstruction, even more controversial than that on the Civil War, similarly reflects the patterns of thought that have prevailed from time to time. The first professional historian of Reconstruction, William A. Dunning, who taught at Columbia University from the 1880s to the 1920s, carried on his work during a period when scholars generally held that certain racial and ethnic groups were inherently superior to others. Dunning assumed that Negroes were inferior and hence unfit to receive the vote. Many of his students wrote books dealing with Reconstruction in particular states, and he himself provided a general account, *Reconstruction, Political and Economic* (1907), which for many years was accepted as authoritative. According to Dunning and the members of the "Dunning school," the Republicans imposed their Radical program upon the South mainly to keep their party in power. (Some later writers, notably Howard K. Beale, added an economic motive – to protect Northern business interests.) Under the Radical plan, the Southern states suffered the agonies of "bayonet rule" and "Negro rule," when with army support the blacks and their unscrupulous white accomplices plundered the people in an unbelievable orgy of corruption, ruinous taxation, and astronomical increases in the public debt.

The first historian seriously to challenge the Dunning interpretation was the Negro scholar William E. B. Du Bois. In an article in the *American Historical Review* (1910) Du Bois pointed out that the misdeeds of the Reconstruction state governments had been exaggerated and their achievements overlooked. These governments were expensive, he explained, because they undertook to provide public education and other public services on a scale never before attempted in the South. In a long book, *Black Reconstruction* (1935), Du Bois described Reconstruction politics in the Southern states as an effort on the part of the masses, black and white, to create a true democratic society. Writing under the influence of Marxism, he assumed a class consciousness for which few other historians could find much evidence.

By the 1940s the attitudes toward race, on the part of scholars at least, had drastically changed. Since that time a new generation of historians has arisen – among them C. Vann Woodward, John Hope Franklin, Eric McKitrick, and John and La Wanda Cox – who assume that the freedmen of the 1860s and 1870s, despite the handicaps of their previous servitude, were by nature quite capable of participating in self-government. According to the new historians, the Radical Republicans were motivated less by partisan or economic interests than by a determination to guarantee basic rights to the former slaves and thus to secure the war aims of reunion and freedom. There was little if anything in the South that could properly be called either military rule or Negro rule, and the Negro, carpetbagger, and scalawag politicians were at least as honest and capable as others of their time. The mistake in Reconstruction was not the attempt to confer civil and political rights upon blacks, but the failure to provide an adequate economic and educational basis and sufficient governmental protection for the assurance of those rights. The recent views are ably synthesized in Kenneth M. Stampp, *The Era of Reconstruction* (1965).

---

The most numerous Republicans in the South were the freedmen, the vast majority of whom had no formal education and no previous experience in the management of affairs. Among the Negro leaders, however, were well-educated, highly intelligent men, most of whom had never been slaves and many of whom had been brought up in the North or abroad. The blacks quickly became politically self-conscious. In various states they held their own conventions, the one in Alabama announcing (1867): "We claim exactly *the same rights, privileges and immunities as are enjoyed by white men*—we ask nothing more and will be content with nothing less."

Negroes served as delegates to the conventions that, under the congressional plan, drew up new state constitutions in the South. Then, in the reconstructed states, Negroes were elected to public offices of practically every kind. All together (between 1869 and 1901) twenty of them were sent to the House of Representatives in Washington. Two went to the United States Senate, both of them from Mississippi. Hiram R. Revels—an ordained minister of the African Methodist Episcopal Church and a former North Carolina free Negro who had been educated at Knox College in Illinois—took the Senate seat (1870) that Jefferson Davis once had occupied. Blanche K. Bruce, who had escaped from slavery in Virginia and studied in the North, was made a senator in 1874 (he was the only Negro to be elected to a full term in the Senate until the election of Edward Brooke, of Massachusetts, in 1966).

Yet no such thing as "Negro rule" ever existed in any of the states. In the South as a whole the number of Negro officeholders was less than proportionate to the number of Negroes in the population. Nor did the state governments show much if any favoritism toward blacks as a group. Constitutions or statutes prohibited, on paper, discrimination on the basis of color, but segregation remained the common practice. Only in New Orleans were there, for a time, a few integrated schools.

The record of the Reconstruction governments is many-sided. As some of the leaders in the convention that framed the new state constitutions were Northerners, they put into these documents the most advanced provisions in those of the most progressive Northern states—provisions embodying the latest advances in local government, judicial organization, public finance, and poor relief.

The financial program of the Republican governments was a compound of blatant corruption and well-designed, if sometimes impractical, social legislation. State budgets expanded and state debts soared. In large measure, the corruption in the South was a phase of a national phe-

nomenon, with the same social force—an expanding capitalism eager to secure quick results—acting as the corrupting agent. Included in the spending programs of the Reconstruction governments were subsidies for railroads and other internal improvements, some of which materialized and some of which did not—because the promoters and the politicians pocketed the subsidies.

The state expenditures of the Reconstruction years seem huge only in comparison with the niggardly budgets of the conservative governments of the prewar era. The reconstructed governments undertook public education, public-works programs, poor relief, and other services that cost money. If there were thieving and foolish spending there were also positive and permanent accomplishments, particularly in education. One example is offered by South Carolina, which in 1860 had only 20,000 children in public schools; by 1873 some 50,000 white and 70,000 Negro students were enrolled.


## A Soldier in the White House

At the end of the war both parties had angled to make General Grant their candidate, and he could have had the nomination of either party. As he watched the congressional Radicals triumph over President Johnson, he concluded that the Radical Reconstruction policy expressed the real wishes of the people. He was receptive when the Radical leaders approached him with offers of the Republican nomination.

The Republicans endorsed Radical Reconstruction and Negro suffrage for the South, but declared that in the North the question of Negro voting should be determined by each state. (Thus during the campaign the Republicans opposed the suffrage amendment, the Fifteenth, which they were to pass soon after the election.)

Unwisely the Democrats decided to meet the Republican challenge. Their platform also emphasized Reconstruction, denouncing in extravagant terms the Radical program and demanding restoration of "home rule" in the South. Thus the Democrats chose to fight the campaign on an issue that was related to the war and its emotions—an issue that enabled their opponents to associate them with rebellion. They did, however, attempt to inject a new question of an economic nature into the contest. In 1868 approximately $356 million of the Civil War greenbacks were in circulation, and Middle Western Democrats wanted to keep the paper currency and use it when legally possible to pay off the national debt. Behind this so-called "Ohio idea" was the larger question of retaining the greenbacks as a permanent part of the money supply. This proposal appealed to the debtor farmers of the West and also to many hard-pressed businessmen of the East. The Westerners succeeded in writing the Ohio idea into the platform, but the party nominated Horatio Seymour of New York, a gold or "sound money" man, who repudiated the currency plank.

After a bitter campaign revolving around Reconstruction and Seymour's war record as governor of New York (he had been a Peace Democrat), Grant carried twenty-six states and Seymour only eight. But Grant got only 3,012,000 popular votes to Seymour's 2,703,-000, a scant majority of 310,000, and this majority was due to Negro votes in the reconstructed states of the South.

Ulysses S. Grant was the second professional soldier to be elected to the Presidency (Zachary Taylor having been the first), and the last to be chosen until Dwight D. Eisenhower was selected in 1952. Grant had little knowledge of political issues or political ways, and he was naïve in choosing men to help him, often appointing rascals or mediocrities. His greatest defect was that he did not understand his function as President. He regarded the Presidency as a cermonial and administrative office and failed to provide real leadership in trying times.

## Successes in Foreign Affairs

In foreign affairs the Grant administration achieved its most brilliant successes, as the Johnson administration also had done. These were the accomplishments of two outstanding Secretaries of State: William H. Seward (1861–1869) and Hamilton Fish (1869–1877).

An ardent expansionist and advocate of a vigorous foreign policy, Seward acted with as much daring as the demands of Reconstruction politics and the Republican hatred of President Johnson would permit. By exercising firm but patient pressure, he persuaded Napoleon III of France to abandon his Mexican empire, which was established during the war when the United States was in no position to protest. Napoleon withdrew his troops in 1867, his puppet Emperor Maximilian was executed by the Mexicans, and the validity of the Monroe Doctrine was strikingly reaffirmed.

When Russia let it be known that she would like to sell Alaska to the United States, the two nations long having been on friendly terms, Seward readily agreed to pay the asking price of $7.2 million. Only by strenuous efforts was he able to induce the Senate to ratify the treaty and the House to appropriate the money (1867–1868). Critics jeered that the secretary had bought a useless frozen wasteland — "Seward's Icebox" and "Walrussia" were some of the terms employed to describe it — but Alaska, a center for the fishing industry in the North Pacific and potentially rich in such resources as gold, was a distinct bargain. Seward was not content with expansion in continental North America. In 1867 he engineered the annexation of the tiny Midway Islands west of Hawaii.

The United States had a burning grievance against Great Britain which had originated during the Civil War. At that time the British government, according to the American interpretation, had violated the laws of neutrality by permitting Confederate cruisers, the *Alabama* and others, to be built and armed in English shipyards and let loose to prey on Northern commerce. American demands that England pay for the damages committed by these vessels became known as the "Alabama claims." Although the British government realized its diplomatic error in condoning construction of the cruisers (in a future war American-built *Alabamas* might operate against Britain), it at first hesitated to submit the issue to arbitration.

Seward tried earnestly to settle the Alabama claims before leaving office. Secretary Fish continued to work for a solution, and finally in 1871 the two countries agreed to the Treaty of Washington, one of the great landmarks in international pacification, providing for arbitration of the cruiser issue and other pending controversies. The Alabama claims were to be laid before a five-member tribunal appointed by the governments of the United States, England, Italy, Switzerland, and Brazil. In the covenant Britain expressed regret for the escape of the *Alabama* and agreed to a set of rules governing neutral obligations that virtually gave the British case away. In effect, this meant that the tribunal would have only to fix the sum to be paid by Britain. Convening at Geneva in Switzerland, the arbitrators awarded $15.5 million to the United States.

## The Evils of "Grantism"

Through both his foreign and his domestic policies, President Grant antagonized and alienated a number of prominent Republicans, among them the famous Radical, Charles Sumner.

Sumner and other Republican leaders joined with civil-service reformers to criticize Grant for his use of the spoils system, his reliance on ruthless machine politicians. Republican critics of the President also denounced him for his support of Radical Reconstruction. He continued to station federal troops in the South, and on numerous occasions he sent them to the support of Negro-and-carpetbag governments that were on the point of collapsing. To growing numbers in the North this seemed like dangerous militarism, and they were more and more disgusted by the stories of governmental corruption and extravagance that came up from the South. Some Republicans were beginning to suspect that there was corruption not only in the Southern state governments but also in the federal government itself. Still others criticized Grant because he had declined to speak out in favor of a reduction of the tariff. The high wartime duties, used as a means of paying off the war debt, remained substantially unchanged.

In 1872, hoping to prevent Grant's reelection, his opponents bolted the party. Referring to themselves as Liberal Republicans, they proceeded to set up their own organization for running presidential and vice-presidential candidates. For the Presidency they named Horace Greeley, veteran editor and publisher of the New York *Tribune*. The Democratic convention, seeing in his candidacy the only chance to unseat the Republicans, endorsed him with no great enthusiasm. Despite his recent attacks on Radical Reconstruction, many Southerners, remembering Greeley's own Radical past, prepared to stay at home on election day. Greeley carried only two Southern and four border states.

During the campaign the first of a series of political scandals had come to light. Although the wrongdoing had occurred before Grant took office, it involved his party and the onus for it fell on his administration. This scandal originated with the Crédit Mobilier construction company that helped build the Union Pacific Railroad. In reality, the Crédit Mobilier was controlled by a few Union Pacific stockholders who awarded huge and fraudulent contracts to the construction company, thus milking the Union Pacific, a company of which they owned a minor share, of money that in part came from government subsidies. To avert a congressional inquiry into the deal, the directors sold at a discount (in effect gave) Crédit Mobilier stock to key members of Congress. A congressional investigation revealed that some high-placed Republicans had accepted stock, including Schuyler Colfax, now Grant's Vice President.

One dreary episode followed another during Grant's second term. Benjamin H. Bristow, secretary of the treasury, discovered that some of his officials and a group of distillers operating as a "Whiskey Ring" were cheating the government out of taxes by means of false reports. Among the prominent Republicans involved was the President's private secretary, Orville E. Babcock. Grant defended Babcock, appointed him to another office, and eased Bristow out of the cabinet. A House investigation revealed that William W. Belknap, secretary of war, had accepted bribes to retain an Indian-post trader in office. Belknap resigned with Grant's blessing before the Senate could act on impeachment charges brought by the House. Lesser scandals involved the Navy Department, which was suspected of selling business to contractors, and the Treasury, where John D. Sanborn, a special agent appointed to handle overdue taxes, collected $427,000 and retained a 50 percent commission for himself and the Republican bigwigs who had placed him in the job. Not to be left out of the picture, Congress passed an act doubling the annual salary of the President from $25,000 to $50,000 (the first increase since George Washington's time), and raising the salaries of members of Congress from $5,000 to $7,500 a year. The increases were justifiable, but the country was enraged to learn that its representatives had also voted themselves two years of back pay. Bowing before a storm of denunciation, the next Congress hastened to repeal the so-called "Salary Grab."

## The Greenback Question

Meanwhile the Grant administration along with the country as a whole had suffered another blow when the Panic of 1873 struck. It was touched off by the failure of a leading investment banking firm, Jay Cooke and Company, the "financier of the Civil War," which had done well in the handling of government war bonds but had sunk excessive amounts in postwar railroad building. Depressions had come before with almost rhythmic regularity—in 1819, 1837, and 1857—but this was the worst one yet. It lasted four years, during which unemployment rose to 3 million, and agricultural prices fell so far that thousands of farmers, unable to meet mortgage payments, went more deeply into debt or lost their farms.

Debtors hoped the government would follow an inflationary, easy-money policy, which would have made it easier for them to pay their debts and would have helped to stimulate recovery from the depression. But President Grant and most Republicans preferred what they called a "sound" currency, which was to the advantage of the banks, money-lenders, and other creditors.

As a relief measure after the Panic of 1873, the Treasury increased the amount of greenbacks in circulation. For the same reason Congress, in the following year, voted to raise the total again. Grant, responding to pressures from the financial interests, vetoed the measure. In 1875 the Republican Congress enacted the Resumption Act, providing that after January 1, 1879, the government would exchange gold dollars for greenbacks and directing the government to acquire a gold reserve for redemption purposes. The law had its intended result: with the specie value of greenbacks assured, they were equal in worth to gold. The fundamental impact of the law was to produce deflation and thus protect the interests of the creditor classes, but at the same time, the debtor groups could take some comfort in the retention of the greenbacks.

## Southern Republicans Lose

The period of Republican control in the South varied from state to state. In a few states the Democrats (or Conservatives) got into power as soon or almost as soon as restoration occurred. The longest that Republican rule lasted in any of the states was about ten years. It was ended in Virginia, North Carolina, and Georgia in 1870; in Texas in 1873; in Alabama and Arkansas in 1874; in Mississippi in 1875; and in South Carolina, Louisiana, and Florida in 1877.

In the states where the whites constituted a majority—the upper South states—overthrow of Republican control was a relatively simple matter. The whites had only to organize and win the elections. Their success was facilitated by the early restoration of the suffrage to those whites who had been deprived of it by national or state action. Presidential and congressional pardons returned the privilege to numerous individuals, and in 1872 Congress, responding to public demands to forgive the penalties of the war, enacted the Amnesty Act, which restored political rights to 150,000 ex-Confederates and left only 500 excluded from political life.

In other states, where the Negroes were in the majority or the population difference between the races was small, the whites resorted to intimidation and violence. Secret societies that were frankly terroristic appeared in many parts of the South—the Ku Klux Klan, the Knights of the White Camellia, and others. They attempted to frighten or physically prevent Negroes from voting. To stamp out these societies, Congress passed two Force Acts (1870–1871) and the Ku Klux Klan Act (1871), which authorized the President to use military force and martial law in areas where the orders were active.

More potent than the secret orders were the open semimilitary organizations that operated under such names as Rifle clubs, Red Shirts, and White Leagues. After the first such society was founded in Mississippi, the idea spread to other states, and the procedure employed by the clubs was called the Mississippi Plan. Briefly stated, the plan called for the whites in each community to organize and arm, and to be prepared, if necessary, to resort to force to win elections.

Perhaps an even stronger influence than the techniques practiced by the armed bands was the simple and direct weapon of economic pressure. The war had freed the Negro, but he was still a laborer—a hired worker or a tenant—dependent upon the whites for his livelihood. The whites readily discovered that this dependence placed the Negro in their power. Planters refused to rent land to Republican Negroes, storekeepers refused to extend them credit, employers refused to give them work.

Certainly the Negro's political position was hopeless without the continued backing of the Republican party and the federal government. But he was losing the support of people in the North, even of many humanitarian reformers who had worked for emancipation and Negro rights. After the adoption of the Fifteenth Amendment (1870), most of the reformers convinced themselves that their long campaign in his behalf at last was over, that with the vote he ought to be able to take care of himself.

When the depression came in 1873, the hard times aggravated political discontent both North and South. In the congressional elections of 1874 the Democrats gained a majority of the seats in the national House of Representatives. After 1875, when the new House met, the Republicans no longer controlled the whole Congress, as they had done since the beginning of the war. And President Grant, in view of the changing temper of the North, no longer was willing to use military force to save from violent overthrow the Republican regimes that were still standing in the South.

## The Compromise of 1877

In 1876 the Republican managers, seeking to reunite the party, secured the nomination of Rutherford B. Hayes, governor of Ohio and a symbol of honest government. The Democrats nominated Samuel J. Tilden, governor of New York and also a symbol of honest government. Between the two candidates there was little difference. Both were conservative on economic issues and both were on record as favoring the withdrawal of troops from the South.

The November election revealed an apparent electoral and popular majority for Tilden. But disputed returns had come in from three Southern states, Louisiana, South Carolina, and Florida, whose total electoral vote was nineteen. In addition, there was a technical dispute in Oregon about one elector. Tilden had for certain 184 electoral votes, one short of a majority. The twenty votes in controversy would determine who would be President.

With surprise and consternation, the public now learned that no measure or method existed to determine the validity of disputed returns.

The Constitution stated: "The President of the Senate shall, in the presence of the Senate and House of Representatives, open all the certificates and the votes shall then be counted." The question was how and by whom? The Senate was Republican and so, of course, was its president, and the House was Democratic. The country was threatened with crisis—and possibly with chaos.

Not until the last days of January 1877 did Congress act to break the deadlock. Then it created a special Electoral Commission to pass on all the disputed votes. The Commission was to be composed of five Senators, five Representatives, and five Justices of the Supreme Court. Because of the party lineup, the Congressional delegation would consist of five Republicans and five Democrats. The creating law named four of the judicial commissioners, two Republicans and two Democrats. The four were to select their fifth colleague, and it was understood that they would choose David Davis, an independent Republican, thus ensuring that the deciding vote would be wielded by a relatively unbiased judge. But at this stage Davis was elected to the Senate from Illinois and refused to serve. His place on the Commission fell to a Republican. Sitting throughout February, the Commission by a partisan vote of eight to seven decided every disputed vote for Hayes. Congress accepted the final verdict of the agency on March 2, only two days before the inauguration of the new President.

But the findings of the Commission were not final until approved by Congress, and the Democrats could have prevented action by filibustering. The success of a filibuster, however, depended on concert between Northern and Southern Democrats, and this the Republicans disrupted by offering the Southerners sufficient inducement to accept the Commission's finds. They promised to the Southerners control of federal patronage in their states, generous internal improvements, federal aid for a Southern transcontinental railroad, and withdrawal of federal troops from the South. The Southerners accepted the package, and the crisis was over.

The withdrawal of the troops, which President Hayes effected soon after his inauguration, was a symbol that the national government was giving up its attempt to control Southern politics and to determine the place of the Negro in Southern society.

The controversy between the sections that finally erupted in civil war is treated in a number of general studies. Among the best of these are Allan Nevins, *Ordeal of the Union* (2 vols., 1947), and *The Emergence of Lincoln* (2 vols., 1950); A. O. Craven, *The Growth of Southern Nationalism, 1848–1861* (1953); A. C. Cole, *The Irrepressible Conflict, 1850–1865* (1934); R. F. Nichols, *The Disruption of American Democracy\** (1948); and E. B. Smith, *The Death of Slavery, 1837–1865\** (1967). Special aspects of the sectional quarrel are treated in Louis Filler, *The Crusade Against Slavery\** (1960), and Holman Hamilton, *Prologue to Conflict\** (1964), the Compromise of 1850. Lincoln's role in the developing crisis is subjected to searching analysis in D. E. Fehrenbacher, *Prelude to Greatness\** (1962). On the ideas motivating Republicans there is Eric Foner's *Free Soil, Free Labor, Free Men: The Ideology of the Republican Party before the Civil War* (1970).

Some of the biographies cited in the immediately preceding section, especially those of Calhoun, Webster, and Clay, are useful for the decade of the fifties. Other good studies are Holman Hamilton, *Zachary Taylor, Soldier in the White House* (1951); G. F. Milton, *The Eve of Conflict* (1934), Stephen A. Douglas; David Donald, *Charles Sumner and the Coming of the Civil War* (1960); A. D. Kirwan, *John J. Crittenden* (1962); P. S. Klein, *President James Buchanan* (1962); and S. B. Oates, *To Purge This Land with Blood* (1970), John Brown. The critical events of 1860–1861 are related in D. M. Potter, *Lincoln and His Party in the Secession Crisis\** (1942); K. M. Stampp, *And the War Came* (1950); and R. N. Current, *Lincoln and the First Shot\** (1963).

The literature on the Civil War is so vast as to defy summary. Excellent bibliographies appear in the convenient survey by J. G. Randall and David Donald, *The Civil War and Reconstruction* (1961). There is the massive survey of Allan Nevins, *The War for the Union* (4 vols., 1959–1972). See also Bruce Catton, *This Hallowed Ground* (1956). Informative for the Southern side are Clement Eaton, *A History of the Southern Confederacy\** (1954), and C. P. Roland, *The Confederacy\** (1960).

On special aspects of the North at war see T. H. Williams, *Lincoln and the Radicals\** (1941), and H. L. Trefousse, *The Radical Republicans* (1969), which offer somewhat contrasting views; Wood Gray, *The Hidden Civil War\** (1942), the opposition to the war; F. L. Klement, *The Copperheads in the Middle West* (1960); B. I. Wiley, *The Life of Billy Yank\** (1952), the common soldier; Dudley Cornish, *The Sable Arm\** (1956), the Negro soldier; Benjamin Quarles, *The Negro in the Civil War* (1953); J. M. McPherson, *The Struggle for Equality* (1964), the abolitionists in the war; and P. W. Gates, *Agriculture and the Civil War* (1965). For Northern diplomacy see G. G. Van Deusen, *William Henry Seward* (1967). On the South at war consult B. I. Wiley, *The Life of Johnny Reb\** (1943); F. E. Vandiver, *Rebel Brass* (1956), Southern command; A. B. Moore, *Conscription and Conflict in the Confederacy* (1924); and F. L. Owsley, *States Rights in the Confederacy* (1925), and *King Cotton Diplomacy* (1931, 1959).

Civil War biographies are many but vary in quality. There is no good life of Jefferson Davis. On Lincoln see B. F. Thomas, *Abraham Lincoln* (1952), and J. G. Randall, *Mr. Lincoln* (1957), distilled by R. N. Current from Randall's four-volumed *Lincoln the President*. See also R. N. Current, *Old Thad Stevens* (1942); Fawn Brodie, *Thaddeus Stevens* (1959), which presents a contrasting view; and David Donald, *Charles Sumner and the Rights of Man* (1970). A classic Confederate item is D. S. Freeman, *R. E. Lee* (4 vols., 1934–1935), abridged to one volume by Richard Harwell, *Lee* (1951).

**SELECTED READINGS**

Of the shelves of books treating Civil War campaigns, begin with J. B. Mitchell, *Decisive Battles of the Civil War** (1955); T. H. Williams, *Lincoln and His Generals** (1952); and Bern Anderson, *By Sea and By River* (1962), the navies. Eventually any serious student will have to get into D. S. Freeman, *Lee's Lieutenants* (3 vols., 1942–1944).

The older but now questioned view of Reconstruction appears in W. A. Dunning, *Reconstruction, Political and Economic** (1907), and W. L. Fleming, *The Sequel to Appomattox* (1919). It was first challenged by W. E. B. DuBois in *Black Reconstruction* (1935). Later and more telling challenges came in E. L. McKitrick, *Andrew Johnson and Reconstruction** (1966); J. H. Franklin, *Reconstruction** (1965); and David Donald, *The Politics of Reconstruction* (1965). Representative of a number of books treating the role of the Negro is Joel Williamson, *After Slavery* (1966). On the New South see C. V. Woodward, *Origins of the New South, 1877–1913** (1951), and *The Strange Career of Jim Crow** (1953). The best overall account is K. M. Stampp's *Era of Reconstruction* (1965).

* Titles available in paperback.

# Appendices

## The Declaration of Independence

*In Congress, July 4, 1776,*

THE UNANIMOUS DECLARATION OF THE THIRTEEN UNITED STATES OF AMERICA

When, in the course of human events, it becomes necessary for one people to dissolve the political bands which have connected them with another, and to assume, among the powers of the earth, the separate and equal station to which the laws of nature and of nature's God entitle them, a decent respect to the opinions of mankind requires that they should declare the causes which impel them to the separation.

We hold these truths to be self-evident, that all men are created equal; that they are endowed by their Creator with certain unalienable rights; that among these, are life, liberty, and the pursuit of happiness. That, to secure these rights, governments are instituted among men, deriving their just powers from the consent of the governed; that, whenever any form of government becomes destructive of these ends, it is the right of the people to alter or to abolish it, and to institute a new government, laying its foundation on such principles, and organizing its powers in such form, as to them shall seem most likely to effect their safety and happiness. Prudence, indeed, will dictate that governments long established, should not be changed for light and transient causes; and, accordingly, all experience hath shown, that mankind are more disposed to suffer, while evils are sufferable, than to right themselves by abolishing the forms to which they are accustomed. But, when a long train of abuses and usurpations, pursuing invariably the same object, evinces a design to reduce them under absolute despotism, it is their right, it is their duty, to throw off such government and to provide new guards for their future security. Such has been the patient sufferance of these colonies, and such is now the necessity which constrains them to alter their former systems of government. The history of the present King of Great Britain is a history of repeated injuries and usurpations, all having, in direct object, the establishment of an absolute tyranny over these States. To prove this, let facts be submitted to a candid world: —

He has refused his assent to laws the most wholesome and necessary for the public good.

He has forbidden his governors to pass laws of immediate and pressing importance, unless suspended in their operation till his assent should be obtained; and, when so suspended, he has utterly neglected to attend to them.

He has refused to pass other laws for the accommodation of large districts of people, unless those people would relinquish the right of representation in the legislature; a right inestimable to them, and formidable to tyrants only.

He has called together legislative bodies at places unusual, uncomfortable, and distant from the depository of their public records, for the sole purpose of fatiguing them into compliance with his measures.

He has dissolved representative houses repeatedly for opposing, with manly firmness, his invasions on the rights of the people.

He has refused, for a long time after such dissolutions, to cause others to be elected; whereby the legislative powers, incapable of annihilation, have returned to the people at large for their exercise; the state remaining, in the meantime, exposed to all the danger of invasion from without, and convulsions within.

He has endeavored to prevent the population of these States; for that purpose, obstructing the laws for naturalization of foreigners, refusing to pass others to encourage their migration hither, and raising the conditions of new appropriations of lands.

He has obstructed the administration of justice, by refusing his assent to laws for establishing judiciary powers.

He has made judges dependent on his will alone, for the tenure of their offices, and the amount and payment of their salaries.

He has erected a multitude of new offices, and sent hither swarms of officers to harass our people, and eat out their substance.

He has kept among us, in time of peace, standing armies, without the consent of our legislatures.

He has affected to render the military independent of, and superior to, the civil power.

He has combined, with others, to subject us to a jurisdiction foreign to our Constitution, and unacknowledged by our laws; giving his assent to their acts of pretended legislation:

For quartering large bodies of armed troops among us:

For protecting them by a mock trial, from punishment, for any murders which they should commit on the inhabitants of these States:

For cutting off our trade with all parts of the world:

For imposing taxes on us without our consent:

For depriving us, in many cases, of the benefit of trial by jury:

For transporting us beyond seas to be tried for pretended offences:

For abolishing the free system of English laws in a neighboring province, establishing therein an arbitrary government, and enlarging its boundaries, so as to render it at once an example and fit instrument for introducing the same absolute rule into these colonies:

For taking away our charters, abolishing our most valuable laws, and altering, fundamentally, the powers of our governments:

For suspending our own legislatures, and declaring themselves invested with power to legislate for us in all cases whatsoever.

He has abdicated government here, by declaring us out of his protection, and waging war against us.

He has plundered our seas, ravaged our coasts, burnt our towns, and destroyed the lives of our people.

He is, at this time, transporting large armies of foreign mercenaries to complete the works of death, desolation, and tyranny, already begun, with circumstances of cruelty and perfidy scarcely paralleled in the most barbarous ages, and totally unworthy the head of a civilized nation.

He has constrained our fellow citizens, taken captive on the high seas, to bear arms against their country, to become the executioners of their friends, and brethren, or to fall themselves by their hands.

He has excited domestic insurrections amongst us, and has endeavored to bring on the inhabitants of our frontiers, the merciless Indian savages, whose known rule of warfare is an undistinguished destruction of all ages, sexes, and conditions.

In every stage of these oppressions, we have petitioned for redress, in the most humble terms; our repeated petitions have been answered only by repeated injury. A prince, whose character is thus marked by every act which may define a tyrant, is unfit to be the ruler of a free people.

Nor have we been wanting in attention to our British brethren. We have warned them, from time to time, of attempts made by their legislature to extend an unwarrantable jurisdiction over us. We have reminded them of the circumstances of our emigration and settlement here. We have appealed to their native justice and magnanimity, and we have conjured them, by the ties of our common kindred, to disavow these usurpations, which would inevitably interrupt our connections and correspondence. They, too, have been deaf to the voice of justice and consanguinity. We must, therefore, acquiesce in the necessity which denounces our separation, and hold them as we hold the rest of mankind, enemies in war, in peace, friends.

We, therefore, the representatives of the United States of America, in general Congress assembled, appealing to the Supreme Judge of the world for the rectitude of our intentions, do, in the name, and by the authority of the good people of these colonies, solemnly publish and declare, that these united colonies are, and of right ought to be, free and independent states: that they are absolved from all allegiance to the British Crown, and that all political connection between them and the state of Great Britain is, and ought to be, totally dissolved; and that, as free and independent states, they have full power to levy war, conclude peace, contract alliances, establish commerce, and to do all other acts and things which independent states may of right do. And, for the support of this declaration, with a firm reliance on the protection of Divine Providence, we mutually pledge to each other our lives, our fortunes, and our sacred honor.

The foregoing Declaration was, by order of Congress, engrossed, and signed by the following members:

### JOHN HANCOCK

**New Hampshire**

Josiah Bartlett
William Whipple
Matthew Thornton

**Massachusetts Bay**

Samuel Adams
John Adams
Robert Treat Paine
Elbridge Gerry

**Rhode Island**

Stephen Hopkins
William Ellery

**Connecticut**

Roger Sherman
Samuel Huntington
William Williams
Oliver Wolcott

**New York**

William Floyd
Philip Livingston
Francis Lewis
Lewis Morris

**New Jersey**

Richard Stockton
John Witherspoon
Francis Hopkinson
John Hart
Abraham Clark

**Pennsylvania**

Robert Morris
Benjamin Rush
Benjamin Franklin
John Morton
George Clymer
James Smith
George Taylor
James Wilson
George Ross

**Delaware**

Caesar Rodney
George Read
Thomas M'Kean

**Maryland**

Samuel Chase
William Paca
Thomas Stone
Charles Carroll,
    of Carrollton

**Virginia**

George Wythe
Richard Henry Lee
Thomas Jefferson
Benjamin Harrison
Thomas Nelson, Jr.
Francis Lightfoot Lee
Carter Braxton

**North Carolina**

William Hooper
Joseph Hewes
John Penn

**South Carolina**

Edward Rutledge
Thomas Heyward, Jr.
Thomas Lynch, Jr.
Arthur Middleton

**Georgia**

Button Gwinnett
Lyman Hall
George Walton

*Resolved,* That copies of the Declaration be sent to the several assemblies, conventions, and committees, or councils of safety, and to the several commanding officers of the continental troops; that it be proclaimed in each of the United States, at the head of the army.

# The Constitution of the United States of America[1]

WE the People of the United States, in Order to form a more perfect Union, establish Justice, insure domestic Tranquility, provide for the common defence, promote the general Welfare, and secure the Blessings of Liberty to ourselves and our Posterity, do ordain and establish this CONSTITUTION for the United States of America.

## Article I

### SECTION 1.

All legislative Powers herein granted shall be vested in a Congress of the United States, which shall consist of a Senate and House of Representatives.

### SECTION 2.

The House of Representatives shall be composed of Members chosen every second Year by the People of the several States, and the Electors in each State shall have the Qualifications requisite for Electors of the most numerous Branch of the State Legislature.

No Person shall be a Representative who shall not have attained to the Age of twenty-five Years, and been seven Years a Citizen of the United States, and who shall not, when elected, be an Inhabitant of that State in which he shall be chosen.

[Representatives and direct Taxes[2] shall be apportioned among the several States which may be included within this Union, according to their respective Numbers, which shall be determined by adding to the whole Number of free Persons, including those bound to Service for a Term of Years, and excluding Indians not taxed, three fifths of all other Persons.][3] The actual Enumeration shall be made within three Years after the first Meeting of the Congress of the United States, and within every subsequent Term of ten Years, in such Manner as they shall by Law direct. The Number of Representatives shall not exceed one for every thirty Thousand, but each State shall have at Least one Representative; and until such enumeration shall be made, the State of New Hampshire shall be entitled to chuse three, Massachusetts eight, Rhode-Island and Providence Plantations one, Connecticut five, New York six, New Jersey four, Pennsylvania eight, Delaware one, Maryland six, Virginia ten, North Carolina five, South Carolina five, and Georgia three.

When vacancies happen in the Representation from any State, the Executive Authority thereof shall issue Writs of Election to fill such Vacancies.

The House of Representatives shall chuse their Speaker and other Officers; and shall have the sole Power of Impeachment.

### SECTION 3.

The Senate of the United States shall be composed of two Senators from each State, chosen by the Legislature thereof, for six Years; and each Senator shall have one Vote.

Immediately after they shall be assembled in Consequence of the first Election, they shall be divided as equally as may be into three Classes. The Seats of the Senators of the first Class shall be vacated at the Expiration of the second Year, of the second Class at the Expiration of the fourth Year, and of the third Class at the Expiration of the sixth Year, so that one-third may be chosen every second Year; and if Vacancies happen by Resignation, or otherwise, during the Recess of the Legislature of any State, the Executive thereof may make temporary Appointments until the next Meeting of the Legislature, which shall then fill such Vacancies.

No Person shall be a Senator who shall not have attained to the Age of thirty Years, and been nine Years a Citizen of the United States, and who shall not, when elected, be an Inhabitant of that State for which he shall be chosen.

[1]This version, which follows the original Constitution in capitalization and spelling, was published by the United States Department of the Interior, Office of Education, in 1935.
[2]Altered by the Sixteenth Amendment.
[3]Negated by the Fourteenth Amendment.

The Vice President of the United States shall be President of the Senate, but shall have no vote, unless they be equally divided.

The Senate shall chuse their other Officers, and also a President pro tempore, in the absence of the Vice President, or when he shall exercise the Office of President of the United States.

The Senate shall have the sole Power to try all Impeachments. When sitting for that purpose, they shall be on Oath or Affirmation. When the President of the United States is tried, the Chief Justice shall preside: And no person shall be convicted without the Concurrence of two thirds of the Members present.

Judgment in Cases of Impeachment shall not extend further than to removal from Office, and disqualification to hold and enjoy any Office of honor, Trust, or Profit under the United States: but the Party convicted shall nevertheless be liable and subject to Indictment, Trial, Judgment, and Punishment, according to Law.

### SECTION 4.

The Times, Places and Manner of holding Elections for Senators and Representatives, shall be prescribed in each State by the Legislature thereof; but the Congress may at any time by Law make or alter such Regulations, except as to the Places of Chusing Senators.

The Congress shall assemble at least once in every Year, and such Meeting shall be on the first Monday in December, unless they shall by Law appoint a different Day.

### SECTION 5.

Each House shall be the Judge of the Elections, Returns and Qualifications of its own Members, and a Majority of each shall constitute a Quorum to do Business; but a smaller number may adjourn from day to day, and may be authorized to compel the Attendance of absent Members, in such Manner, and under such Penalties, as each House may provide.

Each House may determine the Rules of its Proceedings, punish its Members for disorderly Behaviour, and, with the Concurrence of two thirds, expel a Member.

Each House shall keep a Journal of its Proceedings, and from time to time publish the same, excepting such Parts as may in their Judgment require Secrecy; and the Yeas and Nays of the Members of either House on any question shall, at the Desire of one fifth of those Present, be entered on the Journal.

Neither House, during the Session of Congress, shall, without the Consent of the other, adjourn for more than three days, nor to any other Place than that in which the two Houses shall be sitting.

### SECTION 6.

The Senators and Representatives shall receive a Compensation for their Services, to be ascertained by Law, and paid out of the Treasury of the United States. They shall in all Cases, except Treason, Felony, and Breach of the Peace, be privileged from Arrest during their Attendance at the Session of their respective Houses, and in going to and returning from the same; and for any Speech or Debate in either House, they shall not be questioned in any other Place.

No Senator or Representative shall, during the Time for which he was elected, be appointed to any civil Office under the Authority of the United States, which shall have been created, or the Emoluments whereof shall have been increased, during such time; and no Person holding any Office under the United States shall be a Member of either House during his continuance in Office.

### SECTION 7.

All Bills for raising Revenue shall originate in the House of Representatives; but the Senate may propose or concur with Amendments as on other bills.

Every Bill which shall have passed the House of Representatives and the Senate, shall, before it become a Law, be presented to the President of the United States; If he approve he shall sign it, but if not he shall return it, with his Objections, to that House in which it shall have originated, who shall enter the Objections at large on their Journal, and proceed to reconsider it. If after such Reconsideration two thirds of that House shall agree to pass the bill, it shall be sent, together with the objections, to the other House, by which it shall likewise be reconsidered, and if approved by two thirds of that House, it shall become a Law. But in all such Cases the Votes of both Houses shall be determined by Yeas and Nays, and the Names of the Persons voting for and against the Bill shall be entered on the Journal of each House respectively. If any Bill shall not be returned by the President within ten Days (Sundays excepted) after it shall have been presented to him, the Same shall be a Law, in like Manner as if he had signed it, unless the Congress by their Adjournment prevent its Return, in which Case it shall not be a Law.

Every Order, Resolution, or Vote to which the Concurrence of the Senate and House of Representatives may be necessary (except on a question of Adjournment) shall be presented to the President of the United States; and before the Same shall take Effect, shall be approved by him, or being disapproved by him, shall be repassed by two thirds of the Senate and House of Representatives, according to the Rules and Limitations prescribed in the Case of a Bill.

## SECTION 8.

The Congress shall have Power To lay and collect Taxes, Duties, Imposts and Excises, to pay the Debts and provide for the common Defence and general Welfare of the United States; but all Duties, Imposts and Excises shall be uniform throughout the United States;

To borrow money on the credit of the United States;

To regulate Commerce with foreign Nations, and among the several States, and with the Indian Tribes;

To establish an uniform Rule of Naturalization, and uniform Laws on the subject of Bankruptcies throughout the United States;

To coin Money, regulate the Value thereof, and of foreign Coin, and fix the Standard of Weights and Measures;

To provide for the Punishment of counterfeiting the Securities and current Coin of the United States;

To establish Post Offices and post Roads;

To promote the Progress of Science and useful Arts, by securing for limited Times to Authors and Inventors the exclusive Right to their respective Writings and Discoveries;

To constitute Tribunals inferior to the Supreme Court;

To define and punish Piracies and Felonies committed on the high Seas, and Offenses against the Law of Nations;

To declare War, grant Letters of Marque and Reprisal, and make Rules concerning Captures on Land and Water;

To raise and support Armies, but no Appropriation of Money to that Use shall be for a longer Term than two Years;

To provide and maintain a Navy;

To make Rules for the Government and Regulation of the land and naval forces;

To provide for calling forth the Militia to execute the Laws of the Union, suppress Insurrections and repel Invasions;

To provide for organizing, arming, and disciplining the Militia, and for governing such Part of them as may be employed in the Service of the United States, reserving to the States respectively, the Appointment of the Officers, and the Authority of training the Militia according to the discipline prescribed by Congress;

To exercise exclusive Legislation in all Cases whatsoever, over such District (not exceeding ten Miles square) as may, by Cession of particular States, and the acceptance of Congress, become the Seat of the Government of the United States, and to exercise like Authority over all Places purchased by the Consent of the Legislature of the State in which the Same shall be, for the Erection of Forts, Magazines, Arsenals, Dock-yards, and other needful Buildings; – And

To make all Laws which shall be necessary and proper for carrying into Execution the foregoing Powers, and all other Powers vested by this Constitution in the Government of the United States, or in any Department or Officer thereof.

## SECTION 9.

The Migration or Importation of such Persons as any of the States now existing shall think proper to admit, shall not be prohibited by the Congress prior to the Year one thousand eight hundred and eight, but a tax or duty may be imposed on such Importation, not exceeding ten dollars for each Person.

The privilege of the Writ of Habeas Corpus shall not be suspended, unless when in Cases of Rebellion or Invasion the public Safety may require it.

No bill of Attainder or ex post facto Law shall be passed.

No capitation, or other direct, Tax shall be laid unless in Proportion to the Census or Enumeration herein before directed to be taken.

No Tax or Duty shall be laid on Articles exported from any State.

No Preference shall be given by any Regulation of Commerce or Revenue to the Ports of one State over those of another: nor shall Vessels bound to, or from, one State, be obliged to enter, clear, or pay Duties in another.

No Money shall be drawn from the Treasury, but in Consequence of Appropriations made by Law; and a regular Statement and Account of the Receipts and Expenditures of all public Money shall be published from time to time.

No Title of Nobility shall be granted by the United States: And no Person holding any Office of Profit or Trust under them, shall, without the Consent of the Congress, accept of any present, Emolument, Office, or Title, of any kind whatever, from any King, Prince, or foreign State.

**SECTION 10.**

No State shall enter into any Treaty, Alliance, or Confederation; grant Letters of Marque and Reprisal; coin Money; emit Bills of Credit; make any Thing but gold and silver Coin a Tender in Payment of Debts; pass any Bill of Attainder, ex post facto Law, or Law impairing the Obligation of Contracts, or grant any Title of Nobility.

No State shall, without the Consent of the Congress, lay any Imposts or Duties on Imports or Exports, except what may be absolutely necessary for executing its inspection Laws: and the net Produce of all Duties and Imposts, laid by any State on Imports or Exports, shall be for the Use of the Treasury of the United States; and all such Laws shall be subject to the Revision and Control of the Congress.

No state shall, without the Consent of Congress, lay any duty of Tonnage, keep Troops, or Ships of War in time of Peace, enter into any Agreement or Compact with another State, or with a foreign Power, or engage in War, unless actually invaded, or in such imminent Danger as will not admit of delay.

## Article II

**SECTION 1.**

The executive Power shall be vested in a President of the United States of America. He shall hold his Office during the Term of four years, and, together with the Vice President, chosen for the same Term, be elected, as follows:

Each State shall appoint, in such Manner as the Legislature thereof may direct, a Number of Electors, equal to the whole Number of Senators and Representatives to which the State may be entitled in the Congress: but no Senator or Representative, or Person holding an Office of Trust or Profit under the United States, shall be appointed an Elector.

[The Electors shall meet in their respective States, and vote by Ballot for two persons, of whom one at least shall not be an Inhabitant of the same State with themselves. And they shall make a List of all the Persons voted for, and of the Number of Votes for each; which List they shall sign and certify, and transmit sealed to the Seat of the Government of the United States, directed to the President of the Senate. The President of the Senate shall, in the Presence of the Senate and House of Representatives, open all the Certificates, and the Votes shall then be counted. The Person having the greatest Number of Votes shall be the President, if such Number be a Majority of the whole Number of Electors appointed; and if there be more than one who have such Majority, and have an equal Number of Votes, then the House of Representatives shall immediately chuse by Ballot one of them for President; and if no Person have a Majority, then from the five highest on the List the said House shall in the Manner chuse the President. But in chusing the President, the Votes shall be taken by States, the Representation from each State having one Vote; a quorum for this Purpose shall consist of a Member or Members from two-thirds of the States, and a Majority of all the States shall be necessary to a Choice. In every Case, after the Choice of the President, the Person having the greatest Number of Votes of the Electors shall be the Vice President. But if there should remain two or more who have equal votes, the Senate shall chuse from them by Ballot the Vice President.][4]

The Congress may determine the Time of chusing the Electors, and the Day on which they shall give their Votes; which Day shall be the same throughout the United States.

No person except a natural-born Citizen, or a Citizen of the United States, at the time of the Adoption of this Constitution, shall be eligible to the Office of President; neither shall any Person be eligible to that Office who shall not have attained to the Age of thirty-five years, and been fourteen Years a Resident within the United States.

[4]Revised by the Twelfth Amendment.

In Case of the Removal of the President from Office, or of his Death, Resignation, or Inability to discharge the Powers and Duties of the said Office, the same shall devolve on the Vice President, and the Congress may by Law provide for the Case of Removal, Death, Resignation, or Inability, both of the President and Vice President, declaring what Officer shall then act as President, and such Officer shall act accordingly, until the disability be removed, or a President shall be elected.

The President shall, at stated Times, receive for his Services a Compensation, which shall neither be increased nor diminished during the Period for which he shall have been elected, and he shall not receive within that Period any other Emolument from the United States, or any of them.

Before he enter on the execution of his Office, he shall take the following Oath or Affirmation: — "I do solemnly swear (or affirm) that I will faithfully execute the Office of President of the United States, and will, to the best of my Ability, preserve, protect, and defend the Constitution of the United States."

### SECTION 2.

The President shall be Commander in Chief of the Army and Navy of the United States, and of the Militia of the several States, when called into the actual Service of the United States; he may require the Opinion, in writing, of the principal Officer in each of the executive Departments, upon any subject relating to the Duties of their respective Offices, and he shall have Power to Grant Reprieves and Pardons for Offenses against the United States, except in Cases of Impeachment.

He shall have Power, by and with the Advice and Consent of the Senate, to make Treaties, provided two-thirds of the Senators present concur; and he shall nominate, and by and with the Advice and Consent of the Senate, shall appoint Ambassadors, other public Ministers and Consuls, Judges of the supreme Court, and all other Officers of the United States, whose Appointments are not herein otherwise provided for, and which shall be established by Law: but the Congress may by Law vest the Appointment of such inferior Officers, as they think proper, in the President alone, in the Courts of Law, or in the Heads of Departments.

The President shall have Power to fill up all Vacancies that may happen during the Recess of the Senate, by granting Commissions which shall expire at the End of their next Session.

### SECTION 3.

He shall from time to time give to the Congress Information of the State of the Union, and recommend to their Consideration such Measures as he shall judge necessary and expedient; he may, on extraordinary occasions, convene both Houses, or either of them, and in Case of Disagreement between them, with respect to the Time of Adjournment, he may adjourn them to such Time as he shall think proper; he shall receive Ambassadors and other public Ministers; he shall take care that the Laws be faithfully executed, and shall Commission all the Officers of the United States.

### SECTION 4.

The President, Vice President and all civil Officers of the United States, shall be removed from Office on Impeachment for, and Conviction of, Treason, Bribery, or other high Crimes and Misdemeanors.

## Article III

### SECTION 1.

The judicial Power of the United States, shall be vested in one supreme Court, and in such inferior Courts as the Congress may from time to time ordain and establish. The Judges, both of the supreme and inferior Courts, shall hold their Offices during good Behaviour, and shall, at stated Times, receive for their Services, a Compensation, which shall not be diminished during their Continuance in Office.

### SECTION 2.

The judicial Power shall extend to all Cases, in Law and Equity, arising under this Constitution, the Laws of the United States, and Treaties made, or which shall be made, under their Authority; — to all Cases affecting ambassadors, other public ministers and consuls; — to all cases of admiralty and maritime Jurisdiction; — to Controversies to which the United States shall be a Party; — to Controversies between two or more States; — between a State and Citizens of another State;[5] — between Citizens of

[5]Qualified by the Eleventh Amendment.

different States, – between Citizens of the same State claiming Lands under Grants of different States, and between a State, or the Citizens thereof, and foreign States, Citizens or Subjects.

In all Cases affecting Ambassadors, other public Ministers and Consuls, and those in which a State shall be Party, the supreme Court shall have original Jurisdiction. In all the other Cases before mentioned, the supreme Court shall have appellate Jurisdiction, both as to Law and Fact, with such Exceptions, and under such Regulations as the Congress shall make.

The trial of all Crimes, except in Cases of Impeachment, shall be by Jury; and such Trial shall be held in the State where the said Crimes shall have been committed; but when not committed within any State, the Trial shall be at such Place or Places as the Congress may by Law have directed.

### SECTION 3.

Treason against the United States, shall consist only in levying War against them, or in adhering to their Enemies, giving them Aid and Comfort. No Person shall be convicted of Treason unless on the Testimony of two Witnesses to the same overt Act, or on Confession in open Court.

The Congress shall have power to declare the Punishment of Treason, but no Attainder of Treason shall work Corruption of Blood, or Forfeiture except during the Life of the Person attainted.

## Article IV

### SECTION 1.

Full Faith and Credit shall be given in each State to the public Acts, Records, and judicial Proceedings of every other State. And the Congress may by general Laws prescribe the Manner in which such Acts, Records and Proceedings shall be proved, and the Effect thereof.

### SECTION 2.

The Citizens of each State shall be entitled to all Privileges and Immunities of Citizens in the several States.

A Person charged in any State with Treason, Felony, or other Crime, who shall flee from Justice, and be found in another State, shall on demand of the executive Authority of the State from which he fled, be delivered up, to be removed to the State having Jurisdiction of the crime.

No Person held to Service or Labour in one State, under the Laws thereof, escaping into another, shall, in Consequence of any Law or Regulation therein, be discharged from such Service or Labour, but shall be delivered up on Claim of the Party to whom such Service or Labour may be due.

### SECTION 3.

New States may be admitted by the Congress into this Union; but no new State shall be formed or erected within the Jurisdiction of any other State; nor any State be formed by the Junction of two or more States, or parts of States, without the Consent of the Legislatures of the States concerned as well as of the Congress.

The Congress shall have Power to dispose of and make all needful Rules and Regulations respecting the Territory or other Property belonging to the United States; and nothing in this Constitution shall be so construed as to Prejudice any Claims of the United States, or of any particular State.

### SECTION 4.

The United States shall guarantee to every State in this Union a Republican Form of Government, and shall protect each of them against Invasion; and on Application of the Legislature, or of the Executive (when the Legislature cannot be convened) against domestic Violence.

## Article V

The Congress, whenever two-thirds of both Houses shall deem it necessary, shall propose Amendments to this Constitution, or, on the Application of the Legislatures of two-thirds of the several States, shall call a Convention for proposing Amendments, which, in either Case, shall be valid to all Intents and Purposes, as part of this Constitution, when ratified by the Legislatures of three-fourths of the several States, or by Conventions in three-fourths thereof, as the one or the other Mode of Ratification may be proposed by the Congress; Provided that no Amendment which may be made prior to the Year One thousand eight hundred and eight shall in any Manner affect the first and fourth Clauses in the Ninth Section of the first Article; and that no State, without its Consent, shall be deprived of its equal Suffrage in the Senate.

## Article VI

All Debts contracted and Engagements entered into, before the Adoption of this Constitution, shall be as valid against the United States under this Constitution, as under the Confederation.

This Constitution, and the Laws of the United States which shall be made in Pursuance thereof; and all Treaties made, or which shall be made, under the Authority of the United States, shall be the supreme Law of the Land; and the Judges in every State shall be bound thereby, any Thing in the Constitution or Laws of any State to the Contrary notwithstanding.

The Senators and Representatives before mentioned, and the Members of the several State Legislatures, and all executive and judicial Officers, both of the United States and of the several States, shall be bound by Oath or Affirmation to support this Constitution; but no religious Test shall ever be required as a qualification to any Office or public Trust under the United States.

## Article VII

The Ratification of the Conventions of nine States shall be sufficient for the Establishment of this Constitution between the States so ratifying the same.

Done in Convention by the Unanimous Consent of the States present the Seventeenth Day of September in the Year of our Lord one thousand seven hundred and Eighty seven, and of the Independence of the United States of America the Twelfth. In Witness whereof We have hereunto subscribed our Names.[6]

George Washington
*President and deputy from Virginia*

### New Hampshire

John Langdon
Nicholas Gilman

### Massachusetts

Nathaniel Gorham
Rufus King

### Connecticut

William Samuel Johnson
Roger Sherman

### New York

Alexander Hamilton

### New Jersey

William Livingston
David Brearley
William Paterson
Jonathan Dayton

### Pennsylvania

Benjamin Franklin
Thomas Mifflin
Robert Morris
George Clymer
Thomas FitzSimons
Jared Ingersoll
James Wilson
Gouverneur Morris

### Delaware

George Read
Gunning Bedford, Jr.
John Dickinson
Richard Bassett
Jacob Broom

### Maryland

James McHenry
Daniel of St. Thomas Jenifer
Daniel Carroll

### Virginia

John Blair
James Madison, Jr.

### North Carolina

William Blount
Richard Dobbs Spaight
Hugh Williamson

### South Carolina

John Rutledge
Charles Cotesworth Pinckney
Charles Pinckney
Pierce Butler

### Georgia

William Few
Abraham Baldwin

[6]These are the full names of the signers, which in some cases are not the signatures on the document.

*Articles in Addition to, and Amendment of, the Constitution of the United States of America, Proposed by Congress, and Ratified by the Legislatures of the Several States, Pursuant to the Fifth Article of the Original Constitution*[7]

## [Article I]

Congress shall make no law respecting an establishment of religion, or prohibiting the free exercise thereof; or abridging the freedom of speech, or of the press; or the right of the people peaceably to assemble, and to petition the Government for a redress of grievances.

## [Article II]

A well regulated Militia, being necessary to the security of a free State, the right of the people to keep and bear Arms shall not be infringed.

## [Article III]

No Soldier shall, in time of peace, be quartered in any house, without the consent of the Owner, nor in time of war, but in a manner to be prescribed by law.

## [Article IV]

The right of the people to be secure in their persons, houses, papers, and effects, against unreasonable searches and seizures, shall not be violated, and no Warrants shall issue, but upon probable cause, supported by Oath or affirmation, and particularly describing the place to be searched, and the persons or things to be seized.

## [Article V]

No person shall be held to answer for a capital or otherwise infamous crime, unless on a presentment or indictment of a Grand Jury, except in cases arising in the land or naval forces, or in

[7]This heading appears only in the joint resolution submitting the first ten amendments.

the Militia, when in actual service in time of War or public danger; nor shall any person be subject for the same offence to be twice put in jeopardy of life or limb; nor shall be compelled in any criminal case to be a witness against himself, nor be deprived of life, liberty, or property, without due process of law; nor shall private property be taken for public use, without just compensation.

## [Article VI]

In all criminal prosecutions, the accused shall enjoy the right to a speedy and public trial, by an impartial jury of the State and district wherein the crime shall have been committed, which district shall have been previously ascertained by law, and to be informed of the nature and cause of the accusation; to be confronted with the witnesses against him; to have compulsory process for obtaining witnesses in his favour, and to have the Assistance of Counsel for his defence.

## [Article VII]

In suits at common law, where the value in controversy shall exceed twenty dollars, the right of trial by jury shall be preserved, and no fact tried by a jury, shall be otherwise reexamined in any Court of the United States, than according to the rules of the common law.

## [Article VIII]

Excessive bail shall not be required, nor excessive fines imposed, nor cruel and unusual punishments inflicted.

## [Article IX]

The enumeration in the Constitution, of certain rights, shall not be construed to deny or disparage others retained by the people.

## [Article X]

The powers not delegated to the United States by the Constitution, nor prohibited by it to the

States, are reserved to the States respectively, or to the people.

[Amendments I – X, in force 1791.]

## [Article XI][8]

The Judicial power of the United States shall not be construed to extend to any suit in law or equity, commenced or prosecuted against one of the United States by Citizens of another State, or by Citizens or Subjects of any Foreign State.

## [Article XII][9]

The Electors shall meet in their respective States and vote by ballot for President and Vice-President, one of whom, at least, shall not be an inhabitant of the same State with themselves; they shall name in their ballots the person voted for as President, and in distinct ballots the person voted for as Vice-President, and they shall make distinct lists of all persons voted for as President, and of all persons voted for as Vice-President, and of the number of votes for each, which lists they shall sign and certify, and transmit sealed to the seat of the government of the United States, directed to the President of the Senate; — The President of the Senate shall, in the presence of the Senate and House of Representatives, open all the certificates and the votes shall then be counted; — The person having the greatest number of votes for President, shall be the President, if such number be a majority of the whole number of Electors appointed; and if no person have such majority, then from the persons having the highest numbers not exceeding three on the list of those voted for as President, the House of Representatives shall choose immediately, by ballot, the President. But in choosing the President, the votes shall be taken by states, the representation from each state having one vote; a quorum for this purpose shall consist of a member or members from two-thirds of the states, and a majority of all the

states shall be necessary to a choice. And if the House of Representatives shall not choose a President whenever the right of choice shall devolve upon them, before the fourth day of March next following, then the Vice-President shall act as President, as in the case of the death or other constitutional disability of the President. – The person having the greatest number of votes as Vice-President, shall be the Vice-President, if such number be a majority of the whole number of Electors appointed, and if no person have a majority, then from the two highest numbers on the list, the Senate shall choose the Vice-President: a quorum for the purpose shall consist of two-thirds of the whole number of Senators, and a majority of the whole number shall be necessary to a choice. But no person constitutionally ineligible to the office of President shall be eligible to that of Vice-President of the United States.

## [Article XIII][10]

### SECTION 1.
Neither slavery nor involuntary servitude, except as a punishment for crime whereof the party shall have been duly convicted, shall exist within the United States, or any place subject to their jurisdiction.

### SECTION 2.
Congress shall have power to enforce this article by appropriate legislation.

## [Article XIV][11]

### SECTION 1.
All persons born or naturalized in the United States, and subject to the jurisdiction thereof, are citizens of the United States and of the State wherein they reside. No State shall abridge the privileges or immunities of citizens of the United States; nor shall any State deprive any person of life, liberty, or property, without due process of law; nor deny to any person within its jurisdiction the equal protection of the laws.

---

[8]Adopted in 1798.
[9]Adopted in 1804.

[10]Adopted in 1865.
[11]Adopted in 1868.

## SECTION 2.

Representatives shall be apportioned among the several States according to their respective numbers, counting the whole number of persons in each State, excluding Indians not taxed. But when the right to vote at any election for the choice of electors for President and Vice-President of the United States, Representatives in Congress, the Executive and Judicial officers of a State, or the members of the Legislature thereof, is denied to any of the male inhabitants of such State, being twenty-one years of age, and citizens of the United States, or in any way abridged, except for participation in rebellion, or other crime, the basis of representation therein shall be reduced in the proportion which the number of such male citizens shall bear to the whole number of male citizens twenty-one years of age in such State.

## SECTION 3.

No person shall be a Senator or Representative in Congress, or elector of President and Vice-President, or hold any office, civil or military, under the United States, or under any State, who, having previously taken an oath, as a member of Congress, or as an officer of the United States, or as a member of any State legislature, or as an executive or judicial officer of any State, to support the Constitution of the United States, shall have engaged in insurrection or rebellion against the same, or given aid or comfort to the enemies thereof. But Congress may by a vote of two-thirds of each House, remove such disability.

## SECTION 4.

The validity of the public debt of the United States, authorized by law, including debts incurred for payment of pensions and bounties for services in suppressing insurrection or rebellion, shall not be questioned. But neither the United States nor any State shall assume or pay any debts or obligation incurred in aid of insurrection or rebellion against the United States, or any claim for the loss or emancipation of any slave; but all such debts, obligations, and claims shall be held illegal and void.

## SECTION 5.

The Congress shall have the power to enforce, by appropriate legislation, the provisions of this article.

## [Article XV][12]

### SECTION 1.

The right of citizens of the United States to vote shall not be denied or abridged by the United States or by any State on account of race, color, or previous condition of servitude —

### SECTION 2.

The Congress shall have power to enforce this article by appropriate legislation.

## [Article XVI][13]

The Congress shall have power to lay and collect taxes on incomes, from whatever source derived, without apportionment among the several States, and without regard to any census or enumeration.

## [Article XVII][14]

The Senate of the United States shall be composed of two Senators from each State, elected by the people thereof, for six years; and each Senator shall have one vote. The electors in each State shall have the qualifications requisite for electors of the most numerous branch of the State legislatures.

When vacancies happen in the representation of any State in the Senate, the executive authority of such State shall issue writs of election to fill such vacancies: *Provided,* That the legislature of any State may empower the executive thereof to make temporary appointments until the people fill the vacancies by election as the legislature may direct.

This amendment shall not be so construed as to affect the election or term of any Senator chosen before it becomes valid as part of the Constitution.

## [Article XVIII][15]

### SECTION 1.

After one year from the ratification of this article the manufacture, sale, or transportation of

[12]Adopted in 1870.
[13]Adopted in 1913.
[14]Adopted in 1913.
[15]Adopted in 1918.

intoxicating liquors within, the importation thereof into, or the exportation thereof from the United States and all territory subject to the jurisdiction thereof for beverage purposes is hereby prohibited.

### SECTION 2.

The Congress and the several States shall have concurrent power to enforce this article by appropriate legislation.

### SECTION 3.

This article shall be inoperative unless it shall have been ratified as an amendment to the Constitution by the legislatures of the several States, as provided in the Constitution, within seven years from the date of the submission hereof to the States by the Congress.

## [Article XIX][16]

The right of citizens of the United States to vote shall not be denied or abridged by the United States or by any State on account of sex.

Congress shall have power to enforce this article by appropriate legislation.

## [Article XX][17]

### SECTION 1.

The terms of the President and Vice-President shall end at noon on the 20th day of January, and the terms of Senators and Representatives at noon on the 3d day of January, of the years in which such terms would have ended if this article had not been ratified; and the terms of their successors shall then begin.

### SECTION 2.

The Congress shall assemble at least once in every year, and such meeting shall begin at noon on the 3d day of January, unless they shall by law appoint a different day.

### SECTION 3.

If, at the time fixed for the beginning of the term of the President, the President elect shall have died, the Vice-President elect shall become President. If a President shall not have been chosen before the time fixed for the be-

ginning of his term, or if the President elect shall have failed to qualify, then the Vice-President elect shall act as President until a President shall have qualified; and the Congress may by law provide for the case wherein neither a President elect nor a Vice-President elect shall have qualified, declaring who shall then act as President, or the manner in which one who is to act shall be selected, and such person shall act accordingly until a President or Vice-President shall have qualified.

### SECTION 4.

The Congress may by law provide for the case of the death of any of the persons from whom the House of Representatives may choose a President whenever the right of choice shall have devolved upon them, and for the case of the death of any of the persons from whom the Senate may choose a Vice-President whenever the right of choice shall have devolved upon them.

### SECTION 5.

Sections 1 and 2 shall take effect on the 15th day of October following the ratification of this article.

### SECTION 6.

This article shall be inoperative unless it shall have been ratified as an amendment to the Constitution by the legislatures of three-fourths of the several States within seven years from the date of its submission.

## [Article XXI][18]

### SECTION 1.

The eighteenth article of amendment to the Constitution of the United States is hereby repealed.

### SECTION 2.

The transportation or importation into any State, Territory, or possession of the United States for delivery or use therein of intoxicating liquors, in violation of the laws thereof, is hereby prohibited.

### SECTION 3.

This article shall be inoperative unless it shall have been ratified as an amendment to the

---

[16]Adopted in 1920.
[17]Adopted in 1933.

[18]Adopted in 1933.

Constitution by conventions in the several States, as provided in the Constitution, within seven years from the date of the submission hereof to the States by the Congress.

## [Article XXII][19]

No person shall be elected to the office of the President more than twice, and no person who has held the office of President, or acted as President, for more than two years of a term to which some other person was elected President shall be elected to the office of the President more than once.

But this Article shall not apply to any person holding the office of President when this Article was proposed by the Congress, and shall not prevent any person who may be holding the office of President, or acting as President, during the term within which this Article becomes operative from holding the office of President or acting as President during the remainder of such term.

This article shall be inoperative unless it shall have been ratified as an amendment to the Constitution by the legislatures of three-fourths of the several states within seven years from the date of its submission to the states by the Congress.

## [Article XXIII][20]

### SECTION 1.

The District constituting the seat of Government of the United States shall appoint in such manner as the Congress may direct:

A number of electors of President and Vice-President equal to the whole number of Senators and Representatives in Congress to which the District would be entitled if it were a State, but in no event more than the least populous State; they shall be in addition to those appointed by the States, but they shall be considered, for the purposes of the election of President and Vice-President, to be electors appointed by a State; and they shall meet in the District and perform such duties as provided by the twelfth article of amendment.

[19]Adopted in 1951.
[20]Adopted in 1961.

### SECTION 2.

The Congress shall have power to enforce this article by appropriate legislation.

## [Article XXIV][21]

### SECTION 1.

The right of citizens of the United States to vote in any primary or other election for President or Vice President, for electors for President or Vice President, or for Senator or Representative in Congress, shall not be denied or abridged by the United States or any state by reason of failure to pay any poll tax or other tax.

### SECTION 2.

The Congress shall have the power to enforce this article by appropriate legislation.

## [Article XXV][22]

### SECTION 1.

In case of the removal of the President from office or of his death or resignation, the Vice President shall become President.

### SECTION 2.

Whenever there is a vacancy in the office of the Vice President, the President shall nominate a Vice President who shall take office upon confirmation by a majority vote of both Houses of Congress.

### SECTION 3.

Whenever the President transmits to the President Pro Tempore of the Senate and the Speaker of the House of Representatives his written declaration that he is unable to discharge the powers and duties of his office, and until he transmits to them a written declaration to the contrary, such powers and duties shall be discharged by the Vice President as Acting President.

### SECTION 4.

Whenever the Vice President and a majority of either the principal officers of the executive departments or of such other body as Congress may by law provide, transmit to the President Pro Tempore of the Senate and the Speaker of

[21]Adopted in 1964.
[22]Adopted in 1967.

the House of Representatives their written declaration that the President is unable to discharge the powers and duties of his office, the Vice President shall immediately assume the powers and duties of the office as Acting President.

Thereafter, when the President transmits to the President Pro Tempore of the Senate and the Speaker of the House of Representatives his written declaration that no inability exists, he shall resume the powers and duties of his office unless the Vice President and a majority of either the principal officers of the executive departments or of such other body as Congress may by law provide, transmit within four days to the President Pro Tempore of the Senate and the Speaker of the House of Representatives their written declaration that the President is unable to discharge the powers and duties of his office. Thereupon Congress shall decide the issue, assembling within forty-eight hours for that purpose if not in session. If the Congress, within twenty-one days after receipt of the latter

written declaration, or, if Congress is not in session, within twenty-one days after Congress is required to assemble, determines by two-thirds vote of both Houses that the President is unable to discharge the powers and duties of his office, the Vice President shall continue to discharge the same as Acting President; otherwise, the President shall resume the powers and duties of his office.

## [Article XXVI][23]

### SECTION 1.

The right of citizens of the United States, who are eighteen years of age or older, to vote shall not be denied or abridged by the United States or by any State on account of age.

### SECTION 2.

The Congress shall have power to enforce this article by appropriate legislation.

[23]Adopted in 1971.

# Admission of States to the Union*

| | | | | | |
|---|---|---|---|---|---|
| 1 | Delaware | Dec. 7, 1787 | 26 | Michigan | Jan. 26, 1837 |
| 2 | Pennsylvania | Dec. 12, 1787 | 27 | Florida | Mar. 3, 1845 |
| 3 | New Jersey | Dec. 18, 1787 | 28 | Texas | Dec. 29, 1845 |
| 4 | Georgia | Jan. 2, 1788 | 29 | Iowa | Dec. 28, 1846 |
| 5 | Connecticut | Jan. 9, 1788 | 30 | Wisconsin | May 29, 1848 |
| 6 | Massachusetts | Feb. 6, 1788 | 31 | California | Sept. 9, 1850 |
| 7 | Maryland | Apr. 28, 1788 | 32 | Minnesota | May 11, 1858 |
| 8 | South Carolina | May 23, 1788 | 33 | Oregon | Feb. 14, 1859 |
| 9 | New Hampshire | June 21, 1788 | 34 | Kansas | Jan. 29, 1861 |
| 10 | Virginia | June 25, 1788 | 35 | West Virginia | June 19, 1863 |
| 11 | New York | July 26, 1788 | 36 | Nevada | Oct. 31, 1864 |
| 12 | North Carolina | Nov. 21, 1789 | 37 | Nebraska | Mar. 1, 1867 |
| 13 | Rhode Island | May 29, 1790 | 38 | Colorado | Aug. 1, 1876 |
| 14 | Vermont | Mar. 4, 1791 | 39 | North Dakota | Nov. 2, 1889 |
| 15 | Kentucky | June 1, 1792 | 40 | South Dakota | Nov. 2, 1889 |
| 16 | Tennessee | June 1, 1796 | 41 | Montana | Nov. 8, 1889 |
| 17 | Ohio | Mar. 1, 1803 | 42 | Washington | Nov. 11, 1889 |
| 18 | Louisiana | Apr. 30, 1812 | 43 | Idaho | July 3, 1890 |
| 19 | Indiana | Dec. 11, 1816 | 44 | Wyoming | July 10, 1890 |
| 20 | Mississippi | Dec. 10, 1817 | 45 | Utah | Jan. 4, 1896 |
| 21 | Illinois | Dec. 3, 1818 | 46 | Oklahoma | Nov. 16, 1907 |
| 22 | Alabama | Dec. 14, 1819 | 47 | New Mexico | Jan. 6, 1912 |
| 23 | Maine | Mar. 15, 1820 | 48 | Arizona | Feb. 14, 1912 |
| 24 | Missouri | Aug. 10, 1821 | 49 | Alaska | Jan. 3, 1959 |
| 25 | Arkansas | June 15, 1836 | 50 | Hawaii | Aug. 21, 1959 |

*In the case of the first thirteen states, the date given is that of ratification of the Constitution.

| Year | Candidates | Parties | Popular Vote | Electoral Vote |
|------|-----------|---------|-------------|----------------|
| 1789 | **GEORGE WASHINGTON** (Va.)* | | | 69 |
| | John Adams | | | 34 |
| | Others | | | 35 |
| 1792 | **GEORGE WASHINGTON** (Va.) | | | 132 |
| | John Adams | | | 77 |
| | George Clinton | | | 50 |
| | Others | | | 5 |
| 1796 | **JOHN ADAMS** (Mass.) | Federalist | | 71 |
| | Thomas Jefferson | Democratic-Republican | | 68 |
| | Thomas Pinckney | Federalist | | 59 |
| | Aaron Burr | Dem.-Rep. | | 30 |
| | Others | | | 48 |
| 1800 | **THOMAS JEFFERSON** (Va.) | Dem.-Rep. | | 73 |
| | Aaron Burr | Dem.-Rep. | | 73 |
| | John Adams | Federalist | | 65 |
| | C. C. Pinckney | Federalist | | 64 |
| | John Jay | Federalist | | 1 |
| 1804 | **THOMAS JEFFERSON** (Va.) | Dem.-Rep. | | 162 |
| | C. C. Pinckney | Federalist | | 14 |
| 1808 | **JAMES MADISON** (Va.) | Dem.-Rep. | | 122 |
| | C. C. Pinckney | Federalist | | 47 |
| | George Clinton | Dem.-Rep. | | 6 |
| 1812 | **JAMES MADISON** (Va.) | Dem.-Rep. | | 128 |
| | De Witt Clinton | Federalist | | 89 |
| 1816 | **JAMES MONROE** (Va.) | Dem.-Rep. | | 183 |
| | Rufus King | Federalist | | 34 |
| 1820 | **JAMES MONROE** (Va.) | Dem.-Rep. | | 231 |
| | John Quincy Adams | Dem.-Rep. | | 1 |
| 1824 | **JOHN Q. ADAMS** (Mass.) | Dem.-Rep. | 108,740 | 84 |
| | Andrew Jackson | Dem.-Rep. | 153,544 | 99 |
| | William H. Crawford | Dem.-Rep. | 46,618 | 41 |
| | Henry Clay | Dem.-Rep. | 47,136 | 37 |
| 1828 | **ANDREW JACKSON** (Tenn.) | Democrat | 647,286 | 178 |
| | John Quincy Adams | National Republican | 508,064 | 83 |

*State of residence at time of election.

| Year | Candidates | Parties | Popular Vote | Electoral Vote |
|------|-----------|---------|-------------|----------------|
| 1832 | **ANDREW JACKSON (Tenn.)** | Democrat | 687,502 | 219 |
|      | Henry Clay | National Republican | 530,189 | 49 |
|      | John Floyd | Independent | | 11 |
|      | William Wirt | Anti-Mason | 33,108 | 7 |
| 1836 | **MARTIN VAN BUREN (N.Y.)** | Democrat | 765,483 | 170 |
|      | W. H. Harrison | Whig | | 73 |
|      | Hugh L. White | Whig | 739,795 | 26 |
|      | Daniel Webster | Whig | | 14 |
|      | W. P. Mangum | Independent | | 11 |
| 1840 | **WILLIAM H. HARRISON (Ohio)** | Whig | 1,274,624 | 234 |
|      | Martin Van Buren | Democrat | 1,127,781 | 60 |
|      | J. G. Birney | Liberty | 7,069 | — |
| 1844 | **JAMES K. POLK (Tenn.)** | Democrat | 1,338,464 | 170 |
|      | Henry Clay | Whig | 1,300,097 | 105 |
|      | J. G. Birney | Liberty | 62,300 | — |
| 1848 | **ZACHARY TAYLOR (La.)** | Whig | 1,360,967 | 163 |
|      | Lewis Cass | Democrat | 1,222,342 | 127 |
|      | Martin Van Buren | Free-Soil | 291,263 | — |
| 1852 | **FRANKLIN PIERCE (N.H.)** | Democrat | 1,601,117 | 254 |
|      | Winfield Scott | Whig | 1,385,453 | 42 |
|      | John P. Hale | Free-Soil | 155,825 | — |
| 1856 | **JAMES BUCHANAN (Pa.)** | Democrat | 1,832,955 | 174 |
|      | John C. Frémont | Republican | 1,339,932 | 114 |
|      | Millard Fillmore | American | 871,731 | 8 |
| 1860 | **ABRAHAM LINCOLN (Ill.)** | Republican | 1,865,593 | 180 |
|      | Stephen A. Douglas | Democrat | 1,382,713 | 12 |
|      | John C. Breckinridge | Democrat | 848,356 | 72 |
|      | John Bell | Union | 592,906 | 39 |
| 1864 | **ABRAHAM LINCOLN (Ill.)** | Republican | 2,213,655 | 212 |
|      | George B. McClellan | Democrat | 1,805,237 | 21 |
| 1868 | **ULYSSES S. GRANT (Ill.)** | Republican | 3,012,833 | 214 |
|      | Horatio Seymour | Democrat | 2,703,249 | 80 |
| 1872 | **ULYSSES S. GRANT (Ill.)** | Republican | 3,597,132 | 286 |
|      | Horace Greeley | Democrat; Liberal Republican | 2,834,125 | 66 |
| 1876 | **RUTHERFORD B. HAYES (Ohio)** | Republican | 4,036,298 | 185 |
|      | Samuel J. Tilden | Democrat | 4,300,590 | 184 |
| 1880 | **JAMES A. GARFIELD (Ohio)** | Republican | 4,454,416 | 214 |
|      | Winfield S. Hancock | Democrat | 4,444,952 | 155 |

| Year | Candidates | Parties | Popular Vote | Electoral Vote |
|------|-----------|---------|-------------|---------------|
| 1884 | **GROVER CLEVELAND (N.Y.)** | Democrat | 4,874,986 | 219 |
|      | James G. Blaine | Republican | 4,851,981 | 182 |
| 1888 | **BENJAMIN HARRISON (Ind.)** | Republican | 5,439,853 | 233 |
|      | Grover Cleveland | Democrat | 5,540,309 | 168 |
| 1892 | **GROVER CLEVELAND (N.Y.)** | Democrat | 5,556,918 | 277 |
|      | Benjamin Harrison | Republican | 5,176,108 | 145 |
|      | James B. Weaver | People's | 1,041,028 | 22 |
| 1896 | **WILLIAM McKINLEY (Ohio)** | Republican | 7,104,779 | 271 |
|      | William J. Bryan | Democrat-People's | 6,502,925 | 176 |
| 1900 | **WILLIAM McKINLEY (Ohio)** | Republican | 7,207,923 | 292 |
|      | William J. Bryan | Dem.-Populist | 6,358,133 | 155 |
| 1904 | **THEODORE ROOSEVELT (N.Y.)** | Republican | 7,623,486 | 336 |
|      | Alton B. Parker | Democrat | 5,077,911 | 140 |
|      | Eugene V. Debs | Socialist | 402,283 | – |
| 1908 | **WILLIAM H. TAFT (Ohio)** | Republican | 7,678,908 | 321 |
|      | William J. Bryan | Democrat | 6,409,104 | 162 |
|      | Eugene V. Debs | Socialist | 420,793 | – |
| 1912 | **WOODROW WILSON (N.J.)** | Democrat | 6,293,454 | 435 |
|      | Theodore Roosevelt | Progressive | 4,119,538 | 88 |
|      | William H. Taft | Republican | 3,484,980 | 8 |
|      | Eugene V. Debs | Socialist | 900,672 | – |
| 1916 | **WOODROW WILSON (N.J.)** | Democrat | 9,129,606 | 277 |
|      | Charles E. Hughes | Republican | 8,538,221 | 254 |
|      | A. L. Benson | Socialist | 585,113 | – |
| 1920 | **WARREN G. HARDING (Ohio)** | Republican | 16,152,200 | 404 |
|      | James M. Cox | Democrat | 9,147,353 | 127 |
|      | Eugene V. Debs | Socialist | 919,799 | – |
| 1924 | **CALVIN COOLIDGE (Mass.)** | Republican | 15,725,016 | 382 |
|      | John W. Davis | Democrat | 8,386,503 | 136 |
|      | Robert M. LaFollette | Progressive | 4,822,856 | 13 |
| 1928 | **HERBERT HOOVER (Calif.)** | Republican | 21,391,381 | 444 |
|      | Alfred E. Smith | Democrat | 15,016,443 | 87 |
|      | Norman Thomas | Socialist | 267,835 | – |
| 1932 | **FRANKLIN D. ROOSEVELT (N.Y.)** | Democrat | 22,821,857 | 472 |
|      | Herbert Hoover | Republican | 15,761,841 | 59 |
|      | Norman Thomas | Socialist | 881,951 | – |
| 1936 | **FRANKLIN D. ROOSEVELT (N.Y.)** | Democrat | 27,751,597 | 523 |
|      | Alfred M. Landon | Republican | 16,679,583 | 8 |
|      | William Lemke | Union and others | 882,479 | – |
| 1940 | **FRANKLIN D. ROOSEVELT (N.Y.)** | Democrat | 27,244,160 | 449 |
|      | Wendell L. Willkie | Republican | 22,305,198 | 82 |

| Year | Candidates | Parties | Popular Vote | Electoral Vote |
|------|-----------|---------|-------------|----------------|
| 1944 | **FRANKLIN D. ROOSEVELT (N.Y.)** | Democrat | 25,602,504 | 432 |
|      | Thomas E. Dewey | Republican | 22,006,285 | 99 |
| 1948 | **HARRY S. TRUMAN (Mo.)** | Democrat | 24,105,695 | 304 |
|      | Thomas E. Dewey | Republican | 21,969,170 | 189 |
|      | J. Strom Thurmond | State-Rights Democrat | 1,169,021 | 38 |
|      | Henry A. Wallace | Progressive | 1,156,103 | — |
| 1952 | **DWIGHT D. EISENHOWER (N.Y.)** | Republican | 33,936,252 | 442 |
|      | Adlai E. Stevenson | Democrat | 27,314,992 | 89 |
| 1956 | **DWIGHT D. EISENHOWER (N.Y.)** | Republican | 35,575,420 | 457 |
|      | Adlai E. Stevenson | Democrat | 26,033,066 | 73 |
|      | Other | — | — | 1 |
| 1960 | **JOHN F. KENNEDY (Mass.)** | Democrat | 34,227,096 | 303 |
|      | Richard M. Nixon | Republican | 34,108,546 | 219 |
|      | Other | — | — | 15 |
| 1964 | **LYNDON B. JOHNSON (Tex.)** | Democrat | 43,126,506 | 486 |
|      | Barry M. Goldwater | Republican | 27,176,799 | 52 |
| 1968 | **RICHARD M. NIXON (N.Y.)** | Republican | 31,770,237 | 301 |
|      | Hubert H. Humphrey | Democrat | 31,270,533 | 191 |
|      | George Wallace | American Indep. | 9,906,141 | 46 |
| 1972 | **RICHARD M. NIXON (N.Y.)** | Republican | 47,169,911 | 520 |
|      | George S. McGovern | Democrat | 29,170,383 | 17 |
|      | Other | — | — | 1 |
| 1976 | **\*JAMES E. CARTER, JR. (Ga.)** | Democrat | 40,287,283 | 297 |
|      | Gerald R. Ford | Republican | 38,557,855 | 241 |

*Based on returns from 99 percent of the precincts.

# Presidents and Vice Presidents

| President | Vice President |
|---|---|
| 1. George Washington, Federalist<br>1789 | John Adams, Federalist<br>1789 |
| 2. John Adams, Federalist<br>1797 | Thomas Jefferson, Dem.-Rep.<br>1797 |
| 3. Thomas Jefferson, Dem.-Rep.<br>1801 | Aaron Burr, Dem.-Rep.<br>1801<br>George Clinton, Dem.-Rep.<br>1805 |
| 4. James Madison, Dem.-Rep.<br>1809 | George Clinton, Dem.-Rep.<br>1809<br>Elbridge Gerry, Dem.-Rep.<br>1813 |
| 5. James Monroe, Dem.-Rep.<br>1817 | D. D. Tompkins, Dem.-Rep.<br>1817 |
| 6. John Quincy Adams, Dem.-Rep.<br>1825 | John C. Calhoun, Dem.-Rep.<br>1825 |
| 7. Andrew Jackson, Democratic<br>1829 | John C. Calhoun, Democratic<br>1829<br>Martin Van Buren, Democratic<br>1833 |
| 8. Martin Van Buren, Democratic<br>1837 | Richard M. Johnson, Democratic<br>1837 |
| 9. William H. Harrison, Whig<br>1841 | John Tyler, Whig<br>1841 |
| 10. John Tyler, Whig and Democratic<br>1841 | |

| | |
|---|---|
| 11. James K. Polk, Democratic<br>1845 | George M. Dallas, Democratic<br>1845 |
| 12. Zachary Taylor, Whig<br>1849 | Millard Fillmore, Whig<br>1849 |
| 13. Millard Fillmore, Whig<br>1850 | |
| 14. Franklin Pierce, Democratic<br>1853 | William R. D. King, Democratic<br>1853 |
| 15. James Buchanan, Democratic<br>1857 | John C. Breckinridge,<br>Democratic 1857 |
| 16. Abraham Lincoln, Republican<br>1861 | Hannibal Hamlin, Republican<br>1861<br>Andrew Johnson, Unionist<br>1865 |
| 17. Andrew Johnson, Unionist<br>1865 | |
| 18. Ulysses S. Grant, Republican<br>1869 | Schuyler Colfax, Republican<br>1869<br>Henry Wilson, Republican<br>1873 |
| 19. Rutherford B. Hayes, Republican<br>1877 | William A. Wheeler, Republican<br>1877 |
| 20. James A. Garfield, Republican<br>1881 | Chester A. Arthur, Republican<br>1881 |
| 21. Chester A. Arthur, Republican<br>1881 | |
| 22. Grover Cleveland, Democratic<br>1885 | T. A. Hendricks, Democratic<br>1885 |
| 23. Benjamin Harrison, Republican<br>1889 | Levi P. Morton, Republican<br>1889 |
| 24. Grover Cleveland, Democratic<br>1893 | Adlai E. Stevenson, Democratic<br>1893 |
| 25. William McKinley, Republican<br>1897 | Garret A. Hobart, Republican<br>1897<br>Theodore Roosevelt, Republican<br>1901 |

| President | Vice President |
| --- | --- |
| 26. Theodore Roosevelt, Republican<br>1901 | Chas. W. Fairbanks, Republican<br>1905 |
| 27. William H. Taft, Republican<br>1909 | James S. Sherman, Republican<br>1909 |
| 28. Woodrow Wilson, Democratic<br>1913 | Thomas R. Marshall, Democratic<br>1913 |
| 29. Warren G. Harding, Republican<br>1921 | Calvin Coolidge, Republican<br>1921 |
| 30. Calvin Coolidge, Republican<br>1923 | Charles G. Dawes, Republican<br>1925 |
| 31. Herbert Hoover, Republican<br>1929 | Charles Curtis, Republican<br>1929 |
| 32. Franklin D. Roosevelt, Democratic<br>1933 | John Nance Garner, Democratic<br>1933<br>Henry A. Wallace, Democratic<br>1941<br>Harry S. Truman, Democratic<br>1945 |
| 33. Harry S. Truman, Democratic<br>1945 | Alben W. Barkley, Democratic<br>1949 |
| 34. Dwight D. Eisenhower, Republican<br>1953 | Richard M. Nixon, Republican<br>1953 |
| 35. John F. Kennedy, Democratic<br>1961 | Lyndon B. Johnson, Democratic<br>1961 |
| 36. Lyndon B. Johnson, Democratic<br>1963 | Hubert H. Humphrey, Democratic<br>1965 |
| 37. Richard M. Nixon, Republican<br>1969 | Spiro T. Agnew, Republican<br>1969<br>Gerald R. Ford, Republican<br>1973 |
| 38. Gerald R. Ford, Republican<br>1974 | Nelson A. Rockefeller, Republican<br>1974 |
| 39. James E. Carter, Jr., Democrat<br>1977 | Walter F. Mondale, Democrat<br>1977 |

# Population of the United States

| Division and State | 1790 | 1800 | 1810 | 1820 | 1830 | 1840 | 1850 | 1860 | 1870 |
|---|---|---|---|---|---|---|---|---|---|
| United States | 3,929,214 | 5,308,483 | 7,239,881 | 9,638,453 | 12,866,020 | 17,069,453 | 23,191,876 | 31,443,321 | 39,818,449 |
| **GEOGRAPHIC DIVISIONS** | | | | | | | | | |
| New England | 1,009,408 | 1,233,011 | 1,471,973 | 1,660,071 | 1,954,717 | 2,234,822 | 2,728,116 | 3,135,283 | 3,487,924 |
| Middle Atlantic | 952,632 | 1,402,565 | 2,014,702 | 2,699,845 | 3,587,664 | 4,526,260 | 5,898,735 | 7,458,985 | 8,810,806 |
| South Atlantic | 1,851,806 | 2,286,494 | 2,674,891 | 3,061,063 | 3,645,752 | 3,925,299 | 4,679,090 | 5,364,703 | 5,853,610 |
| East South Central | 109,368 | 335,407 | 708,590 | 1,190,489 | 1,815,969 | 2,575,445 | 3,363,271 | 4,020,991 | 4,404,445 |
| West South Central | | | 77,618 | 167,680 | 246,127 | 449,985 | 940,251 | 1,747,667 | 2,029,965 |
| East North Central | | 51,006 | 272,324 | 792,719 | 1,470,018 | 2,924,728 | 4,523,260 | 6,926,884 | 9,124,517 |
| West North Central | | | 19,783 | 66,586 | 140,455 | 426,814 | 880,335 | 2,169,832 | 3,856,594 |
| Mountain | | | | | | | 72,927 | 174,923 | 315,385 |
| Pacific | | | | | | | 105,871 | 444,053 | 675,125 |
| **NEW ENGLAND** | | | | | | | | | |
| Maine | 96,540 | 151,719 | 228,705 | 298,335 | 399,455 | 501,793 | 583,169 | 628,279 | 626,915 |
| New Hampshire | 141,885 | 183,858 | 214,460 | 244,161 | 269,328 | 284,574 | 317,976 | 326,073 | 318,300 |
| Vermont | 85,425 | 154,465 | 217,895 | 235,981 | 280,652 | 291,948 | 314,120 | 315,098 | 330,551 |
| Massachusetts | 378,787 | 422,845 | 472,040 | 523,287 | 610,408 | 737,699 | 994,514 | 1,231,066 | 1,457,351 |
| Rhode Island | 68,825 | 69,122 | 76,931 | 83,059 | 97,199 | 108,830 | 147,545 | 174,620 | 217,353 |
| Connecticut | 237,946 | 251,002 | 261,942 | 275,248 | 297,675 | 309,978 | 370,792 | 460,147 | 537,454 |
| **MIDDLE ATLANTIC** | | | | | | | | | |
| New York | 340,120 | 589,051 | 959,049 | 1,372,812 | 1,918,608 | 2,428,921 | 3,097,394 | 3,880,735 | 4,382,759 |
| New Jersey | 184,139 | 211,149 | 245,562 | 277,575 | 320,823 | 373,306 | 489,555 | 672,035 | 906,096 |
| Pennsylvania | 434,373 | 602,365 | 810,091 | 1,049,458 | 1,348,233 | 1,724,033 | 2,311,786 | 2,906,215 | 3,521,951 |
| **SOUTH ATLANTIC** | | | | | | | | | |
| Delaware | 59,096 | 64,273 | 72,674 | 72,749 | 76,748 | 78,085 | 91,532 | 112,216 | 125,015 |
| Maryland | 319,728 | 341,548 | 380,546 | 407,350 | 447,040 | 470,019 | 583,034 | 687,049 | 780,894 |
| Dist. of Columbia | | 14,093 | 24,023 | 33,039 | 39,834 | 43,712 | 51,687 | 75,080 | 131,700 |
| Virginia | 747,610 | 880,200 | 974,600 | 1,065,366 | 1,211,405 | 1,239,797 | 1,421,661 | 1,596,318 | 1,225,163 |
| West Virginia | | | | | | | | | 442,014 |
| North Carolina | 393,751 | 478,103 | 555,500 | 638,829 | 737,987 | 753,419 | 869,039 | 992,622 | 1,071,361 |
| South Carolina | 249,073 | 345,591 | 415,115 | 502,741 | 581,185 | 594,398 | 668,507 | 703,708 | 705,606 |
| Georgia | 82,548 | 162,686 | 252,433 | 340,989 | 516,823 | 691,392 | 906,185 | 1,057,286 | 1,184,109 |
| Florida | | | | | 34,730 | 54,477 | 87,445 | 140,424 | 187,748 |
| **EAST SOUTH CENTRAL** | | | | | | | | | |
| Kentucky | 73,677 | 220,955 | 406,511 | 564,317 | 687,917 | 779,828 | 982,405 | 1,155,684 | 1,321,011 |
| Tennessee | 35,691 | 105,602 | 261,727 | 422,823 | 681,904 | 829,210 | 1,002,717 | 1,109,801 | 1,258,520 |
| Alabama | | | | 127,901 | 309,527 | 590,756 | 771,623 | 964,201 | 996,992 |
| Mississippi | | 8,850 | 40,352 | 75,448 | 136,621 | 375,651 | 606,526 | 791,305 | 827,922 |
| **WEST SOUTH CENTRAL** | | | | | | | | | |
| Arkansas | | | 1,062 | 14,273 | 30,388 | 97,574 | 209,897 | 435,450 | 484,471 |
| Louisiana | | | 76,556 | 153,407 | 215,739 | 352,411 | 517,762 | 708,002 | 726,915 |
| Texas | | | | | | | 212,592 | 604,215 | 818,579 |

| | | | | | | | | |
|---|--:|--:|--:|--:|--:|--:|--:|--:|
| **EAST NORTH CENTRAL** | | | | | | | | |
| Ohio | 45,365 | 230,760 | 581,434 | 937,903 | 1,519,467 | 1,980,329 | 2,339,511 | 2,665,260 |
| Indiana | 5,641 | 24,520 | 147,178 | 343,031 | 685,866 | 988,416 | 1,350,428 | 1,680,637 |
| Illinois | | 12,282 | 55,211 | 157,445 | 476,183 | 851,470 | 1,711,951 | 2,539,981 |
| Michigan | | 4,762 | 8,896 | 31,639 | 212,267 | 397,654 | 749,113 | 1,184,059 |
| Wisconsin | | | | | 30,945 | 305,391 | 775,881 | 1,054,670 |
| **WEST NORTH CENTRAL** | | | | | | | | |
| Minnesota | | | | | | 6,077 | 172,023 | 439,706 |
| Iowa | | | | | 43,112 | 192,214 | 674,913 | 1,194,020 |
| Missouri | | 19,783 | 66,586 | 140,455 | 383,702 | 682,044 | 1,182,012 | 1,721,295 |
| North Dakota | | | | | | | | 2,405 |
| South Dakota | | | | | | | | 11,776 |
| Nebraska | | | | | | | 28,841 | 122,993 |
| Kansas | | | | | | | 107,206 | 364,399 |
| **MOUNTAIN** | | | | | | | | |
| Montana | | | | | | | | 20,595 |
| Idaho | | | | | | | | 14,999 |
| Wyoming | | | | | | | | 9,118 |
| Colorado | | | | | | | 34,277 | 39,864 |
| New Mexico | | | | | | 61,547 | 93,516 | 91,874 |
| Arizona | | | | | | | | 9,658 |
| Utah | | | | | | 11,380 | 40,273 | 86,786 |
| Nevada | | | | | | | 6,857 | 42,491 |
| **PACIFIC** | | | | | | | | |
| Washington | | | | | | | 11,594 | 23,955 |
| Oregon | | | | | | 13,294 | 52,465 | 90,923 |
| California | | | | | | 92,597 | 379,994 | 560,247 |

| Division and State | 1880 | 1890 | 1900 | 1910 | 1920 | 1930 | 1940 | 1950 | 1960 | 1970 |
|---|---|---|---|---|---|---|---|---|---|---|
| UNITED STATES | 50,155,783 | 62,947,714 | 75,994,575 | 91,972,266 | 105,710,620 | 122,775,046 | 131,669,275 | 150,697,361 | 179,323,175 | 203,211,926 |
| GEOGRAPHIC DIVISIONS | | | | | | | | | | |
| New England | 4,010,529 | 4,700,749 | 5,592,017 | 6,552,681 | 7,400,909 | 8,166,341 | 8,437,290 | 9,314,453 | 10,509,367 | 11,841,663 |
| Middle Atlantic | 10,496,878 | 12,706,220 | 15,454,678 | 19,315,892 | 22,261,144 | 26,260,750 | 27,539,487 | 30,163,533 | 34,168,452 | 37,199,040 |
| South Atlantic | 7,597,197 | 8,857,922 | 10,443,480 | 12,194,895 | 13,990,272 | 15,793,589 | 17,823,151 | 21,182,335 | 25,971,732 | 30,671,337 |
| East South Central | 5,585,151 | 6,429,154 | 7,547,757 | 8,409,901 | 8,893,307 | 9,887,214 | 10,778,225 | 11,477,181 | 12,050,126 | 12,803,470 |
| West South Central | 3,334,220 | 4,740,983 | 6,532,290 | 8,784,534 | 10,242,224 | 12,176,830 | 13,064,525 | 14,537,572 | 16,951,255 | 19,320,560 |
| East North Central | 11,206,668 | 13,478,305 | 15,985,581 | 18,250,621 | 21,475,543 | 25,297,185 | 26,626,342 | 30,399,368 | 36,225,024 | 40,252,476 |
| West North Central | 6,157,443 | 8,932,112 | 10,347,423 | 11,637,921 | 12,544,249 | 13,296,915 | 13,516,990 | 14,061,394 | 15,394,115 | 16,319,187 |
| Mountain | 653,119 | 1,213,935 | 1,674,657 | 2,633,517 | 3,336,101 | 3,701,789 | 4,150,003 | 5,074,998 | 6,855,060 | 8,281,562 |
| Pacific | 1,114,578 | 1,888,334 | 2,416,692 | 4,192,304 | 5,566,871 | 8,194,433 | 9,733,262 | 14,486,527 | 20,339,105 | 25,453,688 |
| Noncontiguous | | | | | | | | | 858,939 | 1,068,943 |
| NEW ENGLAND | | | | | | | | | | |
| Maine | 648,936 | 661,086 | 694,466 | 742,371 | 768,014 | 797,423 | 847,226 | 913,774 | 969,265 | 992,048 |
| New Hampshire | 346,991 | 376,530 | 411,588 | 430,572 | 443,083 | 465,293 | 491,524 | 533,242 | 606,921 | 731,681 |
| Vermont | 332,286 | 332,422 | 343,641 | 355,956 | 352,428 | 359,611 | 359,231 | 377,747 | 389,881 | 444,330 |
| Massachusetts | 1,783,085 | 2,238,947 | 2,805,346 | 3,366,416 | 3,852,356 | 4,249,614 | 4,316,721 | 4,690,514 | 5,148,578 | 5,689,110 |
| Rhode Island | 276,531 | 345,506 | 428,556 | 542,610 | 604,397 | 687,497 | 713,346 | 791,896 | 859,488 | 946,725 |
| Connecticut | 622,700 | 746,258 | 908,420 | 1,114,756 | 1,380,631 | 1,606,903 | 1,709,242 | 2,007,280 | 2,535,234 | 3,031,709 |
| MIDDLE ATLANTIC | | | | | | | | | | |
| New York | 5,082,871 | 6,003,174 | 7,268,894 | 9,113,614 | 10,385,227 | 12,588,066 | 13,479,142 | 14,830,192 | 16,782,304 | 18,236,967 |
| New Jersey | 1,131,116 | 1,444,933 | 1,883,669 | 2,537,167 | 3,155,900 | 4,041,334 | 4,160,165 | 4,835,329 | 6,066,782 | 7,168,164 |
| Pennsylvania | 4,282,891 | 5,258,113 | 6,302,115 | 7,665,111 | 8,720,017 | 9,631,350 | 9,900,180 | 10,498,012 | 11,319,366 | 11,793,909 |
| SOUTH ATLANTIC | | | | | | | | | | |
| Delaware | 146,608 | 168,493 | 184,735 | 202,322 | 223,003 | 238,380 | 266,505 | 318,085 | 446,292 | 548,104 |
| Maryland | 934,943 | 1,042,390 | 1,188,044 | 1,295,346 | 1,449,661 | 1,631,526 | 1,821,244 | 2,343,001 | 3,100,689 | 3,922,399 |
| Dist. of Columbia | 177,624 | 230,392 | 278,718 | 331,069 | 437,571 | 486,869 | 663,091 | 802,178 | 763,956 | 756,510 |
| Virginia | 1,512,565 | 1,655,980 | 1,854,184 | 2,061,612 | 2,309,187 | 2,421,851 | 2,677,773 | 3,318,680 | 3,966,949 | 4,648,494 |
| West Virginia | 618,457 | 762,794 | 958,800 | 1,221,119 | 1,463,701 | 1,729,205 | 1,901,974 | 2,005,552 | 1,860,421 | 1,744,237 |
| North Carolina | 1,399,750 | 1,617,949 | 1,893,810 | 2,206,287 | 2,559,123 | 3,170,276 | 3,571,623 | 4,061,929 | 4,556,155 | 5,082,059 |
| South Carolina | 995,577 | 1,151,149 | 1,340,316 | 1,515,400 | 1,683,724 | 1,738,765 | 1,899,804 | 2,117,027 | 2,382,594 | 2,590,516 |
| Georgia | 1,542,180 | 1,837,353 | 2,216,331 | 2,609,121 | 2,895,832 | 2,908,506 | 3,123,723 | 3,444,578 | 3,943,116 | 4,589,575 |
| Florida | 269,493 | 391,422 | 528,542 | 752,619 | 968,470 | 1,468,211 | 1,897,414 | 2,771,305 | 4,951,560 | 6,789,443 |
| EAST SOUTH CENTRAL | | | | | | | | | | |
| Kentucky | 1,648,690 | 1,858,635 | 2,147,174 | 2,289,905 | 2,416,630 | 2,614,589 | 2,845,627 | 2,944,806 | 3,038,156 | 3,218,706 |
| Tennessee | 1,542,359 | 1,767,518 | 2,020,616 | 2,184,789 | 2,337,885 | 2,616,556 | 2,915,841 | 3,291,718 | 3,567,089 | 3,923,687 |
| Alabama | 1,262,505 | 1,513,401 | 1,828,697 | 2,138,093 | 2,348,174 | 2,646,248 | 2,832,961 | 3,061,743 | 3,266,740 | 3,444,165 |
| Mississippi | 1,131,597 | 1,289,600 | 1,551,270 | 1,797,114 | 1,790,618 | 2,009,821 | 2,183,796 | 2,178,914 | 2,178,141 | 2,216,912 |
| WEST SOUTH CENTRAL | | | | | | | | | | |
| Arkansas | 802,525 | 1,128,211 | 1,311,564 | 1,574,449 | 1,752,204 | 1,854,482 | 1,949,387 | 1,909,511 | 1,786,272 | 1,923,285 |
| Louisiana | 939,946 | 1,118,588 | 1,381,625 | 1,656,388 | 1,798,509 | 2,101,593 | 2,363,880 | 2,683,516 | 3,257,022 | 3,641,306 |
| Oklahoma | | 258,657 | 790,391 | 1,657,155 | 2,028,283 | 2,396,040 | 2,336,434 | 2,233,351 | 2,328,284 | 2,559,229 |
| Texas | 1,591,749 | 2,235,527 | 3,048,710 | 3,896,542 | 4,663,228 | 5,824,715 | 6,414,824 | 7,711,194 | 9,579,677 | 11,196,730 |
| EAST NORTH CENTRAL | | | | | | | | | | |
| Ohio | 3,198,062 | 3,672,329 | 4,157,545 | 4,767,121 | 5,759,394 | 6,646,697 | 6,907,612 | 7,946,627 | 9,706,397 | 10,652,017 |
| Indiana | 1,978,301 | 2,192,404 | 2,516,462 | 2,700,876 | 2,930,390 | 3,238,503 | 3,427,796 | 3,934,224 | 4,662,498 | 5,193,669 |
| Illinois | 3,077,871 | 3,826,352 | 4,821,550 | 5,638,591 | 6,485,280 | 7,630,654 | 7,897,241 | 8,712,176 | 10,081,158 | 11,113,976 |
| Michigan | 1,636,937 | 2,093,890 | 2,420,982 | 2,810,173 | 3,668,412 | 4,842,325 | 5,256,106 | 6,371,766 | 7,823,194 | 8,875,083 |
| Wisconsin | 1,315,497 | 1,693,330 | 2,069,042 | 2,333,860 | 2,632,067 | 2,939,006 | 3,137,587 | 3,434,576 | 3,951,777 | 4,417,731 |

| | | | | | | | | | |
|---|---|---|---|---|---|---|---|---|---|
| **WEST NORTH CENTRAL** | | | | | | | | | |
| Minnesota | 780,773 | 1,310,283 | 1,751,394 | 2,075,708 | 2,387,125 | 2,563,953 | 2,792,300 | 2,982,483 | 3,413,864 | 3,804,971 |
| Iowa | 1,624,615 | 1,912,297 | 2,231,853 | 2,224,771 | 2,404,021 | 2,470,939 | 2,538,268 | 2,621,073 | 2,757,537 | 2,824,376 |
| Missouri | 2,168,380 | 2,679,185 | 3,106,665 | 3,293,335 | 3,404,055 | 3,629,367 | 3,784,664 | 3,954,653 | 4,319,813 | 4,676,501 |
| North Dakota | 36,909 | 190,983 | 319,146 | 577,056 | 646,872 | 680,845 | 641,935 | 619,636 | 632,446 | 617,761 |
| South Dakota | 98,268 | 348,600 | 401,570 | 583,888 | 636,547 | 692,849 | 642,961 | 652,740 | 680,514 | 665,507 |
| Nebraska | 452,402 | 1,062,656 | 1,066,300 | 1,192,214 | 1,296,372 | 1,377,963 | 1,315,834 | 1,325,510 | 1,411,330 | 1,483,493 |
| Kansas | 996,096 | 1,428,108 | 1,470,495 | 1,690,949 | 1,769,257 | 1,880,999 | 1,801,028 | 1,905,299 | 2,178,611 | 2,246,578 |
| **MOUNTAIN** | | | | | | | | | |
| Montana | 39,159 | 142,924 | 243,329 | 376,053 | 548,889 | 537,606 | 559,456 | 591,024 | 674,767 | 694,409 |
| Idaho | 32,610 | 88,548 | 161,772 | 325,594 | 431,866 | 445,032 | 524,873 | 588,637 | 667,191 | 712,567 |
| Wyoming | 20,789 | 62,555 | 92,531 | 145,965 | 194,402 | 225,565 | 250,742 | 290,529 | 330,066 | 332,416 |
| Colorado | 194,327 | 413,249 | 539,700 | 799,024 | 939,629 | 1,035,791 | 1,123,296 | 1,325,089 | 1,753,947 | 2,207,259 |
| New Mexico | 119,565 | 160,282 | 195,310 | 327,301 | 360,350 | 423,317 | 531,818 | 681,187 | 951,023 | 1,016,000 |
| Arizona | 40,440 | 88,243 | 122,931 | 204,354 | 334,162 | 435,573 | 499,261 | 749,587 | 1,302,161 | 1,770,900 |
| Utah | 143,963 | 210,779 | 276,749 | 373,351 | 449,396 | 507,847 | 550,310 | 688,862 | 890,627 | 1,059,273 |
| Nevada | 62,266 | 47,355 | 42,335 | 81,875 | 77,407 | 91,058 | 110,247 | 160,083 | 285,278 | 488,738 |
| **PACIFIC** | | | | | | | | | |
| Washington | 75,116 | 357,232 | 518,103 | 1,141,990 | 1,356,621 | 1,563,396 | 1,736,191 | 2,378,963 | 2,853,214 | 3,409,169 |
| Oregon | 174,768 | 317,704 | 413,536 | 672,765 | 783,389 | 953,786 | 1,089,684 | 1,521,341 | 1,768,687 | 2,091,385 |
| California | 864,694 | 1,213,398 | 1,485,053 | 2,377,549 | 3,426,861 | 5,677,251 | 6,907,387 | 10,586,223 | 15,717,204 | 19,953,134 |
| **NONCONTIGUOUS** | | | | | | | | | |
| Alaska | | | | | | | | | 226,167 | 300,382 |
| Hawaii | | | | | | | | | 632,772 | 786,561 |

# About the Authors

RICHARD N. CURRENT is University Distinguished Professor of History at the University of North Carolina at Greensboro. He is co-author of the Bancroft Prize-winning *Lincoln the President*. His books include: *Three Carpetbag Governors; The Lincoln Nobody Knows; Daniel Webster and the Rise of National Conservatism;* and *Secretary Stimson*. Professor Current has lectured on U.S. history in Europe, Asia, South America, Australia, and Antarctica. He has been a Fulbright Lecturer at the University of Munich and the University of Chile at Santiago, and has served as Harmsworth Professor of American History at Oxford. He is President of the Southern Historical Association.

T. HARRY WILLIAMS is Boyd Professor of History at Louisiana State University. He was awarded both the 1969 Pulitzer Prize and National Book Award for his biography of *Huey Long*. His books include: *Lincoln and His Generals; Lincoln and the Radicals; P. G. T. Beauregard; Americans at War; Romance and Realism in Southern Politics; Hayes of the Twenty-Third; McClellan, Sherman, and Grant; The Union Sundered;* and *The Union Restored*. Professor Williams has been a Harmsworth Professor of American History at Oxford and President of both the Southern Historical Association and the Organization of American Historians.

FRANK FREIDEL is Charles Warren Professor of History at Harvard University. He is writing a six-volume biography of Franklin D. Roosevelt, four volumes of which have been published. Among his other books are: *Our Country's Presidents; F.D.R. and the South;* and *America in the Twentieth Century*. He is co-editor of the 1974 edition of the *Harvard Guide to American History,* and Vice President of the Organization of American Historians. He is also a former president of the New England Historical Society.

W. ELLIOT BROWNLEE is an Associate Professor of History at the University of California, Santa Barbara. He received his Ph.D. from the University of Wisconsin. His area of specialization is U.S. economic history. He received a Haynes Foundation Fellowship in 1969. His published works include *Progressivism and Economic Growth: The Wisconsin Income Tax, 1911–1929; Women in the American Economy: A Documentary History, 1675 to 1929;* and *Dynamics of Ascent: A History of the American Economy*. In addition he has contributed to professional journals that include *Explorations in Economic History, Economic History Review,* and *Wisconsin Magazine of History*.

# A NOTE ON THE TYPE

The text of this book was set in Linofilm Times Roman, adapted from the Linotype face designed by Stanley Morison for The Times (London), and introduced by that newspaper in 1932.

Among typographers and designers of the twentieth century, Stanley Morison has been a strong forming influence, as typographical advisor to the English Monotype Corporation, as a director of two distinguished English publishing houses, and as a writer of sensibility, erudition, and keen practical sense.